THE COUNTRY LIFE BOOK OF
CASTLES
AND
HOUSES
IN BRITAIN

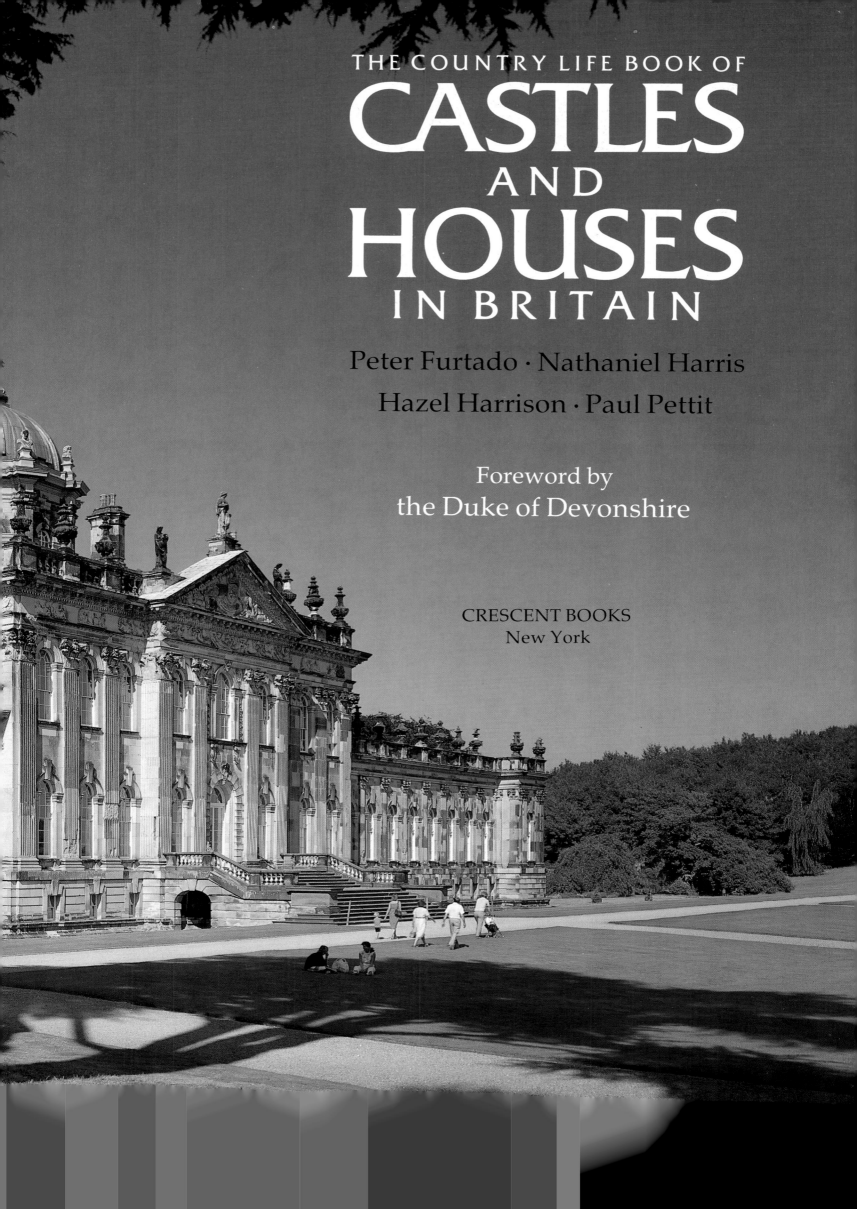

THE COUNTRY LIFE BOOK OF
CASTLES
AND
HOUSES
IN BRITAIN

Peter Furtado · Nathaniel Harris
Hazel Harrison · Paul Pettit

Foreword by
the Duke of Devonshire

CRESCENT BOOKS
New York

Key to Symbols

- ⊖   Public transport available
- ℗   Car park available
- WC   Toilets
- ♿   Access for the disabled
- ⌸   Parties welcome
- D   Dogs welcome
- ♠   Gardens or grounds open to the public
- ☕   Refreshments or meals available
- ⩙   Picnic site available
- ★   Free entry
- ◆   Shop
- ✿   Garden centre
- ✼   Guide book
- ✗   Guided tours
- ●   Restrictions on photography
- ✶   Playground
- ⚲   Nature trail

The National Grid four-figure reference (AZ 1234) and the Ordnance Survey Landranger 1:50 000 series sheet map reference number (OS 999) are given for every house and castle in this book, to assist detailed route planning.

Preceding page photograph
Castle Howard, North Yorkshire
Photograph: Andy Williams, London

1986 edition published by
Crescent Books
distributed by Crown Publishers, Inc.

First published in Britain by
Newnes Books
a division of The Hamlyn Publishing Group Limited
Bridge House, 69 London Road, Twickenham, Middlesex TW1 3SB, England

ISBN 0-517-46806-9

The contents of this book are believed correct at the time of publication; while every effort has been made to ensure that the factual information given is accurate, no liability can be accepted by the publishers for the consequences of any error. The representation on the maps of any road or track is not evidence of the existence of a public right of way.

Printed in Italy

h g f e d c b a

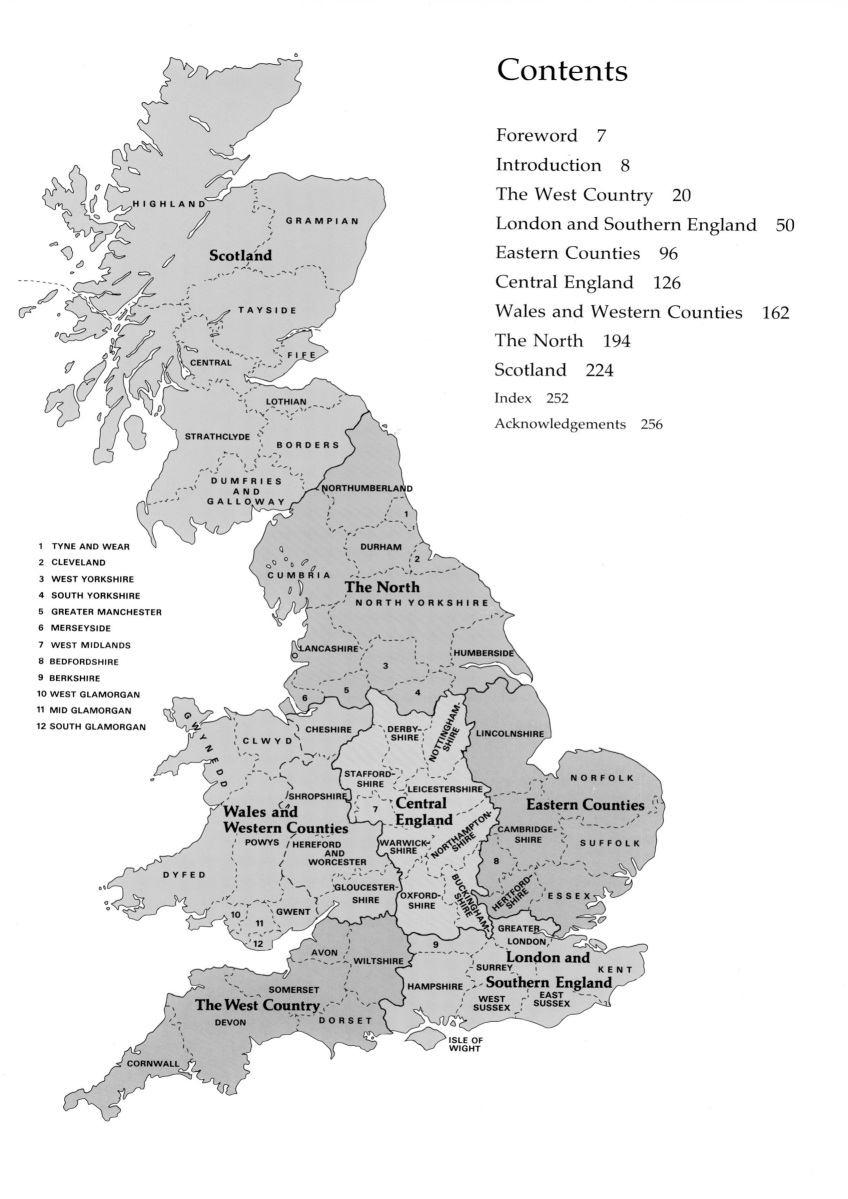

Contents

1 TYNE AND WEAR
2 CLEVELAND
3 WEST YORKSHIRE
4 SOUTH YORKSHIRE
5 GREATER MANCHESTER
6 MERSEYSIDE
7 WEST MIDLANDS
8 BEDFORDSHIRE
9 BERKSHIRE
10 WEST GLAMORGAN
11 MID GLAMORGAN
12 SOUTH GLAMORGAN

HIGHLAND

GRAMPIAN

Scotland

TAYSIDE

FIFE

CENTRAL

LOTHIAN

STRATHCLYDE

BORDERS

DUMFRIES
AND
GALLOWAY

NORTHUMBERLAND

1

DURHAM

2

CUMBRIA

The North

NORTH YORKSHIRE

LANCASHIRE

HUMBERSIDE

3

5

4

6

G W Y N E D D

CLWYD

CHESHIRE

DERBY-
SHIRE

NOTTINGHAM-
SHIRE

LINCOLNSHIRE

STAFFORD-
SHIRE

LEICESTERSHIRE

SHROPSHIRE

NORFOLK

**Wales and
Western Counties**

7

**Central
England**

Eastern Counties

POWYS

HEREFORD
AND
WORCESTER

WARWICK-
SHIRE

NORTHAMPTON-SHIRE

CAMBRIDGE-
SHIRE

SUFFOLK

DYFED

8

GLOUCESTER-
SHIRE

OXFORD-
SHIRE

BUCKINGHAM-SHIRE

HERTFORD-
SHIRE

ESSEX

10

GWENT

GREATER
LONDON

11

9

**London and
Southern England**

12

AVON

WILTSHIRE

SURREY

KENT

SOMERSET

HAMPSHIRE

WEST
SUSSEX

EAST
SUSSEX

The West Country

DEVON

D O R S E T

ISLE OF
WIGHT

CORNWALL

Foreword

While many aspects of our national life are giving rise to concern there are others which are a matter for rejoicing. High among these is the increasing awareness among people of all ages and all walks of life of the need to conserve what has come to be known as our national heritage.

In that heritage houses, whether they be castles, medieval manors or country houses of later centuries, together with their parks and gardens, are among these great assets, and in this field no other country in Europe can boast such riches as Britain. This book will make a most valuable addition to the literature of the nation's country houses, providing much information on the subject and thereby giving added enjoyment to those visiting the houses and castles described.

Much of this country's history is linked with its great houses; from Knowle, closely associated with Henry VIII, and indeed Hardwick Hall, the great Elizabethan house built by my forebear Bess, to Blenheim Palace, architectural masterpiece of Sir John Vanbrugh and birthplace of Sir Winston Churchill. Those wishing to study English history have a rich field open to them in learning about the country houses of Britain large and small.

From the number of visitors who come to Chatsworth each year I know what an enormous source of interest these houses are and what pleasure they give to countless numbers of people. Their future maintenance and wellbeing is of paramount importance and the publication of this book will be of inestimable value to this end.

The Duke of Devonshire

Opposite, the drawing room at Chatsworth House, showing some of the Mortlake tapestries which depict the Acts of the Apostles; the wood carving is by Samuel Watson, a local carver whose work was similar to that of the more well-known Grinling Gibbons.

Introduction

The buildings of Britain have been spared much of the havoc that wars and revolutions have wrought in other countries. From the end of the Roman occupation in the 5th century AD to the Second World War, the only large-scale damage done to the fabric of British buildings – apart from the natural ravages of time and the innovations of the new generations of architects – was the battering given to castles and fortified houses by cannoneers during the English Civil War of the 1640s. The relative security of British history encouraged building with an eye to permanence and posterity; and the stability and continuity of the social order ensured that much survived, despite individual whims and changes in taste and fashion.

New owners did of course replace or neglect the buildings they inherited from past generations, and one of the pleasures offered by historic houses and castles is the nostalgic 'pleasure of ruins'. But more often British houses have been modified or adapted over the centuries – enlarged in new styles, provided with the conveniences felt to be indispensable in a particular era, more or less redecorated inside, or given a face-lift outside by landscaping or the addition of the latest in the way of garden architecture or statuary. In such places, time has weathered and made a unity of the most apparently disparate elements. They have become part of the national heritage, preserving the past in stone, brick, timber, plaster and other materials. Naturally it is possible to admire the end result with only the vaguest notions of history and architecture; but there is a richer pleasure in deciphering and relating the various human and material elements that go to make up a historic building. It is hoped that this introduction, outlining the development of houses, homes and castles in Britain, will assist the reader and visitor to experience that richer pleaure.

Before the Normans

Until the late Middle Ages, most of Britain was heavily forested, so that wood was the cheapest and most convenient – and therefore the most natural – material for building. To the prehistoric Briton, only burial and worship seem to have been thought important enough to justify building in stone, as at Stonehenge. But the disadvantage of wood, from the historian's point of view, is that it rots and, in the British climate, generally disappears entirely within a few centuries. Bronze and Iron Age dwellings therefore mostly exist only in archaeologists' reconstructions. A few prehistoric houses survive in the remoter parts of Scotland and the Hebrides, where the shortage of suitable timber meant that people were forced to build in stone even for domestic purposes; some imposing fortifications, known as duns and brochs (high round towers) also survive in those regions. Throughout Britain Iron Age hillforts – some, like Maiden Castle in Dorset, on a truly massive scale – bear witness to the ancient British skill in military architecture. But with the coming of the Romans these native castles-cum-fortified villages (*oppida*) were abandoned, being replaced by the invaders' military camps, laid out on a grid-iron pattern near the new roads, and serving as the nucleus for many later towns and villages. The Romans built fine towns, especially in the south of Britain, and their economic system was based upon the large estate or villa, which sometimes took the form of a grand palace, as at Fishbourne in West Sussex. Little remains above ground of most of the Roman villas and camps, however (except for the fine examples near Hadrian's Wall); some were destroyed by invaders or the ravages of time (Fishbourne, like other villas, succumbed to a disastrous fire), others were neglected and abandoned, while still more were incorporated into later works until their origins were entirely hidden from view. Archaeologists have done an excellent job in revealing the range and quality of life in Roman Britain, but the interest of many Roman sites for the visitor is very different from that of most later houses and castles, and for this reason they receive only a passing mention here.

The Anglo-Saxons and Vikings and indigenous Britons were not greatly interested in Roman architecture – indeed there is some evidence that the Anglo-Saxons, at least, were so awed by its scale that they preferred to stay well clear of Roman sites when they could – and apart from churches and monasteries they built little in stone. Again, their cottages and thatched halls have been reconstructed admirably, but even their fortifications were built mainly in wood, and fewer traces of these can be found than of earlier periods of military architecture.

With the coming of the Normans, their innovation of the stone castle, and their introduction of stone for some other domestic architecture, the long story of the British heritage of houses and castles that we know today really begins. Many were erected on more ancient sites, but few incorporate more than a vestige of pre-Norman work in their walls or their ground-plan. Most Norman buildings have been altered, extended and rebuilt and, in some cases, they have been changed out of all recognition over the centuries; but this process can be seen as one of evolution, with a strong element of continuity; and for this reason we have chosen to regard the Conquest of 1066 as a crucial date in establishing the origins of the British historic house and castle.

The Norman Conquest gave Anglo-Saxon England a new set of foreign masters and a new social system: feudalism. The Norman king was the apex of a hierarchy of lords and vassals, and landlords and tenants, that included barons, knights and ecclesiastics; at the bottom of the hierarchy, the Anglo-Saxon serfs were tied to the land and toiled on it to produce the food that supported the entire system. In theory the lord justified his privileges by protecting his serfs; in practice, protection benefited the protector most, since, as the chronicler William of Malmesbury wrote of the Normans, 'they plunder their subjects, although they protect them from others'.

The Norman castle

In the years following the Conquest, William and his Norman barons tried to ensure their security by building castles at strategic points all over England; from his castle the baron could dominate the surrounding countryside and overawe the villagers on his manor. In the first instance, almost all of these were motte-and-bailey castles built of wood. The motte was a mound of earth (artificially built up or, if a natural feature, levelled off at the top) on which a wooden tower was erected. The tower was protected by a palisade with walkways for defence and observation. The banked area below

Above, the great tower of Colchester Castle, by far the largest of the many castle towers constructed by William the Conqueror to control his new territories. The windows were enlarged at a later date, and the top two storeys were demolished in the 17th century.

Opposite, Figsbury Ring, Wiltshire, one of the many Iron-Age forts in Britain, where the massive earthworks served both as military enclosure and as protection for a permanent settlement. Most of the hill-forts were abandoned after the Roman invasions.

Left, the White Tower of the Tower of London, as painted in the 15th century, when it still dominated the city just as it had done when William built it some four hundred years before. British Library, London.

and around the motte – the bailey – was also enclosed by a timber palisade. There was no watery 'moat' unless the surrounding ditch happened to lie on low, marshy ground and filled up naturally through seepage.

These early castles were built of wood because the Normans were in a hurry to secure their authority (the use of stone demanded time, resources and transport), and because wood was the only material which the hard-driven local Saxon workforces were capable of handling properly. Nonetheless the Normans were already passionate builders in stone and King William and his most powerful supporters brought this enthusiasm to England within a few years of the Conquest. They brought with them the style which became known as 'Norman' in this country, though it is really the British version of the continental Romanesque. This had developed in the mid-10th century in western Europe, and initially represented an attempt by people emerging from barbarism to learn from what was known of Roman building; hence the round arches and columns, and the barrel- or tunnel-vaults, characteristic of Romanesque. (A vault is an arched ceiling or roof; the barrel-vault is its simplest form, resembling a continuous arch.) Lacking the Romans' engineering skills, Romanesque builders kept their plans simple, and relied on sheer mass to stabilise their structures, making their walls, columns and piers (vertical supports, more massive than columns) immensely thick. The superb effects which can be obtained with these limited means are apparent in two great Romanesque cathedrals begun within thirty years of the Conquest, Norwich and Durham; many people consider Durham the finest of all English cathedrals.

Norman stone castles have the same massive quality, but the rounded forms of Romanesque are absent in the main feature: the keep or great tower. This square or rectangular tower was constructed with walls several yards thick, and involved quarrying large quantities of stone and transporting it considerable distances to the site. Most of the early examples were located at ultra-sensitive spots. In 1078 William the Conqueror began replacing his earth-and-timber castle in the south-east corner of his new capital, London, with a stone keep tucked into the city walls. This, the White Tower, received its name from being repainted regularly in that colour, perhaps to remind Londoners of their master's might; it forms the earliest part of what is now the Tower of London. It was built for William by Gundulf, Bishop of Rochester, who later supervised the construction of the even bigger royal castle at Colchester. Even before Gundulf started the White Tower, the Breton earl, Alan the Red, had begun Richmond Castle to strengthen the Norman grip on the rebellious North; while other trusted lords built castles at Chepstow and Ludlow to hold the Marches (borderlands) against the Welsh.

These and other early Norman keeps varied in shape and arrangement; but by the time Rochester Castle was built, in the second quarter of the 12th century, the tall tower keep had become the norm. Typically, it was three or four storeys high. The walls were made of rubble – uncut stone laid out in rough lines – with dressed stone (ashlar) giving a more finished look to the corners and the doors and window surrounds; in places such as London and Colchester the economical Normans embedded Roman tiles in the walls, often arranging them in the ancient herringbone pattern. The wooden roof was disguised and protected by a parapet that was often crenellated – that is, provided with the familiar alternation of spaces and upright rectangular projections. The motte became redundant, and the keep now stood inside the bailey, which was protected by a stone wall (the curtain wall) equipped with a more or less formidable gatehouse and mural towers.

Inside the bailey, or enclosure, were kitchens, workshops, stables, a smithy and all the other items needed to maintain a great household in both war and peace. But if necesary in time of war the lord and his retainers could withdraw into the keep itself and still be self-sufficient, although more austerely so. The entire ground floor was a storehouse, which also contained the most vital resource of all in times of siege – a well. The windows of the ground-floor storehouse were tiny, so that no enemy could squeeze through them into the keep. To make life harder for the attackers, the entrance to the keep was on the first floor, up a flight of stairs; from the 12th century the steps led to a drawbridge and an additional building (the forebuilding) which had to be captured before the besieging army could even reach the entrance to the main keep, itself protected by a formidable portcullis (the metal grid that slid down to seal off the entrance).

The most important room in the upper storeys was the hall, the large common living- and eating-room in which the lord, his family and his retainers spent most of their time. In essentials it differed little from the halls in which Homeric heroes, Viking chiefs and Teutonic war-lords had feasted over many centuries – or from the unfortified great hall, built by William II (r. 1087-1100), which formed part of his Palace of Westminster. It was, in fact, a natural arrangement while master and followers retained something of the war-band mentality; and the hall, and the mentality it represented, long survived the demise of the castle as a building seriously intended for military purposes.

Even in Norman times, however, there was some physical separation between master and man. The lord and his family occupied a dais, raised a step or two above the rest of the hall, and had a separate private room (the solar) adjacent to the hall or just above it. The hall itself was a lofty place, usually two storeys high, if only to make sure that the inhabitants were not stifled by the smoke that rose from the central hearth and lingered in the rafters; there was no chimney, and the fumes gradually seeped out through lateral holes or louvres in the roof. Windows in the hall were relatively large (placed high up, out of the reach of scaling ladders), and except in fine weather they were covered by wooden shutters, since glass had not yet come into general use and was reserved for church windows.

The well-equipped keep contained all the necessities of Norman life, including at least one chapel and a garderobe or latrine. This last consisted of a stone seat above a shaft leading down to a cesspit; it was not unheard-of for a castle to be taken by soldiers intrepid enough to climb the shaft and risk the consequences!

Apotheosis of the castle

During the century following the Conquest, large numbers of timber motte-and-bailey castles were converted to stone. Within a stone keep and curtain wall, a baron was not only more secure from resentful serfs and marauders: he was also able to contemplate defying his overlord, even if that overlord were the king himself. 'They filled the land with castles,' lamented a chronicler during the reign of King Stephen (r. 1135-54), when England was racked by the civil war between Stephen and the Empress Matilda. During this period, 'the Anarchy', central authority virtually disappeared while the royal combatants devoted all their energies to a seemingly endless succession of sieges.

Order was restored by Matilda's son Henry II (r. 1154-89), the first Angevin or Plantagenet king, who razed many castles that had been erected without the necessary royal licence. The next wave of building was influenced by military lessons learned from the sieges of the previous reign, and by ideas brought back from the sophisticated East by the Crusaders. Rectangular keeps were still built (including those in the royal castles at Scarborough and Peveril), but experiments began with other shapes. From circular and polygonal keeps the defenders could more easily see everything their enemies were doing below them and respond appropriately.

The royal castle at Orford in Suffolk, with its virtually circular (actually 18-faceted) tower and three tall turrets, was under construction from 1165; Conisbrough in South Yorkshire, built by Henry's half-brother, followed in 1180-90.

The surviving curtain wall of Roger Bigod's castle at Framlingham, in Suffolk, provides a splendid early example of an even more important trend, towards active defence based on the curtain wall rather than passive reliance on the strength of the keep. The curtain wall at Framlingham is equipped with no fewer than thirteen towers. The obvious advantage of this arrangement was that, no matter what the direction of an attack, the enemy could be caught in devastating crossfire from two of the towers. The popularity of shell-keeps also favoured the trend towards active defence, although the motive for building them was usually more pedestrian – to make a direct substitution of stone for wood. The shell-keep was basically a stone wall built round a motte, and in most cases directly replaced the palisade that had stood on the same spot. The wooden tower inside might be rebuilt in stone, or new buildings of wood or stone might be put up against the walls of the shell-keep. The most famous shell-keep in Britain is the round tower of Windsor Castle, built by Henry II.

The most vulnerable place in a curtain wall was inevitably the entrance. To remedy this, great twin-towered gateways were erected, with formidable outworks (known as barbicans) to protect them; a drawbridge and portcullis controlled the entrance, and those who did penetrate into the entrance lobby were likely to be dealt with by something shot or dropped through the aptly-named 'murder hole' in the lobby ceiling. A similar purpose was served by machicolations, which were stone galleries projecting in front of and above the outside walls, with spaces through which objects or bucketfuls of water could be dropped. (Cold water to put out a fire; boiling water to dampen the enemy's enthusiasm for climbing the walls.)

These developments foreshadowed the new castle style which reached a climax in terms of magnificence, engineering skill and ruinous expenditure during the reign of Edward I (r. 1272-1307). The earliest 'Edwardian' castle was Caerphilly, built by a subject, Gilbert de Clare, who actually started it the year before Edward's accession. But the most spectacular castles were the king's own – above all the massive fortresses constructed to hold down north Wales, whose long history as a more or less independent principality was brought to an end by Edward's ruthless determination. For once the name of the chief architect is known – he was Master James of St George – although of course no such profession yet existed: James was simply a master mason, like the builders of the great medieval cathedrals.

At Beaumaris, Caernarfon, Conwy, Harlech and the other Welsh royal castles, the idea of defending the walls actively was taken to its logical conclusion. The mural towers (in the walls) became huge, turreted drums, and massive, elaborate gateways and barbicans proliferated, making the would-be besieger's task well-nigh hopeless. (The more gateways a castle possessed – provided they could be adequately defended – the more difficulty a besieger experienced in blockading it without fatally dividing his own forces.) At Beaumaris and Harlech the builders copied de Clare's innovation at Caerphilly: instead of one curtain wall, two were raised, one inside the other; which is why these structures are known as concentric castles. The outer wall was always the lower of the two, so that archers on the inner wall could shoot over it at the enemy forces beyond. The bailey was now divided into two areas, called wards; the entire inner ward, defended by massive gatehouses, became the equivalent of the old Norman keep, housing suites of rooms, abundant stores and most other necessities and comforts of 13th-century life.

The great Edwardian castles of north Wales – still breathtakingly complex even in their ruined state – represent the apotheosis of medieval English military architecture. Castles continued to be built in the 14th century, but considerations of domesticity and comfort at last begin to leave significant traces in the architectural record.

Left, the 15th-century red-brick Herstmonceux Castle, East Sussex, with its magnificent gatehouse, was built when splendour was as important as military strength in castle architecture. It is now the official residence of the Astronomer Royal.

Below, the so-called King John's Hunting Lodge, in Axbridge, Somerset, typical of the countless houses built in timber-framed or 'half-timbered' style in the Middle Ages and Tudor period. Such houses are found wherever oak was readily available as the prime building material; the solid frame was as durable as stone.

The later Middle Ages

For much of the later Middle Ages, most of England and Wales enjoyed a fair degree of peace and prosperity. The distinction (and therefore the enmity) between Norman and Anglo-Saxon had disappeared, and the feudal system was modified as the lord of the manor ceased to be a fighting man and emerged in his familiar role as local squire or country gentleman. For such people – though not, as yet, for the great lords – the manor house, scarcely if at all fortified, became a natural dwelling place.

In the manor house, as in the castle, life was centred on the hall, with its paved dais for the family at one end, raised above the earth floor used by the other inhabitants. At the far end, a moveable screen stood in front of the 'screens passage' leading to the buttery and pantry; the kitchens were usually separately housed. (The buttery – from French, *bouteillerie* – was where the bottles were kept; the pantry – *paneterie*, or place for *pain*, bread – was the food store.) The lord's family had an adjacent or upstairs room which, as the demand for privacy grew stronger, became a comfortable apartment known as a solar. Most early halls were built of wood and have therefore disappeared, but Oakham Castle in Leicestershire is a remarkable example of a 12th-century stone hall, aisled like a church because the timbers used for the roof were not long enough to span the entire width; the aisled sections have separate lean-to roofs.

The timber roof nonetheless became one of the glories of English architecture, at its most elaborate and impressive in the 15th and 16th centuries. Earlier timber roofs were all supported on a tie-beam, which stretched horizontally across the hall or church from the tops of the walls. Then the hammer-beam was introduced – a short beam serving as a bracket from which the rafters could be supported without any need for a tie-beam. The hammer-beam roof could therefore be built far loftier than other types. The earliest dated example is the roof of Westminster Hall, built in 1394 by the carpenter, Hugh Herland. No brief outline can describe the technical and decorative ingenuity lavished on these roofs by English craftsmen, who filled not only halls but many otherwise insignificant churches with superb examples of their skills.

Many buildings, including manor houses, were timber-framed (also called half-timbered). Instead of having stone walls carrying the weight of the structure, a sturdy framework of oak beams carried the load. The spaces between the beams were usually packed with a dense, sticky mass of twigs caked with wet clay that had been mixed with straw or hair. This infilling (wattle-and-daub) was later often replaced by laths (flat strips of wood) or bricks. Finally the exterior would be plastered or covered with weatherboarding (overlapping boards). Half-timbered houses are widely but wrongly thought of as typically 'Tudor'; this only reflects the fact that the great majority of surviving examples date from the 16th and 17th centuries. The technique is far older; an earlier surviving house such as Lower Brockhampton in Herefordshire (late 14th-century) was certainly neither exceptional nor new in its own time.

Castles continued to be built during the later Middle Ages,

but with increasing concern for comfort and ostentation rather than military necessity. As early as the 1290s, a building such as Stokesay Castle in Shropshire was designed as a fortified house rather than a true castle – and arguably even there the fortifications were an afterthought, intended more for show than as a genuine protection against the conquered Welsh. Similar qualifications can be made about even such an ambitious structure as Bodiam Castle in East Sussex, built in the 1380s to protect the south coast after the alarms caused by French raids; its large windows and other unmilitary amenities suggest that it was not seriously expected to withstand a prolonged assault.

In the Border counties of England and Scotland the situation was different. Life was poorer and harsher, Scots and English were often at war, and at all times cross-border banditry was rife. In response to these conditions, both Scots and English built hundreds of pele towers – rectangular stone towers that might be characterised as poor relations of the Norman keep. Dozens of these survive from the 13th and 14th centuries. The pele house was far less substantial than a keep, but sufficiently strong to hold out against fly-by-night raiders; the ground floor served as a storeroom in times of peace, but would be crowded with local people and their cattle in any emergency. One incontrovertible proof that, in England, better times arrived in the Elizabethan period is the conversion of pele towers into country houses at places such as Sizergh and Levens in Cumbria.

Further south, where these changes occurred earlier, the use of bricks marked another stage in the domestication of secular architecture. Bricks were initially imported from the Low Countries, and were not used on any scale until the 15th century, when the brick houses that Englishmen saw while fighting in France helped to make the new material fashionable. Two splendid brick castles, Herstmonceux in East

Sussex and Tattershall in Lincolnshire, date from the 1430s and 1440s. As with other 15th-century castles-cum-mansions, their military role can scarcely have been primary; apart from any other consideration, brick is not the ideal material to use against siege engines or cannon.

The invention of gunpowder is often said to have rendered castles obsolete, and in the long run this was doubtless true. Yet most of these developments took place long before the cannon had become a reliable (let alone a decisive) factor in warfare. Impulses towards domestic comfort, peaceful enjoyment of wealth and competitive display made themselves felt before changes in military technique enforced them. Even more interesting is the fact that such impulses seem to have been largely unaffected by the intermittent civil war – the Wars of the Roses – that apparently dominated English political history for much of the later 15th century: evidently the wider effects of dynastic and aristocratic feuds can be exaggerated. Not surprisingly, however, it was not until the Wars of the Roses had ended and the new Tudor dynasty created a more stable order that the long boom in secular building truly began.

The Tudor Age

Until the 16th century, ecclesiastical building was far more impressive as architecture than anything done for domestic or military purposes. After the erection of the great cathedrals and abbeys of the Middle Ages, the 15th century witnessed the transformation of parish churches through building or rebuilding in the Perpendicular style. Then, quite suddenly, ecclesiastical building came to a halt, and for 150 years virtually every significant architectural achievement was secular in function and spirit. No doubt there were cathedrals and churches enough by 1500; but the completeness of the change indicated that the Tudor outlook was significantly different from that of the past.

Although nobody knew it at the time, Henry Tudor's successful bid for the throne in 1485 effectively ended the Wars of the Roses. For over a century, the Tudor monarchy remained both strong and popular, even though the dynasty had its fair share of plots, intrigues and rebellions. Despite unfamiliar problems – notably inflation – the propertied classes and people of 'the middling sort' became better-off and more comfortably lodged. The most important social upheaval of the century operated to their benefit. In the 1530s, as part of the chain of events that were to turn England into a Protestant nation, all the monasteries were closed, and the King (Henry VIII) took over their accumulated wealth and huge landholdings. Henry was an extravagant monarch, and put most of the lands up for sale; they were avidly purchased by the gentry and nobility, who thereby also acquired stately abbeys that were quite often converted into stately homes (for example Newstead Abbey, Woburn Abbey and many other properties included in this book). The 'Dissolution of the Monasteries' proved to be the biggest redistribution of land since the Norman Conquest; and new land, which meant new wealth, provided new incentives for building.

Stylistically, the change to secular building was not very significant. Manor houses and other substantial dwellings were still no more than functional agglomerations with various Gothic trappings. But although timber-framed houses continued to be built in traditional fashion, and the availability of local materials often determined what might be done, brick now became extremely popular – and virtually mandatory for houses with pretensions to grandeur. Display and comfort were increasingly important considerations, but they were not yet refined by any underlying sense of style. The visitor to a Tudor 'Great House' is struck first of all by the enormous twin-towered gatehouse, often adorned with coats of arms, and then by the fantastically jumbled skyline of twisted chimneys, vanes and turrets. Battlements and other mock-military features emphasise the assertive spirit behind the entire structure. The hall was still the central feature of the house, but the number and size of the other room grew steadily, thanks to both a desire for greater privacy and a wish to emphasise social differences. A new and distinctively English feature, the long gallery, appeared on the first floor –

Above, the chimneys of Lacock Abbey, Wiltshire, one of the many monastery buildings converted from their original use to become the homes of the 'new men' of Elizabeth England. The houses of the 16th century frequently had as much imagination devoted to their roofs as to the façade or interior.

Opposite, Longleat House, Wiltshire, painted by Jan Siberechts in the late 17th century. Longleat was one of the finest examples of the exuberant but academically naive interpretation of Classical architecture found in the great houses of Elizabethan England.

a room spacious and comfortable enough for the proprietorial family to enjoy spending most of their indoor leisure time in it, away from their retainers and dependants; and, as the name implies, it was long enough to be strolled about in. Walls were generally panelled in wood, which was often carved with the distinctive linenfold design, tremendously popular in Tudor times. (It was exactly what the name indicates: a stylised image of a piece of folded linen.) Otherwise, such style as there was derived mainly from Perpendicular: window tracery and stained glass; oriel windows (bay windows above ground-floor level); and depressed arches in gatehouse entrances and windows, and above fireplaces. The introduction of the proper fireplace, equipped with a flue leading to a chimney, was perhaps the aspect of 'the general amendment of lodging' in early Tudor times that impressed contemporaries most; the insistent corkscrew shape of the chimney-stacks was no doubt the owner's way of advertising that his house was absolutely up to date. One advantage of the fireplace was that it made it possible to use coal – an important advantage since, in the 16th century, Britain's forests were rapidly disappearing. Coal fumes were so intolerable that even the loftiest hall was unbearable unless there was a chimney to keep the smoke out of the living area. But the installation of chimneys made lofty living rooms unnecessary, a fact that contributed to an eventual change in the function of the hall.

The Renaissance and Tudor architecture

The first significant English contacts with Renaissance art took place during the reign of Henry VIII (r. 1509-47). The King himself imported an Italian sculptor, Pietro Torrigiano, to carve the tomb of his father, Henry VII, in Westminster Abbey. His chief minister, Cardinal Wolsey, built Hampton Court Palace, which Henry later took over and extended, in a style that revealed the limits of English feeling for Renaissance architecture: the structure, including Henry's great hall, remained traditionally Gothic, and the Renaissance elements were confined to some aspects of the decoration – notably the medallions on the gateways containing busts of Roman emperors executed in terracotta, which had been unknown in England until Torrigiano introduced it.

Thereafter Renaissance influences made very slow progress in England, partly at least because the Reformation virtually excluded direct Anglo-Italian contact. After about 1536 English notions of Renaissance art and architecture were derived from French, and later Flemish, sources which inevitably distorted them in transmission. And even after the publication of the first English book describing the Classical Orders, John Shute's *First and Chief Groundes of Architecture* (1563), English taste remained eccentrically provincial and eclectic, and during Queen Elizabeth's reign created a number of striking buildings that have become increasingly admired in recent years.

Before moving on to the Elizabethan period, mention must be made of the chain of forts built for Henry VIII along the south coast in 1539-40. At that time a joint Franco-Imperial invasion to restore papal authority in England seemed a real possibility, and Henry's forts represented a major defensive effort. Deal Castle is the best-preserved example, with a moat and three sets of walls culminating in a central keep crowned with a lantern; the outer walls were made massively thick to withstand cannon-fire, and gunports at every level gave the garrison command of a wide area. Though now deceptively medieval in appearance (crenellated parapets were added to the walls in the fanciful 18th century), Deal is not a true castle: like Henry's other forts, it had a small garrison but was never a family residence. Many 16th-century gentlemen were capable of roughing it when duty called, but the unfortified house, with its rituals and comforts, had become the sole centre of English family life.

Under Elizabeth I (r. 1558-1603), the upper and middle ranks of English society prospered greatly and enjoyed a variety of amenities that were either new or or more widely available than ever before. Among these were items such as pewter, plate, glass, chimneys and silk stockings! Consequently, despite the crises of the reign – by no means over even when the Spanish Armada had been defeated – the dominant classes were full of self-confidence, and almost manically self-assertive. Their taste for competitive display helped to sustain a long surge of building and rebuilding, which reached extravagant heights in the 'prodigy houses' commissioned by the great men of the realm. Many of these massive showpieces were partly justified by the hope that the Queen would deign to stay at them during one of her regular summer tours ('progresses'), when the entire Court had to be accommodated at one place after another. The supreme privilege in Elizabethan England was to be allowed to ruin yourself entertaining the monarch, as the Earl of Leicester did with the most famous of all such jamborees, held at Kenilworth in 1575. Even Elizabeth's sober chief minister, William Cecil, Lord Burghley, shared the prodigy house mania, building both Burghley House in Northamptonshire and Theobalds in Hertfordshire. Theobalds, one of the most vast and splendid palaces of the time, was demolished in the 17th century, but Burghley remains as an interesting example of the mixture of elements in the Elizabethan house. It was built of stone (brick had gone out of fashion again) with a twin-towered gatehouse leading to a courtyard, in a style that was already old-fashioned; the skyline is still cluttered with spires and cupolas; and inside the courtyard stands a spectacular clock tower rising to a pyramid – and with a different Classical Order applied to each of its three storeys.

The most famous of the prodigy houses are associated with the name of Robert Smythson (c. 1536-1614), an architect of very great ability although his status was still that of a mason or 'surveyor'. His patrons undoubtedly made many of the critical decisions about the larger design features of their houses, and this may account for the otherwise curious fact that Smythson's first major commission, Longleat in Wiltshire, is the most Classically compact of his buildings. In the next, Wollaton Hall, Nottinghamshire, the corners were drawn up and out to make towers, suggesting that Englishmen had not yet abandoned a certain military style – now pure fantasy – even while they submitted to the foreign (Renaissance) fashion for unmistakably civilian balustrades and colonnades.

This tendency is even more marked at Hardwick Hall in Derbyshire, where the three-storey main block is surrounded by six four-storey towers. Hardwick is probably also Smythson's work, and again combines Renaissance features such as the colonnaded façade and balustraded skyline with the Elizabethan taste for a weighty, vaguely castellated general appearance embellished by bays and quantities of glass. The well-known jingle 'Hardwick Hall/More glass than wall' conveys some of the pride and wonder evoked by vistas of this material, whose lavish use had not long before been an ecclesiastical monopoly. The interior of Hardwick confirmed the changed function of the hall, now placed neatly on the axis of the main entrance to form a grand reception area, while separate state and private rooms on different floors catered for the two sides of the owner's life.

In Elizabethan houses, ornament ran riot, as if people were positively uncomfortable when forced to contemplate un-filled spaces. Fabrics were densely embroidered, and walls hung with tapestries and portraits; woodwork was carved and plasterwork moulded into a wide variety of designs. The most popular involved strapwork, imported from Flanders, and similar geometric or floral patterns.

The building boom went on into the reign of the first Stuart king of England, James I (r. 1603-25), who had been king of Scotland (as James VI) since 1567. James's prodigality and chronic shortage of money led him to bestow or sell titles on an unprecedented scale, and this served to encourage his subjects to build dwellings appropriate to their new rank. The first great Jacobean house was Knole in Kent, remodelled by Queen Elizabeth's cousin Thomas Sackville, Earl of Dorset; the outside is characteristically English and eclectic, combin-ing a colonnade in a minor Order, the Tuscan, with carved Dutch gables, which became a very popular feature on Jacobean buildings. The greatest Jacobean prodigy house that has survived intact is Hatfield House in Hertfordshire, built in brick (which had come back into fashion) by Robert Cecil, the son of Elizabeth's chief minister. Cecil had been con-firmed in power and created Earl of Salisbury by James I, to whom he had felt obliged to present the palatial Theobalds; in return he received the one-time ecclesiastical palace of Hatfield, which he plundered for building materials to use in his new prodigy house. This episode is characteristic of the way in which the new country-house England supplanted the medieval order.

The Elizabethans and Jacobeans loved allegory and symbolism, and there are undoubtedly many 'messages' contained in their buildings (as there are in the miniature paintings of, for example, Hans Eworth and Nicholas Hilliard) that most of us cannot hope to decipher. One remarkable and relatively clear example is the Triangular Lodge built by Sir Thomas Tresham at Rushton in North-amptonshire, with its multiple triangles representing the Trinity and making a kind of covert declaration of his Roman Catholic faith. Another type of allusion occurs on the grand scale in Bolsover Castle, Derbyshire, built on the site of a medieval castle and including a crenellated 'keep' or 'hall'. This is the first sham castle, exploiting what we can only suppose to be an early case of nostalgia for the 'Age of Chivalry' – an emotion more familiar in an urbane 18th-century setting.

The buildings of the early Jacobean period seemed to show that English architecture was as far as ever from any concept of stylistic unity. Yet in fact the first self-proclaimed English architect and exponent of pure Classicism was about to appear on the scene.

Inigo Jones and 17th-century Classicism

Inigo Jones (1573-1652) was the son of a Smithfield cloth-worker. Almost nothing is known of his early life except that, as a young man, he somehow managed to visit Italy and Denmark. In 1605, already in his thirties, he began his career at Court as an omnicompetent designer, notably of costumes and sets for masques – pageant-like performances, combining poetry, music and spectacle, in which the entire Court took part. Jones produced masques in collaboration with the dramatist Ben Jonson until 1632, and created unusual stage effects that he may well have learned from contemporary Italian masters of the craft. In 1613-14 he revisited Italy in the train of the Earl of Arundel, studying antique architecture with the help of the Paduan architect Palladio's book *I Quattro Libri dell'Architettura* (1570); Jones's copy, containing his notes, still survives. Both as a writer and as a practitioner of domestic architecture in a superbly harmonious Classical

Above, the Banqueting House, Whitehall, built by Inigo Jones in 1622. It introduced the ideas of Palladio and the Italian Classical architects to England, and proved enormously influential.

Opposite, the house and gardens of Westbury Court, Gloucestershire, as depicted by Johannes Kip in about 1707. The formal water garden (of which this is a rare surviving example) with its long vistas, canals and regular plantations, was inspired by Continental models.

style, Palladio was to have an enormous influence on English architecture. Jones became the first English Palladian after he was appointed Surveyor of the Works, in charge of all royal building, in 1615. His principal surviving works are the Queen's House at Greenwich (now part of the National Maritime Museum) and the Banqueting House at Whitehall; he is less certainly associated with several country houses, including Wilton House in Wiltshire.

After the heavy self-assertion and idiosyncrasies of the prodigy houses, the cool, elegant simplicity of Jones's buildings comes as a relief and a surprise; it is hard to believe that James I's courtiers were not astonished when they saw the Banqueting House take shape in 1619-22. It revealed that the Renaissance style was not just a glorious repertoire of decorative devices – as English builders had assumed on the basis of second-hand information – but an intellectually precise system of relationships which determined the propor-tions of all the component parts.

The simplicity of Jones's designs is deceptive – an 'art that conceals art'. Instead of the far-flung E- and H-plans of Elizabethan and Jacobean houses, the Queen's House and the Banqueting House are compact rectangles, with flat balustraded roofs, neatly grouped chimneys, and closely integrated, regular decorative details including columns, pilasters, swags (leafy chains) and pedimented windows. Their interiors demonstrated that the mass of ornament which had increasingly overwhelmed the English house was not necessary to create an effect of grandeur; while Peter Paul Rubens's great ceiling decorations at Whitehall, in which heroic figures apparently soar into an open sky, offered the greatest possible contrast to the intimate, icon-like quality of Elizabethan painting.

The English Civil War (1642-46) effectively ended Jones's career. But despite the disruptions caused by the fighting, the execution in 1649 of King Charles I, and the eventual establishment of the Cromwellian protectorate (1654-58), Jones's assistant John Webb (1611-72) and a highly talented gentleman-amateur, Sir Roger Pratt (1620-85), applied Clas-sical principles to the building of country houses; at the Vyne, in Hampshire, Webb introduced the temple-style portico, with columns supporting a pediment, which was to become one of the most popular features of English country houses.

These artists remained active after the Restoration of 1660 brought Charles II (r. 1660-85) to the throne. Another influential figure was Hugh May (1621-84), who had shared the King's exile in Holland and brought back with him a knowledge of the Dutch version of Palladianism. This entailed the use of brick – a material that English builders

understood well – and evolved into a type of building popular for generations because its plain, quiet dignity so admirably suited well-to-do people without any aristocratic pretensions. Its standard features included various Classical elements that were used only decoratively, notably a large central pediment on the main façade; a hipped (four-sided) roof which, by dispensing with gables, allowed the placing of a characteristically elegant, unbroken cornice along the line of the eaves; and dormer windows lighting a top storey placed within the roof to avoid spoiling the proportions of the building. In this and other types of house, the sash window – in its day an ingeniously designed convenience – became commonplace from about 1700.

Although the type of building just described has often been called a 'Wren house' (when it has not been labelled 'Queen Anne'), it has no significant connection with Sir Christopher Wren (1632-1723). It is in fact ironical that the greatest British architect should warrant only the briefest mention here. Most of the famous Wren buildings – St Paul's Cathedral, the City of London churches, the Sheldonian Theatre in Oxford, Greenwich Hospital – are outside the scope of this book. However, the fountain court at Hampton Court Palace is his work, as is Flamsteed House (the Royal Observatory, Greenwich Park), built in 1675 for the first Astronomer Royal, John Flamsteed – an appropriate conjunction since Wren himself had been a professor of astronomy before turning to architecture.

Wren's extraordinary genius, and the sheer scale and number of his buildings, established Classicism as *the* English style for all imaginable purposes. And at almost the same time, Scottish architecture, which had previously developed along rather different lines, also succumbed to Classicism.

Scottish castle style

Scotland was a much poorer country than England, and life there remained harsh and dangerous for much longer; the pele tower continued to be the typical dwelling of most nobles right through to the 16th century. The chief outside influence was not England – the old enemy across the border – but France, Scotland's partner in 'the auld alliance'. As a result, when a surge of building activity did occur from the 1560s, the new residences had something of the character of expanded pele towers; in particular, the structure normally included a central tower with the main entrance at its base. Combined with the influence of French castle style, which in the Loire Valley reached heights of fantasy undreamed-of in

England, this produced what the Victorians christened 'Scottish Baronial style' – splendid story-book castles such as Glamis, whose skylines are crowded with cupolas or conical turrets springing from the angles of the walls. The Baronial style continued to flourish even when the Scottish monarchs became domiciled in London as kings of England, and it was only after the Restoration of 1660 that Scotland was seriously invaded by Classicism of the sort favoured by the English; Drumlanrig Castle in Dumfriesshire (1675-89) represents the last Baronial fling, already oddly embellished with Classical features in a distinctly alien mood. Meanwhile Sir William Bruce (d. 1710), as Surveyor-General for Scotland, had introduced a thoroughgoing Classicism in his work on Holyroodhouse, Edinburgh, and in his own Kinross House, Tayside; and this supplanted the native style. For better or worse, Scottish architecture became part of the main British tradition, with at least one favourable result, in that Scotland produced a series of major architects who were able to seize the opportunities offered by the growing wealth and power of Britain.

The English Baroque

For most of the 17th century Italy remained the dynamic centre of European art. One of its most astonishing creations was the Baroque style, which united architecture, painting and sculpture in a vast, all-embracing celebration of grandeur and glory – above all, in Italy, the grandeur and glory of the Catholic Church. The supreme exponents of Baroque, the Italians Bernini and Borromini, worked on the largest possible scale to create a heroic art in which sweeping curvaceous forms were organised with a sculptor's sense of the effective interplay between masses and voids. These fluent forms, and the wealth of carved and moulded ornament, blurred the lines between sculpture and architecture; and painting too was recruited into the service of drama and illusion: the Baroque painter – especially the ceiling painter – carries the spectator's eyes straight out of the house and up into the heavens without breaking the spell under which he has fallen.

As it travelled north-west, the Baroque was put into the service of new patrons. At Versailles it became an element in the glorification of the absolute monarchy of Louis XIV (r. 1643-1715), the Sun King; and in Britain this ultra-Catholic and absolutist style was modified by the great landowners who had increasingly become the real masters in the evolving constitutional-but-oligarchic (and Protestant) Whig political system. Chatsworth House, Castle Howard and Blenheim

Palace are magnificent monuments to the generation of Whig grandees who saw through the long wars against France and survived political perils at home before settling the Hanoverians on the throne as kings of a thoroughly Protestant, Whig-dominated Great Britain.

For all its extravagance and complexity, the Baroque was a development of Renaissance Classicism – a wayward one in which the dignified Classical vocabulary was manipulated and distorted in the interests of a theatrically heroic emotion. English architects never fully embraced the ecstatic curvilinearity of full-blooded Continental Baroque, and the work of Wren and his successors is sometimes described by the compromise term 'Baroque Classicism' to indicate the continuing presence in it of a certain restraint or a temperamental preference for the foursquare. All the same, English Baroque proved a grandiose though brief episode. Chatsworth in Derbyshire was remodelled for the Duke of Devonshire by William Talman (1650-1719) in 1687-96. Then in 1699 Sir John Vanbrugh (1664-1726), soldier of fortune and fashionable playwright, turned architect and designed Castle Howard in North Yorkshire for the Earl of Carlisle. In 1705, while this huge house was still under construction, Vanbrugh won the commission for Blenheim Palace, which was built at the national expense as a home for (and monument to) the Duke of Marlborough, who had led the victorious Allied armies against Louis XIV. At Castle Howard, and even more so at Blenheim, Vanbrugh was able to indulge his taste for the colossal, creating buildings that in size and complex interaction of parts had no parallel in earlier British architecture. Although each element is individually 'Classical', his assemblages of giant Orders, far-flung wings, tall domes, towers, and assorted urns and sculpted figures on the skyline are a world away from the cool, compact style of Palladio and his disciple Inigo Jones.

Vanbrugh was assisted by Nicholas Hawksmoor (1661-1736), who had previously spent twenty years working for Wren; quite why this gifted architect allowed himself to be overshadowed in this fashion is not clear. Apart from his famous City churches, Hawksmoor designed the striking Mausoleum at Castle Howard. Other Baroque architects of distinction were Thomas Archer (c. 1668-1743), who worked at Chatsworth, and James Gibbs (1682-1754), whose career was impeded by Catholic and Tory affiliations; as well as such famous buildings as St Martin-in-the-Fields, in Trafalgar Square, London, and the Radcliffe Camera at Oxford, he designed Orleans House, Twickenham, and created a very late Baroque hall at Ragley, Warwickshire (begun c. 1750).

The complex, ornate interiors of Baroque houses called on a wide range of native skills. However, for the illusionistic decorative painting characteristic of Baroque interiors, foreigners – notably the team of Verrio and Laguerre – were imported. One British painter of some distinction emerged in the person of Sir James Thornhill (1675-1734), who worked at Blenheim and elsewhere, and was also the architect of Moor Park, Hertfordshire.

The Palladian revival

Early in the 18th century, one of the most extraordinary revivals in the history of architecture took place: Baroque was vigorously attacked and overthrown even before Vanbrugh's two major projects had been completed, and strict adherence to the Classicism of Inigo Jones and Palladio became the order of the day. The publication in 1715 of two books, *Vitruvius Britannicus* by Colen Campbell, and a new translation of Palladio, began the new trend. Campbell (d. 1729) converted the wealthy and cultured Lord Burlington, who dismissed Gibbs and gave the previously obscure Scottish architect the job of finishing his London mansion, Burlington House. Campbell went on to design the most slavish of all tributes to Palladio, Mereworth Castle in Kent, which is a virtual copy of the Italian master's famous Rotunda. He then worked on the grand scale at Houghton Hall, Norfolk, built for the Prime Minister, Sir Robert Walpole, and more modestly at Stourhead, Wiltshire, and elsewhere.

Meanwhile, Campbell's patron, Lord Burlington (1694-1753), made himself into an architect of some distinction.

After taking on Campbell, he studied Palladio at first hand in Italy (1719-20) and returned to Britain to become the high priest of the new movement. His wealth, influence and puritanical insistence on 'correctness' combined to make the Palladian country house the norm for an entire generation. Burlington's best surviving works are his own villa, Chiswick House, and the Assembly Rooms, York.

Burlington brought back with him from Italy a curious, only semi-literate artist named William Kent (c. 1685-1748), who had seriously mistaken his vocation. Kent believed he was a good history painter in the grand manner, but he was wrong; and even Burlington's powerful influence failed to forward a career punctuated with rebuffs and humiliations. But Kent *was* a designer of genius. In his forties he became an architect (Holkham Hall, Norfolk), but he was more original as an interior designer – if only because almost nothing was known about ancient Roman interiors, so that this gifted designer was left free to combine and permutate antique elements in accordance with his own tastes.

Kent also initiated the 18th-century revolution in landcape gardening. Until his day, the main influence on British landscaping was the French formal garden, developed during the reign of Louis XIV by André Le Nôtre. In this, Nature was utterly subdued – reduced to strictly geometrical vistas of radiating, straight, gravelled paths, regularly placed trees and bushes that had been trimmed into an impeccable symmetry, and efficiently marshalled beds of flowers; fountains, canals, urns and statuary emphasised the subjugation of Nature to Man. Kent and his successors, Lancelot 'Capability' Brown (1716-83) and Humphry Repton (1752-1818), swept all this away and created the 'English' garden, in which Nature ruled supreme. Or appeared to do so: in fact, large-scale operations were usually necessary to create the rolling landscape, clumps of trees, lakes and other aesthetically satisfying features of 'untouched' vistas. It is sad that we have lost the formal gardens which were the intended setting for the great Baroque houses (though some efforts have been made to re-create them); but the mellow integration brought about between the house and the English garden – both products of time as well as art – now provides one of the great pleasures of the English scene.

As towns became centres of fashionable, professional and commercial life, the need for new forms of housing became apparent. The problem arose relatively early at Bath, which was the first example of a new phenomenon: the fashionable spa and resort town, thronged with visitors. The response was the earliest of the great town-planning schemes characteristic of the Georgian period (others were the New Town, Edinburgh, and Regent's Park, London). From 1729 John Wood the Elder (1704-54) built Queen Square and the Circus, finished by his son John Wood the Younger (1728-81), who went on to build the magnificent Royal Crescent (1767-74). The Woods' inspired adaptation of Classicism to substantial terrace houses, conceived on the grand scale as collective units, provided a model for generations of British builders.

Above, the Rotunda at Stowe, Buckinghamshire, painted by Jacques Rigaud (1681-1754). The gardens at Stowe were laid out by Bridgman, Kent, Brown, Gibbs and Vanbrugh – a galaxy of 18th-century talent. Classical temples and statuary served a triple purpose: they were picturesque; they were elevating; and they provided a focal point for the vistas created by the landscape gardeners.

Opposite, the romantic English landscape garden, as created at Stourhead in Wiltshire by Henry Hoare to the inspiration of the paintings of Claude Lorrain. This painting was done by C.W. Bampfylde in 1758.

Right, the Royal Crescent, Bath, designed by John Wood the Younger and built between 1767 and 1774. The Royal Crescent provided a model for urban house and street design for a century or more, adapting the country-house idiom to a new urban setting. Engraving by John Claude Nathes, 1806. Victoria Art Galley, Bath.

Neo-Classicism

With the passing of Burlington's generation of Palladians, a number of different tendencies appeared in British Classicism. Although no fundamental change was involved, the label 'Neo-Classical' tends to be used of art and architecture produced in this tradition after about 1750 – partly, at least, to accommodate it to the genuinely new Neo-Classical movement developing on the Continent, which did entail a significant break with the immediate past (dominated by Baroque and its offshoot, Rococo).

One advantage possessed by the new generation was the ability to study antiquity at first hand, rather than through the writings of Palladio and other Renaissance architects. Wealthy enthusiasts for the Antique even made it possible for James Stuart and Nicholas Revett to make the first accurate measurements and drawings of the masterpieces of Greek architecture, and their book *The Antiquities of Athens* (1762, 1789) revealed the austere simplicity of the Greek style to readers whose notions of Classicism were based entirely on Roman and Renaissance buildings. However, although Stuart designed a thorough-going Greek temple at Hagley

(West Midlands), the Greek Revival proper did not begin until the 19th century, when it was essentially an institutional style for banks, insurance companies and the like.

From our point of view, the major figure of this generation was the Scottish architect Robert Adam (1728-92), who worked at many places described in this book – Syon House, Osterley Park and Kenwood, all in or near London; Nostell Priory and Harewood House in West Yorkshire; Kedleston Hall, Derbyshire; and Saltram House, Devon. In most cases his task was to remodel an existing building or finish off another architect's work, for by this time most of the great 18th-century houses had been built or were already under construction.

Nonetheless all Adam's best houses carry his individual stamp. His exteriors are Palladian, but with a more sculpturesque feeling than Campbell's or Burlington's; Adam admitted to being influenced by Vanbrugh and wrote that he regarded 'movement' as his most important contribution to architecture. However, Adam's interiors are undoubtedly his greatest achievements – dazzling displays of polished marble, gilding, beautifully moulded plasterwork, bronze, glass,

wood and so on, combining lightness with sumptuousness. Like Stuart, Adam was a scholar; he had published measured drawings of Diocletian's Palace at Spalato (now Split, Yugoslavia), studied the interiors of newly excavated Roman houses at Pompeii, and drew on a variety of Renaissance and even 'Etruscan' (actually Greek) sources in his decorative work. The fusion of these influences is a unique feat, made possible by the fact that Adam was the first British interior designer in the modern sense, meticulously overseeing every detail of the work in hand, whatever the medium.

Castles, pagodas and the Picturesque

There were other sides to Adam's activities. In his native Scotland he worked on a number of houses such as Mellerstain, in which he adapted himself to the old 'castle style' or produced new designs for owners who were developing a taste for castellation. In England, for the dilettante and connoisseur Horace Walpole (1717-97), he designed the round tower at Strawberry Hill, Twickenham. This small 'castle', created by Walpole and his friends over a number of years, was an early example of the 'Gothick' – a revival of the medieval style that, while not necessarily unscholarly, was certainly more playful than antiquarian in spirit; some years earlier Walpole had published a hugely successful 'Gothick' novel, *The Castle of Otranto*, which also showed this ultra-civilised man squeezing pleasurable thrills from the rude passions and incredible supernatural horrors of a barbarian past.

The Gothick was only one of several manifestations of discontent with 18th-century Classicism and sweet reasonableness; these did not overthrow Neo-Classicism, but coexisted with it, and sometimes modified its impact. Chinoiserie, the cult of things Chinese (or mock-Chinese), made its greatest impact on interior decoration, but a respectable Neo-Classical architect, Sir William Chambers, designed the pagoda at Kew and a Chinese dairy at Woburn Abbey. Much more important, and closely related to Gothick, was the theory of 'the Picturesque', which emphasised the distinctly unclassical virtues of irregularity and ruggedness, making a cult of rocks and ruins that transformed many country house landscapes, filling them with brand-new crumbling abbeys and similar 'follies'. One of the champions of the Picturesque, Richard Payne Knight, built himself the massive Downton Castle in Hereford and Worcester, which gave a great impetus to the medievalising vogue; and, once established, the taste for castles or at least the 'castle look' persisted throughout the 19th century.

Confronted with a choice of styles, some architects – notably Henry Holland (1745-1806) – remained faithful to Neo-Classicism. Most, however, proved willing to adapt, following the example of the prolific James Wyatt (1747-1813). He designed the classically elegant Heaton Hall, Greater Manchester; created a number of Adam-style interiors; built Gothic castles of varying eccentricity; and is rather unfairly remembered for the most fantastic of all follies, built for the

'oriental-Gothick' writer William Beckford – Fonthill Abbey, whose 225-foot tower collapsed in 1825.

Wyatt's near-contemporary John Nash (1753-1835) was an equally versatile designer of country houses, but his career reached its climax a generation later, during the Regency period. He was taken up by the Prince Regent (later George IV), and devised the last of the great Georgian achievements in town planning, the Regent's Park and Regent Street development in London. In an utterly different vein, he built the extraordinary but delightful Royal Pavilion, Brighton, in fantasy-Indian style as a holiday home for his master. He also began Buckingham Palace, but was abruptly forced into retirement after the death of George IV in 1830.

The other great architect of the period was Sir John Soane (1753-1837), famous during his lifetime for his work on the Bank of England. He manipulated the Neo-Classical style in a highly original manner to produce romantic and mysterious effects. This is now best seen at his own house (Sir John Soane's Museum) in Lincoln's Inn Fields, London; its complicated layout, changing floor-levels, top lighting and multitude of mirrors create a striking, enclosed but surprisingly comfortable atmosphere.

The Victorians

The reign of Queen Victoria (r. 1837-1901) transformed Britain. This was the age of rapid industrialisation, huge population growth, cities, factories, railways, world-wide commerce and far-flung Empire. Masterful engineers tunnelled through the Pennines, bridged the Forth and raised vast structures of metal and sheet glass such as the Crystal Palace and the great railway stations. Buildings of all sorts were needed and provided in quantities – slums and suburbs, churches and clubs, factories, mills, warehouses, banks, big business and civic buildings. And, of course, houses for the old and new rich, including enormous country houses and castles.

One of the striking things about Victorian architecture is the absence of any dominant style. Styles had overlapped or

Opposite left, the gallery of Strawberry Hill, Twickenham, Middlesex, built by Horace Walpole in 1776; the 'Gothick' fantasy of his style sought charm and idiosyncrasy in medieval architecture irrespective of its structural relevance.

Opposite above right, an elevation of a wall for the glass drawing room at Northumberland House, London, by Robert Adam, about 1773. Adam's designs combined a monumental vision with a concern for every last detail, and his scholarly accuracy was enhanced by a vision that was his alone.

Opposite below right, a design (1869-71) for Knightshayes Court, Devon, by William Burges. Little of this decorative work at Knightshayes was ever completed.

Right, in the Romantic era people began to become aware of the grandeur, monumentality and drama of ruined castles, as in this painting of Conwy by Paul Sandby (1725-1809). Once this appeal had been recognised, the castles were rescued from oblivion, restored, preserved, copied, and finally turned into some of the most popular examples of the British heritage.

coexisted in earlier periods, but there had never before been anything like the Victorians' eclecticism – their willingness to build in any manner, whether ancient, medieval or modern, native, foreign or sheerly exotic. No new, distinctively 'Victorian' style emerged from this profusion: the age was one of successive or simultaneous revivals. The style with the strongest claim to high seriousness was Gothic, which, thanks to the influence of A.W.N. Pugin (1812-52), ceased to be associated with the picturesque and mysterious; in the hands of such eminent High Victorians as William Butterfield (1814-1900) and Sir George Gilbert Scott (1811-78) it was used with scholarship and vigour for ecclesiastical building – and also for the Houses of Parliament and St Pancras Railway Station and Hotel.

By contrast, Neo-Classicism ceased to be high fashion, although it was still found appropriate for many civic buildings (especially in the new cities and towns created by industrialism) and for solid middle-class terraces. The Victorians' taste for mass and ornament – one of several respects in which they resembled the Elizabethans – was better served by the neo-Renaissance *palazzo* style, with its powerful arches and rusticated surfaces (that is, surfaces in which the masonry consists of blocks whose edges have been chiselled away, creating an emphatic pattern of blocks and grooves). The major pioneer of the style was Sir Charles Barry (1795-1860), who (literally) acclimatised it to Britain by roofing over the Italianate open courtyard, which became a grand balconied hall. Followers of the style included Albert, the Prince Consort, who designed the royal residence, Osborne House, on the Isle of Wight.

There were many more styles, and also sub-styles – for the Victorian blend of eclecticism and scholarship encouraged architects to seek a spurious orginality by working in some national or period version of a style (for example, Dutch or French, rather than Italian, Renaissance). This proliferation was nowhere more marked than in country houses, where size, spectacle and instant historic effect were at a premium – notoriously so with the vulgar new-rich magnates and financiers who were setting themselves up as 'lords of the manor', but also with the many supposedly unvulgar aristocrats who managed to benefit from the booming Victorian economy.

The size of Victorian country houses was partly the result of a new pattern of weekend entertaining, made possible by the railways, which could bring or take away hordes of visitors within a few hours; these had to be accommodated, and so did the hordes of servants who looked after them. New rooms – for example the smoking-room and gun-room – gave guests the opportunity to spread out, and also catered for the Victorian obsession with specialisation, which was

even more apparent 'below stairs'. The Victorian country house has plausibly been likened to a rabbit warren, and the achievement of architects in making it work effectively should not be underestimated.

As accomplished professionals, most architects produced designs in whatever style their clients required. Barry adopted his preferred Renaissance style for Cliveden in Buckinghamshire, but also enlarged Dunrobin Castle in Scottish Baronial – and rebuilt the Houses of Parliament in Gothic. Joseph Paxton (1801-65), designer of the severely functional iron-and-glass Crystal Palace, had no qualms about building Mentmore Towers, Buckinghamshire, in the Elizabethan manner of Wollaton. Anthony Salvin (1799-1881) was a prolific designer of Gothic, Elizabethan and Jacobean mansions. One architect with firm convictions was William Burges (1827-81), who seems to have lived in a private Gothic fantasy-world which, finding the ideal patron, he expressed lavishly at Cardiff Castle and Castell Coch, South Glamorgan . . . . But sometimes no British architect would do: to build Waddesdon Manor, Buckinghamshire, in the style of a Loire *château*, Baron de Rothschild thought it necessary to import a bona fide Frenchman in the person of Gabriel-Hippolyte Destailleur!

Into the 20th century

Eventually a reaction did set in against Victorian revivalism, especially in more modest (though still substantial) domestic building. Pugin, John Ruskin, William Morris and the Arts & Crafts movement all contributed to a new emphasis on honest craftsmanship, the use of local and appropriate materials, and the avoidance of period styles – or at any rate a restrained and tasteful use of them. Philip Webb (1831-1915) was the first significant architect of the movement, and the Red House he built in 1859 for Morris at Bexleyheath was its first monument. Houses in this tradition were generally informal and unpretentious, horizontal in emphasis, respectful of local materials and associations, and 'Old English' in feeling, with a more or less definite medieval manor-house atmosphere. Richard Norman Shaw (1831-1912) was influenced by this tradition, for example at Adcote in Shropshire, though he worked in other manners including his own 'Queen Anne' version of the 17th-century town house.

C.F.A.Voysey (1857-1941) took the 'Old English' manner into the 20th century, as did Sir Edwin Lutyens (1869-1944). However, the spectacularly successful Lutyens later turned to a grandiose Neo-Classicism which reached a literally imperial apotheosis with the Viceroy's House, New Delhi. He is an appropriate figure with whom to end this outline, since his immense granite Castle Drogo (1910-30) was the very last of country seats in the grand manner.

Dunster Castle, Somerset

The West Country

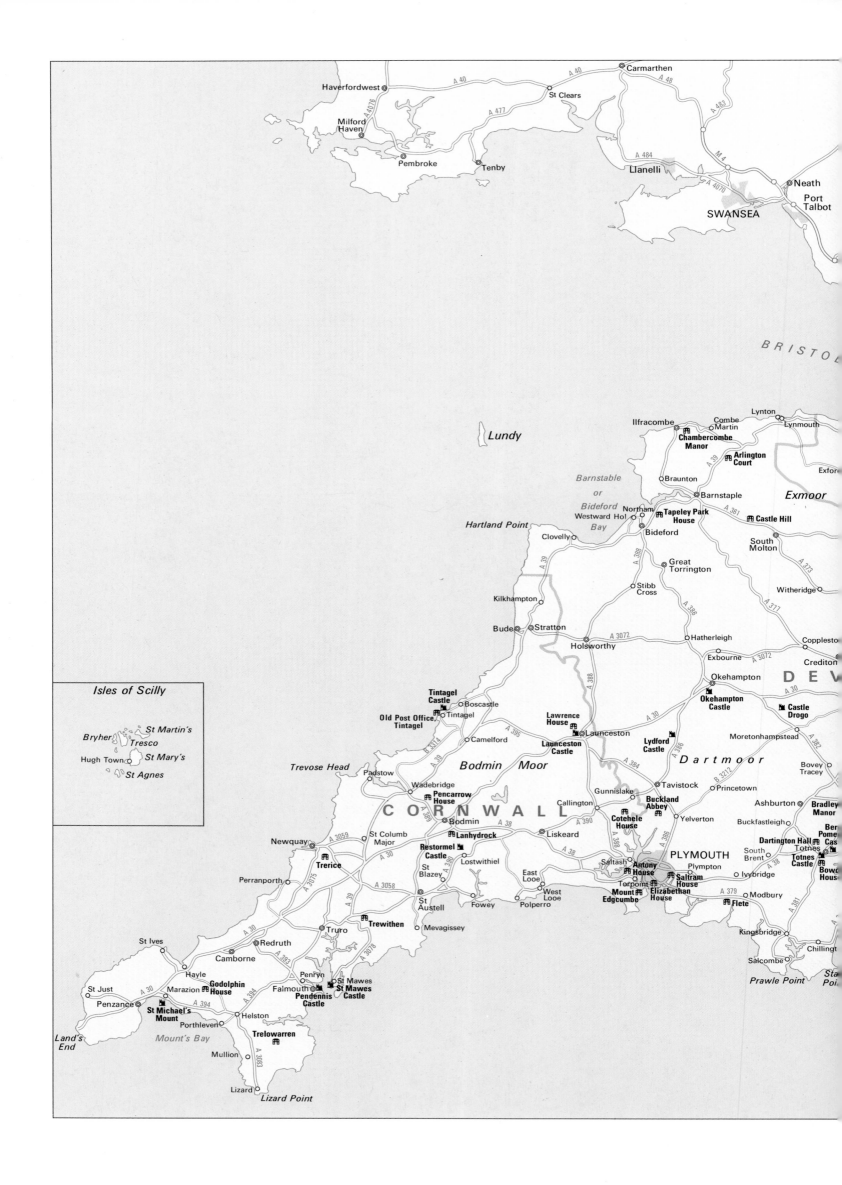

Athelhampton Hall

Athelhampton, Dorset

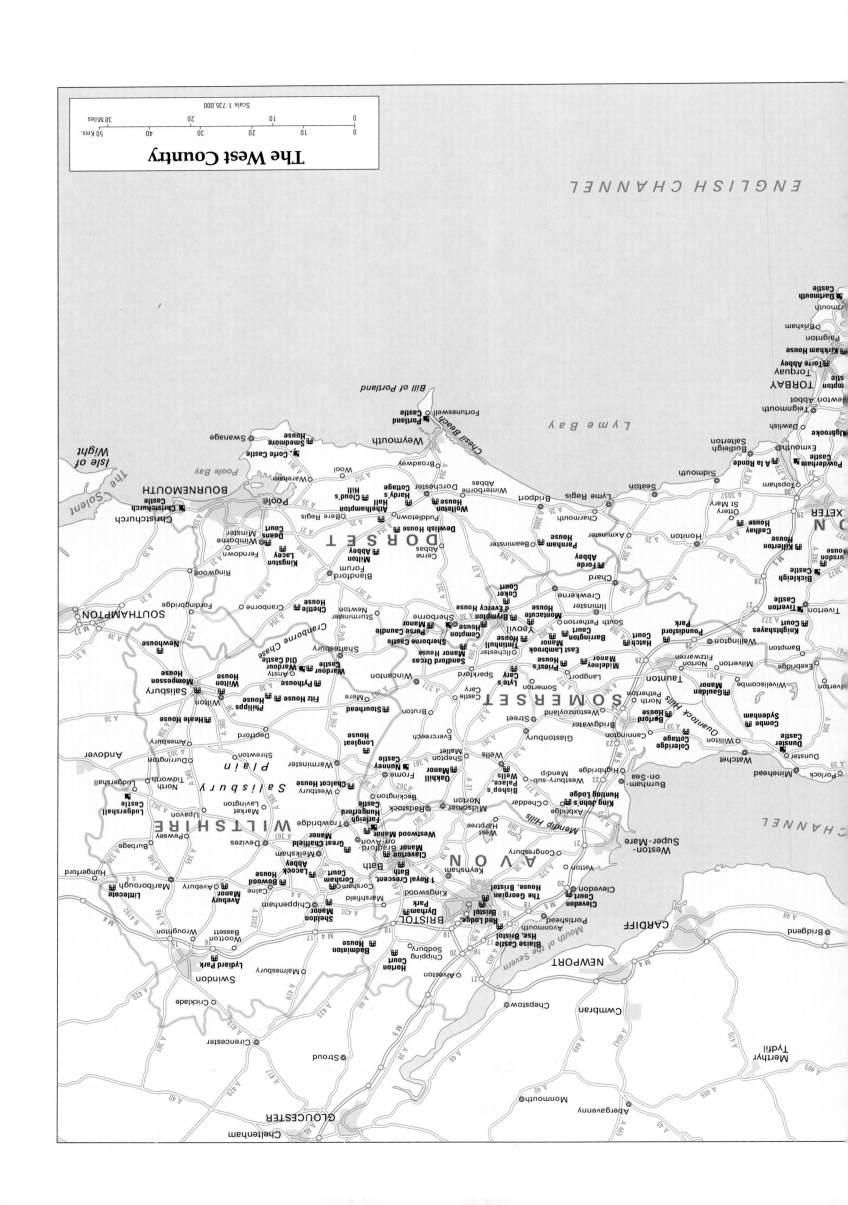

The West Country

Scale 1:735,000

Deep in Thomas Hardy's Wessex the house stands among trees close to the River Piddle. In spite of partial destruction and much alteration and restoration, it is an important example of Tudor domestic architecture. The comparatively modest scale of this Tudor gentleman's rural retreat affords an interesting comparison to the great houses of the nobility.

The name indicates the homestead or settlement of a Saxon leader but no records or archaeological evidence exist. The earliest known Lords of the Manor were the de Loundres and then the de Pydeles. From the latter the estate passed by marriage to Sir Richard Martyn about the middle of the 14th century. His descendant, Sir William Martyn, Lord Mayor of London in 1493, obtained permission to enclose 160 acres of parkland and to erect a residence incorporating the status symbols of towers and ornamental battlements. He built a typical early Tudor country house round a small court and with an impressive entrance. To the right of the porch an extra storey was added soon afterwards and the original battlements can be seen embedded in the later masonry.

After Sir William's death in 1504, his son Christopher added the two-storey wing on the west side with rather top-heavy dormers which are not aligned with the lower windows. The wing is not at right-angles to the earlier block, giving a slightly splayed effect. The general lack of symmetry of both the main fronts is one of the attractions of the house.

Opposite, the great hall of Athelhampton, a fine example of 15th-century domestic building, with the original timber roof.

Below, the great chamber, with 17th-century plasterwork ceiling and oak panelling. The harpsichord dates from 1761.

Christopher died in 1525 and his son Robert formed an outer courtyard on the south-west side, with an imposing gatehouse. The last male Martyn died in 1596 and the estate passed in equal shares to his four daughters. The eldest married a Brune who soon afterwards acquired two of the other shares. The youngest daughter married a Floyer, the fourth share remaining in that family's possession until the middle of the 19th century. In 1848 the whole estate was acquired from the Brune descendants and the Floyers by George Wood. He was a wealthy Congregationalist who started a Noncomformist school at Athelhampton.

By this time only the foundations remained of the north and east wings round the small court and the rest of the house was becoming derelict. Wood pulled down the decaying gatehouse and walls of the outer court-yard, leaving the open front as it exists today. He compensated for this destruction by beginning the restoration of the house, most importantly saving the roof of the great hall. Later in the 19th century Alfred Cart de Lafontaine purchased the estate and continued the restoration. He reconstructed part of the south wing which had been truncated when the east wing was demolished. He collected many items to furnish the rooms and started to create the gardens on a formal Italian pattern.

The present owners are Sir Robert and Lady Cooke. For nearly twenty years they have preserved the house as a family home and extended and improved the delightful gardens.

The great hall of pre-1500, a modest 38 feet in length, has a simple and superb timber roof. The braces are boldly curved to form unusual cusps, the main braces shaped like flattened horseshoes. The roof is matched by some fine linenfold panelling round the walls. The

striking bay window at the north-west corner does not rise to the height of the house wall and so has its own, slightly lower battlements. The bay is four-sided, vaulted, the windows tall and slender with simple tracery. All the windows of the hall have either original heraldic glass or copies. The Martyn crest is prominent: a chained ape (a martin in heraldic language) on a tree stump holding a mirror in its right paw. Their motto was 'He who looks at Martyn's ape, Martyn's ape shall look at him'. The screen below the minstrels' gallery is contemporary but brought from elsewhere to replace the neglected and decayed original. On the north wall a fine Flemish tapestry depicts Samson slaying the Philistines with the jawbone of an ass.

A doorway at the side of the bay window leads to an anteroom with more oak panelling and a timbered roof. From this two archways give access to the great chamber which occupies the ground floor of the west wing. More heraldic glass shows the Martyn crest and the arms of the families with whom the Martyns intermarried. Worcester porcelain is displayed in an 18th-century cabinet. The harpsichord in a marquetry case belonged to Queen Charlotte. It is dated 1761, the year of her marriage to George III (r. 1760-1820), presumably a wedding gift.

From the ante-room a newel staircase of stone steps changing to oak steps ascends to the former gallery, much restored, which occupies the upper floor of the west wing. It is a small version of the long galleries of the great Tudor mansions. On the upper floor of the older block the state bedroom has an admirable 15th-century chimneypiece, rectangular and bold, decorated with the crests of Sir William Martyn and his wife.

The gardens make a lovely setting for the Hall. The formal sections are divided by walls of Ham stone, with four separate plots radiating from a circular, central court. One contains yew trees clipped to the shape of

Above, the formal gardens to the south-east of the house contrast the Ham stone of their walls with the dark green clipped yews, planted and cut in the Elizabethan manner.

Opposite above, Athelhampton Hall is a typical and irregular Elizabethan country house.

Opposite below, the statue of Hygeia, goddess of health, one of the features of the lime walk.

pyramids, another a long pool with the ends imitating horizontally and in stone the braces of the great hall roof. Elsewhere the gardens are less formal with woodland and riverside walks and, notably, an early 16th-century dovecote. The revolving ladder inside, to facilitate collection of eggs and squabs from the nests, is still in place.

Thomas Hardy (1840-1928), born a few miles away at Bockhampton, knew Athelhampton from childhood. It is probable that his stonemason father worked there on restoration work for George Wood. Hardy shortened the name to Athelhall in two poems ('The Dame of Athelhall' and 'The Children and Sir Nameless') and in his short story 'The Waiting Supper'. He had good reason to remember Athelhampton through his attachment as a young man to his clever and attractive cousin Tryphena Sparks. She attended the school started by George Wood and began her teaching career there. She remained in Hardy's thoughts for many years to inspire more than one of his moving poems on the theme of lost love.

☎ Puddletown (030 584) 363

7 m NE of Dorchester on A35, 1 m E of Puddletown

SY 7794 (OS 194)

Open mid Apr to mid Oct W, Th, Su, Good Fri and Bank Hol M also M and T in Aug 1400-1800

⊖ 🅿 WC ♿ (limited access) 🚼 D (car park only) ♣ 🍴 ⌓ ● ⚲

Longleat House

Warminster, Wiltshire

The stimulus for the building of the great Elizabethan country houses came from the Queen herself. Each summer she travelled through the provinces to visit her most powerful subjects, particularly the new land-owners who had risen to high position and wealth in Tudor times. They vied with each other to entertain her and her retinue on a grand scale. The frugal Elizabeth had no objection to her subjects paying out vast sums for this purpose. The first of these Elizabethan man-sions, built by Sir John Thynne, was Longleat.

Thynne had been a favourite of the Duke of Somer-set, the Lord Protector during the minority of Edward VI. He fought and was wounded at the Duke's victory over the Scots at Pinkie in 1547. Somerset knighted him on the battlefield and allowed him to quarter the Scottish lion, with a twisted tail, on his coat of arms. When Somerset fell from power Thynne was impris-oned in the Tower of London, but he obtained his release on payment of a large fine. Meanwhile, in 1540, he had purchased an Augustinian Priory close to the

Wiltshire-Somerset border and watered by a stream known as the Long Leat. In the same year as Pinkie he began to build a mansion on the site. Work continued for many years but almost as soon as completed the house was destroyed by fire. Sir John, undeterred, immediately started to build again. The earlier house seems to have been entirely his design but now he enlisted the aid of his master mason, Robert Smythson, who was to become the only noteworthy architect of Elizabethan times. Whatever Smythson's exact con-tribution, the result was the first important Renaissance building in England. In 1575 Sir John was able to entertain the Queen there in suitable style.

The building is a vast square with two inner spaces designed not as courtyards but as light-wells for the rooms around them, a remarkable innovation. The three-storeyed fronts have big mullioned windows in and between bays to light the outer rooms while the balustrades, chimneys and domed turrets above give a classical finish. The north front, however, is an early

19th-century imitation of the other three. Other alterations to the exterior were the placing of statues on the balustrades and the addition of an ornamental doorway on the south front, late in the 17th century. These embellishments were the work of Sir Thomas Thynne who inherited Longleat when his cousin, another Thomas, was murdered in Pall Mall in 1682.

Sir Thomas was created Viscount Weymouth in the same year that he inherited. He was a cultured man and made many improvements to the interior of the house and to the gardens, though most of these have since been swept away. A notable exception is the room on the top floor known as Bishop Ken's library where most of the family's 30,000 books are housed. Bishop Ken, one of the Seven Bishops in the famous trial in 1688, was given asylum by the 1st Viscount after his acquittal and died at Longleat in 1711.

The 3rd Viscount was raised to the dignity of Marquis of Bath in 1789 and employed Capability Brown to arrange the park. The formal gardens were destroyed,

Opposite, Longleat is one of the most coherent and controlled of the great Elizabethan houses; its plan distantly recalls castle architecture.

Above, the saloon, formerly the long gallery, was remodelled in the Italian fashion in the late 19th century, and given mainly 18th-century French furniture.

lakes formed from the Long Leat and the valley planted with woods and clumps of trees. It must be counted one of Brown's most successful creations.

After the death of the 1st Marquis the estate descended from father to son down to the present 6th Marquis who inherited in 1946 after active service in the Second World War.

The great hall is the least changed part of the Elizabethan interior. The chimneypiece and the fine screen and minstrel's gallery were added about 1600, the small balcony at the other end about 1660. Later in the 17th century the present ceiling was inserted above the braces of the hammer-beam roof, to enable a room to be built above, a sad distortion of the Elizabethan

Left, the orangery and 'half mile pond', products of the 18th-century reworking of Longleat's grounds, in some of Capability Brown's most effective work.

Opposite, the great hall, unlike much of the rest of the house interior, retains its Elizabethan quality, and remains substantially as it was planned by Sir John Thynne in the 1550s.

Below, the red library houses some 6000 volumes, a small part of those collected by the family over many centuries.

proportions. The set of paintings by John Wootton are mid-18th century; they tell the story of a homeless boy found on the estate by the 2nd Viscount and given employment in the stables only to be killed, at the age of fourteen, trying to separate two stallions.

The great staircase and the lower east corridor were part of a reconstruction by Sir Jeffry Wyattville for the 2nd Marquis, in the first decade of the 19th century. The simple ceiling of the latter is in contrast to the elaborate work in the red library and the state rooms carried out in the 1870s for the 4th Marquis. He had been Ambassador at Lisbon and Vienna, and brought over Italian craftsmen to transform the house, particularly by a series of ceilings in imitation of those in Italian palaces. The state drawing room ceiling is adapted from the library of St Mark's, Venice, the state dining room has an Italianate frieze and an elaborate ceiling displaying a dozen pictures of the School of Titian. Perhaps the saloon, the former Elizabethan long gallery, is the most impressive of these rooms. The 90-foot long ceiling was inspired by one in the Palazzo Massimo in Rome and the huge fireplace copied from one in the Doge's Palace at Venice. The big Elizabethan windows continue to light the Victorian intrusions and the early 16th-century tapestries covering the inner wall.

Longleat exhibits all the furnishings of a great house, notable silver and ceramics and exotic furniture. The collection of paintings includes *The Holy Family*, which

is attributed to Titian, and a range of portraits from Tudor times to Sir William Orpen's painting of the 5th Marquis and Graham Sutherland's informal and delightful study of the present owner.

Notwithstanding the importance of the house and its treasures, it is the wild animals roaming Capability Brown's park that have given Longleat an extra dimension during the last twenty years. The proposal to create a wild life park in the Wiltshire countryside came from Chipperfield, the well-known circus owner. The present Marquis adopted the idea with enthusiasm and the first 'safari park' in Britain was opened in 1966. Soon 'the lions of Longleat' became familiar to people all over Britain. Many less dangerous animals also live in the park, camels, giraffes, monkeys and notably white rhinoceros, until comparatively recently an endangered species in its African homeland. In 1984 a baby white rhino was born at Longleat and has delighted visitors from all over the world ever since.

☎ Maiden Bradley (098 53) 551

3½ m W of Warminster on A362

ST 8043 (OS 183)

Open throughout year daily 1000-1800, closes 1600 Oct to Easter

🅿 WC ♿ (by appt) 🚻 D
♣ ♟ ⛺ ◆ ☷ ♨ (available in French and German)
🏃 (compulsory)

Wilton House

Salisbury, Wiltshire

Three miles west of Salisbury, at the meeting of the Rivers Wylye and Nadder, Wilton House stands on the site of a Saxon abbey. Only a small medieval building to the west of the stable block remains of the older foundation. In 1544 Henry VIII gave the abbey and lands to William Herbert, a gentleman of Welsh origin who had married Anne, sister to the King's sixth wife, Catherine Parr.

The portrait of William Herbert at Wilton shows a shrewd, able man of Tudor times. He managed to survive in high office in four successive reigns while many others were disgraced or sent to the scaffold. He was one of the regents appointed by Henry VIII's will to govern on behalf of the young Edward VI, and in 1551 he was created Earl of Pembroke.

Meanwhile the abbey at Wilton had been pulled down and a house built fit for such a powerful man. A contemporary drawing suggests that the plan, four blocks round a courtyard, was essentially similar to the present one.

Future earls would also hold high office, but another aspect of Wilton came about through the marriage of the 2nd Earl to Mary (1561-1621), the sister of Sir Philip Sidney. She was a great patroness of literature and learning and her brother wrote his influential *Arcadia* at Wilton. Later the first folio edition of Shakespeare's plays was dedicated to her two sons. Already the house had become the cultural centre that is still manifest in its appearance and contents.

About 1647 a fire destroyed most of the Tudor house and all the contents. Rebuilding in grey stone from Chilmark, a dozen miles away along the Nadder valley, began at once. The work, supervised by Inigo Jones and his nephew John Webb, was completed about 1653. The north and west blocks were drastically altered at the beginning of the 19th centuy by James Wyatt in Gothick style, and at the same time the surviving Tudor entrance porch block moved to its present position in the garden. But the east and south fronts have all the marks of Inigo Jones' style: a restrained dignity uncluttered by unnecessary ornament. Inside these blocks the state apartments are 17th-century rooms little altered structurally though the contents owe much to later acquisitions, notably by Thomas, the 8th Earl, who succeeded in 1683. His most famous purchase, the 14th-century *Wilton Diptych*, was sold to the National Gallery in 1929 but so many great works of art remain that this need not be regretted.

The grandest room at Wilton, called 'the double cube', occupies the middle of the south block. Measuring 60 by 30 feet, and 30 foot high, experts often claim that it is the best proportioned room in England. Its main purpose was to show off the family portraits painted by Van Dyck for the 4th Earl. These had previously been in the Earl's London house and so escaped the fire of 1647. Everything else in the room, both contemporary and of later date, makes a superbly contrived setting for the portraits.

Left and below, Wilton House, the home of the Earls of Pembroke for over 400 years. The house was planned in the 1630s with a much longer façade and a central portico; misfortune in the Civil War period reduced the scale finally adopted.

The large picture of the 4th Earl and his family occupies most of the west wall and dominates the room. The elegant figures are grouped with all Van Dyck's skill as portrayer of royalty and nobility. By comparison the smaller portraits of Charles I and Queen Henrietta Maria above the doors on either side are in a minor position. Charles had been a frequent visitor to Wilton before the Civil War and thought himself betrayed when the Earl sided with Parliament. On the north and east walls large individual family portraits hang in splendour, and over the fireplace is a painting of Charles I's children similar to one at Windsor Castle. The furniture, all gilt and red velvet, is by Thomas Chippendale and William Kent. The ceiling of this huge room is reduced to proper size by a wide, flamboyantly painted coving. Gilded friezes and wall decorations complete a room of unsurpassed distinction.

Impressive double-doors connect with the great ante room, a gracious, less overwhelming apartment. It contains more red velvet and gilded chairs and settees, a showcase for part of a 19th-century Viennese dinner service of 250 pieces and some interesting portraits. Outstanding is Rembrandt's realistic but sympathetic painting of his mother, spectacles on nose, a large book open on her lap.

Beyond the white and gold colonnade room, formerly the state bedroom and displaying several portraits by Reynolds, is the corner room in the south-east angle of the house. Paintings by Andrea del Sarto, Lorenzo Lotto, Rubens and Poussin share the walls with a *Leda and the Swan* of particular interest though by a lesser artist. Cesare da Sesto was a pupil of Leonardo da Vinci and his picture is regarded as the closest copy known of a lost painting by Leonardo. The face and hair exactly imitate one of the master's studies (now at Windsor Castle) for his own painting.

Leaving the state apartments the large smoking room recalls the 10th Earl, a soldier who wrote books on equitation and built the riding school at Wilton. A feature of the room is the set of sixty-six pictures of the disciplines of *haute-école* horsemanship. In their original, attractive frames, they are gouache paintings by a famous Austrian riding master, Baron d'Eisenburg. A picture of the Baron, thought to be a self-portrait, hangs facing the unique paintings which he presented to the Earl. No horseman can fail to be captivated by this record of the skills still demonstrated in the Spanish Riding School at Vienna.

Throughout the house fine Chinese porcelain is much in evidence and many Classical and later sculptures. Busts of Florence Nightingale and Sidney Herbert are a reminder that without his support as War Secretary she might never have reached the Crimea. The sash she wore at Scutari is shown in the so-called upper cloisters. Sidney Herbert rented Wilton from his half-brother, the 12th Earl, who lived abroad and was succeeded by Sidney Herbert's son.

The spacious lawns outside the house, the dark cedar trees and the quiet chalkland streams make a perfect setting for a noble house and one of the finest collections of art in private hands.

Below, the Palladian bridge spanning the River Nadder, built by Henry, 9th Earl of Pembroke in 1737, with Roger Morris.

Below left, a view of the house from the Palladian bridge.

Opposite, the double cube room, designed by Inigo Jones and very lavishly decorated. The paintings are mainly by Van Dyck.

☎ Salisbury (0722) 743115

3 m W of Salisbury on A36 SU 0930 (OS 184)

Open Apr to mid Oct T-S and Bank Hol M 1100-1800, Su 1300-1800

⊖ P WC ♿ ⊟ (by appt) D (guide dogs only) ♣ ☛ ◆ ⊛ ⚹ ✗ (compulsory exc Su; available in foreign languages) ● (not in house) ⚲

A La Ronde

Summer Lane, Exmouth, Devon

An unusual sixteen-sided house, built by two maiden ladies in the last years of the 18th century, and one of the lesser-known curiosities among England's houses. The ladies, Jane Parminter and her orphaned cousin Mary, had spent ten years travelling on the Continent, and they designed the house, supposedly based on the church of San Vitale in Ravenna, on their return in 1794. Later they also built a chapel and almshouses nearby. The house, although it appears small, is actually quite spacious: there are twenty rooms within its solid stone walls, those on the ground floor radiating from a central hall 54 foot high. Between the rooms are closets with lozenge windows, and there are many ingenious space-saving devices such as folding seats and sliding doors. The decorations were all done by the ladies themselves, and provide impressive examples of the handicraft skills that were becoming popular at the time. In the hall, rather than San Vitale's mosaics, the whole upper part is encrusted with shellwork and featherwork pictures of birds. There is more featherwork in the drawing room, while elsewhere there are pictures made of sand and seaweed and some of cut paper. All this would probably have been ridiculed earlier this century, but with today's revival of these 18th- and 19th-century crafts the house has a particular fascination for the modern visitor. The original furniture and pictures are still in the house, which is now owned by a descendant.

☎ Exmouth (0395) 265514

In the N outskirts of Exmouth off B3180

SY 0083 (OS 192)

Open Good Fri to end Oct daily 1000-1800, Su 1400-1900; by appt throughout year

⊖ 🄿 WC ⌸ 🚻 D ♣ 🍴 (by appt)
🪑 ◆ ♨ 🗡 ● (no video cameras in house)

Antony House

Torpoint, Cornwall

This elegant rectangular house was built for Sir William Carew between 1711 and 1721, of silver-grey stone with rose-covered red-brick wings. The present building has a simple design, with identical north and south façades, nine windows along the first storey, eight below, and dormer windows set into the roof. The front porch was added in 1839. Surprisingly, the interior is quite different from the light and graceful exterior, the rooms downstairs being quite small and intimate, panelled in Dutch oak and consequently rather dark. They contain some fine furniture made for the house, including a Queen Anne pier glass and a set of tapestry-covered chairs, and an excellent series of family portraits. There are also collections of sporting paintings and porcelain; the tapestry room contains Soho tapestries, and the library displays a copy of Richard Carew's *Survey of Cornwall*, published in 1602. The ground-floor rooms, all of which face north and only one with windows in more than one wall, are arranged round a central hall, from which a fine if rather heavy staircase rises in two broad flights. The first floor is much more 18th century in feeling, with charming bedrooms leading off a tall-arched central corridor. The beautiful gardens, which run down to the River Lynher, were partly laid out by Humphry Repton, and many of the trees he planted have grown to an enormous size. The stone carvings and the Burmese temple bell were brought back by Sir Reginald Pole-Carew from military campaigns in India and Burma.

☎ Plymouth (0752) 812191

1 m NW of Torpoint on A374 turn NW at Maryfield.
5 m W of Plymouth via Torpoint car ferry

SX 4156 (OS 201)

Open Apr to end Oct T-Th and Bank Hol M 1400-1800

⊖ (limited) 🄿 WC ⌸ (limited access)
🚻 (by appt) ♣ ◆ 🍴 ♨ 🗡

Badminton House

Badminton, Avon

A splendid Palladian mansion, home of the Dukes of Beaufort, and now the setting for the internationally famous annual Badminton Horse Trials. Henry Somerset, created Duke of Beaufort by Charles II, inherited the original manor from a cousin, and after the Restoration the house was entirely rebuilt, with much use of Classical detail. Around the house the Duke planted radiating avenues, which were much admired by visitors and neighbouring gentry. The 1st Duke died in 1700 and the 2nd Duke in 1714; and it was the 3rd Duke, with his architect William Kent, who transformed the house in the mid-18th century. It has been little altered since. Kent added a top storey, as he had noticed that the house was becoming dwarfed by the 1st Duke's planted avenues, and flanked it with low wings ending in pavilions. Finally, he crowned the north front with cupolas and a pediment. He also built the charming Worcester Lodge in the park, and redecorated a great deal of the interior, a particularly fine feature being the entrance hall hung with equestrian paintings by John Wootton (c.1686-1765). The south drawing room is the only one to survive from the earlier period. The house also contains collections of Italian and Dutch paintings, and the stables and hunt kennels are open for viewing.

☎ Badminton (045 421) 202

2½ m E of Chipping Sodbury on A432 turn onto B4040 for 4 m, turn NE at Acton Turville

ST 8082 (OS 172)

Open June to Sept W 1430-1700

🄿 WC 🚻 (by appt) ♣ 🗡

Brympton d'Evercy

Yeovil, Somerset

This house, with all its buildings made of the lovely golden Ham Hill stone, seems at first sight to be uniformly Tudor. But although the west front, which bears the arms of Henry VIII, is a fine example of Tudor architecture, the house went through several different periods of building. The main house, together with the left side of the front, was built by the Sydenhams from about 1520; the central section, church and dower house are older. The Sydenhams lived consistently above their income, and the programme of constant building and renovation they carried out at Brympton, culminating in the splendid south front, was to turn them from wealthy landowners to paupers. The south front is one of the most famous examples of the Classical style of the 1670s, and was the work of Sir John Posthumous Sydenham; but it finally destroyed the family fortunes. Five years after his death in 1692 his son put the house up for sale as 'a Very Large New Built Mansion', and after a short spell of ownership by Thomas Penny, Receiver General of Somerset, it was bought by Francis Fane, whose descendants still live here. The main ground-floor rooms are open to the public, including the hall with its huge staircase, and they contain some good furniture and paintings as well as 18th-century panelling. The layout of the gardens was the work of Lady Georgiana Fane, who never married because she lost her heart to a 'lowly soldier' and her father would not countenance such a match. The 'lowly soldier' in question later became better known as the Duke of Wellington.

☎ West Coker (093 586) 2528
2½ m W of Yeovil on A3088 turn SW to Odcombe for ½ m then S
ST 5215 (OS 183)

Open Easter weekend then May to end Sept S-W 1400-1800
⊖ (limited) 🅿 WC 🔼 🚻 ♣ 🍴
🪑 ◆ 🏵 ⚘

Combe Sydenham Hall

Monksilver, Somerset

This pleasant manor house dates back to about 1360, when it was built for the Sydenham family, who occupied it for over 300 years. Standing in a combe, or hollow, surrounded by trees, Combe Sydenham was originally a semi-fortified house, built round a courtyard with towers at each corner; but it was remodelled by George Sydenham in 1850. Like other comfort- and fashion-conscious Elizabethans he reduced the height of the hall and put in an up-to-date staircase; the present house, with its single tower and two wings, is essentially his creation and, appropriately enough, the visitor is greeted by his initials carved on the porch. Notable features of the interior are the Court Room, with its 15th-century tiles, and the Restoration Chamber; in the latter, the windows were designed to show off the great expanses of glass in which the Elizabethans took such pride. One of the curiosities of the house is a meteorite kept in the entrance hall. According to legend, Sir Francis Drake was betrothed to George Sydenham's daughter, and promised to send her a sign while he was away at sea. The voyage was a long one, and Elizabeth Sydenham grew tired of waiting. She was on the point of marrying another man when the meteorite rolled between them, evidently putting an end to the match; at any rate, she did in fact marry Drake in 1585. In front of Combe Sydenham stands a range of buildings including a well-restored medieval gatehouse.

☎ Stogumber (09846) 284
5 m N of Wiveliscombe on B3188
ST 0736 (OS 181)

Open Spring Bank Hol weeekend, June and Sept T, W, F; July and Aug M-F 1300-1700
🅿 WC 🔼 ♣ 🍴

Corfe Castle

Corfe, near Wareham, Dorset

Corfe Castle, standing on a steep isolated mound in the ridge of the Purbeck hills, was in its time one of the strongest castles in England. Excavation has found traces of a substantial pre-Conquest building, probably a royal house, but the building of the castle proper began in the 11th century and was basically completed by 1285. The early buildings are those near the top of the hill, with the remains of the keep, built during the early part of the 12th century, at the peak. The 'gloriette' (an unfortified house) was built for King John about 1200, while the outer bailey, a new south-west gatehouse and the outer gatehouse were the last to be constructed. From its construction by William the Conqueror to its destruction by Cromwell's forces in the Civil War, Corfe Castle has been a setting for many episodes in England's history. William I's son, Robert, Duke of Normandy, was imprisoned here; King John, whose favourite castle it was, imprisoned his wife here in 1212 and four years later hid his crown and treasures here, and Edward II, who improved and enlarged the castle, was himself imprisoned in it in 1326. Henry VII visited it in 1496, and in 1571 Elizabeth I sold it to Sir Christopher Hatton, whose widow later disposed of it to the Royalist Sir John Bankes. Sir John spent most of his time in attendance on the King, and when the Civil War broke out Lady Bankes was left to defend the castle on her own. She held out bravely, but was eventually defeated, and in 1646 the House of Commons voted to demolish the building.

☎ Corfe Castle (0929) 480442
6 m SW of Wareham on A351 in Corfe village
SY 9582 (OS 195)

Open Mar to Oct daily 1000-dusk; Nov to Feb S and Su 1400-1600
⊖ (limited) 🚻 D ♣ 🪑 ◆ ⚘

☎ Corsham (0249) 712214
4½ m SW of Chippenham on A4, turn S at Corsham
ST 8770 (OS 173)

Open mid Jan to mid Dec T, W, Th, S, Su 1400-1600; June, Sept and Bank Hols 1400-1800
🅿 WC ⓰ (by appt) 🚻 (by appt) D ♠ 🍴
🐕 (occasional) ✕ ● (not in house)

Corsham Court

Corsham, Wiltshire

Corsham Court, a mixture of Elizabethan and 18th century, is best known for its 18th-century rooms with their fine art collections. The original yellow stone manor was built by Thomas Smythe in 1582, and the south front is unchanged, as are the stables on the west side and the riding school on the east. The house was bought in 1745 by Paul Methuen, and in 1760 Capability Brown, famous as a landscape gardener but less so as an architect, was given the job of enlarging both house and grounds. He converted the entire east wing into a suite of sumptuous state rooms to hold Paul Methuen's collection of works of art. In 1800 John Nash was commissioned to make further enlargements, but his 'Gothick' north front and entrance was replaced in 1845 by Thomas Bellamy, and all that now remains of Nash's work is a tiny dairy in the park and some decoration on the east front. Of the rooms open to visitors three, the entrance hall, music room and dining room, are Bellamy's; the rest are all Brown's creations, the finest of them being the picture gallery. This room is hung with pictures up to the ceiling, and the walls are covered in crimson silk damask echoed in the covers of the chairs, sofas and window seats made by Chippendale. The plaster ceiling is from a rejected design by Brown for the hall at Burton Constable, and the carpet reflects this design. The other state rooms are smaller but no less treasure-filled. The paintings include an *Annunciation* from the studio of Filippo Lippi and works by Elsheimer, Jan Breughel and Teniers, and the furniture is of high quality.

☎ Liskeard (0579) 50434
6 m SW of Tavistock on A390 turn S at Drakewalls to Albaston and Newton
SX 4268 (OS 201)

Open Apr to end Oct daily 1100-1800; reduced rates for parties of 15 or over
♿ 🅿 WC ⓰ (limited access) 🚻 (by appt, not Bank Hols) ♠ 🍴 (limited opening) 🍴 ♦ 🐕 ✕

Cotehele House

St Dominick, near Saltash, Cornwall

A romantic granite-built manor house with an authentic medieval atmosphere, very little altered since it was built by Sir Richard Edgcumbe from 1480. The tower was added in 1627. But if the house has not changed much, the setting undoubtedly has. Sir Richard, who was involved in the revolt against Richard III, was a hard-headed soldier; he would neither have recognised nor comprehended the soft lush lawns and vegetation which now surround his house. Woods would never have been allowed so near a house, and gardens were at that time strictly utilitarian. But Cotehele still has tremendous atmosphere, and gives the visitor a sense of stepping back into the past which few houses can achieve. The Edgcumbes more or less left the house after 1700, though they did not neglect it, and tourists, among them George III, had begun to visit it by the end of the 18th century – 'old-fashioned houses' were becoming popular at the time. The great hall is decorated with armour, antlers and oak furniture, while the small, dark, ground-floor rooms are hung with rich tapestries. There are four-poster beds in the bedrooms, and the ground-floor chapel contains an early clock of Sir Richard Edgcumbe's day. However, it is likely that not all the furniture and fittings are actually relics of the old house – some may have come from elsewhere and from antique dealers during the 19th century, when 'Elizabethan' furniture was often skilfully made up from bits and pieces. The estate includes a watermill and a quay on the River Tamar.

☎ Abson (027 582) 2501
4 m N of Bath on A46
ST 7475 (OS 172)

Open Apr, May and Oct: daily exc Th and F (but inc Good Fri); June to end Sept: daily exc F 1400-1800; other times by appt
🅿 (limited) WC ⓰ 🚻 ♠ 🍴 🍴 ✕ ⚳

Dyrham Park

near Chippenham, Avon

This mansion house, grouped together with its parish church and stables in a narrow valley, is rather a curiosity; built in two separate stages, it is really two houses rather clumsily joined together. It was built between 1691 and 1702 for William Blathwayt, an ambitious civil servant with a sincere feeling for architecture. He engaged a little-known French architect, Hauduroy, who added a long two-storey front to the old Tudor house. This, the existing west front, joined to the church, has a definite French look, with its projecting wings breaking the monotony of the fifteen bays. By 1694 the work was complete, and Hauduroy disappeared into the obscurity whence he came. Blathwayt became Secretary of State under William III, and the prestigious William Talman was engaged to improve the house further. Talman added what is really a second house, and the great east front, Italianate in style and decorated with carved ornament, was built from 1700 to 1704. The two houses, back-to-back with each other, are joined only by the large hall and dining room. Talman is also credited with a design for the stables, but this rather crude piece of architecture was actually the work of his carpenter, Edward Wilcox. The interior of the house has not altered much since Blathwayt's time, and most of the furniture dates from that period. There is some fine rich decoration, notably in the balcony room, which also contains some of Blathwayt's Delftware vases and has lovely brass door fittings.

Forde Abbey

near Chard, Dorset

Originally a Cistercian monastery until it was closed by Henry VIII, the house, with its long, low front in the lovely Ham Hill stone, is a fascinating mixture. Unusually, at Forde a great deal of the original monastic building survives, forming the base for the major rebuilding in the 17th century. Thomas Chard, the last abbot, had spent large sums of money on new building just before the Abbey was closed: the great hall and the magnificent gatehouse, both resplendent with Renaissance carving, were built by him. In 1539 he and his twelve monks surrendered the Abbey, and 110 years later it was bought by Edmund Prideaux, Attorney-General to Oliver Cromwell, who set about transforming it into an Italian-style palace. Its monastic layout was well suited to this treatment, and there was little structural alteration, but the interiors were quite transformed, with lavish panelling and plaster-work. The outside was 'modernised' with large mullioned windows (later 'Gothicked'), a saloon was built next to the entrance tower, as well as some small rooms over Abbot Chard's cloister. The alterations were more or less complete by 1660, and little has since been changed. The great hall, which was shortened by Prideaux, has a late Gothic wooden roof and 17th-century panelling, and all the rooms have been furnished in a style suited to the building. The saloon contains five Mortlake tapestries woven from Raphael cartoons, a later present from Queen Anne. A conservatory has been made from the surviving cloister range.

☎ South Chard (0460) 20231
4 m SE of Chard on B3162 turn S at Whatley to bridge
ST 3505 (OS 193)

Open May to Sept Su, W, Bank Hols 1400-1800
🅟 WC ♿ (limited access) 🚻 D ♣ 🍴
🏛 ◆ ✿ ⚘

Fursdon House

near Thorverton, Devon

Fursdon is situated at Cadbury amid unspoiled Devon countryside, in the triangle of land formed by Crediton, Exeter and Tiverton. It is a fine example of a family house that has never been a showpiece but has always functioned as the centre of a busy agricultural estate. Walter de Fursdon lived at Cadbury from about 1259; the property has passed down in the male line ever since, and is still owned by the Fursdons. The present Fursdon House probably originated at about the beginning of the 17th century, but most of the structure now visible was the work of Richard Strong, a Minehead builder employed by George Fursdon in 1732. Strong created a long Georgian building with two wings; the library was added to the west wing in 1815, and three years later the façade was rather clumsily ornamented with an Ionic colonnade. There have been numerous minor and major alterations over the centuries, but exploitation of Fursdon's non-agricultural appeal (for example, by the creation of holiday flats) is quite recent; and the house was only opened to the public in August 1982. The interior contains family portraits, antique furniture and a collection of interesting domestic items in the so-called billiard room (actually a kitchen). There is also a costume collection, including a beautifully preserved mid 18th-century mantua, or court dress, worn by Elizabeth Fursdon. The gardens, parkland and woods are one of the pleasant features of Fursdon, and the walks laid out on the estate include one to the Iron Age hill fort of Cadbury.

☎ Exeter (0392) 860860
6 m SW of Tiverton on A3072, turn S to Fursdon
SS 9204 (OS 192)

Open Easter Su and M; May to end Sept Th and Bank Hol M also W in July and Aug; parties at other times by appt
🅟 WC 🚻 ♣ 🍴 ◆

Gaulden Manor

Tollard, Lydeard St Lawrence, Taunton, Somerset

From the outside Gaulden Manor appears to be simply an attractive but unpretentious ancient farmhouse, but its rough stone walls are a front for some of the most extraordinary and sumptuous plasterwork in the country. There is some disagreement about the dates of this work, but it seems that in 1565 the house became the retreat of the ex-Bishop of Exeter, James Turberville, after he had been imprisoned in the Tower of London for refusing to take the Oath of Supremacy to Queen Elizabeth I. Some experts believe that the plasterwork in the hall, by far the most elaborate, was put in by him, while others claim that it is mid-17th century and was put in by his great-nephew John Turberville, who bought the house in 1639. The hall has a deep plaster frieze running right round the walls, with intricately modelled religious scenes (possibly representing the life and trials of the Bishop), and the ceiling has three large plaster roundels, the central one with a pendant. The fireplace is Tudor, and there is a fine mantelpiece bearing the Turberville arms. Opening off the hall, and divided from it by a carved 16th-century oak screen, is a small room known as the chapel, with more plasterwork, and the upstairs bedroom has a fine decorative plaster overmantel which was unfortunately cut in half by a later ceiling. This and the ceiling of the hall were probably done for John Turberville. There is a very attractive garden, which was entirely created by the present owners, who have lived at the Manor since 1966.

☎ Lydeard St Lawrence (09847) 213
8½ m NW of Taunton on A358 turn W to Handy Cross then S for 1 m and N for ½ m
ST 1131 (OS 181)

Open Easter, May to mid Sept Su and Th, also W July to Sept 1400-1730; parties other times by appt
🅟 WC ♿ 🚻 (by appt) ♣ 🍴 🏛 ◆ ✿
⚘ ✗ ● (in house by permission)

☎ Hatch Beauchamp (0823) 480208

8 m SE of Taunton on A358 turn NE to Curry Mallet

ST 3021 (OS 193)

Open July to mid Sept Th 1430-1730

♿ 🅿 WC 🚻 (by appt only from May)

♣ ☕ 🎋 ⚘ ⚔

Hatch Court

Hatch Beauchamp, Taunton, Somerset

This elegant 18th-century house was built by John Collins, who had become wealthy in the wool trade and needed a house worthy of his new status. Instead of engaging a professional architect, Collins approached Thomas Prowse, a sophisticated amateur and local gentleman, to provide a design. Prowse was a friend of a more famous amateur architect, Sanderson Miller, who built Hagley Hall near Birmingham, and Hatch Court, though smaller than Hagley, is very similar. The two buildings are exact contemporaries, both being built in 1775. Prowse may have been an amateur, but there is nothing clumsy about Hatch Court, with its four towers, its charming arcaded piazza and its fine, restrained architectural detail beautifully executed in Bath stone. The curving wings, added around 1800, are successful additions, giving the house a satisfying quality. The finest feature of the interior is a marvellous staircase, which fills the entire centre of the house, dividing and doubling back on itself at the half-landing. There is a fine old oak table in the hall, dating from about 1630, and the drawing room has an elaborate Rococo plaster ceiling. The furniture is largely Georgian, and the paintings, as well as family portraits, include several wild Canadian landscapes which belonged to Andrew Gault, who lived here in the 1920s. A dynamic figure, Gault was responsible for raising a Canadian regiment, Princess Caroline's Light Infantry, to fight in the First World War, and a small regimental museum commemorates his achievement.

☎ Wimborne (0202) 883402

2 m NW of Wimborne on B3082

ST 9701 (OS 195)

Open May to end Oct Th and F 1400-1800

♿ 🅿 WC 🚻 (by appt only) ♣ ☕

🎋 ♦ ⚘

Kingston Lacy House

near Wimborne, Dorset

This is one of the earliest surviving houses built in a Classical style after the Restoration of 1660, with such features as pediments, hipped roofs, dormer windows and cornices. The manor of Kingston Lacy took its name from its medieval owners, the de Lacys, who were Earls of Lincoln. It belonged to members of the royal family for long periods until 1637, when Sir John Bankes bought it from the Earl of Newport. Until 1643 the main Bankes family residence was Corfe Castle, which Lady Mary Bankes defended vigorously for six weeks against Parliament during the Civil War. As a result the castle was thoroughly slighted, and after the Restoration Lady Mary's son, Sir Ralph Bankes, had a new family seat built at Kingston Lacy in the mainly urban style that was becoming fashionable. The architect was Inigo Jones's disciple, Sir Roger Pratt, under whom the work was executed between 1663 and 1665. The original house consisted of two storeys and a semi-basement, built in red brick with stone dressings. Kingston Lacy was much altered in the 18th century, but in 1835-39 Sir Charles Barry restored the cupola and other features; however, he also 'improved' it in various ways, for example adding the present chimneys and lowering the ground level to convert the basement into a full floor on the main front. The interior was lavishly remodelled in Barry's favoured Renaissance style, the *pièce de resistance* being the splendid marble staircase. The formal garden is also Barry's creation. The collection of paintings at Kingston Lacy is famous.

☎ Lacock (024 973) 227

4 m S of Chippenham on A350

ST 9168 (OS 173)

Open Apr to end Oct daily exc T and Good Fri 1400-1800; parties by appt at other times

♿ (exc Su) 🅿 WC 🚻 (by appt) D ♣

⚔ Concerts

Lacock Abbey

near Chippenham, Wiltshire

Lacock owes its 18th-century appearance to the gentleman architect Sanderson Miller, who enlarged it in the 1750s in the 'Gothick' style, but in fact it has a much longer history. Originally an Augustinian convent, it was closed down in 1539 and bought by Sir William Sharrington, whose descendants have lived here ever since. Sharrington, unlike many of his contemporaries who built on old abbeys, retained a great deal of the original building, making most of his alterations upstairs where the living accommodation was (and still is). The result is that one enters a country house and finds oneself inside a medieval convent, with its lovely fan-vaulted cloister, stately chapter house and refectory. Among Sharrington's alterations that survived the 18th-century rebuilding are the octagonal tower, four storeys high, at the south-east corner of the building, and the stable block. The house is entered through Miller's splendid 'Gothick' entrance hall, and visitors can wander freely through the monastic buildings and the stable court as well as most of the first-floor rooms. Lacock is famous as the home of the pioneer of photography, William Henry Fox Talbot, who also built the oriel windows on the south front, the last alteration to be made to the house. Hanging by one of these windows is a photograph of it, a print from the negative made in 1835, and a converted barn houses the Fox Talbot Museum of the History of Photography. The Abbey and village were given to the National Trust by William Henry's granddaughter, Miss Matilda Fox Talbot, in 1944.

Littlecote House

near Hungerford, Wiltshire

Littlecote, a Tudor manor house set in an ancient park, is probably the oldest brick building in Wiltshire. In defiance of its name, it is a very large house, long and low, the entrance front of the 1590s being of the usual Tudor E-shape, but pulled out to a much greater width. The garden side, faced with flint, is older, dating from about 1490. Littlecote was owned by the Darrell family until 1589, when it was bought by Sir John Popham, later Lord Chief Justice of England, remaining in the Popham family until 1922. It was then acquired by Sir Ernest Salter Wills, whose grandson and family live here today. The Pophams were Puritans, and the great hall, a fine room with excellent panelling and furniture, displays Cromwellian weapons and uniforms, as well as a finger stock said to have been used by Sir John to confine prisoners in the dock. The chapel, one of the few examples of a Puritan religious building to survive complete, is typical in its arrangement, the elevated pulpit taking the place of the altar. The brick hall, so-called for its brick floor, has good 17th-century panelling, and there are some unusual paintings of nudes in Classical settings in the Dutch parlour. The bedrooms contain some fine oak furniture, including a four-poster bed contemporary with Elizabeth I's visit in 1601, and a marvellous set of crewel work bed curtains in the 'haunted bedroom', which is associated with a gruesome child murder by William Darrell in 1575. The lovely long gallery contains a good collection of furniture and family portraits.

☎ Hungerford (0488) 82170
2 m NW of Hungerford on A419, continue on road to Littlecote
SU 3070 (OS 174)

Open Apr to end June S, Su, Bank Hol M; July to Sept daily 1400-1800; parties at other times by appt
🅿 WC 🚹 (limited access) 🍴 (by appt) D ♠ 🐕
🎪 ♦ ✂ ✗ (compulsory) ● (not in house)

Montacute House

Montacute, near Yeovil, Somerset

Montacute, built of the honey-coloured Ham Hill stone and glittering with glass, is one of the finest Elizabethan mansions in England, and one of the least changed. It was completed about 1600 for Sir Edward Phelps, a West Country landowner and lawyer, who was Speaker of the House of Commons from 1598, and the architect was probably William Arnold, a brilliant local master-mason. There were some alterations in the late 18th century, when the lovely Renaissance porch now on the west front was brought from Clifton Maybank, and Lord Curzon, who lived here from 1915 to 1925, made some changes to the interior, but the character of the house was unaltered. The interior is also almost pure Elizabethan, and retains much of its original decoration, including fine ornamental plasterwork, carved fireplaces, and a fine carved screen in the great hall. The rooms themselves are large, light and airy, the finest being the library, once the great chamber, where the manorial courts would have been held. There is a splendid chimneypiece of Portland stone, a carved wooden porch, Elizabethan panelling and four great windows. The panelling in the other rooms is 19th century, dating from Lord Curzon's occupancy, and the house has been entirely furnished by the National Trust with the help of a magnificent bequest of furniture and tapestries belonging to Sir Malcolm Stewart. The long gallery shows a large collection of 16th-century portraits from the National Portrait Gallery.

☎ Martock (0935) 823289
4½ m W of Yeovil on A3088
ST 5117 (OS 193)

Open Apr to mid Nov daily exc T 123:-1800 (or dusk if earlier); other times by written appt
🅿 WC 🍴 (by appt) ♠ 🐕 🎪 ♦ ✂

Newhouse

Redlynch, near Salisbury, Wiltshire

Newhouse, originally called Tychebourne Park, was built for the owner of Longford Castle, Sir Edward Gorges, probably as a hunting lodge. It is a curious shape, in the form of a Y, the central part of which was completed by 1619 and the 'arms' extended in the 18th century. Only one other house of this shape is known. In 1633 Gorges sold the house to Giles Eyre, whose descendants still live there, and the two wings were added in 1742 and 1760. The furnishings have been collected over the years by the Eyre-Matcham family (Harriet Eyre married George Matcham in 1817) and are not exceptional, though there are some interesting pieces, including a child's cot made for Horatia Nelson, daughter of Lord Nelson and Lady Hamilton. Catherine Matcham was Nelson's sister, and more or less brought up Horatia. The parlour has Louis XVI armchairs with covers embroidered by Catherine Matcham, and the east room contains a lovely Queen Anne embroidered quilt. The house has some good family portraits, but the most interesting picture is the 'Hare picture', thought to have been painted about 1640. It apparently shows the triumph of hares over men, but it may have been a pun ('Hare' for 'Eyre') or an allegory of some kind. The drawing room was lavishly refurnished in 1906 in the 'Carolean' style by Maples, but the furnishings are now badly decayed and the room is being restored. It is used to display a collection of costume dating from the 1750s to the 1930s. One of the outhouses has collection of agricultural implements found nearby.

☎ Downton (0725) 20055
9 m S of Salisbury on A338, turn E onto B3080 then N to Redlynch
SU 2021 (OS 184)

Open Easter and Spring Bank Hol M, June to Aug S, Su and Bank Hol M 1400-1800
🅿 WC 🍴 (by appt) 🐕

41

Parnham House

Beaminster, Dorset

For 300 years the family seat of the Strodes, Parnham was largely built about 1550, and it retains a charmingly Tudor appearance, with gables and pinnacles and mellow golden stone. But in fact there were three main periods of building, as the whole right half of the house was built about 1600, while in 1810 John Nash was commissioned to enlarge the house. The castellations, buttresses and pinnacles, together with the other two sides of the house, were added at this time. Extensive renovations were carried out in 1910 by Hans Sauer, who reinstated the Tudor interiors altered by Nash and landscaped the grounds, building terraces, water channels, balustrades, rotundas and the front court. Parnham has had a chequered history and, like other historic houses, has several times been under threat. In 1896 it was owned by Vincent Robinson, who lived surrounded by pets and Renaissance furniture; in 1912 it was bought by the Rhodes-Moorhouse family, whose son William was the first pilot to be awarded the Victoria Cross; in the 1920s it became a country club; in the Second World War it was an army hospital and afterwards it became a private nursing home. In 1976 it was bought by John Makepeace, and it is now the home of the John Makepeace Furniture Workshop and the School for Craftsmen in Wood. The main rooms now display, not only their original carving and panelling, but also fine examples of modern furniture, and visitors can see young craftsmen at work in the workshop.

☎ Beaminster (0308) 862204

7 m N of Bridport on A3066 just before Beaminster

ST 4700 (OS 193)

Open Apr to Oct Su, W, Bank Hols; parties only T, Th 1000-1700

⊖ P WC ⅏ ⊟ D ♥ ☞ ⊼ ◆ ※ ✗ (compulsory for parties) �

Pencarrow

Washaway, Bodmin, Cornwall

This well-proportioned stuccoed Palladian house has a particularly exciting approach, through beautiful woodlands and into a drive with massed hydrangeas, rhododendrons and azaleas which suddenly reveals the house. In the 1760s Sir John Molesworth, 4th Baronet, employed an architect from York, Robert Allanson, to rebuild the family house. Allanson added the south and east fronts in the Palladian style, but traces of the original building can still be seen on the west. The first room to be visited is the music-room; this owes much to Sir William Molesworth, the 8th Baronet, who in 1844 engaged the architect George Wightwick to carry out alterations. He extended the room by adding the alcove, and carried out the maple-graining on the walls. He also used old panelling from another house, both here and in the entrance hall, which he turned into a library. Most of the rooms, however, are mid-Georgian and very charming, with good chimneypieces and fine furniture. The house is well known for its large collection of 18th-century paintings including portraits by Reynolds, a landscape by Richard Wilson and a conversation-piece by Arthur Devis with St Michael's Mount in the background. The nursery, upstairs, contains a bedspread showing the flora and fauna of Cornwall, embroidered by the Cornwall Federation of Women's Institutes, as well as several antique dolls dressed in hand-made baby clothes. In the ante-room a lovely 19th-century linen wallpaper patterned with birds and butterflies was found beneath layers of later paper.

☎ St Mabyn (020884) 369

5 m NW of Bodmin on A389 turn NE to Croanford

SX 0471 (OS 200)

Open Easter to end Sept M, T, W, Th, Su 1330-1730; June to mid Sept and Bank Hol M 1100-1730

⊖ (limited) P WC ⅏ ⊟ D ♥ ☞ ⊼ ◆ ⬚ ※ ✗ (by appt for parties; available in French) �

Poundisford Park

Poundisford, Taunton, Somerset

A compact Tudor gabled house built on an H-plan and dating from about 1546, it is unusual for its time in that it stands by itself in the midst of fields instead of being built on a previously fortified or ecclesiastical site. It also still retains its detached kitchen, where spit roasting and brewing would have been done. The house is owned by the Vivian-Neal family, whose home it is, and there are guided tours of the rooms. The entrance door leads into a screens passage and then the great hall, a fine, large room with a 16th-century plaster ceiling. There are several of these in the house, and they are believed to be early examples of the work of a School of West Somerset Plasterers. A spiral stair leads to the porcelain gallery on the upper floor, where there is a ribbed plaster ceiling contemporary with the one in the hall. The glass in the bow window is also 16th century, as are the window fastenings. The gallery contains an English longcase clock in a Chinese-style case, and the cabinets hold china and curios collected over generations. Next comes a bedroom with a fine 19th-century patchwork quilt, and then a room in which 18th- and 19th-century costumes are displayed. A modern staircase leads down to the original pantry, and thence to the pretty 18th-century parlour formed from what was the buttery. The dining room was built on in 1692, but altered in 1737, and is totally 18th century in style. The pleasant, simply planted garden has an unusual 17th-century gazebo and a decorated water-butt bearing the date 1671.

☎ Blagdon Hill (082342) 244

5 m S of Taunton on B3170 turn W

ST 2220 (OS 193)

Open May to mid Sept W, Th and Bank Hol M also F in July and Aug 1100-1700

⊖ (limited) P WC ⅏ (limited access) ⊟ (by appt) D ♥ ◆ ⬚ ※ ✗ ● (not in house)

Powderham Castle

Kenton, Exeter, Devon

Powderham was a fortified manor house, the home of the Courtenay family since the 14th century. In medieval times the house stood on a dry knoll above the marshy ground of the Exe estuary, but in the 18th century the marsh was drained and reclaimed as parkland. The 14th-century house consisted of the centre building and six towers, one of which survives, as does the interior of the chapel and various bits and pieces of stonework. Several improvements were made in the 18th century, and many of the interiors are still of that time, with pretty Rococo plasterwork. There was another building campaign in the 19th century, and the entrance courtyard and banqueting hall, dating from about 1840, are the work of the architect Charles Fowler. The new hall is in the ornate Gothic style of the time, and chimneypiece, panelling and roof are resplendent with the heraldry of the Courtenays' illustrious descent. There is also a large painting of the 1st Viscount Courtenay by a local artist, Thomas Hudson, who preceded Reynolds as London's fashionable portrait painter. Of the 18th-century interior work by far the best is the staircase, which rises the entire height of the building and has an elaborately carved balustrade and walls which are a cornucopia of modelled plaster fruit and flowers. It is dated 1755 and was made by James Garrett and John Jenkins of Exeter. The elegant music room with its bow window and central dome was added by James Wyatt in the 1770s, and contains fine furniture and a marble chimneypiece.

☎ Starcross (0626) 890243
4 m S of Exeter on A379 turn E to Powderham
SX 9683 (OS 192)

Open late May to mid Sept Su-Th 1400-1730; parties at other times by appt
⊖ P WC ♿ ♣ ☕ ⛩ ◆ ✵ (available in foreign languages)

St Michael's Mount

Marazion, near Penzance, Cornwall

St Michael's Mount, the conical-shaped island just off the coast of Cornwall, is the twin of Mont St Michel in France, and both are the home of monastic foundations. The fortified Benedictine priory in Cornwall was built by the Abbot of Mont St Michel in 1135 and remained attached to the French foundation for nearly 350 years, after which it passed into the hands of the convent of Syon. After the Dissolution in the 1530s the Mount was primarily used as a fortress, and was frequently garrisoned; it was held for the King in the Civil War. The St Aubyn family acquired it in 1657, but for some time it remained more or less unoccupied, until in the 18th century the family began to use it as a summer home. In 1875 it was transformed into a comfortable, usable country house, under the guidance of Piers St Aubyn, known as a church restorer. Today his restorations are generally deplored but St Michael's Mount is a remarkable achievement. He took great care not to alter the famous silhouette of rock-perched buildings. The finest rooms are the Chevy Chase Room, originally the monks' refectory, with its plaster hunting frieze, banners and coat-of-arms, and the two drawing rooms made from the Lady Chapel. These both have charming Rococo decoration and Chippendale chairs, and the larger one has a portrait of Sir John St Aubyn, a copy by Opie of an original by Reynolds. The little church is still basically the 14th-century building, although the seats and much of the decoration are modern, and it retains its serene monastic atmosphere.

☎ Marazion (0736) 710507
3 m E of Penzance on A30 turn E to Marazion
SW 5130 (OS 203)

Open Nov to end Mar M, W, F, guided tours only depending on tides etc; Apr to end May T, W, F; Jun to end Oct M-F 1030-1745
⊖ WC 🚌 D ♣ ☕ (limited opening) ⛩ ◆ ✵ 🚶

Saltram House

Plympton, Plymouth, Devon

Saltram, a large, square Georgian house, its brickwork rendered and whitewashed, can only be described as plain, but inside these very ordinary walls lie the most out-of-the-ordinary rooms imaginable. The original house was Tudor, and in the 1740s John Parker and his wife Lady Catherine set about enlarging it. The main south front was built at this time; the porch was a Regency addition. This part of the building, and the rooms within it, is Rococo in style, and the charming interiors contain some lovely plasterwork. In 1768 John Parker died, and his son of the same name called in Robert Adam to fit up the east range, which had not been finished. The dining room and saloon were completely remodelled by Adam, down to the last detail, and represent some of his finest work. The saloon, or ballroom, is on the grand scale that was fashionable at the time, and occupies the whole central part of the wing. The dining room, its long, low proportions the result of an earlier phase of building, is pale green and white, with a splendid ceiling the design of which is reflected in the specially woven carpet. Adam's work did not extend to the first-floor rooms, but several of these are quite delightful, and include a Chinese Chippendale room and another which is hung with Chinese paintings on glass. There are also some beautiful and unusual oriental wallpapers in several rooms. All the furniture and paintings, including fourteen by Reynolds, belong in the house, and the Adam rooms are carefully preserved from the harmful effects of light.

☎ Plymouth (0752) 336546
3 m E of Plymouth on A379 turn NE for 1½m at Billacombe and NW to Saltram House
SX 5255 (OS 201)

Open Apr to end Oct T-Su, Bank Hol M and Good Fri
⊖ (¾ m walk) P WC ♿ (by appt)
🚌 D ♣ ☕ ⛩ ◆ ✵

☎ Chippenham (0249) 653120
1½ m NW of Chippenham on A420, turn S to
Biddestone for 1 m
ST 8874 (OS 173)

Open Apr to early Oct Th, Su, Bank Hols 1400-1800
1 (1½ m walk) P WC ⓖ (by appt)
🚻 (by appt) D ♣ ■ ◆ ⊛ (occasional)
✂ ● (in house by permission only)

Sheldon Manor

Chippenham, Wiltshire

This attractive stone manor house has a long history. The manor of Sheldon, as well as that of Chippenham, came to Sir Geoffrey Gascelyn in 1256, and his family held them until 1424, when Sheldon was bought by the Hungerfords, a powerful landowning family. They rebuilt one wing and added a chapel, but then evidently decided to live elsewhere, and let the house to the first in a long line of tenant farmers. By the end of the Civil War it was in a very run-down condition, and the current tenant, William Forster, had to obtain permission to rebuild it himself. In 1659 he rebuilt the entire left-hand side, with its tall gables and mullioned windows, but in 1684 the spendthrift Sir Edward Hungerford sold the property, and no further building was done, although two barns were added in the 1720s. Sheldon remained a farm until 1911, and the Gibbs family, the present owners, bought it in 1917 and have made it their home since 1957. The house has one of the finest 13th-century porches in the country, all that remains of the Gascelyn manor house. The first floor has a stone vault, and it contains the original stone water cistern, fed by pipes from the roof, while the room above, the priest's room, has a fine timber waggon roof. The rooms in the house are snug and lived-in, and there is a fine oak staircase in the 17th-century wing and the original tie-beams in the dining room. The interesting collection of furniture includes early oak pieces, Lancashire chairs, a country-made painted cupboard and two 17th-century Dutch cabinets.

☎ Sherborne (093 581) 3182
In the E outskirts of Sherborne, 5 m E of Yeovil
off A30
ST 6416 (OS 183)

Open Easter S to end Sept Th, S, Su and Bank Hols
1400-1800
⊖ (1 m walk) P WC ⓖ (limited access) 🚻 D ♣
■ 🍴 ◆ ⊛ ✂ ● (with permission)

Sherborne Castle

New Road, Sherborne, Dorset

This is not one but two castles, standing on opposing hills and separated by a lake. The older castle, now a ruin, was owned by the Bishop of Salisbury and coveted by Sir Walter Raleigh. In 1592 Elizabeth I leased it to him, and when, two years later, he was banished from Court he built himself a new house, tall and square, with a picturesque skyline and walls rendered a pleasant yellow ochre. He called it 'The Lodge', and the name stuck until 1800, when it was rechristened, and in fact the name 'castle' describes it better, with its towers and pinnacles, heraldic beasts and forest of chimneys. Sir John Digby, later Earl of Bristol, whose descendants still own the castle, was granted the Sherborne estates in 1617, and added four long wings terminating in towers. The rooms inside contrast with the rather outlandish romanticism of the exterior, being quite small in scale and domestic in feeling. Much redecoration was done in the 19th century by P. C. Hardwicke in the 'Jacobean' style, and some of the plaster ceilings as well as the alabaster fireplace in the dining room are his work. One Georgian interior has survived – the delightful library in the Strawberry Hill 'Gothick' style – and the panelled Jacobean oak room has changed little since the early 17th century. There is some very good Georgian furniture, and there is also a large collection of porcelain. The family portraits, stretching in an unbroken line from the 17th century, include works by Van Dyck, Lely, Reynolds and Gainsborough.

☎ Bourton (0747) 840348
14 m S of Frome on B3092, turn W at Stourton
ST 7734 (OS 183)

Open Apr and Oct to mid Nov S-W, May to end
Sept daily exc F 1400-1800 (dusk if earlier)
P WC ⓖ 🚻 (by appt) D (Oct to Feb only)
♣ ■ 🍴 ◆ ⊛ ✂ ✗

Stourhead

Stourton, Warminster, Wiltshire

The house, built by Colen Campbell for the wealthy banker Sir Henry Hoare, and completed in 1725, is one of the earliest of the English Palladian mansions. Stourhead is famous for its grounds, which were laid out from 1744 by Henry Hoare II and the architect Henry Flitcroft, and take the form of an idealised Italian landscape; the house itself, lying on high ground above the lake, is also very fine. Colen Campbell's severely Classical stone house with its porticoed entrance forms the centre of the present building (the portico was actually added in 1840, but to a design left by Campbell). The main additions were made in the 1790s by Sir Richard Colt Hoare, grandson of Henry Hoare II. He was an antiquarian, scholar and amateur painter, and he built the two projecting wings, each containing one room, for his collection of books and paintings. The central block was gutted by fire in 1902, but well reconstructed. Sir Richard's wings, with their splendid Regency interiors, were unharmed. His library, Roman in inspiration, is a fine room with a barrel-vaulted ceiling and a carpet based on a mosaic pattern, and the furniture, including the flight of library steps, was designed and made by Thomas Chippendale the Younger, who made much of the furniture for the house. The picture gallery in the other wing, with a red and green colour scheme, has two tiers of windows on the east side, all with gilt and ebonised pelmets. Many of the paintings collected by the family remain, including Classical landscapes of the type that inspired the garden.

Tintagel Castle

Tintagel, Cornwall

Tintagel Castle is often referred to as 'King Arthur's Castle', but although the local tourist industry leans heavily on the Arthurian connection, there is no real evidence for it, as the earliest reference is in the fanciful and highly coloured *History of Britain* by the 12th-century monk Geoffrey of Monmouth. He was writing in about 1140 when the Norman castle was being built, and it was possibly the discovery of early monastic remains that gave him the idea of a much earlier castle on the site. This idea has appealed to the popular imagination ever since. Tintagel Castle is full of romance and atmosphere, particularly on a fine day, and its site, on a high, wave-lashed promontory, could not be more spectacular. The Norman castle and keep was built by Reginald, Earl of Cornwall, in the 12th century, and the Celtic monastery probably dates from before the 9th century. The original great hall, of which little more than foundations remain, was evidently built before the mid-13th-century curtain wall. The buildings were considerably extended by Earl Richard, younger brother of Henry III, who held Tintagel from 1236 to 1272, and the major part of the building on the mainland is his work (the castle is divided into two, with a narrow causeway between). During the 14th century it began to show signs of dilapidation, although it was used as a prison towards the end of the century. In 1377 the castle was made the property of the Black Prince, Duke of Cornwall, but from the 15th century onwards it was allowed to fall into disrepair.

2 m N of Camelford on B3266 turn W onto B3263

SX 0588 (OS 200)

Open daily throughout year; Mar to Oct 0930-1830
Oct to Mar 0930-1600 (Su 1400-1600)

🅿 WC ⊟ D ♣ ☙

Wardour Castle

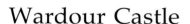

Tisbury, Wiltshire

Wardour Castle, despite its name, is not a castle but an extremely fine Palladian house, built on the site of an older, once-fortified mansion. The Arundells, owners of the estate, were Catholics and improverished through the 17th and much of the 18th centuries, but in 1768 the 8th Lord Arundell married an heiress and was able to rebuild his ancestral home on a grand scale. The house, designed by James Paine and built between 1770 and 1776, is most imposing, with a massive central block containing splendid reception rooms and the two wings containing a Catholic chapel on one side and kitchens on the other. There is an impressive central pediment on the garden side. The low, columned entrance hall leads directly into the marvellous 'Pantheon' or staircase hall, the best feature of the interior, where the two semi-circular flights of the staircase curve up to a first-floor gallery, and the dome above is carried by eight soaring columns. The house is now a girls' school, and the contents and many of the mural decorations have been dispersed, but there are some family portraits, and the finely proportioned rooms contain fine plaster decoration, the most notable example being the ceiling of the music room. The chapel, part of Paine's original design but extended by Sir John Soane in 1788, is rich and splendid. The decorator was an Italian called Quarenghi, who may also have been responsible for the music room ceiling. The romantic ruins of Wardour Old Castle can be seen from the house.

21 m SW of Salisbury on A30, turn N to Donhead St Andrew

ST 9227 (OS 184)

Open late July to early Sept M, W, F, S 1430-1800

🅿 WC ♿ ⊟ (by appt)
D ♣ 🖤 ◆ ☙ 🍴 (compulsory)
● (not in house)

Wolfeton House

Dorchester, Dorset

A grey, oddly shaped, mainly Elizabethan manor house is the seat of the Trenchards, a Wessex landowning family who made their money in sheep farming. It was built by two members of the family, Sir Thomas and his great-grandson Sir George. The gatehouse, which has an inscription dating it to 1534, was Sir Thomas' work, and once led to a courtyard house also built by Sir Thomas on the site of a yet earlier house. Unfortunately, most of this house was demolished around 1800, and even the hall was removed. The taller range has large mullioned windows reminiscent of Longleat; it was built by Sir George around 1580; Thomas Hardy described the house as 'an ivied manor house . . . more than usually distinguished by the size of its mullioned windows'. The interior shows a mixture of decorations, but there are some splendid fireplaces, and a vaulted corridor, stone staircase and doorway. All are beautifully carved in Renaissance style, possibly the work of one of the Longleat carvers. When the last Trenchard of Wolfeton departed, taking with him the armorial glass and probably other treasures, the house lost much of its status and was sold and partly demolished, although some restoration was attempted in the mid-19th century. Since the Second World War, the house has been let as three separate residences, but the present owner is making many improvements, and restoration work is in hand. The outbuildings contain a cider house, where old presses are still used, and visitors given a glass of home-made cider on leaving.

☎ Dorchester (0305) 63500

2 m N of Dorchester on road to Charminster

SY 6892 (OS 194)

Open May, Jun, Jul, Sept T, F, Su, Bank Hol M; Aug daily exc S 1400-1800; at other times by appt

❸ (1½ m walk) 🅿 ♿ (limited access)
⊟ D ♣ 🖤 🎋 ☙

Arlington Court, Barnstaple, Devon (tel Shirwell [027 182] 296). 8 m NE of Barnstaple on A39, turn E. SS 6140 (OS 180). Neo-Classical style Regency house virtually unchanged since the mid-19th century and containing the collection of its last private owner, Miss Rosalie Chichester, which includes shells, pewter, model ships, *objets d'art* and costume. The stables include a collection of 19th-century vehicles. There is a formal garden and a park. House open Apr to Oct daily (exc S) am and pm; garden and park open all year am and pm. ⊖ 🅿 WC 🔊 🚻 (by appt) ♣ 🐾

Avebury Manor, Avebury, Wiltshire (tel Avebury [067 23] 203). 15 m SW of Swindon on A361. SU 0970 (OS 173). 16th-century manor house built on the site of an old monastery. The interiors are 16th-century to Victorian and contain fine plasterwork and fireplaces. The woodwork of the dining room is notable, and the oak staircase is the work of the 17th century. The gardens are laid out in formal Elizabethan style. Open Apr to end Sept daily pm; Oct to end March S and Su only; other times by appt. ⊖ 🅿 WC ♣ 🐾 🎍

Barford Park, near Enmore, Somerset (tel Spaxton [027 867] 269). 5 m N of Bridgwater on A39, turn SW then N. ST 2335 (OS 182). Miniature Queen Anne period red-brick country house in a park with fine trees. There is a formal garden and a water garden. Open May to Sept W, Th and Bank Hol S-M pm; other times by appt. 🅿 WC ♣ ★

Barrington Court, Ilminster, Somerset (tel Ilminster [046 05] 2242). 3 m NE of Ilminster on B368, turn SE. ST 3918 (OS 193). Attractive 16th-century E-shaped house, restored in the early 20th century. The gardens were laid out by Gertrude Jekyll in the 1920s, and there is a late 17th-century stable block. House open end Apr to end Sept W pm; gardens open end Apr to end Sept Su-W pm. ⊖ 🅿 🔊 🚻 (by appt) ♣

Berry Pomeroy Castle, near Totnes, Devon (tel Totnes [0803] 863397). 1 m E of Totnes on A385, turn NE. SX 8462 (OS 202). Ruined castle built in about 1300 by the Pomeroy family, with remains of a manor house inside the walls, built by the Duke of Somerset, Lord Protector in Edward VI's reign. Open March to Oct daily am and pm; Nov to Feb M-F am and pm exc Christmas. 🅿 WC 🐾

Bickleigh Castle, near Tiverton, Devon (tel Bickleigh [088 45] 363). 7 m S of Tiverton on A396 turn SW onto A3072. SS 9306 (OS 192). Pretty and romantic home of the Courtenays, heirs of the Earls of Devon. The chapel is believed to be the oldest complete building in Devon, dating from the late 11th century. The gatehouse is moated and there is an attractive water garden. Open Easter Week and W, Su and Bank Hol M to end May; June to Oct daily (Exc S) pm. ⊖ 🅿 🚻 ♣ 🐾

Bishop's Palace, Wells, Somerset (tel Wells [0749] 78691). In city centre. ST 5545 (OS 182). Fortified and moated palace, dating in part to the 13th century, and with a 14th-century gatehouse. The great hall, now ruined, was built in 1280. The interior of the palace was remodelled in the 17th century, with a fine staircase and the creation of a long gallery; it was restored in the mid-19th century. Open Easter to Oct Th, Su and Bank Hol M pm; Aug daily pm. ⊖ 🅿 WC 🔊 🐾

Blaise Castle House, Henbury, Bristol, Avon (tel Bristol [0272] 25777). 4 m NW of Bristol on A4018. ST 5678 (OS 172). 18th-century house containing social history museum covering West Country life from 1750 to 1900. Extensive picturesque gardens laid out by Humphry Repton with buildings by John Nash. Blaise Hamlet, also by Nash, is nearby. Open S-W pm all year, exc Bank Hols. ⊖ 🅿 WC 🔊 🚻 ♣ 🐾 ★

Bowden House, Totnes, Devon (tel Totnes [0803] 863664). 1 m S of town centre on A381, turn SE. SX 8058 (OS 202). Ancient house, with parts dating back to the 13th century but primarily an early 18th-century façade on an early Tudor mansion. The hall is decorated in Baroque style. Open Apr to Oct T pm. ⊖ 🅿 WC 🚻 (by appt) ♣

Bowood House, Calne, Wiltshire (tel Calne [0249] 812102). 5 m SE of Chippenham on A4, turn S. ST 9769 (OS 173). 18th-century house designed by Robert Adam, once the 'Little House' to the main Bowood House which was demolished in 1955. It houses Adam's library, and the room in which Joseph Priestley discovered oxygen. The old orangery now houses a picture gallery, with Old Master works; there is also a collection of Indian silver caskets, and antique sculpture. The beautiful grounds were laid out by Capability Brown and Humphry Repton in the 1760s; among the features are a rose garden, an Italian garden, an 18th-century aboretum, a mausoleum by Nash, a temple, and a lake. Open June and Aug daily am and pm; Sept to May daily exc M. ⊖ 🅿 WC 🔊 🚻 ♣ 🐾 🎍

Bradley Manor, Newton Abbot, Devon. On west side of Newton Abbot, on A381. SX 8470 (OS 202). Small manor house mainly dating from about 1420. The interior contains many architectural features of the 15th and 16th century, including great hall, buttery and chapel. Open Apr to Sept W pm, also the last Th in each month pm. ⊖ 🅿 🚻 (by appt) ⊗

Buckland Abbey, near Yelverton, Devon (tel Yelverton [082 285] 3607). 7 m SE of Tavistock on A386, turn SW. SX 4866 (OS 201). 13th-century Cistercian monastery, bought by Richard Grenville in 1541, converted in the 1570s, and bought by Sir Francis Drake in 1581 after his voyage around the world. The house now contains relics of Drake and the Grenville family, including 'Drake's Drum', naval exhibits and a Devon folk museum. The grounds contain a large tithe barn. Open Easter to Sept daily am and pm (Su pm only); Oct to Apr W, S and Su pm only. ⊖ 🅿 WC 🚻 (by appt) ♣ 🐾

Cadhay, Ottery St Mary, Devon (tel Ottery St Mary [040 481] 2432). 5 m SW of Honiton on A30, turn SE. ST 0896 (OS 192). Mid-Tudor house, built from proceeds of the Dissolution of the Monasteries; extended around 1600, and with a new front added in the 1730s. Open Spring and Summer Bank Hols, and July to Aug, T-Th pm. ⊖ 🅿 WC 🚻 (by appt) ♣

Castle Drogo, Drewsteignton, Devon (tel Chagford [064 73] 3306). 12 m W of Exeter, 4 m NE of Chagford. SS 6728 (OS 180). Mock castle built in 1910-30 by Edwin Lutyens for Julius Drewe, one of the last great houses to be built in Britain. It is made of granite, and sited high above the gorge of the River Teign. There are extensive formal gardens and grounds. Open Apr to end Oct daily am and pm. ⊖ 🅿 WC 🔊 🚻 (by appt) ♣ 🐾

Castle Hill, Filleigh, Barnstaple, Devon (tel Filleigh [059 86] 227). 3½ m W of South Molton on A361. SS 6728 (OS 180). Grand Neo-Classical house built 1730-40, family home of the Fortescue family. The house contains a notable collection of 18th-century furniture and *objets d'art*. The gardens are extensive and varied, and include an aboretum. Open Apr to Oct by appt. ⊖ 🅿 ♣

Chalcot House, Westbury, Wiltshire (tel Chapmanslade [037 388] 466). 2 m W of Westbury, on A3098. ST 8448 (OS 173). Small late 17th-century Classical manor house, recently restored and with attractive 18th- and 19th-century furniture. Open July and Aug daily pm. 🅿 🔊 🚻 (by appt) ♣

Chambercombe Manor, Ilfracombe, Devon (tel Ilfracombe [0271] 62624). 1 m SE of Ilfracombe on A399, turn S. SS 5346 (OS 180). Small and attractive early medieval manor, mainly rebuilt in the 16th and 17th centuries, and containing furniture of that period. Open Easter to Sept M-F am and pm, Su pm only. 🅿 WC ♣ 🐾

Chettle House, Blandford Forum, Dorset (tel Tarrant Hinton [025 889] 209). 8 m NE of Blandford Forum on A354, turn NW. ST 9513 (OS 195). House in the English Baroque style, built by Thomas Archer in the 1710s. Much of the house has been modified, but the staircase remains a dramatic example of the style. Open daily am and pm. 🅿 ♣ ★

Christchurch Castle, Christchurch, Dorset. In town centre. SZ 1692 (OS 195). Norman motte, with a great tower of around 1300, and the ruins of a rare earlier Norman hall within the castle enclosure. Open daily am and pm (Su pm only). ⊖ 🅿 ★

Arlington Court, Devon

Fitz House, Wiltshire

Claverton Manor, near Bath, Avon (tel Bath [0225] 60503). 3¾ m SE of Bath on A36, turn W. ST 7864 (OS 172). Classical villa built c. 1820 and now housing the American Museum in Britain, with exhibits illustrating many aspects of American domestic life from 17th to 19th centuries, notably of American Indians, Pennsylvania Germans and Shakers. Open daily (exc M) pm, am and pm Bank Hols and preceding Su, end Mar to end Oct. Other times by appt. ⊖ ▯ WC 🖾 🚌 ♣ 💬

Clevedon Court, Clevedon, Avon (tel Clevedon [0272] 872257). 1 m E of Clevedon on B3130. ST 4271 (OS 172). Manor house originally built in the 14th century, with a restored hall and 14th-century chapel. The house was extended continuously over the centuries. It has associations with Charles Makepeace Thackeray, and with Sir Edmund Elton, a well-known late 19th-century potter. Open Apr to end Sept W, Th, Su and Bank Hol M pm. ⊖ ▯ WC ♣

Cloud's Hill, near Wool, Dorset. 9 m E of Dorchester. SY 8290 (OS 194). Cottage that was the home of T.E. Lawrence (Lawrence of Arabia) from 1925 when he rejoined the RAF under an assumed name. The house contains a collection of items relating to Lawrence. Open Apr to Sept W-F, Su and Bank Hols pm; Oct to March, Su pm only. ▯

Coker Court, East Coker, Somerset (tel West Coker [093 586] 3146). 2 m S of Yeovil on A352, turn N. ST 5412 (OS 194). Old manor house, former home of the Helyar family. There is a 15th-century great hall with tapestries of the period, and the house was modified in the 18th century. Open Apr to Sept F and Bank Hols pm. ▯

Coleridge Cottage, Nether Stowey, Somerset (tel Nether Stowey [0278] 732662). 8 m W of Bridgwater, on A39. ST 1939 (OS 182). The home of the poet Samuel Taylor Coleridge from 1797 to 1800, during which he wrote *The Ancient Mariner*. The parlour and reading room are open to the public. Open Apr to end Sept T-Th, Su pm, by appt if possible. ⊖

Compton Castle, near Paignton, Devon (tel Kingkerswell [080 47] 2112). 2 m W of Torquay on A380, turn SW onto A3022 for 2 m, then NW. SX 8664 (OS 202). Fortified house with spectacular façade, built between 1340 and 1520 and associated with the Gilbert family, which included Sir Humphrey Gilbert, the explorer. The house has been extensively restored since the 1930s. Open Apr to end Oct M, W, Th am and pm; Nov to Apr by appt only. ▯ WC 🖾

Compton House, near Sherborne, Dorset (tel Yeovil [0935] 74608). 4 m W of Sherborne on A30. ST 5916 (OS 183). 16th-century manor house greatly embellished in period style in the 19th century, now used to breed and display butterflies. These can been seen in all stages of development and several different environments. There is also a silk farm at which silk worms and silk-making can be seen. Open Apr to end Oct daily am and pm. ⊖ ▯ WC 🖾 ♣ 💬

Dartington Hall, near Totnes, Devon (tel Totnes [0803] 862271). 2 m NW of Totnes, on A384. SX 7962 (OS 202). Late 14th-century house, with original great hall, outer courtyard and other buildings. Since the 1920s the house has been devoted to an educational trust, providing a progressive school and many craft activities, notably glassware. ⊖ ▯ WC ♣ 💬 ★ ◆

Dartmouth Castle, Dartmouth, Devon. 1 m SE of Dartmouth on B3205. SX 8850 (OS 202). Castle built in the 1480s to protect the harbour entrance with artillery and a chain stretched across the river to Kingswear Castle. The castle was used again during the Second World War. It now contains Civil War armour and guns of the late 19th century. Open daily am and pm (Oct to Apr S pm only). ⊖ ▯ 💬

Deans Court, Wimborne, Dorset. Close to town centre. SZ 0199 (OS 195). House built as the deanery for the Minster, and extended in the 18th century. The gardens are partly wild, and retain the monastery fishpond and an 18th-century kitchen garden. There are interesting trees and a sanctuary for threatened vegetables. House open by appt only; gardens open Easter, Spring and Summer Bank Hols M am and pm; June to end Sept Th and Su pm. ⊖ ▯ 🖾 ♣ 💬

Dewlish House, Dewlish, Dorset (tel Milborne St Andrew [025 887] 224). 8 m NE of Dorchester on A354, turn W. SY 7797 (OS 194). House built in the early years of the 18th century, and modified some 50 years later. The staircase and chimney-pieces are notable. Open May to Sept Th pm (not Bank Hols). ▯ ♣

Dunster Castle, Dunster, Somerset (tel Dunster [064 382] 314). 3 m SE of Minehead on A39, turn S onto A396. SS 9943 (OS 181). Fortified manor house of the 14th century built on the site of a Norman fortification. It came into the possession of the Luttrell family in 1376, who owned it until 1976. There is a fine 17th-century staircase, and notable plasterwork. The castle was remodelled in Victorian Gothic style in the 19th century by Anthony Salvin. There are terraced gardens and a deer park. Open Apr to Sept S-W am and pm; Oct to early Nov pm only. ⊖ ▯ WC 🚌 (by appt) ♣

East Lambrook Manor, South Petherton, Somerset (tel South Petherton [0460] 40328). 8 m W of Yeovil, 2 m N of South Petherton. ST 4318 (OS 193). Manor house first built in about 1470 and extended in the late 16th century, when the great hall was divided in two. There is a well-stocked cottage-style garden, which belonged to the gardening writer Margery Fish from 1938. Open gardens daily am and pm; house March to Oct Th pm, other times by appt. ⊖ ▯ WC 🖾 ♣

Elizabethan House, 32 New St, Plymouth, Devon (tel Plymouth [0752] 668000 ext 4380). In town centre, off the quay. SX 4854 (OS 201). Elizabethan merchant's house, restored in 1926. Its staircase is built around a ship's mast. The house contains 16th-century furniture. Open Apr to Sept daily am and pm (Su pm only); Oct to Apr closed Su. ⊖

Farleigh Hungerford Castle, near Trowbridge, Somerset (tel Trowbridge [022 14] 2582). 3 m W of Trowbridge, on A366. ST 8057 (OS 173). Early medieval manor house fortified as a double-courtyard castle by Thomas Hungerford, one of the first Speakers of the House of Commons, in the 1370s. The castle was extended in the 15th century to incorporate the church of St Leonard, which contains notable tombs and paintings. The castle is now a ruin. Open daily am and pm (Su pm only). ▯ WC 🖾

Fitz House, Teffont Magna, Wiltshire. 10 m W of Salisbury on B3089. ST 9832 (OS 184). Attractive Tudor farmhouse, with 14th-century tithe barn. There is a four-acre garden with terraces, yew and beech hedges, roses and an orchard. The house has been lived in by Edith Oliver and Siegfried Sassoon. Only the gardens are open, Apr to end Oct W, Su and Bank Hol M pm. ⊖ ▯ ♣ 💬

Flete, Ermington, Ivybridge, Devon (tel Holbeton [075 530] 308. 11 m E of Plymouth on A379, turn S. SX 6251 (OS 202). Jacobean house rebuilt by Richard Norman Shaw in the 19th century. Open May to Sept W and Th pm. ⊖ ▯ WC ♣

Georgian House, 7 Great George St, Bristol, Avon (tel Bristol [0272] 299771). Close to city centre. ST 5972 (OS 172). Late 18th-century town house now completely restored to recreate the home of the wealthy merchant and West Indies sugar plantation manager, John Pinney. The kitchen is particularly interesting. Open daily (exc Su) am and pm. ⊖ 🖾 ★

Godolphin House, near Helston, Cornwall (tel Germoe [073 676] 2409). 2 m NW of Helston on A394, turn N onto B3302 for 3 m then W. SW 6031 (OS 203). 16th- and 17th-century house built for the Earls of Godolphin, with unusual granite colonnaded front of 1635. The house is said to have been used by the future King Charles II on his escape from Pendennis Castle. Open May and June Th pm; July to Sept T and Th pm. ▯ 🚌 (by appt)

Horton Court, Avon

Great Chalfield Manor, Melksham, Wiltshire. 2½ m NE of Bradford-on-Avon off B3109. ST 8563 (OS 173). Manor house of the late 15th century with a moat, adjoining a parish church of the same date. There is a great hall, with a restored screen and a contemporary mural of the builder. Open Apr to end Oct W pm. 🅿🚻 (by appt)

Hardy's Cottage, Higher Bockhampton, Dorset (Dorchester [0305] 62366). 4 m E of Dorchester on A35, turn S. SY 7292 (OS 194). Small thatched cottage in which the novelist and poet Thomas Hardy was born in 1840. The interior is little altered since that time. Open by appt only, Apr to Oct am and pm. ⊖ 🅿

Heale House, Woodford, Salisbury, Wiltshire (tel Middle Woodford [072 273] 207). 4 m N of Salisbury on A345, turn W. SU 1235 (OS 184). Manor house of the Carolean period, one of several in which the future King Charles II hid after the battle of Worcester (1651). The River Avon runs through the grounds, which comprise a varied garden with herbaceous borders, a water garden with magnolias, and an authentic Japanese tea house. Only the garden is open to visitors, Easter to end Sept M-S and first Su in month am and pm. ⊖ 🅿♿🚻 (by appt) ♣ 🐾 (by appt)

Horton Court, Horton, Avon. 3 m NE of Chipping Sodbury on A46, turn W. ST 7684 (OS 172). Cotswold manor house, with north wing and hall built c. 1140. There is a 16th-century porch, and an ambulatory or covered walk in garden. Open W and S pm, Apr to end Oct, other times by appt. 🅿♿♣

Killerton House, near Exeter, Devon (tel Exeter [0392] 881345). 6 m NE of Exeter on A396, turn E onto B3181. SS 9700 (OS 192). Georgian house erected in the late 1770s for the Acland family. The interior contains an extensive collection of period costume. The grounds were laid out around 1800 by John Veitch with many rare trees and sweeping lawns. House open Apr to end Oct daily am and pm; grounds open all year daily am and pm. ⊖ WC 🚻 (by appt) ♣ 🐾

King John's Hunting Lodge, Axbridge, Somerset. 12½ m NW of Wells on A371. ST 4255 (OS 182). Early 15th-century merchant's timber-framed house. It has no apparent connection with King John, or with hunting, but it was used as an alehouse in the 17th and 18th centuries. The house is now a museum of local history. Open Apr to Sept daily pm. ⊖ 🅿 ★

Kirkham House, Kirkham St, Paignton, Devon (tel Paignton [0803] 522775). In town centre. SX 8860 (OS 202). Late medieval manor house, now restored and known as the Priest's House. It contains a collection of locally made furniture. Open Apr to Sept daily am and pm (Su pm only). ⊖ ♿

Knightshayes Court, near Tiverton, Devon (tel Tiverton [0884] 254665). 3 m N of Tiverton on A396. SS 9615 (OS 181). Victorian house begun by William Burges in 1869 in Gothic Revival style, and decorated by J.D. Crace. The gardens are highly regarded. Gardens open Apr to end Oct am and pm; house pm only. 🅿WC ♿🚻 (by appt) ♣ 🐾

Lanhydrock, near Bodmin, Cornwall (tel Bodmin [0208] 3320). 2½ miles SE of Bodmin. SX 0863 (OS 200). House built in 1630-42, and rebuilt 1881 after a fire. The gatehouse and finely decorated long gallery are 17th-century; the rest of the interior has Victorian decoration. Extensive kitchens. The 19th-century formal gardens lead down to the River Fowey. House and gardens open Apr to Oct daily am and pm; Nov to March, gardens only. ⊖ 🅿WC 🚻 (by appt) D ♣ 🐾

Launceston Castle, Launceston, Cornwall (tel Launceston [0566] 2365). Close to town centre on A388. SX 3284 (OS 201). Ruined 13th-century shell keep castle with extra concentric wall, on a mound used for defence since pre-Conquest times. A large hall has been excavated within the bailey, probably used as a courtroom. Open daily am and pm. ⊖ 🚻

Lawrence House, 9 Castle St, Launceston, Cornwall (tel Launceston [0566] 2833). Close to town centre. SX 3284 (OS 201). 18th-century house, now containing a museum of curious items of local interest, including the feudal dues owed by the town to the Duke of Cornwall. Open Apr to Sept M-F am and pm (not Bank Hols), other times by appt. ⊖ WC ★

Ludgershall Castle, Ludgershall, Wiltshire. 7 m NW of Andover on A342. SU 2651 (OS 201). Norman motte-and-bailey castle, with building works in stone beginning in the 12th century, converting it into a royal residence and hunting lodge by the mid-13th century. Ruins and earthworks open daily am and pm. ⊖ 🅿 ★

Lydford Castle, Lydford, near Okehampton, Devon. 8 m SW of Okehampton on A386, turn W. SX 5084 (OS 201). Ruined keep dating from 1195 on the site of an Iron Age hillfort and a flourishing Anglo-Saxon town. The motte was created around the keep in the late 13th century. Until the 19th century the castle was used as the local courthouse for administering the local tin-mines. Open daily am and pm. ⊖ 🅿 ★

Lydiard Park, Purton, Wiltshire (tel Purton [0793] 770401). 4 m W of Swindon on A420, turn N. SU 1084 (OS 173). Mid-Georgian Classical house, with fine plasterwork interiors and contemporary furniture. The parish church is set in the extensive park. Open daily am and pm (Su pm only). ⊖ 🅿WC ♿🚻 (by appt) ♣ 🐾

Lytes Cary, Ilchester, Somerset (tel Castle Cary [0963] 50586). 2½ m NE of Ilchester off A37. ST 5326 (OS 183). Manor house built in the 14th to 16th centuries, the home of Henry Lyte, the Elizabethan herbalist. The chapel is the oldest part of the house, and the hall is mid-15th century, with a timber roof. The house is furnished in styles ranging from the 16th to 18th centuries, and the gardens have been replanted in the fashion of about 1600. Open March to Oct W and Su pm. ⊖ 🅿♿♣

Midelney Manor, Drayton, near Langport, Somerset (tel Langport [0458] 251229). 15 m E of Taunton, on A378. ST 4024 (OS 193). Medieval manor belonging to the abbot of nearby Muchelney Abbey, which became a private house in the 1530s. The house dates from the 1540s. There is an unusual 17th-century falconry mews, and a heronry in the gardens. Open June to Sept W pm; Bank Hol M pm. ⊖ 🅿WC ♿🚻 (by appt) ♣

Milton Abbey, near Blandford Forum, Dorset (tel Milton Abbas [0258] 880484). 12 m SW of Blandford Forum on A354, turn N. ST 7902 (OS 194). 14th-century abbey church and, beside it, a Georgian Gothick house constructed by William Chambers and James Wyatt from the original hall (completed 1498) of the abbey. The house now is used as a school, for which the hall is the dining room. Its carved screen and hammer-beam roof are notable. House open mid-Apr, and late July to end Aug daily am and pm; church open at all times. ⊖ 🅿WC ♿♣🐾

Mompesson House, Choristers' Green, Cathedral Close, Salisbury, Wiltshire. In city centre. SU 1429 (OS 184). Small stone house built in 1701, a fine example of Georgian provincial town architecture. The panelling and plasterwork are impressive; the oak staircase was added in the 1740s. There is also a collection of English 18th-century drinking glasses, and an attractive garden. Open Apr to end Oct M-W, S and Su pm. ⊖ ♿🚻♣

Mount Edgcumbe House, near Plymouth, Cornwall (tel Plymouth [0752] 82311). By ferry from Plymouth, or on B3247. SX 4552 (OS 201). 16th-century house adapted in the 18th century and rebuilt after the Second World War. The large 18th-century grounds are varied, with formal gardens, open parkland and mature woods, and enjoy outstanding views over Plymouth Sound. House open May to Sept, M and T pm; gardens daily all year. ⊖ WC ♣🐾

Nunney Castle, Nunney, Somerset. 3 m SW of Frome on A361, turn NW. ST 7345 (OS 183). Late 14th-century comprising four corner towers linked by high machicolated connecting walls, built by John de la Mare in the style of French military architecture. The castle was damaged in the Civil War, and the floors were removed. Open daily am and pm. ⊖ 🅿♿ ★

Oakhill Manor, Oakhill, near Bath, Avon (tel Oakhill [0749] 840210). 4 m N of Shepton Mallet on A37, turn E. ST 6347 (OS 183). Attractive country house in 45-acre park, containing a notable collection of model transport exhibits, covering air, land and sea transport. Miniature railway through gardens. Open daily Easter to Oct pm. ⊖ 🅿WC ♿🚻D ♣🐾🚃

Okehampton Castle, Okehampton, Devon (tel Okehampton [0837] 2844). ½ m S of town centre on A30. SX 5894 (OS 191). Extensive ruined castle, with an artificial motte on a natural ridge. It dates from the 11th to the 14th centuries, belonging to the Courtenay family from 1172. The castle was dismantled in the late 1530s after a rebellion against Henry VIII. Open daily am and pm (Su pm only). ⊖ 🅿WC

Old Post Office, Tintagel, Cornwall. In village centre, 13 miles N of Bodmin, on B3263. SX 0588 (OS 200). Medieval 14th-century manor house, with large hall and parlour. It was used between 1844 and 1892 as a village post office, and has now been restored as such. Open Apr to Oct daily am and pm. ⊖ 🅿♿

Pendennis Castle, Falmouth, Cornwall. Near town centre. SW 8231 (OS 204). Coastal fort built in 1540 by Henry VIII on a circular plan with two rings of walls to guard the harbour, and extended later in the 16th century with star-point bastions and earthworks. The castle was besieged for six months by Parliamentary forces in 1646. There is a collection of arms and armour. Open daily (exc S, Christmas and New Year) am and pm. ⊖ WC

Philipps House, Dinton Park, Dinton, Wiltshire (tel Teffont [072 276] 208). 12 m W of Salisbury on B3089. SU 0031 (OS 184). Neo-Classical house built in the early 19th century by Jeffry Wyattville for the Wyndham family. The house is now used as a conference centre for the YWCA. Open Apr to Oct daily am and pm. ⊖ 🅿♿

Portland Castle, Portland, Dorset. 3 m S of Weymouth, off A354. SY 6874 (OS 194). Castle built by Henry VIII in c. 1540 as part of his defences for the south coast; extended in the 17th and 18th centuries. There is an octagonal great tower within an enclosure. It is probably the best-preserved of all Henry's castles. Open Apr to Sept daily am and pm (Su pm only). 🅿

Priest's House, Muchelney, Somerset. 17 m E of Taunton on A378, turn SE. ST 4325 (OS 193). Late medieval house with large Gothic hall window, originally the residence of the parish priest. Open by appt only. ⊖

Purse Caundle Manor, Purse Caundle, Dorset (tel Milborne Port [0963] 250400). 5 m E of Sherborne on A30, turn NE. ST 6917 (OS 183). Typical manor house, mainly of the mid-16th century but with a somewhat earlier hall, and with interesting woodwork throughout. Open Apr to Oct Th, Su and Bank Hols pm, other times by appt. ⊖🅿♣

Pythouse, Tisbury, Wiltshire (tel Tisbury [0747] 870210). 4½ m N of Shaftesbury, 2½ m W of Tisbury. ST 9028 (OS 184). Palladian-style early 19th-century mansion. The reception rooms contain large 16th-century Italian fireplaces. There is an extensive garden with an orangery. Open May to Sept W and Th pm. ⊖🅿WC ♣

Red Lodge, Park Row, Bristol, Avon (tel Bristol [0272] 299771). Close to city centre. ST 5972 (OS 172). House built c. 1570 by merchant John Yonge; upper parts rebuilt in 18th century. The interiors are the oldest in Bristol; they contain original panelling and plasterwork, and 17th- and 18th-century furniture. Open M-S am and pm (exc Bank Hols).⊖ 🅿WC 🚻 ★

Restormel Castle, Lostwithiel, Cornwall (tel Lostwithiel [0208] 872687). 1 m N of Lostwithiel. SX 1061 (OS 200). Classic example of a shell keep castle, built in about 1200, in which the buildings were arranged in a ring just inside the oval wall, leaving a courtyard in the centre. A barbican was added in the 13th century. The castle was held by the Earls of Cornwall in the 13th century. Open daily am and pm (Oct to March, Su pm only). ⊖🅿WC 🔲♣

1 Royal Crescent, Bath, Avon (tel Bath [0225] 28126). Close to city centre. ST 5972 (OS 172). Stone-built Georgian house in the Crescent built by John Wood the Younger in 1767. Interior carefully restored in 1970 and furnished in authentic 18th-century style. Open daily (exc M) am and pm March to Oct; (S and Bank Hols pm only). ⊖🚻 (by appt)

St Mawes Castle, St Mawes, Cornwall (St Mawes [032 66] 526). In town centre. SW 8432 (OS 203). Clover-leaf shaped castle built by Henry VIII in 1543 as part of his coastal defences; guarding Carrick Roads together with Pendennis Castle in Falmouth. The garrison surrendered to the Parliamentary forces in 1646 without a fight. Open daily am and pm. ⊖ WC 🚻 ♣

Sandford Orcas Manor House, Sandford Orcas, Dorset (tel Corton Denham [096322] 206). 5 m E of Yeovil, in village centre. ST 6221 (OS 183). Fine Tudor manor house of stone, preserved as it was in about 1500. The interior contains a fine collection of stained glass and 16th-century furnishings. Open Easter M and May to Sept M am and pm, Su pm only. ⊖ 🚻 (by appt)

Smedmore House, Kimmeridge, Dorset (tel Corfe Castle [0929ß 480717). 6 m S of Wareham on A351, turn SW.SZ 9278 (OS 195). Manor house begun in the 1620s (for a project involving the use of the local oil shale for a glass factory), but mainly of the mid-18th century. It contains Dutch marquetry furniture and paintings, and a collection of antique dolls. There is a walled garden and an interesting shrubbery. Open June to mid-Sept W pm. 🅿WC 🔲🚻 (by appt) ♣

Tapeley Park House, Instow, Devon (tel Instow [0271] 860528). 1 m S of Instow, on A39. SS 4729 (OS 180). House built in the early 18th century, and modified around 1900. There are Georgian interiors, a collection of porcelain and distinctive plasterwork. The beautiful terraced Italian gardens were laid out in the early 20th century, and the house overlooks the estuary of the Rivers Taw

and Torridge. Open Apr to Oct daily (exc M) am and pm; Nov to Apr gardens only open. ⊖ 🅿 WC 🔲🚻 (by appt) D ♣ 🐾

Tintinhull House, Tintinhull, near Yeovil, Somerset (tel Martock [093 582] 2509). 5 m NW of Yeovil on A303, turn S. ST 5019 (OS 183). House of 1600 with an elegant façade of the 1720s. Its gardens were laid out by the botanist Dr Price in the early 20th century. Open Apr to Sept W, Th, S and Bank Hol M pm. ⊖🅿WC 🔲🚻 (by appt) ♣

Tiverton Castle, Tiverton, Devon (tel Tiverton [0884] 253200). On NW outskirts of Tiverton. SS 9513 (OS 181). Castle begun in 1106, with 14th-century gatehouse and additions made in the 16th and 17th centuries. The interior contains a collection of old clocks, and a gallery devoted to Joan of Arc. Open Easter, mid-May to mid-Sept Su-Th pm. ⊖🅿WC 🚻 (by appt)

Torre Abbey, Torquay, Devon (tel Torquay [0803] 23593). On Torquay sea front. SX 9164 (OS 202). 12th-century monastery converted into a private house after the Dissolution of the Monasteries, and much rebuilt in the 18th century. It contains period rooms and a large collection of paintings and other works of art. The medieval ruins and tithe barn can also be visited. Open Apr to Oct daily am and pm, other times by appt. ⊖🅿🐾

Totnes Castle, Totnes, Devon. In town centre. SX 8060 (OS 202). Early Norman motte topped by a well-preserved shell keep, built in the 13th and 14th centuries, and curtain wall. Open daily am and pm (Oct to March, Su pm only). ⊖🅿

Trelowarren House, Mawgan in Meneage, near Helston, Cornwall (tel Mawgan [032 622] 366). 3 m SE of Helston on A3083, turn NE onto B3293 for 2 m then NE. SW 7125 (OS 203). Home of the Vyvyan family since 1427, the main part of the house dates from the early 16th century. The notable chapel was rebuilt in the 18th century in a bright Gothick style. Part of the house is used by the Trelowarren Fellowship, an Ecumenical Charity. House open Easter to Oct, W and Bank Hols pm; also June to Sept Su pm. Chapel open Easter to Oct daily am and pm. 🅿WC 🐾

Trerice, St Newlyn East, near Newquay, Cornwall (Newquay [063 73] 5404). 4½ m SE of New-

Trerice, Cornwall

quay on A3058, turn SW. SW 8458 (OS 200). Manor house built by Sir John Arundell in 1572 on an E-plan. The interior contains a collection of 17th- and 18th-century furniture. The barn contains an exhibition tracing the history of the lawn mower; the garden has only recently been planted. Open Apr to Oct daily am and pm. ⊖ 🅿 WC 🔲🚻 (by appt) ♣ 🐾

Trewithen, near Probus, Cornwall (tel St Austell [0726] 882418). 6 m E of Truro on A390. SW 9147 (OS 204). Early 18th-century house, built by Thomas Edwards and decorated in Rococo style. The gardens were laid out by George Johnstone in the 1920s and are known internationally for their camellias, rhododendrons, magnolias and other exotic trees and shrubs.House open Apr to July M and T pm; garden open March to Sept daily (exc Su) pm. ⊖ WC ♣

Ugbrooke, near Chudleigh, Devon (tel Chudleigh [0626] 852179). 12 m SW of Exeter on A38, turn S onto A380 for 7 m then NW. SX 8778 (OS 192). Medieval house substantially rebuilt in the 1770s by the young Robert Adam in his 'castle' style for the Clifford family. Collection of embroidery and tapestry. There is a separate private chapel. The grounds were laid out by Capability Brown. Open June to Sept Su-Th pm; Easter and May Su and Bank Hols only, pm. 🅿WC 🔲♣ 🐾 🚃

Wardour Old Castle, Tisbury, Wiltshire. 19 m SW of Salisbury on A30, turn N. ST 9326 (OS 184). Ruined castle of 1393, rebuilt by Robert Smythson in the late 16th century. The castle is hexagonal in plan, with the great hall over the entrance. The castle was ruined in the Civil War, after which Wardour Castle was built in the grounds and the grounds landscaped. There is an elaborate late 18th-century grotto. Open late July to early Sept M, W, F, S pm. 🅿WC 🚻 D ♣

Westwood Manor, Bradford-on-Avon, Wiltshire. 14 m SW of Bradford-on-Avon on B3109, turn W. ST 8058 (OS 173). 15th-century stone manor house, with Tudor and Stuart additions. The 'king's room' and great chamber contain excellent plasterwork of the early 17th century. There is also a modern topiary garden. Open Apr to end Sept M, W, Su pm; other times by appt. ⊖🅿 🚻 (by appt) ♣

London and
Southern England

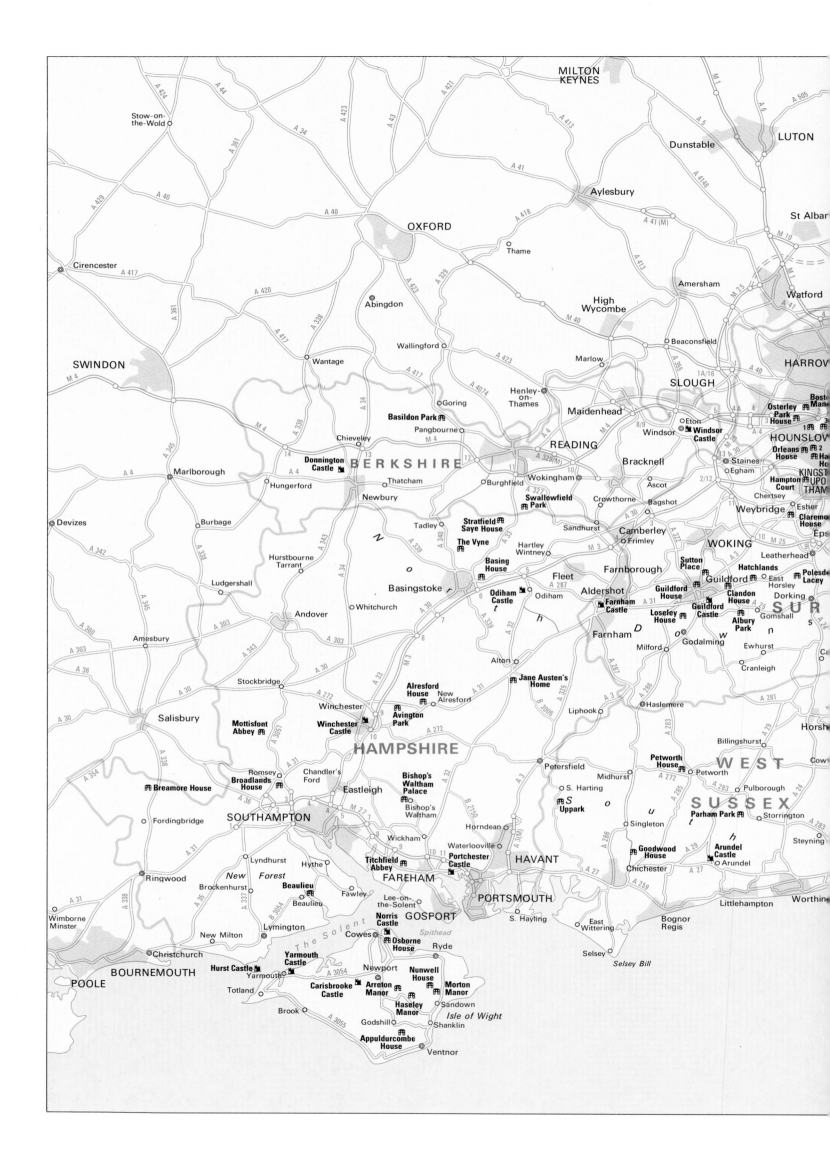

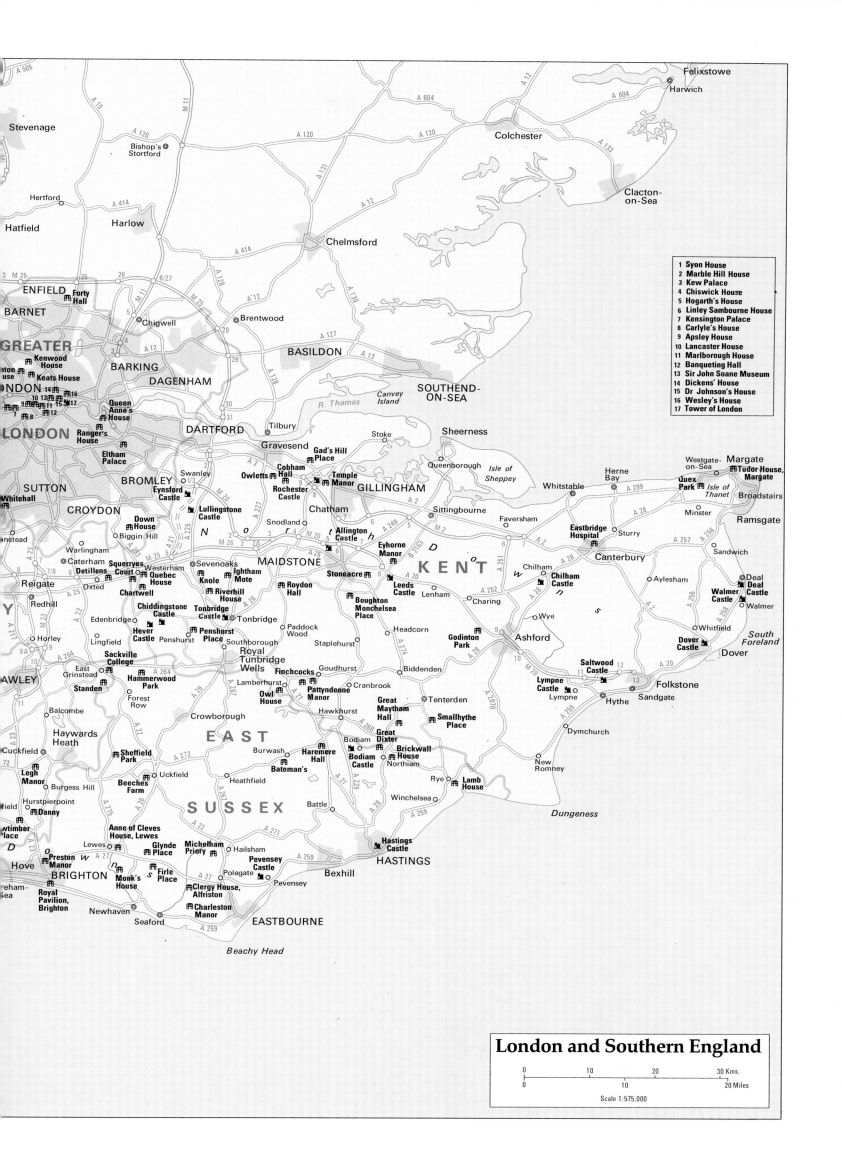

Stevenage

Hertford

Hatfield

Harlow

A 505

A 10

A 120

A 120

A 414

M 11

M 11

Bishop's
Stortford

A 120

Chelmsford

A 414

Colchester

Felixstowe
Harwich

A 12

A 604

A 604

A 133

Clacton-
on-Sea

ENFIELD

BARNET

GREATER

Forty
Hall

Kenwood
House

Keats House

14

10 13

9

8 12

16

15 17

11

7

3 M 25

25

26

6/27

28

29

30

31

M 11

M 25

A 128

A 12

A 130

A 127

BRENTWOOD

BASILDON

A 13

A 178

A 128

Brentwood

Chigwell

BARKING

DAGENHAM

LONDON

LONDON

SUTTON

CROYDON

BROMLEY

Whitehall

Queen
Anne's
House

Ranger's
House

Eltham
Palace

DARTFORD

Swanley

A 1/3

Eynsford
Castle

Down
House

Lullingstone
Castle

Biggin Hill

Tilbury

Gravesend

Gad's Hill
Place

Owletts

Cobham
Hall

Rochester
Castle

Temple
Manor

Stoke

R. Thames

Canvey
Island

SOUTHEND-
ON-SEA

Sheerness

Queenborough

Isle of
Sheppey

Whitstable

Herne
Bay

A 299

Westgate-
on-Sea

Margate

Tudor House,
Margate

Quex
Park

Isle of
Thanet

Broadstairs

Minster

Ramsgate

A 28

A 256

Sandwich

GILLINGHAM

Chatham

A 2

Sittingbourne

Faversham

A 2

Sturry

M 2

Eastbridge
Hospital

Canterbury

A 257

A 256

Deal
Deal
Castle

Walmer
Castle

Walmer

1 Syon House
2 Marble Hill House
3 Kew Palace
4 Chiswick House
5 Hogarth's House
6 Linley Sambourne House
7 Kensington Palace
8 Carlyle's House
9 Apsley House
10 Lancaster House
11 Marlborough House
12 Banqueting Hall
13 Sir John Soane Museum
14 Dickens' House
15 Dr Johnson's House
16 Wesley's House
17 Tower of London

Warlingham

Caterham

Reigate

Redhill

A 23

M 23

A 211

Horley

A 264

East
Grinstead

Standen

Balcombe

Haywards
Heath

Cuckfield

Legh
Manor

Burgess Hill

Hurstpierpoint

Danny

HOVE

BRIGHTON

Royal
Pavilion,
Brighton

Newhaven

Seaford

Oxted

Detillens

Squerryes
Court

Quebec
House

Chartwell

Westerham

Sevenoaks

Knole

Ightham
Mote

Snodland

MAIDSTONE

Allington
Castle

Eyhorne
Manor

Stoneacre

Roydon
Hall

Leeds
Castle

Lenham

Charing

Boughton
Monchelsea
Place

Headcorn

Godinton
Park

Ashford

Chilham

Chilham
Castle

Wye

Whitfield

Dover
Castle

A 2

A 20

A 252

A 251

A 28

A 251

KENT

South
Foreland

Dover

Folkstone

Sandgate

Hythe

Lympne

Dymchurch

New
Romney

Saltwood
Castle

Lympne
Castle

Dungeness

Chiddingstone
Castle

Hever
Castle

Penshurst

Riverhill
House

Tonbridge
Castle

Tonbridge

Penshurst
Place

Paddock
Wood

Southborough

Staplehurst

Royal
Tunbridge
Wells

Finchcocks

Goudhurst

Biddenden

Sackville
College

Hammerwood
Park

Forest
Row

Crowborough

Lamberhurst

Owl
House

Pattyndenne
Manor

Cranbrook

Tenterden

Great
Maytham
Hall

Smallhythe
Place

EAST

SUSSEX

Sheffield
Park

Uckfield

Heathfield

Beeches
Farm

Burwash

Haremere
Hall

Bateman's

Bodiam

Bodiam
Castle

Great
Dixter

Brickwall
House

Northiam

Rye

Winchelsea

Lamb
House

Battle

Hastings
Castle

HASTINGS

Bexhill

Anne of Cleves
House, Lewes

Lewes

Michelham
Priory

Glynde
Place

Firle
Place

Monk's
House

Preston
Manor

Clergy House,
Alfriston

Charleston
Manor

Hailsham

Polegate

Pevensey
Castle

Pevensey

EASTBOURNE

Beachy Head

London and Southern England

0   10   20   30 Kms.

0   10   20 Miles

Scale 1:575,000

Arundel Castle

Arundel, West Sussex

The majestic keep and long walls of Arundel command the lower reach of the river Arun between the South Downs and the sea. A large castle of motte-and-bailey type was erected not long after the Norman Conquest to guard the important gap carved by the river through the Downs. The motte is 70 feet high, and the baileys extend north and south from it along a chalk spur. In the 12th century a battlemented shell-keep was built on south end of this bailey. The gatehouse was heightened late in the 13th century and strengthened by the addition of a two-towered barbican. At this time the castle was held by Richard Fitzalan, created Earl of Arundel in 1290. Except for short intervals the Fitzalan family continued to hold the castle down to 1580, when Henry, the 12th Earl, died without male heir. His daughter Mary had married Thomas Howard, the 4th

the motte, and curtain walls round the baileys. The walls of the keep are 9 foot thick, supported externally by flat buttresses. An arched entrance in the wall, ornamented with Norman mouldings, was blocked up and replaced by a strong gate-tower late in the 12th century.

From the summit of the tower, the highest part of the castle, flies the banner of the Duke of Norfolk, premier Duke of England and hereditary Earl Marshal. The great office of Earl Marshal was bestowed on the 1st Duke in 1483. His duties are to preside at the College of Arms, which controls matters relating to heraldry and honours, and to manage all state processions and ceremonial.

The entrance to the castle is through a 12th-century gatehouse built on the curtain of the south bailey and from an early date the domestic buildings occupied the

Duke of Norfolk, who was beheaded for treason in 1572. The Dukedom was forfeited and not restored for nearly a hundred years. Nevertheless his son Philip Howard succeeded his maternal grandfather as 13th Earl of Arundel. In 1584 he became an avowed Catholic and after failing to escape from England was fined and imprisoned in the Tower of London. Released, he was soon re-arrested and condemned to death, allegedly for saying a Mass for the success of the Spanish Armada. He died in the Tower in 1595, to be canonised by the Catholic Church nearly four hundred years later.

Philip's son Thomas was restored to the Earldom of Arundel by James I in 1604 and the Howards have held the castle ever since. Thomas, a patron of arts and a great collector, escorted Queen Henrietta Maria to safety on the Continent in 1642 and lived abroad until his death at Padua. In his absence the Civil War raged.

Sir William Waller captured Arundel for Parliament and Lord Hopton won it back for the King. Early in 1644 Waller returned, mounting his guns on top of the tower of the parish church in order to fire over the castle walls. Marks of his cannon balls can be seen above the archway of the barbican. Waller's troops sacked the castle and it remained ruined and neglected for fifty years.

The 16th Earl was restored to the Dukedom of Norfolk in 1660 by Charles II. Neither he nor his immediate successors lived at Arundel. Some repairs and extensions were carried out about 1716 but it was not until 1787 that the 11th Duke began a substantial reconstruction to make Arundel fit for his principal residence outside London. He was an amateur architect

and the work went on to his designs for many years. Much of this was drastically remodelled later but the library remains an intriguing monument to his tastes. It is 122 feet long, with a sexpartite vault springing from clusters of slender columns. Flat, pointed arches divide it into two bays. Ceiling, arches, panels and bookcases are all of Honduras mahogany, the work of Jonathan Ritson and his son, wood-carvers brought from Cumberland, who later completed the work of Grinling Gibbons at Petworth. The library is an unusually fine example of a Gothick interior, looking like a small church but given an almost voluptuous warmth by the ten thousand books and manuscripts, the red-and-gold carpet covering the whole length of the room and above all by the rich colours of the mahogany. This memorable

Above and right, Arundel Castle presents a dominating exterior, placed on a chalk spur above the River Arun, a strategic site to defend against invasion from the Continent. The action seen by the castle, however, was more often associated with civil war than with foreign invasion.

Left, the drawing room is one of the many state apartments renovated by the 15th Duke of Norfolk in the late 19th century. The ceiling is carved mahogany.

Opposite, the private chapel, built by the 15th Duke in a style inspired by the nave of Salisbury Cathedral.

Below, the motte and 30-foot high shell-keep remain from the original Norman castle, though topped by the 13th-century well tower.

creation displays treasures other than books, particularly a striking silver icon made in 1908 for the 16th Duke by the great Russian jeweller-craftsman, Fabergé.

The 15th Duke restored the keep and barbican and carried out a comprehensive rebuilding of the domestic blocks during the period 1870-90. The buildings today, though resting on 12th-century foundations, are mainly of this period. Victorian Gothic can have a cold effect but at Arundel this is offset by the portraits, furniture, china and tapestries that enrich the main rooms. Many of these were originally at Norfolk House, the Duke's London residence, which was demolished in 1938.

On the site of the medieval hall the present great hall is a noble successor. Oak from the estate was used to fashion the hammer-beam roof. Stained-glass windows tell the long story of the Fitzalan-Howards by heraldic devices and historic scenes. The fireplace has pairs of squat columns supporting a huge overmantel and a chimney like a half-concealed obelisk sloping up between the braces of the roof. Older furniture, tapestries and portraits suit and enhance the fine Victorian craftsmanship.

The grand staircase, the dining room, the private chapel are all solidly Victorian but also contain earlier furniture and ornaments. The 13th Duke, a Protestant, entertained Queen Victoria at the castle in 1846. Prior to the visit, fearing her disapproval, he removed a stained-glass window in the dining room which showed Solomon entertaining the Queen of Sheba. The homage throne used at Queen Victoria's Coronation is displayed in the library. Gold cups presented to the Earl Marshal by the Sovereign at every Coronation since that of George II, and the Earl Marshal's baton, are shown in the dining room.

The 15th Duke died in 1917 and was succeeded by his son, Bernard Marmaduke, still well remembered in his capacity as Earl Marshal. He arranged the celebration of George V's Silver Jubilee, the Coronations of George VI and Elizabeth II, the funerals of George V and George VI. In 1965, at the express command of the Queen, he and his officers presided over a rare event: the Lying-in-State and State funeral of a commoner, Sir Winston Churchill.

☎ Arundel (0903) 883136

In centre of Arundel

TQ 0107 (OS 197)

Open Apr to end Oct daily exc S 1300-1700; reduced rates for parties

⊖ P WC 🅰 🆓 D ♣ 🍴 ⊼ ⚘ 🗡 (by appt) ● (not in house)

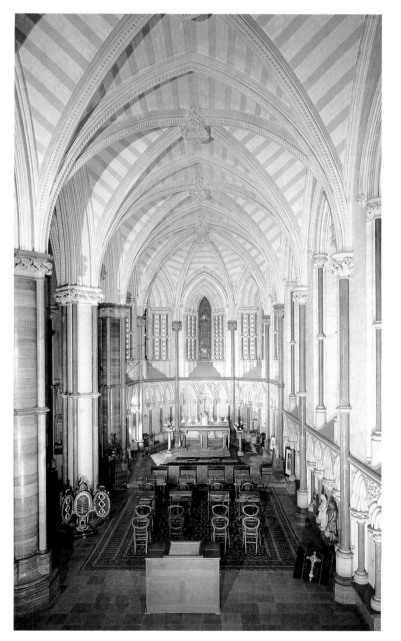

The Royal Pavilion Brighton, West Sussex

At the end of the London Road into Brighton, within sight and smell of the English Channel, the Royal Pavilion must have startled travellers when its domes and minarets first rose skywards. Now an integral feature of the town, it still has the power to amaze and fascinate or to arouse the rancour of puritans. Both reactions are a tribute to its startling originality so carefully restored and maintained by Brighton Borough Council.

George, Prince of Wales, son of George III, first visited Brighton in 1783. Immersion in the sea and drinking of sea water (no doubt with an additive) had been recommended as a cure for his swollen neck glands. Three years later he leased a modest farmhouse near the sea front and employed Henry Holland, who had been working for him at Carlton House in London, to convert it into a large and more comfortable 'marine pavilion'. Much of Holland's structure is contained in the present building but it was in Neo-Classical style and without any trace of oriental influences.

Above, the fantasy Mughal skyline of the Royal Pavilion was made possible by the ingenious use of cast iron.

Opposite, the banqueting hall, with an extraordinary dragon chandelier made of gas. Dragons are ubiquitous in this overpowering room.

Between 1801 and 1803 the interior was entirely redecorated, at huge expense, in the Chinese style which had become popular in Europe during the 18th century. Plans were also prepared for a Chinese exterior. Meanwhile a large stable block in the grounds was constructed in Indian style to designs by William Purdon. Purdon was a pupil of Samuel Pepys Cockerell, the architect responsible for the 'Indian' country house being built at Sezincote in Gloucestershire. This interest in things Indian reflected the growing importance of the sub-continent to England. The Prince was delighted with his stables and at his request Humphry Repton, who had laid out the gardens at Sezincote, made plans for converting the Pavilion itself into a Mughal Palace.

The Royal Pavilion, with the banqueting hall shown in cutaway.

The Prince's financial difficulties, however, prevented further work for the time being. People remarked that the Prince was not so well housed as his horses.

The Prince's enthusiasm for Repton's design faded, and eventually John Nash was employed when the construction of today's Pavilion got under way in 1815. The choice of an adaptable and imaginative architect, who had worked in all sorts of styles, was appropriate. Neither he nor the Prince felt bound by formal rules; accepted styles could 'go hang' so long as the result was picturesque. The Pavilion was a unique building in all respects, without precursor or imitator. The Indian exterior and Chinese interior represented Nash's and the Prince's ideas, not any actual building in those far-off lands. Completed in 1822, it was a glorious fantasy based on eastern themes.

Queen Victoria visited the Pavilion soon after her accession in 1837 and described it as 'a strange, odd, Chinese-looking thing, both inside and out . . .'. She probably disliked it straight away. A palace where the Prince had enjoyed lavish dinners and entertainments, and had invited a succession of mistresses but never his wife, would hardly have appealed to her. And largely through his patronage Brighton had expanded dramatically and was no longer a small, upper-class resort. By 1845, the year of the Queen's last visit, the railway was bringing crowds of trippers from London. The Queen complained that she could not enjoy a walk along the front or on the old Chain Pier without being followed by crowds of 'troublesome' people. In that same year she purchased Osborne in the Isle of Wight for a seaside residence. The Royal Pavilion seemed doomed.

Soon furniture and fittings, and even fixtures such as murals, wallpaper and doorways, were carted away to royal storerooms in London and Windsor. Much damage was done to the fabric by the removers. When the Town, after a lot of legal and civic wrangling, purchased the Pavilion in 1850 to save it from demolition, it was an empty shell. Work to make the main rooms usable began immediately and soon concerts, flower shows, art exhibitions and public meetings were being held in them.

In 1863 Queen Victoria approved the return of selected material that had been lying unpacked in Kensington Palace – wall paintings and papers, chandeliers, decorative dragons and the like – but in spite of this and the initial enthusiasm for restoration the Pavilion was in a shabby condition by the end of the century. Use as a hospital in the First World War did nothing to improve it and during the inter-war period interest in its preservation was kept alive by only a

dedicated few. They were helped by the return of more original articles by George V and by Queen Mary's interest and gifts. Suggestions for demolition were resisted so that at last, after the Second World War, popular interest in the Regency period and a wider appreciation of the Pavilion's importance brought about the sophisticated restoration which is still continuing. Using original pieces or reconstructions from the evidence of fragments and documents, or by making valid substitutes, a wonderfully authentic return to the Pavilion of 1822 has been achieved. Over a hundred original items have been sent on permanent loan by the present Queen.

Visitors enter through the original onion-domed porch and pass into the light and airy octagon hall. Beyond it a vestibule of greys and greens leads to the corridor, 162 foot long, which connects all the main rooms and the Prince's apartments. The dominant colours of the corridor are pinks and reds with waving bamboo plants in blue on the walls, amber panels above and an amber strip down the middle of the red-patterned carpet. The furniture is bamboo, some real and some simulated as it was in 1822. The cast-iron staircases at either end also simulate bamboo. Chinese figures and lanterns, delicate trellis work, mirrors and bamboo friezes contribute to the wealth of decoration.

When guests assembled, walking and talking up and down the long room, waiting to be greeted by the Prince, it must have been an extraordinary scene. And when the guests trooped behind the Prince into the banqueting hall another exotic spectacle dazzled them. Drawing together all the rich threads was the centrepiece: the famous crystal gaselier decorated with lotus leaves of tinted glass and dragons and jewels, suspended from an enormous winged dragon in the dome.

All the restored rooms have a similar exuberance. In the great kitchen royal banquets were prepared among palm-tree pillars, their copper tufts supporting the ceiling. No other palace in Britain contains such inventiveness or conveys the same feeling of unashamed extravagance and enjoyment.

☎ Brighton (0273) 603005

In centre of Brighton near the Palace Pier

TQ 3104 (OS 198)

Open throughout year W-S 1000-1700; T, Su and Bank Hol M 1000-1300 and 1400-1700

♿ WC ⬚ (limited access) ⊟ ♣ ⬛ ◆ ⚹ 𝄢 (available in foreign languages) ● (no tripods allowed)

Left, the kitchen, with a fine array of copper utensils, is supported by slim columns.

Above, the music room was damaged by fire in 1975 but has since been restored.

Top, Chinese staircases of iron and bamboo are placed at either end of the gallery, a wide corridor and meeting place which joins the banqueting hall and the music room.

Hampton Court

Hampton, Greater London

When Thomas Wolsey chose the site for a mansion outside London in 1514 he was approaching the peak of his power and wealth. Later in the year he would become Archbishop of York and, within twelve months, a Cardinal and Henry VIII's Lord High Chancellor. A dozen miles from Westminster by land, though rather longer by barge up the Thames, the red-brick mansion began to rise on the north bank of the river, backed by extensive parkland. Wolsey planned on a large scale, with the buildings grouped round two main and several lesser courts. His household was said to number five hundred people and the mansion to contain a thousand rooms. Pipes were laid to bring a pure water supply from springs some miles away and brick drains to discharge rainwater and soil from many water closets. None of the royal palaces was more comfortable or lavish.

By the late 1520s Wolsey was falling out of favour. To try to placate the King he gave him – surely an incomparable present – Hampton Court and its contents. The gift did not save Wolsey from disgrace though the King accepted it with pleasure and at once began enlargement of the already huge building. He replaced Wolsey's great hall with a greater one, and made a splendid chamber nearby for his Yeomen of the Guard. Wolsey's chapel was given the remarkable fan-vaulted timber roof seen today. Another main courtyard was added with sets of apartments round it for the King and his queens. To serve the royal household even Wolsey's large kitchen quarters had to be extended and remodelled.

Anne Boleyn's gateway between the Base and Clock Courts recalls Henry's second wife. Her arms and initials also appear on the roof timbers of the great hall

Left, the warm red brick of the west front and gatehouse, built by Wolsey in the early 16th century and famous for its myriad chimneys, each one individual in its design.

Above, the astronomical clock built for Henry VIII in 1540, which gives its name to Clock Court. It records the passing hours, days, months, phases of the moon, and tides at London Bridge.

but elsewhere they were removed after her execution in 1536. Eighteen months later Jane Seymour, the third wife, gave birth to the future Edward VI in the state apartments, only to die there within a fortnight. Edward was baptised in Wolsey's chapel with its handsome new vault and spent the first year of his life at the Palace. The fifth wife, Catherine Howard, was placed under guard there before her removal for trial and execution. Henry's last marriage, to Catherine Parr, took place in the Palace chapel.

The later Tudors and the Stuarts used the Palace but left few reminders of their presence. James I (r. 1603-25) celebrated his first Christmas in his new kingdom there and Charles I (r. 1625-49) was briefly held prisoner by the New Model Army in 1647. When the royal properties were sold off after his execution, Cromwell retained Hampton Court for his own use.

After the Restoration in 1660 some repairs were carried out, but by the time Willam and Mary ascended the throne in 1688 the huge building had become outmoded and only the site was to their liking. Plans were prepared for an entirely new building. Christopher Wren, Surveyor of the King's Works since 1669 but not yet knighted, began by demolishing Henry VIII's state apartments and erecting new blocks round the present Fountain Court, a classically severe masterpiece of English Baroque. Brick was used but richly embellished with Portland stone for the arcades, windows, friezes and parapets. At first-floor level sets of apartments in the latest style were provided for the

King and Queen, each with its own staircase. On the west side of the court was the communication gallery which linked the sets of rooms for formal occasions. While the work progressed, and with the King often absent on state affairs, the Queen occupied a Tudor pavilion by the riverside which had been refurbished for her use. But the new apartments were still unfinished when she died at Kensington Palace in 1694. A few years later the Tudor pavilion was pulled down but the plan for demolishing the rest of the Tudor palace was abandoned.

William liked Hampton Court and it was after a fall while riding in its park that he died. The interiors of Wren's buildings were completed under Queen Anne and the first two Georges. After the death of George II in 1760 no sovereign occupied the Palace again.

A survivor from the earliest building is the small room called Wolsey's Closet near the north end of the communication gallery. The panelling was renewed in the 19th century but all else is original. Beautifully coloured panels of scenes from the Passion, a frieze of mermaids, dolphins and Tudor badges with Wolsey's motto endlessly repeated underneath, a dazzling ceiling of interlacing ribs and Tudor roses give some indication of the luxury with which Wolsey furnished his country seat.

Henry VIII's great hall is the most impressive of all Tudor halls. Over 100 foot in length, the carved and moulded hammer-beam roof spans 40 feet with a solid serenity. The Flemish tapestries on the walls tell the

story of Abraham and are dated about 1540. At the east end a fan-vaulted window lights the dais where important people sat.

Wren's apartments for William III are approached by the King's staircase, which has a superb wrought-iron balustrade by the Frenchman, Jean Tijou. Antonio Verrio painted the walls and ceiling with his familiar columns and sprawling figures. On the ceiling the Gods are banqueting and below William III, in the guise of Alexander the Great, is presented to them by the hero Hercules. A line of Roman emperors are respectful spectators.

Pictures, tapestries and furnishings, the important 15th-century cartoons by Andrea Mantegna displayed in the lower orangery, Wren's confident east façade looking down on the Great Fountain and beyond to the Long Water and the lime avenues of Home Park, the famous maze and the famous great vine of Black Hamburgh grapes planted in 1768, the varied gardens – Hampton Court's delights are innumerable. The best way to approach them is by boat, up-river from Westminster or Richmond, like Wolsey and the Tudor and later monarchs. They went to Hampton Court to escape the smoke and mists of London, and the plague, to enjoy country air with masques and plays, dancing, 'real' tennis, tournaments and riding in the park. Today their anticipation of pleasure can be appreciated as the launch rounds the great curve of the Thames where the Home Park lies and slowly approaches the landing stage where the royal barges once moored.

Opposite, the East Front, built by Wren for William and Mary, containing the state apartments.

Below, the Tudor wine cellars; in Henry's day, 1000 people worked at Hampton Court.

Above, a number of small, formal gardens have been laid out in historical style, offering moments of intimacy around this otherwise grand and sprawling building.

☎ (01) 977 1328

Kingston upon Thames at junction of A308 and A309

TQ 1568 (OS 176)

Open May to end Sept M-S 0930-1800, Su 1100-1800; Mar, Apr and Oct closes 1700; Nov to end Feb closes 1600. Closed Good Fri, 24, 25, 26 Dec

⊖ Ⓟ WC 🚻 ♣ ☕ 🎪 ◆ ♨ 🚶

Penshurst Place

Tunbridge Wells, Kent

Right, the north front, mostly made up of the family wing built by the Sidneys in the 16th century.

Below, the 15th- and 16th-century south front of Penshurst, with the great hall distinguished by its tall windows.

One of the few 14th-century domestic buildings to survive in England, the great hall at Penshurst is justly renowned. It was built early in the 1340s by Sir John Pulteney, a wool merchant and financier, four times Lord Mayor of London. He did not live long to enjoy his fine country seat in the upper valley of the River Medway, being struck down by the Black Death in 1349.

His building consisted of the great hall with private apartments at one end and service quarters at the other. Later in the 14th century, possibly as a result of the Peasants' Revolt in 1381 and continuing unrest in the countryside, a wall with corner and intermediate towers was erected round the buildings. These fortifications would have availed little against a properly armed force but would no doubt have deterred bands of discontented peasants. Although only fragments of these medieval walls remain and only one of the towers (the 'garden tower'), their previous existence helps to explain the extraordinary layout of the present buildings. Additional buildings were pushed out to and along the walls but when these disappeared the rectangular plan was lost.

In 1430 the Duke of Bedford, the third son of Henry IV, purchased the estate. A new building was added at this date or soon afterwards extending from the south-west corner of the great hall out to the west wall of the fortifications. It consisted of a crypt and one large room where guests could be entertained away from the household eating in the great hall. It is illogically known as the 'Buckingham building' after the 1st Duke of that name who owned the estate later in the 15th century.

The modern story of Penshurst begins when Edward VI granted it to Sir William Sidney in 1552. He was a veteran soldier who had fought at Flodden Field and later been appointed tutor and steward to the young Prince Edward. He is buried in Penshurst church and his descendants have held the estate since. His son Sir Henry Sidney, three times Lord Deputy of Ireland and for over twenty-five years Lord President of Wales, spent little time at Penshurst because of these and other duties but made many additions and alterations to the medieval buildings. Notably he rebuilt the entrance tower in the middle of the north wall (the King's tower) and the graceful loggia adjoining the north-west or President's tower.

All the Tudor Sidneys were able and zealous servants of the Crown, distinguished from many other high officials by their unselfish disregard of money and titles. Sir Henry's eldest son Philip, born at Penshurst in 1554, was the youthful paragon of the age. In his brief life he gained renown as soldier, poet and diplomat. In 1586, at the age of thirty-two, he was wounded in a skirmish during the siege of Zutphen in the Low Countries, his thigh shattered by a musket ball. He died several weeks later at Arnhem, leaving the world wondering to what heights he might have attained if he had lived.

Philip died in the same year as his father and was the nominal owner of Penshurst for only a few months. His brother Robert, who had been at his side at Zutphen and Arnhem, inherited. He was created Viscount L'Isle in 1605 and Earl of Leicester in 1618. He built the long gallery running between the south-west corner tower and the Buckingham building and the large room in the latter was divided up, to form the forerunners of today's state rooms, and an attic with dormer windows made in the roof.

The most famous Sidney of the 17th century was the republican Algernon Sidney, son of the 2nd Earl of Leicester. He fought for Parliament during the Civil War and was wounded at the battle of Marston Moor. He opposed the trial of Charles I and disapproved when the Protectorate was established by Cromwell. He was abroad at the Restoration but returned voluntarily to England in 1677. During the anti-republican fervour which followed the failure of the Rye House Plot to kill Charles II and his brother James (1683), in which he played no part, he was tried for treason and executed on Tower Hill in 1683. He was buried at Penshurst and has since been extolled as a martyr for freedom.

The Leicester title became extinct in 1743 and the estate passed twice through the female line to John Shelley, who assumed the name of Sidney by Royal Licence in 1793. He carried out extensive alterations to the private apartments stretching north from the great hall and along the north wall. When the work was completed he handed over Penshurst to his son Philip who was created Baron de L'Isle and Dudley in 1835.

The present owner, the 6th Baron, inherited in 1945 and was created Viscount de L'Isle in 1956. As a Major in the Grenadier Guards he had won the Victoria Cross during the desperate fighting on the Anzio beachhead in February 1944.

The apartments open to the public contain many fine furnishings and portraits but the great hall of Sir John Pulteney, sympathetically maintained by the Sidneys for more than four centuries, remains the outstanding feature of Penshurst. The local sandstone used in its construction gives a striking patchwork appearance to the exterior, enhancing the solid proportions of the battlements, buttresses and arched windows and entrance porches. Size alone would have made the interior remarkable but the windows high in the end wall to illuminate the roof were a novel feature at the time. The hall is 62 foot long, and the apex of the roof about 60 feet above the floor. The roof timbers are a superb example of medieval woodwork, attributed to William Hurley, Edward III's carpenter. King-posts rest on collar beams which rest on moulded braces to span nearly 40 feet. The dais and the octagonal hearth in the centre of the hall have survived even though the opening in the roof above the fire was blocked up during a careful restoration in the 19th century. At the east end the screen, masking the passageway between the entrance porches and the usual three doors to the pantry, buttery and kitchen, has Sir Henry Sidney's arms of Bear-and-Ragged-Staff set in the frieze. But the screen looks medieval and seems to be mainly of material from the original. Traces of large medieval wall paintings can be seen between the side windows. This vast and beautiful room was the core of Penshurst, from which all the later buildings were pushed out almost haphazardly over the centuries. Beneath the hall the simple, vaulted cellar may be part of an even earlier building on the site.

☎ Penshurst (0892) 870307

2 m S of Tonbridge on A26 turn W onto B2176 for 5 m

TQ 5244 (OS 188)

Open Apr to early Oct daily exc M (but inc Bank Hol M) 1400-1800; reduced rates for parties

⊖ P WC 日 ♣ ☞ 戸 ◆ ⚒ ⚔ ☆ ⚓

Top, Queen Elizabeth's room, a medieval chamber with Tudor panelling and 17th- and 18th-century furniture.

Above, the early 17th-century long gallery is lined with portraits of the Sidney family; its plasterwork ceiling is notable.

Opposite, the great hall, built in about 1340, is one of the finest early halls in the country. It has a magnificent chestnut timber roof and the hearth is centrally placed, as was usual at that date.

Windsor Castle Windsor, Berkshire

The castle stands on an isolated chalk hill above the River Thames, its elongated plan determined and preserved by the shape of the ground. Like many others it began as a simple motte-and-bailey fortress, one of a ring built by William the Conqueror a day's march from London and from each other to protect his new capital. While castles such as Berkhamsted were allowed to fall into ruin, Windsor survived because from an early date it became a royal residence as well as a fortress.

From the central mound scarped from the chalk by William I, the spectacular round tower overawes the castle, Windsor town and the landscape. The tower's history reflects something of the complex story of the castle. The original shell-keep, built not long after the Conquest, was a large one, 15 foot high and of irregular shape. Timber buildings were already in existence inside the keep when Henry I (r. 1100-35) held Court there in 1114. Later in the 12th century King Henry II

Left, the wards of Windsor Castle, the central Round Tower and St George's Chapel dominating the lower ward are clearly visible in this aerial view.

Above, the Round Tower was built as the castle's great tower in the 11th century. It was heightened by George IV in the early 19th century.

(r. 1154-89) carried out large defensive works which included remodelling the keep. He built another wall within the original shell and rising nearly 20 feet above it. The wall walk of the earlier keep became the 10-foot wide terrace outside the tower which still exists.

Another reconstruction of the castle took place in the 14th century during the reign of Edward III (r. 1327-77). Two-storey buildings, using some of the older posts and beams, were put up inside the keep, leaving an open courtyard in the centre. These are substantially the buildings seen today.

For 350 years the keep remained undisturbed, only assuming its present appearance in the reign of George IV. Sir Jeffry Wyattville was the architect employed to carry out a large-scale reconstruction of the keep and upper ward. The keep was heightened by 30 feet and given the buttresses, windows, battlements and machicolations which are such a well-known sight today. Henry II's shell was strengthened internally to support the extra weight but otherwise the interior was little altered.

The Queen's private apartments occupy the east and south sides of the upper ward and were built by Wyattville. The state apartments on the north side are basically those fitted out for Charles II (r. 1660-85). Only part of the great hall is earlier, attributable to Edward III's reign. The state apartments were drastically reorganised by Wyattville to suit George IV (r.1820-30), though three ceilings survive of the many painted by

Opposite, Windsor Castle was built to dominate the route along the River Thames from London to the heart of England.

Below, the King Henry VIII gateway, which now serves as the main entrance to the castle.

Left, the grand staircase at Windsor, with an array of 15th-century armour.

Bottom, the gardens and east front, which contains the private apartments of the Royal Family. The walls are 12th-century but the interior was refurbished by Jeffry Wyattville in the early 19th century.

Antonio Verrio for Charles II. The rooms exhibit a rather daunting collection of valuable arms and armour, statuary, tapestries, paintings, carving and furnishings. The pictures include one of Rubens' finest landscapes and the famous triple portrait of Charles I by Van Dyck. This was specially painted for sending to Rome so that the renowned sculptor and architect Bernini could make a bust of the King without travelling to London. The painting was eventually brought back to England and purchased by George IV. The 18th-century American-born artists Benjamin West and John Singleton Copley are represented by accomplished portraits. Some of the Queen's collection of drawings, including works by Holbein and Leonardo da Vinci, are also shown.

In the magnificent Waterloo room a banquet is held each year on 18th June, the anniversary of the battle. George IV, Prince Regent at the time of the victory, was

determined that it should be commemorated in style. Sir Thomas Lawrence was commissioned to do portraits of all the soldiers, statesmen and monarchs who had contributed to Napoleon's final overthrow, and Wyatt-ville was ordered to prepare a suitable gallery to display them at Windsor. His solution was ingenious: an open court in the middle of the state apartments was roofed over and a clerestory formed to light the portraits in daytime. They include some of Lawrence's best work. The room is usually shown to the public with its long table laid ready with some sixty places for the banquet.

The Waterloo room is also used once a year in June by the Knights of the Most Noble Order of the Garter. After luncheon they go down from the upper ward, through the 'Norman' gate of Edward III, to the lower ward for their annual service in St George's Chapel. Preceded by the Heralds in their brilliant tabards, the Knights walk casually in their robes and plumed hats, the Sovereign at the rear with an escort of Yeomen of the Guard. The colourful procession is headed by the Military Knights of Windsor wearing scarlet uniforms of the time of William IV (r. 1830-37). They are officers of

distinguished service who live in houses in the lower ward and represent the Garter Knights at daily service in the chapel.

The Most Noble Order of the Garter, the highest Order of Knighthood, was founded by Edward III in 1348. Membership is limited to the Sovereign and twenty-five Companions. Additional members, such as foreign royalty, may be admitted. At first the Order used the modest 13th-century chapel built in the castle by Henry III. By the time of Edward IV the chapel was in woeful disrepair. Across the river at Eton College, which had been founded by Henry VI (r. 1422-61; 1470-71) in 1440, a new and splendid chapel in Perpendicular style seemed to mock the dilapidated condition of St George's. Edward IV was not to be outdone by the king he had driven from the throne and resolved to build a chapel worthy of a royal castle and the Garter Knights.

The building which the visitor sees when entering the lower ward through Henry VIII's gate took fifty years to complete. Flying buttresses, large windows and, inside, the beautiful vault of nave and choir springing from slender, compound piers – all have the grace and lightness of the last phase of Gothic architecture. The Garter service is held in the choir where each Knight has his stall, his embroidered banner hanging above. The canopies of the stalls are so finely carved as to resemble lacework.

Windsor is one of the Sovereign's three official residences, older by many centuries than either Buckingham Palace or Holyroodhouse. The long continuity of royal use is unrivalled and most of the kings and queens of England have left some reminder within its walls.

In December 1984 Prince Henry, the second son of the Prince and Princess of Wales, was christened in St George's Chapel when the Royal Family celebrated Christmas at the castle.

☎ Windsor (075 35) 68286

In centre of Windsor, on B3022

SU 9777 (OS 175)

Open varied times, subject to change at short notice, phone for details

♿ WC ♿ (access by appt)
🅿 ♣ ◆ ✕ (available in foreign languages) ● (not in house)

Palace House, Beaulieu

Brockenhurst, Hampshire

Most people know Beaulieu as the home of the National Motor Museum, and indeed it is quite possible to miss Palace House and the ruins of the old abbey standing some little distance away. The house is the home of Lord and Lady Montagu, and has been in the family since 1538, when it was acquired after the Dissolution of the Monasteries. The building is a slightly odd combination of three styles: it was begun in the 14th century as the gatehouse to the abbey (the outline of the main entrance, on the south side, can still be seen); modified in the 1730s by the 2nd Duke; and in the 1870s converted and extended as a 'Scottish baronial' mansion by the architect Andrew Blomfield for Henry, 1st Baron Montagu of Beaulieu. The house is very much a family home, and thus only some rooms, those in the old gatehouse, are open to the public. The central arch of the original great gatehouse, in today's lower drawing room, is now filled by a very imposing Victorian fireplace. Throughout the house the decorations are mainly Victorian, and there is some good furniture and interesting family portraits. A novel and unusual feature of the house is that each of the rooms is peopled with a tableau of wax figures in period costume representing members of the family from earlier generations.

☎ Beaulieu (0590) 612345
10 m E of Brockenhurst on B3055
SU 3902 (OS 196)

Open throughout year daily exc 25 Dec 1000-1800

🚻 📷 WC ♿ (limited access) 🚌 D ♣
🍴 ◆ ⛽ (seasonal) ♿ 🎯
Monorail, transporama, old bus etc

Bodiam Castle

Bodiam, near Robertsbridge, East Sussex

In 1385 Sir Edward Dalyngrigge received orders from Richard II to 'strengthen and crenellate his manor house', the purpose being to defend the country from the French raids on the south coast (the river Rother was then navigable as far as Bodiam). But the castle was no sooner built than it became redundant, as by 1388 the English had regained control of the Channel, and for centuries the building was left to its slow decay. But in 1916 Lord Curzon bought it, restored the walls with great sensitivity and landscaped the surrounding land. Bodiam, although not large, is a perfect example of a 14th-century castle, and its strong, high, symmetrical walls and towers reflected in its broad moat present a lovely sight. Its plan is simple, with the curtain walls enclosing a rectangular inner courtyard, round towers at each corner, a square tower in the middle of each flank, a gate tower in front and a smaller one at the back. The idea of building a castle as a courtyard defended by the gatehouse, in which the main defences were concentrated, was then quite new, replacing the earlier notion of the keep, or central fortified tower. The great gatehouse at Bodiam is formed of two huge rectangular towers joined by a deep arch and parapet. The parapet is pierced with machicolations: the walls have gun 'loops' for the new weapon, the cannon; and there were originally no fewer than three portcullises, one of which could be closed against the interior, thus keeping the main gate secure from treachery within as well as foes without.

☎ Staplecross (058 083) 436
18 m N of Hastings on A229 turn E at High Wigsell to Bodiam
TQ 7852 (OS 199)

Open Apr to end Oct daily 1000-1800 (sunset if earlier); Nov to end Mar M-S 1000-sunset

🚻 (exc Su) 📷 WC ♿ (limited access)
🚌 D ♣ 🍴 (limited opening) 🏕 ◆ ♿

Boughton Monchelsea Place

near Maidstone, Kent

A pleasant battlemented manor house on a fine site, with a southerly view of the edge of Romney Marshes. The battlements are in fact an early-19th-century fancy addition, but the house has a long history. The manor (Bolton) belonged to Earl Godwin in the 11th century, and after various Norman grants was held by the Montchensies (of which the name Monchelsea is a corruption) from near the end of the 12th century until 1287, and then by various Kentish families. In 1551 it was bought by Richard Rudstone, whose descendants held it continuously until 1888. Two wings of the originally four-sided house were taken down about 1740, and around 1790 the windows and the hall and red dining room were given the then fashionable 'Gothick' look. Other changes in the romantic taste, both to the house and the gardens and drive, followed in 1818-19, which gave them the appearance they have today. After 1888, the house lapsed into occasional lettings or was empty altogether for long periods, with the result that the kind of 'improvements' indulged in by many owners of other properties in the late 19th century passed Boughton Monchelsea by. In 1903 it came back into regular one-family ownership, but after the Second World War part was converted into flats. The fine staircase of 1685 replaced a more rustic Elizabethan one, the top flights of which can be visited in the upper floor. The Mortlake tapestries hanging in the house were originally hung in a room built for them at the top of the new staircase.

☎ Maidstone (0622) 43120
4½ m S of Maidstone on A229 turn E onto B2163 for 1 m then S
TQ 7750 (OS 188)

Open Good Fri to early Oct Su and Bank Hols, also W in Jul and Aug 1415-1800

🚻 📷 WC ♿ (limited access) 🚌 D ♣
🍴 🏕 ◆ ♿ 🎯 (compulsory)

Breamore House

Breamore, Hampshire

Built of rose-red brick with stone facings, this large Elizabethan manor house was completed in 1583. The Dodingtons, who owned it, were an unfortunate family. On April 11th, 1600 William, in a state of anxiety over a lawsuit, threw himself from the steeple of a London church in broad daylight. His son William, although knighted by James I, fared little better: in 1629 his wife was murdered by their son Henry in Breamore House. Henry was hanged in Winchester jail a year later, though legend claims he was 'hanged within sight of the house in which he was so untimely born'. The house now belongs to descendants of Sir Edward Hulse, who bought it in 1748. The visitor is admitted to the main rooms on the ground floor and to the east wing, where there are Tudor bedrooms and an Elizabethan four-poster bed. A fire in 1856 destroyed much of the original decoration, and much of it dates from the subsequent rebuilding, but the furniture survived. On the first-floor landing hangs a very rare English pile carpet, and at the top of the staircase there is an extraordinary set of fourteen paintings, each showing a different kind of mixed-race marriage possible in 17th-century Mexico. They were painted by an illegitimate son of Murillo, who had a studio in Mexico. The kitchen is interesting, as it was used until quite recently and is complete with all its fittings.

☎ Downton (0725) 22468
12 m S of Salisbury on A338 turn W to North Street and Upper Street
SU 1519 (OS 184)

Open Apr to end Sept T, W, Th, S, Su and Bank Hols 1400-1730
⊖ (1 m walk) P WC க் (limited access)
🖪 D ♣ ⮿ 🗛 ◆ ⚹ 𝄍

Broadlands

Romsey, Hampshire

The elegant Palladian mansion of Broadlands was the home of Lord Mountbatten, and is now that of his grandson Lord Romsey. A previous owner, and the man responsible for transforming it from an ordinary 16th-century house into the fine manor we see today, was the 2nd Viscount Palmerston, who in 1766 employed Capability Brown to landscape the grounds and also make improvements to the house. Brown gave the house a grand new portico and refaced it in the fashionable yellow-grey brick, and in the 1780s his protégé and son-in-law Henry Holland added the east front portico and domed hall. This domed entrance hall leads to the sculpture gallery, both rooms containing parts of Lord Palmerston's collection of antique and 18th-century sculpture. The main ground-floor rooms are decorated in the Adam style. Most of the decorative plasterwork was done by Adam's favourite plasterer, Joseph Rose, that in the saloon being particularly fine. There are four paintings by Van Dyck in the dining room; 18th- and 19th-century portraits in the drawing room, and a collection of Wedgwood. Broadlands has had a great many distinguished visitors during its lifetime, including royalty, and the house has many historical associations. One room is devoted to the 3rd Viscount Palmerston, Britain's popular mid-19th-century prime minister, and contains the desk at which he wrote standing up. There is a display of model warships commanded by Lord Mountbatten, and a permanent Mountbatten exhibition in the 17th-century stables.

☎ Romsey (0794) 516878
S of Romsey off A31
SU 3519 (OS 185)

Open Apr to end July daily exc M (but inc Bank Hol M); Aug, Sept daily 1000-1800
⊖ P WC க் 🖪 ♣ ⮿ 🗛 ◆ ⚹
● (no tripods)

Carisbrooke Castle

Carisbrooke, Isle of Wight

Carisbrooke Castle has been a Roman fort, a medieval castle and an Elizabethan fort, and remains are visible of all three phases of its life. Its general appearance, however, is medieval: the keep and curtain wall were completed by 1136, and the domestic buildings are mainly of the 13th century, with 16th-century additions. The dominating feature is the great gatehouse with drum towers, built partly in the 14th and partly in the 15th century. In the reign of Elizabeth I the castle was considerably altered to resist artillery, and an Italian engineer called Federigo Gianibelli was engaged to build the large earthworks surrounding the castle. This work was completed just bfore the end of the century, and no further alterations were made except minor internal modernisations. The castle, in spite of its long history and strategic position, has seen few major dramatic events, though Charles I was imprisoned here in 1647-48, having fled from the army at Hampton Court, and attempting to set sail for Jersey via Portsmouth found himself conveyed to Carisbrooke instead. The castle became the home of the governors of the island, the last of whom was Princess Beatrice, daughter of Queen Victoria, who succeeded her husband as governor. An upstairs room contains the Isle of Wight Museum, and near the domestic buildings there is a well-house with a wheel still operated by donkeys. The chapel next to the main gate was rebuilt on old foundations in 1906.

In SW outskirts of Newport off B3323
SZ 4887 (OS 196)

Open daily throughout year; Mar to Oct 0930-1830
Oct to Mar 0930-1600 (Su 1400-1600)
⊖ P WC க் (limited access) 🖪 D ♣
⮿ (limited opening) 🗛 ◆ ⚹

☎ Penshurst (0892) 870347
10 m W of Tonbridge on B2027 take road to How
Green and Hever
TQ 4945 (OS 188)

Open Mar to Oct W-S, also T mid June to mid Sept
and S Oct 1400-1730; Su and Bank Hols 1130-1730

♿ (1 m walk) 🅿 WC ♿ (by appt) 🚻 D ♦ 🍴 (for
parties by appt) 🎏 ♦ ⚘ ● (not in house)

Chiddingstone Castle

near Edenbridge, Kent

A solid Caroline house of 1679 replacing a medieval manor, dressed up in the 'castle style' early in the 19th century. Chiddingstone is most notable for the idiosyncratic collection formed by Denys Eyre Bower (1905-77). Bower was a Derbyshire bank employee who was deeply bitten by the collecting bug, and who on retiring in 1942 moved to London to conduct an antiques business. He bought Chiddingstone and opened it to the public in 1956 (long before country-house visiting had generally caught on) with the aim of displaying and sharing his treasures 'in the friendly atmosphere of a private home', as he put it. Three dominant passions informed Mr. Bower's collecting: enthusiasm for the Stuarts and the Jacobite tradition; the art of ancient Egypt; and the art of Japan. All the objects are still laid out in the way he wished. The great hall has a generally historical flavour, with paintings recalling the Streatfeild family which owned Chiddingstone for about three hundred years. Buddhist art from many parts of Asia is in the Buddha room on the ground floor. The 1st Stuart room and the 'white rose' room contain the main part of the collection to which the name refers, but documents elsewhere may be inspected by appointment. Japanese art is in the north Gothic hall and three other rooms designated Japanese. The collection in the Egyptian rooms extends from Pre-Dynastic to Ptolemaic times. Paintings and furniture which are apart from these three main themes are seen on the staircases and some other rooms.

In Chiswick, just off A4 at Hogarth Roundabout
TQ 2177 (OS 176)

Open mid Mar to mid Oct daily exc M 0930-1830;
mid Oct to mid Mar W, F, S, Su 0930-1600. Closed
24, 25, 26 Dec and 1 Jan

♿ WC ♿ (limited access) 🚻 D ♦ 🍴 🎏 ♦ ⚘

Chiswick House

Chiswick, London W4

This fine classical building with its clean, crisp lines was the creation of Lord Burlington, one of the most influential patrons of learning and the arts in the early 18th century, and a most accomplished architect. He was committed to a return to the ancient Roman architectural tradition as exemplified by the buildings of Andrea Palladio in Italy, and had little admiration for the current English styles, the ebullient Baroque of Wren and Vanbrugh. Chiswick House, which he designed in 1723, was based on Palladio's Villa Capra near Vicenza, and built in the grounds of his own house in Chiswick (now demolished). It was not intended as a house for living in, but as a 'temple of the arts', and the rooms were used to display paintings, sculpture and other works. The interiors were designed by William Kent, whose admiration for Palladian ideals matched Lord Burlington's own, though Kent proved to be rather less successful as an interior decorator than as an architect. Although the domed saloon and the gallery both have the grandeur and severity the building demands, in some of the other rooms the profusion of ornament seems to obscure the rigid lines and clean proportions. This is not helped by the fact that the original fabric which gave the red and blue velvet rooms their names has now been replaced with flock wallpapers. The gardens, which are as important as the house, were also designed by Kent, and show a break from the completely formal garden in which everything was laid out in straight lines.

In centre of Deal on coast
TR 3752 (OS 179)

Open daily throughout year; Mar to Oct 0930-1830,
Oct to Mar 0930-1600 (Su 1400-1600)

♿ WC ♿ (limited access) 🚻 D ♦ ⚘

Deal Castle

Deal, Kent

Henry VIII's coastal fort at Deal owes its existence to the anchorage between the North and South Forelands of Kent, called The Downs, where whole fleets could ride out a storm, protected on the east by the Goodwin Sands. Deal Castle is among the last functional forts with a solely military purpose to be built in England, and was erected in answer to a threatened invasion in 1539 by the Catholic powers, France and the Holy Roman Empire. Its field of fire and the positioning of the large wide-angle gunports gave it a formidable sweep over any ships lying in The Downs. Thus it could help to defend an English fleet or bombard an enemy landing-force. With two others of similar type, at Sandown and Walmer in Kent, it was built as part of a defensive programme round the east and south coasts. The danger of invasion passed by 1540, and Deal saw action only once, in the Civil War in 1648, although the present battlements were added as late as 1732. The contractor for the building materials brought the fine Caen stone from the demolished Carmelite friary at Sandgate near Folkestone. The beautiful symmetry of this six-lobed gun-house is not as easily appreciated from the ground as it is in aerial photographs: the central tower, low in profile, is flanked by six smaller bastions at the return of the larger outer bastions, all elements being circular or arcs of a circle. The cross-cover for both artillery and small-arms fire is extremely close. Inside the keep there is a cunningly arranged double staircase.

Detillens

Limpsfield, Surrey

The house, which takes its name from an 18th-century owner, James Detillen, was probably built about 1450. Its early Georgian front, added about 1725 in accordance with current taste, conceals a 15th-century timber-framed house. The earliest known occupier was Richard Kinge, a lawyer, who lived here around 1600, and at some stage the house was evidently owned by the local miller, since a quantity of flour has been found between floorboards and rafters. Originally the centre of the house would have been the large hall, open to the roof, but early in the 16th century this was divided both vertically and horizontally to form the front hall and dining room downstairs and bedrooms upstairs. The roof of the old hall had a central truss resting on a huge tie-beam, and this can still be seen in the main bedroom. The front hall now displays an excellent collection of military and sporting guns. The study, which was once the solar, or main sitting room of the house, has a fine Elizabethan overmantel bearing the figures of three caryatids, and the names of two previous occupants of the house are carved into the wood. The staircase is Jacobean, and the Tudor morning room has a fireback bearing the arms of Elizabeth I. This room also houses a selection from a unique collection of orders and decorations, both British and foreign, which has been amassed over the years. The present owners, who bought the house in 1968, have collected all the contents as well as restoring the house and the topiary garden, which is also open to the public.

☎ Oxted (088 33) 3342
9½ m SW of Sevenoaks on A25, turn NW on B269 for ¼ m
TQ 4052 (OS 187)

Open May and June S and Bank Hols; July to end Sept W, S and Bank Hols 1400-1700; parties at other times by appt

⊖ ⓕ WC 🚻 D ♠ ⚹ 🗡 (compulsory)

Donnington Castle

Donnington, near Newbury, Berkshire

The licence to crenellate at Donnington was granted in 1385, the same year as that for Bodiam, and the castle's plan was of the same courtyard type, rectangular on three sides and semi-octagonal on the fourth. There were round towers on the four corners, central towers on the north and south sides and a fortified gatehouse on the east. The historian William Camden described it in 1586 as 'a small but very neat castle . . . having a fair prospect and windows in all sides being very lightsome.' Unfortunately, sixty years later, in the Civil War, it was reduced almost to its foundations, and only the great gatehouse now stands. This had been built on to an existing building by Richard Abberbury in 1386 as part of the programme of fortification that turned it from a manor house into a castle, and the architect may have been William de Wynford, known as the builder of the nave of Winchester Cathedral. Castles built at this time were in the main more fortified residences than pure military strongholds, and Donnington was no exception. It was seized without much difficulty from its owner at the start of the Civil War, and was then held for the King by John Boys, who set about building sophisticated outer earth defences in line with the latest military thinking. He clearly knew what he was about, and although the stone walls were flattened the earthworks proved their worth, and Boys and his men held out for nearly two years until 1646, earning the admiration of their enemies who at one stage allowed them to clean out their poisoned well.

1 m N of Newbury on B4494 turn W at Donnington
SU 4669 (OS 174)

Open daily throughout year at all reasonable times

⊖ ⓕ ♿ (limited access) 🚻 D ♠ 🏕 ★ ⚹

Dover Castle

Dover, Kent

Dover's history is rich in episodes of invasion and defence, and the castle, high on the cliffs above the town, has been called the 'key of England'. It is one of the largest and best preserved castles in England, and has a long history: the main earthworks were almost certainly part of an Iron Age hill fort built before the Roman Conquest. The great keep was built in the 1180s by Henry II, and the surrounding curtain wall and outer fortifications were begun by him, continued by his son Richard, and completed by King John. In John's reign (1199-1216) the castle was besieged by Prince Louis of France, and the northern gateway successfully undermined, causing the collapse of the eastern tower. Clearly the castle was not impregnable after all, and in Henry III's reign a great deal of money was spent on rebuilding. The splendid 'constable's gate' was built about 1227, and by 1256 the castle had reached its maximum strength and size. During the Civil War of the 1640s it was taken by Cromwell's forces, and remained in their hands until the Restoration, thus escaping the usual slighting (destruction of defences), but it was drastically altered during the Napoleonic Wars, when the tops of many of the towers were cut off to provide artillery platforms. Most of the castle is open to the public, and within the walls is the Saxon church of St Mary in Castro with its free-standing bell-tower which was originally a Roman lighthouse. The roof of the keep, reached by the two great spiral staircases, provides an excellent view of the fortifications.

In E outskirts of Dover
TR 3241 (OS 179)

Open daily throughout year; Mar to Oct 0930-1830, Oct to Mar 0930-1600 (Su 1400-1600)

⊖ ⓕ WC ♿ (limited access) 🚻 D ♠
🍴 (limited opening) 🏕 ◆ ⚹

Eyhorne Manor

Hollingbourne, Kent

Timber-framed houses such as Eyhorne, in the style known as 'Wealden', were built during the 15th and 16th centuries for prosperous yeomen, but this house is unique in that it has been restored by the present owners and their two daughters unaided over a period of twenty years. The furniture, needlework and embroidery have also been made by the family, who live in the house; all the rooms can be seen by visitors, and excellent diagrams and information sheets are provided. The house was built in the early 15th century; in about 1610 the great hall, which was originally open to the roof, was divided both horizontally and vertically to make six rooms, and a huge chimney stack was put in to replace the old hall's central hearth. The 'red and white bedroom', which was part of the old hall, still has blackened timbers from the smoke of the central fire, but the ceiling, which was put in at the same time as the chimney stack, is clean. The L-shaped dining room extension was added later, probably in the 18th century. Large quantities of oyster shells were found under the floor, presumably flung out from the great hall, and among them was a French 15th-century water bottle. The original laundry, which became the kitchen after the division of the hall, illustrates how the smoking of carcases was done in this type of house, with the fire made on the stone floor and the smoke trapped in the 'smoking bay' above. The room also contains an interesting collection of early irons and other laundry equipment, and a selection of herbs once used to scent linen.

☎ Hollingbourne (062780) 514
6 m E of Maidstone on A20 turn NE to Eyhorne Street for ¼ m
TQ 8354 (OS 188)

Open May to July S, Su; Aug T, W, Th, S, Su and Bank Hol M 1400-1800

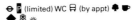

Firle Place

near Lewes, East Sussex

The house lies in its fine parkland beneath the slopes of Firle Beacon. It is the home of the Gage family, and was built for Sir John Gage in the mid-16th century, remaining more or less unchanged until the 18th century. Extensive additions and alterations were made between 1713 and 1754, and although a gable on the south side still survives from the Tudor building and the plan, with its two courtyards, is probably the original one, the old house was otherwise almost entirely swallowed by the new one. The approach is through one of the courtyards, and the Classical front door opens straight into what was once the Tudor great hall. Little that is Tudor now remains even here, however: in the 18th century the room was divided into two, an elegant entrance hall and a superb Palladian staircase hall. One of the finest rooms is the drawing room, also Palladian, with screens of Ionic columns and full-length family portraits set in white and gold panelling. There is also some fine furniture, but the best furniture and paintings are in the upper rooms. Here there is a magnificent collection of mainly French 18th-century furniture, including a roll-top desk in the manner of Riesener, a famous collection of Sèvres porcelain, and several important paintings including Fra Bartolomeo's *The Holy Family and the Infant St John*. The long gallery, built about 1713, and with a fine spectacular view of the South Downs, contains excellent portraits and paintings of the English school, as well as a major work by David Teniers, *The Wine Harvest*.

☎ Glynde (079159) 335
6 m E of Lewes on A27 turn S to West Firle
TQ 4707 (OS 198)

Open Jun to Sept W, Th, Su and Bank Hol M 1415-1700; reduced rates for parties by appt

Goodwood House

near Chichester, West Sussex

The 18th-century house was originally a hunting lodge, which was bought in 1677 by the 1st Duke of Richmond and greatly enlarged to the designs of James Wyatt by the 3rd Duke. The elegant stable block was designed by Sir William Chambers and built in the 1750s, and about twenty years later the Duke began to plan a lavish new house, to be a setting for entertainments, concerts and so on. Wyatt supplied designs, but of these only the tapestry room and kennels (now a golf club) were built, and it was not until about 1800 that the Duke and Wyatt thought again about rebuilding the house. This time the plan was for a great octagon, arranged round a central courtyard containing the older house; but this extremely bold architectural plan never came to fruition, and only three sides were completed. These are built of flint, and are three storeys high with round towers at the corners. The rooms themselves are rather austere, and all except the tapestry room were redecorated in 1970 to form a neutral background to the very fine collection of French furniture, Sèvres porcelain and clocks brought back by the 3rd Duke, who was an ambassador at the court of Louis XV. Wyatt's tapestry room is a fine example of his decorative style, and is hung with superb 18th-century Gobelin tapestries of Don Quixote. The unusual marble chimneypiece was made by John Bacon. The house contains many fine paintings, including several portraits by Van Dyck and Lely, two Canaletto views of London and equestrian paintings by Stubbs and Wootton.

☎ Chichester (0243) 774107
3 m NE of Chichester on A27, turn N to Waterbeach
SU 8808 (OS 197)

Open Easter Su and M and May to mid Oct Su and M, Aug Su-Th 1400-1700

Ham House

Ham, Richmond, Surrey

Originally an H-shaped Jacobean house built in 1610 for Sir Thomas Vavasour, Ham House was completely redecorated in the 1670s, and is now the finest existing example of the interior decoration of the Restoration period. The 1st Earl of Dysart made some alterations in the 1630s, redecorating the older rooms and inserting the staircase, but it was his daughter Elizabeth and her husband, the Duke of Lauderdale (1616-82), who made the house we see today. They enlarged it by adding a new range of rooms, thus filling in the south side of the H, but their work on the exterior was minimal compared to the time, money and skills lavished on the interior, particularly the new rooms. The ground floor contains the private apartments including bedrooms, an arrangement we find rather odd today; and most of these are panelled or hung with leather. The great staircase (c. 1637), with grained and once-gilded panels and an elaborately carved balustrade, leads to the first-floor state rooms which, although relatively small in scale, are furnished with incredible splendour, with painted ceilings, parquetry floors, marble chimneypieces and tapestry, damask or velvet wallhangings. Much of the furniture has no parallel in the country and was specially made for the house, and many of the pieces are mentioned in an inventory of 1679. In several of the rooms the paintwork and fabric have been renewed with the utmost care, and the bright colours (which some people dislike) are those which would have been used originally.

☎ (01) 940 1950
W of Richmond Park at Petersham off A307 on Ham Street
TQ 1773 (OS 176)

Open Apr to end Sept 1400-1800; Oct to end Mar 1200-1600 daily exc M but inc Bank Hol M. Closed Good Fri, 24,25,26 Dec and 1 Jan

⊖ 🅿 WC 🚻 🚻 D ♦ ♥ 🎪 ◆ ✗

Hever Castle

Hever, Edenbridge, Kent

This compact stone castle in its rectangular moat was the home of Anne Boleyn (c. 1507-36), who spent much of her childhood here and was courted by Henry VIII within these walls. The castle dates to about 1270, when the great gatehouse, outer walls and moat were built, and it was improved and enlarged in the 15th and 16th centuries by the Bullen (Boleyn) family. But it was not to remain a fine home for long – Anne's father died soon after her own execution, new owners came and went through the centuries, and by the end of the 19th century Hever had become a humble farmhouse. In 1903 the American millionaire William Waldorf Astor bought it and lavished a fortune on restoring it, building the imitation 'Tudor village' just outside and creating the spectacular gardens and lake. Mr. Astor was a man of taste, and the restoration, carried out by the architect F. L. Pearson, was so careful and meticulous that the outside of the building now looks almost exactly as it did in Anne Boleyn's day. The interior still has some original panelling, but it was almost entirely remade in a lavish pastiche of the Tudor style, with carved woodwork, panelling and plaster ceilings far more elaborate than anything Tudor craftsmen would have produced. The contents, collected from all over Europe, reflect the tastes of this wealthy connoisseur: there are superb tapestries and paintings, sculpture, an outstanding collection of armour and some fine paintings, among them portraits of Anne Boleyn, her sister Mary, Henry VIII and Anne's daughter Elizabeth I.

☎ Edenbridge (0732) 865224
11 m W of Tonbridge on B2027 at Bough Beech take road to How Green and Hever
TQ 4745 (OS 188)

Open Apr to early Oct daily exc Th in Apr; May and Sept 1200-1800; reduced rates for parties

⊖ 🅿 WC 🚻 (limited access) 🚻 (by appt)
D ♦ ♥ 🎪 ◆ 🕸 ✗ 🎣 ● (not in castle) 🐕

Ightham Mote

Ivy Hatch, Sevenoaks, Kent

This 14th-century moated manor house, set in a quiet hollow and partly surrounded by woods, powerfully evokes the past. Its name comes, not from the moat, but from the 'moot' or local council, which was held here in medieval times. The buildings are a delightful mixture, with timber-framed upper storeys, red tile roofs and creamy-yellow stone below. The stone parts of the house are the earliest; the timber-framing and brick is probably 16th century. The house is entered by a bridge across the moat into a very attractive cobbled courtyard, and opposite is the oldest part of the house, a stone hall of about 1340. This still has the original doorway, but the oriel window was put in about 1500. The interior has a timber roof with corbels carved in the form of crouching figures, and the small two-light window is 14th century. The other outstanding early interior is the Tudor chapel, which has a barrel roof with painted decoration in the Tudor colours and fine woodwork on sanctuary, pulpit, screen and pews. The other rooms show a mixture of decorative styles from the Jacobean, through the 17th century to the Victorian, representing the long ownership of the Selby family (1598-1889), and there is some well preserved 18th-century Chinese wallpaper in the drawing room. Since their time the house has changed hands frequently, and was in danger of demolition when the present owner, Mr Robinson, fell in love with it, bought it, repaired and restored it, and now lives in it whenever possible.

☎ Sevenoaks (0732) 62235
7 m N of Tonbridge on A227 turn W on road to Ivy Hatch and Ightham Mote
TQ 5853 (OS 188)

Open Mar and Oct F 1400-1700; Nov to Feb F 1400-1600; Apr to Sept F and Su 1400-1700

🅿 WC 🚻 (limited access) 🚻 D ♦ 🕸
🎣 (for parties by appt)

☎ Alton (420) 83262
1 m SW of Alton off Alton by-pass in Chawton village
SU 7037 (OS 185)

Open Apr to end Oct daily; Nov to end Mar W-Su 100-1630

⊖ P WC ♿ (limited access) ⊟
♣ ☂ ⅋ ◆ ☀

Jane Austen's House

Chawton, Alton, Hampshire

The 300-year-old house, now the Jane Austen Museum, was the author's last home, where she lived with her mother and her sister Cassandra from 1809 until her early death in 1817. Little is known of the house's early history, except that it was built as an inn, and remained so until occupied by Jane's third brother Edward, who offered it to his mother when the Rev. George Austen died. The outside of the house looks very much as it did in Jane's time, but the interior was considerably altered after Cassandra's death in 1845, when it was divided into three separate dwellings for farm workers. However, it has now been restored as far as possible, and visitors can see the drawing room, vestibule, dining room and upstairs parlour. Jane, who wrote *Mansfield Park, Emma* and *Persuasion* here, used the dining room for her writing, and a creaking door warned her when she was about to be interrupted. There is only one piece of her own furniture in the house, a small round table which she is believed to have used for writing, but there are a few personal items including a lock of hair, some jewellery and a patchwork quilt made by her and her mother. She was very fond of embroidering: her younger sister described her as 'a great adept at overcast and satin stitch, the peculiar delight of that day'. The particular feature of the museum is its large collection of documentary material, including many letters written by Jane, and there are also illustrations of her books and of her many other homes.

☎ (01) 937 9561 ext 2
In Kensington on Palace Avenue off Kensington High Street
TQ 2580 (OS 176)

Open throughout year M-S 0900-1700, Su 1300-1700. Closed 24,25,26 Dec and 1 Jan

⊖ P ⊟ D ♣ ☂ ⅋ ☀

Kensington Palace

Kensington, London W8

Kensington Palace, a rather unassuming and un-palatial building on the west side of Kensington Gardens, did not become a palace until William III decided that the air of Kensington might benefit his lungs, and moved here from Whitehall in 1689. It was then called Nottingham House, having been built for the Earl of Nottingham in 1661. Various additions were made to the old house by Sir Christopher Wren in the 1690s, and the process continued in 1720-21 during the reign of George I, when some of the interiors were lavishly redecorated by William Kent, who also laid out the gardens. The orangery and the King's gallery, built in 1695 and 1704 respectively, may have been designed by Nicholas Hawksmoor, and the orangery has a very fine interior with carved panels by Grinling Gibbons. The state apartments, which have been open to the public since 1899, have been returned to their 18th-century appearance, with suitable paintings and pieces of furniture from the Royal Collection, and the painted decorations by William Kent have been restored. It is rather a surprise amid the 18th-century elegance to come to a suite of rooms entirely in the Victorian style, but Queen Victoria was born in Kensington Palace and was very fond of it. The last room to be seen by visitors is the most splendid of the 1720 additions, the cupola room. This was intended to be the main state room, and is decorated with pilasters and gilded statues of Roman gods and emperors.

☎ (01) 348 1286
On Hampstead Heath off B519 Hampstead Lane
TQ 2787 (OS 176)

Open daily, Apr to end Sept 1000-1900; Mar and Oct 1000-1700; Nov to end Jan 1000-1600

⊖ P WC ♿ (limited access) ⊟ D ♣ ☂
⅋ ★ ◆ ☀ ● (by permission) ♟

Kenwood House

Hampstead Lane, London

This elegant mansion on the northern edge of Hampstead Heath was built around 1700, but owes its appearance to Robert Adam who remodelled it in 1764 for the Earl of Mansfield. He designed the grand entrance portico and pediment on the north side, and redesigned the entire south front overlooking the parkland, building a library on the east side to balance the existing orangery on the west. In 1793 the 2nd Earl caused the main Hampstead-to-Highgate road to be moved to its present position (it originally ran closer to the house) so that the house could stand surrounded by its own parkland, and the entrance (north) front is now approached by two winding drives through woods. The two wings, one each side of the entrance portico, were added by George Saunders in the 1790s. The house was bought by Lord Iveagh in 1925, and left to the nation, together with his superb collection of paintings, in 1927. The house is mainly used as a 'display case' for the Iveagh Bequest paintings, and although most of the main rooms were decorated by Adam and still contain some very fine pieces of furniture, the rooms are arranged like a museum, not an occupied country house. The one exception is the library, which is more or less as Adam left it and is one of his finest interiors. The Iveagh Bequest paintings, which include works by Rembrandt and Vermeer as well as outstanding portraits by Gainsborough and Reynolds, are on permanent display in the downstairs rooms, but the upstairs rooms are sometimes used for temporary exhibitions.

Kew Palace

Kew Gardens, near Richmond, Surrey

The building now known as Kew Palace, formerly known as the Dutch House, was built in 1631 by a leading London merchant called Samuel Fortrey. He had Dutch connections, and the tall red-brick house with its curly gables and brick ornament is in the Netherlandish style then popular in England; hence its name. The house is only called 'palace' because by the end of the 18th century it had become part of the royal estates at Kew and Richmond, and a new palace, of which nothing now remains, was built adjoining it. The principal royal residence was then a house called the White Lodge, which was pulled down in 1802 to make room for the new palace (which was never completed). King George III and Queen Charlotte stayed temporarily at the Dutch House, and Queen Charlotte remained there until her death in 1818. All the ground- and first-floor rooms are open to the public, and have been restored to more or less their Georgian appearance, though there is still some of the original 17th-century plasterwork in the Queen's boudoir. One of the rooms has an attractive collection of royal ephemera and playthings. The small garden between the house and the river was first planted in 1696 by Sir Henry and Lady Capel, then owners of the house, and has been restored to give the appearance of a 17th-century garden. The botanical gardens themselves, given to the nation in 1841, were landscaped by Capability Brown for George III and his mother Princess Augusta.

☎ (01) 940 1171

In Kew Gardens, W off Kew Road to Kew Green

TQ 1877 (OS 176)

Open Apr to Sept daily 1100-1730

♿ 🅿 🚻 D (guide dogs only) ♣ 🍵
⛱ ◆ ✳

Knole

Sevenoaks, Kent

Set in a magnificent park studded with ancient trees, Knole is one of England's grandest houses. The vast house, more like a village, is popularly believed to echo the days of the year by having 365 rooms, set around seven separate courtyards. It has a complex building history, but owes its medieval appearance to Thomas Bouchier, Archbishop of Canterbury, who bought it in 1466 and transformed it into an archbishop's palace. It passed to the Crown in the 1530s when Henry VIII's covetous eye fell upon it, and was later given by Elizabeth I to Thomas Sackville, 1st Earl of Dorset, whose descendants still live in the private quarters. Henry had enlarged it by adding an outer courtyard (today's green court) and the long east front with its gatehouse, and Thomas made further alterations, notably creating a series of state rooms above the old palace. Little was done thereafter, as the Sackvilles deliberately cultivated the antique, and the huge grey stone house looks very much as it did in 1618. Knole is famous for the collection of furniture made by Thomas Sackville, and his splendid state rooms, with their lovely plaster-work, panelling and fireplaces, contain one of the finest collections of late 17th-century furniture anywhere in the country, including a set of silver furniture, a state bed with gold tissue hangings and the original 'Knole' sofa, dating from the time of James I. Many of the chairs still have their original upholstery, and the collection is in excellent condition.

☎ Sevenoaks (0732) 450608

S of centre of Sevenoaks on A225 turn E

TQ 5454 (OS 188)

Open Apr to end Oct W-S and Bank Hols 1100-1700, Su 1400-1700; reduced rates for parties

♿ 🅿 WC 🚻 ♣ ⛱ ◆ ✳ ✗
● (not in house)

Lancaster House

Near St James's, London SW1

Lancaster House is an imposing Georgian building with a characteristic buff-coloured exterior of Bath stone. It stands in the heart of royal London, across the road from St James's Palace and just off the Mall leading to Buckingham Palace. It was first designed for King George IV's brother Frederick, Duke of York, by Sir Robert Smirke; but Smirke was superseded by Benjamin Wyatt, who produced new designs and began building 'York House' in 1825. The Duke died in 1827, and the still unfinished building was bought by one of his creditors, the Marquess of Stafford (later Duke of Sutherland). As Stafford House it was long a notable centre of politics, fashion and art, so lavishly furnished that when Queen Victoria arrived she would tell the Duchess: 'I have come from my house to your palace'. In 1912 Viscount Leverhulme bought the house and renamed it Lancaster House in honour of his native country – with the result that, in the course of its history, it has represented both sides in the Wars of the Roses! Leverhulme presented it to the nation, and it is now used as a conference centre. The interiors, mainly by Wyatt and Sir Charles Barry, are still sumptuous, using deeprich colours in an overall setting of white and gold. Outstanding features include the central staircase hall, rising the full height of the building to a coved ceiling supported by caryatids and carrying a huge lantern; Wyatt's grand staircase; and the great gallery on the first floor, over 120 foot long and filling one side of the house.

In Stable Yard, St James's, SW1

TQ 2979 (OS 176)

Open Easter to mid Dec S, Su and Bank Hols 1400-1800; closed for Government functions

♿ WC 🚻 (by appt)

☎ Maidstone (0622) 65400

8 m E of Maidstone on A20 turn S

TQ 8353 (OS 188)

Open Apr to end Oct daily 1100-1700; Nov to end Mar S and Su 1200-1600; reduced rates for parties

⚭ (1 m walk) ⓟ WC ♿ (limited access)
🍴 ♣ ⬤ ⛶ ◆ ⚜ ※ ⬤ (not in castle)

Leeds Castle

Maidstone, Kent

The castle, situated in the middle of its large, lake-like moat, is one of England's oldest and most romantic buildings. But although it looks and feels medieval, and some parts are genuinely so, much rebuilding was done from 1822 by Fiennes Wykeham-Martin, who modernised many of the medieval rooms, cut down the encircling walls to provide a view of the lake, and restored the exterior, which had been given a Jacobean look by a previous owner. This careful restoration led Lord Conway to describe Leeds as 'the loveliest castle . . . in the whole world'. The walls of the gloriette where the royal apartments were, are medieval, but the interior was completely restored and redecorated by Lady Baillie, who bought the castle in 1926 and devoted much of her life to its restoration and care. A magnificent two-tier bridge connects the main building to the gloriette, and the visitor passes through rooms with beamed ceilings, furnished with carved wooden pieces and hung with tapestries, to a Gothic staircase which leads to the seminar room. When Lady Baillie left the castle to the nation she specified that it should be used for international medical meetings as well as for the public benefit, and this is one of the rooms used for meetings. It also contains a fine collection of Impressionist and later paintings. In the main house there are two fine 18th-century rooms, one of which has 17th-century panelling brought from another house. The Norman gate tower contains an unusual collection of medieval dog collars.

☎ Guildford (0483) 571881

4 m S of Guildford on A3100, turn W onto B3000 for ¾ m, then N to Littleton

SU 9747 (OS 186)

Open June to end Sept W-S 1400-1700

⚭ (1½ m walk) ⓟ WC ♿ 🍴
D (guide dogs only) ♣ ⬤ ⛶ ◆ ※
🏃 (compulsory) ⬤ (not in house)

Loseley House

Loseley Park, Guildford, Surrey

A gabled Elizabethan house, built of greenish-grey ragstone from the ruins of nearby Waverley Abbey, with window surrounds of hard white chalk, Loseley House was built between 1562 and 1568 for Sir William More, a kinsman of Sir Thomas More, and a man respected by leading statesmen and trusted by Elizabeth I, who stayed here three times. Sir William's descendants, who married into the Molyneux family, still live here, and now run a well-known dairy farm on the estate. There have been few alterations to the exterior of the house, though the main doorway appears to be a Queen Anne addition. The great hall, a high room with a fine oriel window, heraldic glass and a beamed ceiling, has some good portraits including a large family group painted by Van Somer in 1739. There is also a remarkable series of carved, inlaid and painted panels in the Italian style, which are believed to have come from Henry VIII's palace at Nonsuch (destroyed after the Restoration). The library has some good 16th-century panelling, but most is 19th century, while the drawing room has a plaster ceiling and a striking chimneypiece carved out of chalk. The staircase is 17th century, and the bedrooms upstairs have 16th-century ceilings. The house contains a good collection of furniture as well as some tapestry and needlework, one of the most unusual pieces being a 16th-century German marquetry cabinet with a design showing a fallen city.

☎ Farningham (0322) 862114

8 m N of Sevenoaks on A225 turn W

TQ 5364 (OS 188)

Open Apr to early Oct S, Su and Bank Hols 1400-1800

⚭ (1 m walk) ⓟ WC ♿ (limited access)
🍴 ♣ ⬤ ⛶ ⚜ ※ ⬤ (not in house)

Lullingstone Castle

Eynsford, Kent

The original house was built in the reign of Henry VII by Sir John Peche. The great brick gatehouse of 1497 still survives, and to the west of it is a level area, the old jousting ground, a reminder of Sir John's prowess in the tournament. The house itself has an early 18th-century red-brick façade, but this is only skin-deep; the internal arrangement of the old Tudor house remains almost unchanged, though several of the rooms were panelled. These alterations were carried out for the new owner, Percival Hart, a Jacobite, and friend of Queen Anne who visited the house frequently. The front door opens straight into the great hall, where there is fine 18th-century panelling and a series of full-length family portraits as well as an interesting painting showing the house before the alterations. The dining room also has 18th-century panelling, and the staircase was built for Queen Anne herself, with specially shallow treads. This leads to the Tudor great chamber, known as the state drawing room, which has a lovely barrel-vaulted Tudor ceiling with plaster decoration and exceptional oak panelling. The room also contains some good paintings, and several interesting objects, among them a collection of fans. The state bedroom has an intricately carved four-poster bed, and the furniture throughout the house is varied and interesting. A small room leading off the state bedroom displays a set of fine needlework hangings, the work of the Hon. Mary Bell, maid of honour to Queen Alexandra.

Lympne Castle

near Hythe, Kent

Lympne Castle, which has a spectacular setting on the edge of an escarpment bordering the Romney Marshes, was the home of the archdeacons of Canterbury, one of whom was Thomas à Becket before he became Archbishop. The castle we see today was the main residential block of a complex of buildings, and it has been adapted and altered over the centuries to meet the needs of successive owners. The oldest part is the northern part of the square tower next to the church, which dates from the 13th century. The main part of the building, the hall block, is 14th century, and about 1420 the castle was modernised, and the round part of the great tower, with its newel stairway, was built on. By the end of the 19th century the great hall had been turned into a house by the construction of a first floor, but the other parts were used only for storage, and by the beginning of this century the whole place had become dilapidated. It was saved from ruin by the Scottish architect Robert Lorimer, who in 1906 built on a new wing, restored the old buildings and turned the whole complex into a large house. Only the old parts are open to the public, and the rooms are purposely kept very bare to preserve their medieval atmosphere. The great hall, restored by Lorimer, who removed the first floor, made good the timbers above and fitted new tracery in the windows, is huge and very impressive. There is a toy museum in the west tower, and a fine view of the marshes can be gained from the Second World War observation post on the east tower.

☎ Hythe (0303) 67571
8 m W of Folkestone on A20 turn S onto B2068
TR 1134 (OS 179)

Open Jun to Sept and Bank Hol weekends daily;
Apr, May infrequently 1030-1800
⊖ (1½ m walk) 🅿 WC 🚻 (limited access)
🚻 D ♿ 🍴 (limited opening) 🚻 ◆ ⚘

Marble Hill House

Richmond Road, Twickenham, Middlesex

Marble Hill, a small and beautifully proportioned Palladian villa, was built for Henrietta Howard, Countess of Suffolk – mistress of George II – as a country home. The house was completed in 1729, and as the Palladian style grew more popular it became one of the 'standard models' for the 18th-century villa. The architects appear to have been a partnership consisting of Colen Campbell (who produced the initial designs), Roger Morris and Lord Herbert, connoisseur, amateur architect and contemporary of that great arbiter of taste, Lord Burlington. The house still looks very much as it did when first built, despite many years of neglect in the late 19th century; the interiors of the charming small rooms have been restored and refurnished in the 18th-century style. The hall contains four Ionic columns dividing the room. The most spectacular room is the great room which occupies the centre of the river front, and has lovely carved and gilded ornament and a coved ceiling. It was probably modelled on the cube room at Wilton, built by Inigo Jones. The house is administered by the Greater London Council and some of the 18th-century furniture and paintings have been acquired recently, but in spite of their efforts the house has a rather 'un-lived-in' feeling. The large riverside park which once belonged to the house, and which was laid out by Charles Bridgeman with the help of Alexander Pope, is now a public park.

☎ (01) 892 5115
1 m E of Twickenham, S of A305 Richmond Road
TQ 1773 (OS 176)

Open daily exc F; Feb to end Oct 1000-1700; Nov to
end Jan 1000-1600. Closed 24, 25 Dec
⊖ 🅿 WC 🚻 (limited access) 🚻 (by appt) D
♿ 🍴 (by appt) 🚻 ★ ◆ ⚘ ⚘

Michelham Priory

Upper Dicker, Hailsham, East Sussex

As its name implies, this Tudor house was built on to an old priory. This had been founded in 1229; the buildings were gradually put up over the next hundred years, and the great moat, which encircles today's house, was dug slightly before 1400. The gatehouse was built at the same time, but the bridge leading to it is 16th century. After the Dissolution in 1536 the buildings were destroyed, but later in the century they were repaired and incorporated into a Tudor house which became the centre of a working farm, owned by the Pelham family. The priory buildings were arranged round a cloister, and the house we see today, which was converted into a 'gentleman's residence' early in this century, consists of the south-west corner of the cloister with the Tudor wing at the side. Michelham Priory is now a property of the Sussex Archaeological Society, who have made an effort to illustrate the way of life of the Augustinian monks. Near the entrance is a model of the priory as it probably appeared on completion, and all the priory rooms contain life-size models of monks. The other rooms, arranged to look as though they are still in use, contain 17th-century furniture, tapestries and so on. The 16th-century kitchen still has its great open hearth and some of the original oak beams, while the prior's guest room has a fireplace dating from about 1320. The oak panelling was installed in the 19th century. Two of the rooms are used as a museum, one concerned with local archaeology and the other containing a collection of musical instruments.

☎ Hailsham (0323) 844224
9 m N of Eastbourne on A22 turn W to Upper Dicker
for 2½ m
TQ 5609 (OS 199)

Open Good Fri to late Oct daily 1100-1730
🅿 WC 🚻 🚻 ♿ 🍴 🚻 ◆ ⚘
⚘ ⚔ ● (not in special exhibition)
Forge and working water mill; August Arts Festival

SE of East Cowes, E of A3021

SZ 5194 (OS 196)

Open early Apr to mid Oct M-S 1000-1700,
Su 1400-1700

⊖ 🅿 WC 🅰 (limited access)
🚻 D ♣ 🍴 🛋 ◆ ☀

Osborne House

East Cowes, Isle of Wight

Queen Victoria, who had always loved the Isle of Wight, bought the estate in 1845, five years after her marriage. The house, which replaced a smaller one, was designed by Prince Albert himself with the advice of the architect Thomas Cubitt, and it is based on an Italian villa, with tall towers, a first-floor balcony and terrace gardens adorned with Renaissance-style statuary. When Prince Albert died in 1861 the Queen kept everything just as it had been in his lifetime, and her wishes are still respected. The public entrance to the house is through the extraordinary Durbar room, added in 1890 in honour of the Queen's Indian possessions and decorated with intricate Indian-style plasterwork. The three main ground-floor rooms are reached by the grand corridor, whose walls are lined with statues and pictures as well as cabinets containing gifts presented to the royal family. The billiard room has a table designed by Prince Albert, and in the drawing room is an unusual grand piano with ormolu mounts and porcelain plaques and allegorical statues of the royal children. The main staircase leads to the Queen's private suite. These rooms, in contrast to the grand ground-floor rooms, are full of personal possessions, including paintings by both the Queen and Prince Albert, and the Queen's sitting room, crowded with bric-à-brac, is typical of thousands of similar late-Victorian rooms. About half a mile from the house is the Swiss Cottage, a wooden chalet brought in sections from Switzerland and used by the royal children.

☎ (01) 560 3918
In Osterley S of M4 on Great West Road (A4), turn N
onto Syon Lane and Osterley Lane
TQ 1478 (OS 176)

Open daily exc M (but inc Bank Hol M); Apr to Sept
1400-1800; Oct to Mar 1200-1600.

⊖ 🅿 WC 🅰 🚻 D ♣ 🍴 (limited
opening) 🛋 ★ ◆ ☀ ⚒

Osterley Park House

Osterley, Isleworth, Middlesex

Like Robert Adam's other great masterpieces in the London area, Kenwood and Syon, Osterley is a remodelling of an existing house, in this case an Elizabethan one built in the 1570s for Sir Thomas Gresham. In the mid-18th-century Sir Francis Child, then the owner, had already begun rebuilding (his architect was probably Sir William Chambers), and the entire house was refaced, a long gallery built right across the west front, and various other alterations made. Adam took over in 1761, and his first work was the great pedimented portico which filled the open side of the original courtyard. He then began to redecorate and refurnish seven of the nine ground-floor rooms, and these state rooms, completed in 1780, remain almost exactly as he left them. The architecture of the interiors is dignified and perfect, but the rooms were designed for show rather than comfort, and some of them seem rather austere. As far as possible all the furniture, made to Adam's own designs, has been placed as he intended, standing against the walls as was the fashion in the 18th century, and complemented by paintings of the period. At the end of the tour, in the last room and the passage leading from it, there is a display of Adam's drawings for the furniture and decorations. The large park, with its lakes and ancient yew trees, contains a semi-circular garden house by Adam and a Greek temple which was probably designed by Chambers. The rustic stable block, now a tearoom, is believed to be the remains of the original Tudor house.

☎ Storrington (090 66) 2866

3 m S of Pulborough on A283

TQ 0614 (OS 197)

Open Easter Su to end Sept Su and Bank Hol M
1400-1800; other times by appt

🅿 WC 🅰 (by appt) 🚻 D ♣ 🍴 🛋 ☀ 𝆑 (by
appt M pm, W and Th am) ● (not in house)

Parham Park

Pulborough, West Sussex

This simple grey stone Elizabethan house began to be built in 1577 by Sir Thomas Palmer. Palmer, who went to sea with Drake, evidently preferred sea to land, and in 1610 Parham was sold to the Bysshopp family, branches of which retained it for eleven generations. In 1922 it was bought by the Hon. Clive Pearson, whose daughter and son-in-law now own it. All Parham's owners, including the present ones, have cherished the house, and alterations and restorations have always been carried out with tact and taste. The buildings to the north of the house are 18th century; the range nearest to it was much enlarged in the 1770s, and about 1800 the main entrance was moved from the south porch to the north side and an entrance hall built. These alterations had almost no effect on the interiors, which are nearly all early, with carved panelling and Tudor and Jacobean furniture. The splendid great hall, lit by tall windows, has its original stone fireplace and Renaissance carved screen, and the decorated ceiling, though a 19th-century copy of the original, gives a fine 16th-century effect. The very long gallery (160 feet in length) has its original floor and carved oak wainscot, and the delightful ceiling is a modern interpretation of an Elizabethan theme. The great parlour and great chamber above it are examples of superb restoration work: Edmund Burton did the plasterwork in 1935, using the old method of modelling with the fingers. Parham's paintings include a series of historical portraits and a famous painting of Queen Elizabeth, possibly by Zucchero.

Pattyndenne

Goudhurst, Kent

A delightful old timber-framed house in the local style known as 'Wealden', in which parts of the upper storey and sides project as jetties, but the central part, having no jetties, gives the appearance of being recessed. This central part contained the hall, which was originally open to the roof. At Pattyndenne the whole upper storey rests on four moulded and chamfered corner posts, and the jetties project on all four sides. The plan of the house remains more or less unchanged: the central hall had a parlour on one side and a buttery on the other, with chambers above, and attics above these. When the house was built the only access from one end to the other was through the open hall. The house takes its Saxon name, which means 'a forest clearing by the stream', from the Pattyndenn family, who built it about 1480 as a house suitable not only for living in, but also for holding manor-court proceedings. In the 16th century it was sold to Sir Maurice Berkeley, son of the Lord Berkeley who was Standard Bearer to Henry VIII, Mary Tudor and Queen Elizabeth I. The house has four panes of glass showing the rose of Henry VIII and the pomegranite of Catherine of Aragon. The great fireplace in the hall was installed about 1580. The tiny kitchen wing was built about 1600, and there were no further alterations until 1890, when an extension was built at the back to take a new staircase. The present owners of the house, who bought it in 1972, have carried out considerable restoration work.

☎ Goudhurst (0580) 211361
13½ m E of Royal Tunbridge Wells on A262 turn S at Goudhurst onto B2079 for 1 m
TR 7236 (OS 188)

Open Aug to mid Sept Su and Bank Hol M 1415-1730; parties at other times by appt
🅿 WC 🚻 (by appt) ✸

Petworth House

Petworth, West Sussex

Petworth is famous for its park, the masterpiece of Capability Brown, and its superb collection of paintings, among which are nineteen by J. W. M. Turner, who spent much time here in the 1830s. But although it may be primarily an art gallery, it is also a very impressive country house. The house originally belonged to the Percy family, but almost nothing can now be seen of the medieval building except a 13th-century chapel. In 1682 Charles Seymour, 6th Duke of Somerset, married the Percy heiress, and the present house was built by him between 1686 and 1696. The long main front is very French in appearance, but the architect is not recorded. The visitor enters through the east front, which was partly rebuilt by Anthony Salvin in 1870. The ground-floor rooms are all very opulent, though the only room to survive from the 6th Duke's time is the marble hall. The richly carved decoration is full of French and Dutch features, and it is thought that a Huguenot craftsman and designer, Daniel Marot, may have made the designs. The square dining room, hung with Van Dycks, is among the rooms created by Lord Egremont early in the 19th century. The beauty room, so called because it is devoted to the ladies of Queen Anne's court, has portraits by Kneller and Dahl, while the staircase hall is decorated with murals by Laguerre. The carved room contains a riot of woodcarving by Grinling Gibbons. There is a collection of ancient sculpture made by Turner's patron Lord Egremont, together with his collection of contemporary paintings.

☎ Petworth (0798) 42207
8 m E of Midhurst on A272
SU 9721 (OS 197)

Open Apr to end Oct daily exc M and F but inc Bank Hol M 1400-1800
🅿 WC ♿ 🚻 (by appt) D ♣ 🍴 🎪 ◆ ✸

Polesden Lacey

near Dorking, Surrey

This delightful house, set in the pleasant countryside of the North Downs, was the home of the well-known hostess Mrs Greville, and has seen many distinguished visitors including Edward VII and the Duke and Duchess of York (later George VI and Queen Elizabeth). Originally a Georgian villa, the present house was begun in 1824 to designs of Thomas Cubitt on the site of an earlier house which belonged to the playwright Richard Brinsley Sheridan. Although it was greatly enlarged early in this century it retains something of its Regency flavour, and the south front with its colonnaded portico has been little altered except for an extension to the east. The enlargements were made in 1906 by Ambrose Poynter for the Hon. Ronald Greville and his wife, and the east front is nearly all his work. Mrs Greville was an art collector as well as hostess, and the opulent rooms contain many treasures. The dining room, with rich brocade hangings, contains her collection of English portraits, but the major part of the art collection, which includes important Flemish and early Italian works and Dutch landscapes, hangs in the corridor around the central courtyard. This leads to the airy library, which has been little changed since Mrs Greville's day, and then to the sumptuous drawing room, where the walls are covered in carved and gilt panelling. This room contains some particularly fine furniture and oriental porcelain. The attractive gardens were planted by Mrs Greville, though the long terrace was laid out by Sheridan in the late 18th century.

☎ Bookham (0372) 58203/52048
2 m N of Dorking on A24, turn W to Westhumble
TQ 1352 (OS 187)

Open Mar and Nov S and Su 1400-1700; Apr to end Oct daily exc M and F (open Bank Hol M, closed following T) 1100-1800
🅿 WC ♿ 🚻 D ♣ 🍴 🎪 ◆ ✸

4 m E of Fareham on A27 turn S to Portchester
SU 6204 (OS 196)

Open daily throughout year; Mar to Oct 0930-1830
Oct to Mar 0930-1600 (Su 1400-1600)

♿ 🅿 🖾 (limited access) 🚻 D ♦ ☂
♨ (available in foreign languages)

Portchester Castle

Portchester, Hampshire

Portchester is an extremely unusual castle for two reasons. It stands not on a hill but on a flat piece of land by Portsmouth harbour; and it is a Norman castle built inside a Roman fort, the walls of which still stand to their full height. The Roman fort was square in plan, with entrances on the east and west sides, which were destroyed to make the Norman entrances, rectangular towers with passageways. Most of the walls, however, were left intact, and the Norman castle was built in the north-west corner (about 1120), with a new curtain wall on the south and east meeting the Roman walls to form an enclosure. In 1133 an Augustinian priory was built in the south-east corner, and its chapel still remains. The castle seems to have been appropriated by Henry II at about this time, and it remained in royal hands thereafter. The keep was extended upwards in about 1170, possibly by Henry, making it four storeys high with the basement, and the battlements were added by Richard II (1377-99). Richard was also responsible for the two ranges between the keep and the gatehouse, known as Richard's Palace. These may have replaced earlier Norman buildings, and the main rooms were on the first floor, with the great chamber next to the keep and the great hall against the gatehouse wall. The castle was frequently garrisoned in the 14th century as a defence against French invasions, and in the 18th century it was used as a prison camp for French prisoners of war.

In centre of Rochester facing Bridge Reach
TQ 7468 (OS 178)

Open daily throughout year; Mar to Oct 0930-1830,
Oct to Mar 0930-1600 (Su 1400-1600)

♿ WC 🚻 D ♦ ☂ ♨

Rochester Castle

Rochester, Kent

Although little remains standing except the great square keep, the ruins of Rochester, still one of the most impressive castles in England, dominate the town. The keep itself stands to its full height. In medieval times, barons and bishops both had need of castles, and this one was built by the Bishop of Rochester in about 1090. His building was probably not much more than a stone curtain wall and enclosure; the keep was built in the following century (1127) by the Archbishop of Canterbury, William de Corbeil, who was given the castle by Henry I. It is one of the largest in the country, and was one of the most luxurious. It is four storeys high, with a cross-wall, but the second and third storeys were merged to make the magnificent great hall, with the cross-wall becoming a pierced and columned arcade which divides the room into two. It is lit by a double row of large windows and, although all the floors have now gone, some fine decorative work can still be seen. Staircases in the thickness of the walls give access to the battlements and a close-up view of the four corner turrets, three square and one circular. In 1215 the castle was besieged by King John, whose men undermined the south tower and brought it down, so it had to be rebuilt under Henry III, by which time the circular style had replaced the square. The castle was damaged and repaired again in 1264, restored by Edward III and improved by Richard II, but its great days were over and it was thereafter allowed to decay.

☎ Dane Hill (0825) 790655
11 m N of Lewes on A275 just before Sheffield Green
TQ 4124 (OS 198)

Open Apr to mid Nov T-S 100-1800; Su and Bank
Hol M 1400-1800 (sunset if earlier); closed Good Fri

🅿 WC 🖾 🚻 D ♦ ☛ (limited
opening) ☂ ♦ ♨

Sheffield Park

Uckfield, East Sussex

The house, an early example of the 18th-century 'Gothick' style, is largely the work of the architect James Wyatt. The original house acquired by Lord Sheffield was 16th century, and in 1775 Wyatt was engaged to rebuild it. By 1778 his work was complete, and the east front, facing the lakes, survives virtually unchanged. The west front was given battlements and turrets towards the end of the century, and further additions, notably the delightful orangery, were made by a subsequent owner, Arthur Gilstrap Soames, in 1912. Wyatt's marvellous, huge Gothick window on the east front, the focal point of the house, was put there for artistic effect alone, as on the inside it is blocked by lath and plaster. Unfortunately the house and garden now have different owners – the garden belongs to the National Trust – so in order to walk round the outside of the house as well as the inside one has to pay twice. The present owners of the house, Mr and Mrs Radford, bought it in 1972 totally unfurnished and partially undecorated, and they have been carefully restoring it ever since. Two of its best features are the lovely vaulted staircase hall designed by Wyatt and the first-floor bedroom known as the 'tyger room', which has a ceiling painting showing tigers, lions and leopards done by Charles Catton about 1778. The large triple bay window gives a superb view of lawn and lakes, and there is a fine fireplace. The spacious library where Edward Gibbon is said to have written some of *The Decline and Fall of the Roman Empire* has its original bookcases and marble fireplace.

Southside House

Wimbledon Common, London SW19

This is a pleasant, sturdy house with a long Classical façade crowned by two pediments, square dormer windows and a clock tower. It was built for Robert Pennington, who had shared Charles II's exile in Holland and evidently acquired a taste for Dutch architecture. When the plague carried off his small son he left London with his wife and daughter, and retired to Holme Farm at Wimbledon, which was then still a village several miles from the capital. In 1687 he called in Dutch architects to build Southside House, incorporating the farm building in the structure; this accounts for the asymmetrical placing of the front door and clock tower. Two very large niches, one on each side of the front door, were filled with statues of Plenty and Spring, which are still in place; the faces are said to be likenesses of Pennington's wife and daughter. Southside House remained a family home over the centuries with only one set of major building alterations (in 1776); and Pennington's descendants lived there until after the Second World War. The interiors include a good deal of 17th-century furniture and a range of memorabilia connected with the Penningtons. The 'musik room' was prepared for the entertainment of Frederick, Prince of Wales, who stayed at Southside House in 1750, and later visitors included one of history's most famous *ménages à trois*, Sir William and Lady Hamilton and Lord Nelson. Southside House was damaged during the Second World War, after which it was restored to its late 17th-century condition.

☎ (01) 946 7643
On S side of Wimbledon Common near Crooked Billet inn
TQ 2370 (OS 176)

Open Oct to end Mar (exc Christmas and Easter) T, Th, F 1400-1700; by written appt at other times
⊖ WC ⊟ ♣ ⚹ 𝓴 (compulsory)

Squerryes Court

Westerham, Kent

A modest, symmetrical red-brick house of about 1680, looking out across a lake and small landscaped park. The outside, with its regular windows and matching pediments, is pleasant but plain, and the inside is equally so, reflecting the personalities of the squires who lived here for nearly 250 years. John Warde, son of a Lord Mayor of London, bought the house in 1731, and it now contains the Wardes' accumulation of family contents. There is a very good collection of Dutch and Flemish paintings made by John Warde II, which are hung in the three main downstairs rooms and the staircase hall, and many relics of James Wolfe (1727-59), captor of Quebec, came into the house through John's brother George, who was a friend of his. These are in one of the upstairs rooms. A room downstairs houses the regimental museum of the Kent and County of London Yeomanry, containing banners, military uniforms and so on. There is some good 18th-century furniture, some of which was made for John Warde's father, the Lord Mayor, before the family built Squerryes. The tapestry room contains some interesting decorative tapestries of about 1720 showing vases of flowers on marble tables, which were woven at the Soho factory by the well-known Joshua Morris. In the same room there is an original fireplace, one of several in the house.

☎ Westerham (0959) 62345/63118
7 m SW of Sevenoaks on A25 turn S in W outskirts of Westerham
TQ 4453 (OS 187)

Open Mar Su; Apr to Sept W, S, Su and Bank Hol M 1400-1800; reduced rates for parties by appt
⊖ 🅿 WC ⊟ (by appt only) ♣ ♟ (limited opening by appt for parties) 🛏 ⚹

Stratfield Saye House

Stratfield Saye, near Reading, Hampshire

Stratfield Saye, like Blenheim, was acquired with public money for a national hero, in this case the Duke of Wellington, but there the resemblance ends; Stratfield Saye, originally built between 1630 and 1640 by Sir William Pitt, is as modest as Blenheim is grand. It was originally of red brick, a long, low building with curved gables and small pediments. In the 18th century Lord Rivers stuccoed the brick, washing it over in a warm apricot colour, and entirely redecorated the interior. The Duke looked at several houses before deciding on Stratfield Saye in 1817, and though he originally planned to build a new house, 'Waterloo Palace', on a very grand scale near the present house, in the end nothing was built, as there simply was not enough money. He became fond of the house, though his friends considered it unworthy of him, and lived here quite modestly, only making minor additions, and building a conservatory at one end and a real tennis court at the other. There is a fine colonnaded hall containing Roman mosaics brought from Silchester; the other rooms, quite small, are all Georgian, though they are full of variety, as Lord Rivers' decorations spanned a period of some thirty years. The contents of the house are all Wellington's, and there is a fine collection of paintings, many brought back from Spain as spoils of war. The house has the feeling of a real home; all the Duke's personal possessions have been preserved, and the visitor can see such homely items as spectacles, handkerchiefs and carpet slippers lying about.

☎ Basingstoke (0256) 881337
11 m SE of Reading on A33 turn W for 2 m then S to Stratfield Saye House
SU 7061 (OS 176)

Open Easter to end Apr S and Su; May to end Sept daily exc F 1130-1700; reduced rates for parties
⊖ 🅿 WC ♿ ⊟ ♣
♟ 🛏 ◆ ⚹

Sutton Place

near Guildford, Surrey

Sutton Place, one of the great Tudor houses and an early example of the English Renaissance style, was built in the reign of Henry VIII, who gave the manor to his loyal servant Sir Richard Weston in 1521. The house remained in the Weston family, or various branches of it, until the early years of this century, and since that time it has had many different owners including Lord Northcliffe, the Duke of Sutherland and Paul Getty, who bought it in 1959 largely to house his fabulous art collection. In 1980 Getty Oil granted a lease to Stanley J. Seeger, who has been the motivation behind an immense programme of restoration and renovation. The exterior of the house has been remarkably little changed since it was built, largely because the Westons were often in financial straits, though some 'Georgianising' was done in the 18th century. Inside the house, however, little is left from the 16th century, as it was gutted by fire in Elizabethan times, reconstructed in the 17th century, and altered again in the 19th and 20th centuries. The collection of fine art and furniture, however, more than compensates for any inadequacies in decoration. It is immensely varied, ranging from oak trestle tables contemporary with the house to modern paintings from the Stanley Seeger Collection. The garden was designed by Sir Geoffrey Jellicoe from 1980, and is the most important garden and landscape scheme to be undertaken in Britain for a hundred years. A launching exhibition, 'The Garden at Sutton Place', was held in 1982, and the Trust holds exhibitions and concerts.

Syon House

Syon Park, Brentford, Middlesex

This great house, set in its tree-dotted park, is surprising to find in London's suburbia. Syon takes its name from a monastery founded by Henry V in 1415. After the Dissolution the lands were given to the Duke of Somerset, who built himself a large house, retaining some of the monastic buildings. Basically this is the house we see today, although it was refaced with Bath stone and sash windows put in, which gives it an 18th-century look. Its castellated exterior is not very beautiful but the interior more than makes up for it. This is the house that made Robert Adam's name, and although he was only twenty-nine, the series of rooms he designed here are among the most brilliant of his career. The visitor sees the rooms in the order that Adam intended, starting in the stately Roman-style hall, where the plasterwork was done by Joseph Rose who also made the statuary to Adam's designs. The ante-room, with its gilding and its vivid colouring, is straight out of the Roman Empire at its most lavish. The dining room, the first room Adam completed, is mainly ivory and gold, while the red drawing room takes its name from the crimson Spitalfields silk on the walls. A fine Moorfields carpet designed by Adam fills the room, and the ceiling is an elaborate pattern of coloured octagons and diamonds intersected by bands of gilding. The final room in the series, the long gallery, was planned by Adam as essentially a room for the ladies. The whole room is in pale greens and gold-spangled pinks, and sparkles with delicate ornament.

The Vyne

Sherborne St John, Basingstoke, Hampshire

The Vyne is a Tudor house, but the name itself, meaning 'house of wine', is very old, and it is possible that there was once a Roman inn or villa on the site. The house, a long, low building of rose-red brick with diamond patterning, was built between 1500 and 1520 by the 1st Lord Sandys, Chamberlain to Henry VIII. It is a fine example of Tudor architecture, and many of its features, such as the tall, symmetrical windows, were innovatory. The long gallery (oak gallery) is one of the first to be found in an English country house, and there are outstanding examples of the work of foreign or foreign-influenced craftsmen, notably in the chapel, where the stained glass is Flemish, the choir stalls make use of Renaissance motifs and the tiles are probably from an Antwerp workshop. Sandys' descendants sold the house in about 1650, and the surprising Classical portico, also one of the first in the country, was added by the next owner, Chaloner Chute, who employed John Webb to improve the house. His descendant John Chute, a friend of Horace Walpole, made further improvements. The ground-floor rooms have Tudor woodwork, but the magnificent Palladian staircase was designed by John Chute, as was the tomb chamber. The rooms upstairs include the vast oak gallery; this room, untouched since Tudor times, has four rows of superb linenfold panelling from floor to ceiling, carved with the crests and initials of the King, Sandys himself and his relations and friends. The house is fully furnished, with some good Tudor portraits on the walls.

Tower of London

Tower Hill, London EC3

The most visited castle in England, and one of the most important examples of medieval architecture. It was intended as a royal fortress, and at its core is the White Tower, the huge Norman keep built by William the Conqueror in about 1080. This was built within the Roman city walls, which probably formed part of the fortifications. By the 13th century the building had more or less the form it has today, with the White Tower encircled by two rings of massive walls with towers. Richard I and Henry II built the inner wall and Edward I the outer one, and although they have been much repaired and restored they remain substantially as built. The Tower has so many bloodthirsty associations that it is difficult to envisage it as a palace, but it was the home of royalty as well as a prison, and although the palace buildings were destroyed on the order of Oliver Cromwell, the Crown Jewels are a reminder of this function. The walls, particularly those of the Beauchamp Tower, are carved with inscriptions made by those awaiting trial or death, and the Bowyer Tower still contains the instruments of torture. State prisoners were usually admitted through the Traitor's Gate in St Stephen's Tower, and executions took place both inside the Tower itself and on Tower Hill. The White Tower is now the home of a magnificent collection of medieval arms and armour, including the famous suit of armour made for Henry VIII. St John's Chapel, built about 1080, was restored to its former Romanesque beauty by Prince Albert.

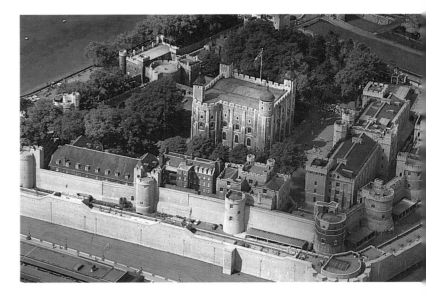

☎ (01) 709 0765

At N end of Tower Bridge off Tower Hill Road

TQ 3380 (OS 176)

Open Mar to end Oct M-S 0930-1700, Su 1400-1700;
Nov to end Feb M-S 0930-1600

♿ 🅿 WC 🅰 (limited access) 🍴 D ♠ 🐕 ⍾
◆ ✾ ✗ ● (not in certain parts of Tower)

Uppark

South Harting, near Petersfield, West Sussex

This attractive house, built on the top of the South Downs, has been nicknamed the 'Sleeping Beauty House' because for most of the 19th century it was occupied by two old ladies who refused to allow any changes. There are many human dramas and stories attached to Uppark. Sarah Wells, the mother of H. G. Wells, was housekeeper here from 1880 to 1893. The house was built in the 1690s for Lord Tankerville, possibly by William Talman, and is typical of houses of this date – built of brick, and three storeys high with a central pediment, the upper storey lit by dormer windows in the roof. It was bought in 1747 by Sir Matthew Fetherstonehaugh, and he and his wife altered and completely redecorated it, leaving only the hall, staircase and dining room as they had been. The exterior was not altered at this time, but the Doric colonnade on the north front was built by Sir Humphry Repton in 1810. The furniture is mainly 18th-century English, and there are Dutch and Italian paintings mostly collected by either Sir Matthew or his son Sir Harry, who turned the house into a favourite haunt of the rich and dissolute society surrounding the Prince Regent. In 1825 Sir Harry, then aged over seventy, married his dairymaid, Mary Ann Bullock – the two ladies who were to preserve the house so well were her sister and former governess. Upstairs the house still has the comfortable feeling of an old ladies' home, while downstairs the housekeeper's room has been arranged just as it was in Sarah Wells' time, with a photograph of her encased in black satin.

☎ Harting (073 085) 317/458

7 m SE of Petersfield on B2146

SU 7717 (OS 197)

Open Apr to end Sept W, Th, Su and Bank Hol M
1400-1800

♿ (1½ m walk) 🅿 WC 🅰 (limited access)
🍴 (by appt) ♠ 🐕 ◆ ✾ ✗

Whitehall

Malden Road, Cheam, Surrey

Built about 1500, Whitehall was probably a yeoman farmer's house attached to East Cheam Manor which was, in turn, owned by the See of Canterbury. In 1539, when the nearby Nonsuch Palace was being built, Henry VIII bought the manor from Archbishop Cranmer, and Whitehall was reputed to have been used to house the Maids of Honour when the King was at Nonsuch. In 1654 Queen Mary granted the manor to Arthur Browne, Viscount Montague and in 1575 it was sold to the Earl of Arundel. From 1645 to 1719 it was the home of Cheam School. Sutton and Cheam Borough Council acquired the property in 1963 and have been responsible for the very careful restoration work. The white-painted weatherboard style of Whitehall is not uncommon in this part of the country but the timber-framed continuous-jettied house has some unusual features, notably a projecting upper storey and a two-storey porch with an attractive depressed Tudor arch. The original house was of two storeys, with three rooms – a hall, stillroom and kitchen-parlour – on the ground floor and a sleeping room and storeroom upstairs. Extensions were added later in the 16th century and also in the 17th and 19th centuries; the weatherboarding itself is a late 18th-century addition.

☎ (01) 661 5050

In centre of Cheam off Malden road

TQ 2464 (OS 176)

Open throughout year W-F, Su 1400-1730,
S 1000-1730; also T Apr to end Sept

♿ 🅿 WC 🍴 🅰 (by appt) ♠ 🐕 ◆ ✾ ✗

Albury Park, Albury, near Guildford, Surrey. 6½ m E of Guildford, on A25. TQ 0647 (OS 187). Country mansion, built in the late 17th century, modified by Sir John Soane, and with the façade designed by A.G.W. Pugin in the mid-19th century; every chimney is different. The interior contains a staircase by Soane. Open May to Sept W and Th pm. ⊖ ⓟ 🔲 ♣

Allington Castle, near Maidstone, Kent (tel Maidstone [0622] 54080). 2 m NW of town centre on A20, turn NE. TQ 7557 (OS 188). Small 13th-century moated castle with corner towers around a rectangular enclosure on the banks of the River Medway. It was converted to a mansion in the Tudor period and restored in the early 20th century by Martin Conway. It is now used as a retreat and conference centre by the Order of Carmelites. Open daily pm. ⓟ WC 🔲 🚻 🐾

Alresford House, Alresford, Hampshire. 8 m E of Winchester on A31. TM 0621 (OS 185). Mid-Georgian country house, built c. 1750 by Admiral Lord Rodney (d. 1792). The grounds offer a variety of catering arrangements, from picnicking and picking fruit to receptions. Open May to Sept W-Su pm; other times by appt. ⊖ ⓟ ♣ 🐾 🍴

Ann of Cleves' House, Southover High St, Lewes, East Sussex (tel Lewes [079 16] 4610). On SE side of Lewes, on A275. TQ 4109 (OS 198). A late medieval house with a varied façade of 1530. The house was part of the divorce settlement of Ann of Cleves from Henry VIII. It now houses a museum of local history, dealing particularly with the ironmaking industry of the Sussex Weald, and there are also collections of children's toys and Victoriana. Open mid-Feb to Nov M-S am and pm; also Su pm, Apr to Oct. ⊖ WC 🚻 ♣

Appuldurcombe House, Wroxall, Isle of Wight. 3 m N of Ventnor on B3327. SZ 5479 (OS 196). Ruins of an 18th-century mansion built for the Worsley family from 1701 in Classical style. The house was irrevocably damaged in 1943 and only the shell of the house remains (though the stonework is in good condition), as does the park, which was the work of Capability Brown. Open daily am and pm (Su pm only). ⊖ WC 🔲

Apsley House, Hyde Park Corner, London SW1 (tel 01-499 5676). At Hyde Park Corner. TQ 2879 (OS 176). Home of the Duke of Wellington from 1817, and built in 1771-78 by Robert Adam for Lord Bathurst. It was given its present Classical façade in 1828. It was converted into a Wellington Museum in 1947, and the interior has been redecorated in early 19th-century style. It contains fine porcelain and silver, as well as the Duke's collection of paintings, which includes works by Velasquez, Van Dyck and Goya. Open T-Th, S am and pm; Su pm only. Closed Christmas and New Year. ⊖ WC 🔲 🚻 ★

Arreton Manor, Arreton, Isle of Wight (tel Newport [0983] 528134). 2 m SE of Newport on A3056. SZ 5386 (OS 196). 17th-century manor house with contemporary furniture. It contains a collection of lacemaking, and a museum of childhood. In the grounds (and connected to the house by a secret passageway) is the Pomeroy museum dolls house, and a collection of wireless receivers dating back to the early 20th century. Open Easter to end Oct, M-S am and pm, Su pm only. ⊖ ⓟ WC 🔲 ♣ 🐾

Avington Park, Winchester, Hampshire (tel Itchen Abbas [0962 78] 202). 2½ m NE of Winchester on A33, turn E onto B3047. SU 5332 (OS 185). Charming brick-built country house mainly erected in the late 17th century in the style of Sir Christopher Wren, and enhanced by the Duke of Chandos a century later. The rooms range in style from the early 18th century to the large mid-Victorian conservatory. Avington Church, in Georgian style, stands in the grounds. Open May to Sept S, Su and Bank Hol pm. ⊖ ⓟ WC 🔲 ♣ 🐾

Banqueting House, Westminster (tel 01-212 4785). On Whitehall. TQ 3080 (OS 176). One of the first Classical-style houses in London, built by Inigo Jones in 1619-22 as part of the vast Whitehall Palace, which was otherwise never completed. It was the centre of court life in the 17th century. The interior is decorated by Rubens, and the house was converted into a royal chapel by Sir Christopher Wren in the early 18th century, and restored in the 1970s. Open daily (exc M) am and pm (Su pm only). ⊖ 🚻

Basildon Park, near Pangbourne, Berkshire (tel Pangbourne [073 57] 3040). 9 m NW of Reading on A329, turn W. SU 6178 (OS 175). Attractive Palladian house built in the 1770s by John Carr in a park overlooking the River Thames. The staircase is an important feature of the house. Much of the decoration is original, and the rooms are furnished in 18th-century style. There is an unusual octagon room, completed in the 1840s. Open Apr to Oct W-Su and Bank Hols pm. ⊖ ⓟ WC 🚻 D (grounds only) ♣ 🐾

Basing House, Old Basing, Hampshire (tel Basingstoke [0256] 67294). 3 m E of Basingstoke, off A30. SU 6652 (OS 185). Ruined Tudor palace built by Henry VIII on the site of four castles. It was an important stronghold for the Royalists during the Civil War, holding out in a two-year siege until 1645. There is a 16th-century gatehouse and tithe barn. Open June to Aug daily pm; Apr, May and Sept S, Su and Bank Hols pm. 🚻 🐾

Bateman's, Burwash, East Sussex (tel Burwash [0435] 882302). 8 m NE of Heathfield, off A265. TQ 6723 (OS 199). Gabled 17th-century house built for a local ironmaster, home of Rudyard Kipling from 1902 to 1936. The ground floor has 17th-century furnishings, and upstairs is Kipling's study preserved as he left it. A watermill adapted by him to supply electricity is nearby. Kipling's Rolls Royce is in the garage. Open June to Sept M-Th am and pm, S and Su pm only; March to May, Oct daily (exc F) pm. ⊖ ⓟ WC 🚻 (by appt) ♣ 🐾

Beeches Farm, near Uckfield, East Sussex. 10 m E of Haywards Heath, off B2102. TQ 4520 (OS 199). A 16th-century timber-framed and tile-hung farmhouse; the gardens and views are notable. Garden open daily am and pm, house open by appointment only. ⊖ ⓟ 🚻 (by appt) ♣ 🐾 (by appt)

Bishop's Waltham Palace, Bishop's Waltham, Hampshire. 6 m E of Eastleigh on A333. SU 5517 (OS 185). Fortified palace dating from the reign of King Stephen, and built by the Bishop of Winchester. William of Wykeham died here in 1404. It has a great tower, gatehouse and Romanesque chapel. Open daily am and pm. ⓟ

Boston Manor, Boston Manor Road, Brentford, Middlesex (tel 01-570 7728 ext 3974). Just N of A4, 2 m E of Hounslow. TQ 1678 (OS 176). Jacobean house dated 1622, with an elaborate plasterwork ceiling, and original fireplace and mantelpieces. The oak staircase is memorable. Open end May to end Sept S pm. ⊖ ⓟ ★

Bramber Castle, near Steyning, West Sussex. 4 m N of Shoreham-by-Sea, off A283. TQ 1810 (OS 198). Early Norman castle on the edge of the Downs; the former home of the Dukes of Norfolk. Only a few ruins remain of the original stonework. Open daily am and pm. ⓟ ★

Brickwall House, Northiam, Rye, East Sussex (tel Northiam [07974] 2494). 7 m NW of Rye off A268. TQ 8323 (OS 199). Gabled Jacobean house, home of the Frewen family since 1666. The drawing room is decorated in original style, and the garden is in the process of restoration in the 18th-century style. The house is now used as a school. Open end Apr to late May, and June to mid-July, W and S pm. ⊖ ⓟ ♣

Carlyle's House, 24 Cheyne Row, Chelsea, London SW3 (tel 01-352 7087). N of Chelsea Embankment. TQ 2777 (OS 176). Early 18th-century town house, the home of philosopher Thomas Carlyle from 1834 to his death in 1881. The house remains as it was at that time and contains many books and relics of Carlyle. There is a small garden. Open Apr to Oct W-Su and Bank Hols am and pm. ⊖ WC 🚻 ♣

Charleston Manor, West Dean, Seaford, East Sussex. 7 m W of Eastbourne, on A259, turn N. TQ 5200 (OS 199). Ancient house comprising Norman, Tudor and Georgian elements. There is a famous Romanesque window, and exquisite rose gardens; in the grounds is a Tudor tithe barn and a Norman dovecote. House not open; gardens open Apr to Oct daily am and pm. ⊖ ⓟ

Appuldurcombe House, Isle of Wight

Chartwell, Westerham, Kent (tel Edenbridge [0732] 866368). 2 m S of Westerham on B2026, turn SE. TQ 4551 (OS 188). 18th-century farmhouse modified in the 1920s, the home of Sir Winston Churchill from 1924 until his death in 1965. The interior is partly preserved as it was in his lifetime, and also contains a museum of Churchill memorabilia; the grounds are attractive and contain a lake, and Churchill's studio hung with many of his paintings. House open March to Nov (gardens Apr to mid-Oct) T-Th pm, S and Su am and pm; also July and Aug W and Th am. ⊖ 🅿 WC 🅰 🖪 (by appt) ♠

Chilham Castle, Chilham, Kent (tel. Canterbury [0227] 730319). 8 m SW of Canterbury on A28, turn W on A252. TR 0653 (OS 189). Castle with an octagonal great tower built in the 1170s by Henry II, extended for use as a house in the Jacobean period by Inigo Jones. There are extensive and attractive gardens, laid out by Tradescant, with woodland and lakeside walks. The castle is not open; gardens open Apr to Oct daily am and pm. ⊖ 🅿 WC 🅰 🖪 (by appt) ♠

Clandon Park, West Clandon, near Guildford, Surrey (tel Guildford [0483] 222482). 3 m NE of Guildford on A247. TQ 0451 (OS 186). Palladian house built in the early 1730s for the Onslow family. It contains one of the finest 18th-century interiors in Britain, recently decorated in original style. There is a Baroque entrance hall, and a collection of fine 18th-century furniture, ceramics and paintings. The Victorian kitchen is on display. There is also a collection of Chinese porcelain birds, and the museum of the Queen's Royal Surrey Regiment. There is a garden containing a Maori house, and a landscaped park (not open to the public). Open Apr to Oct T-Th, S, Su pm; also Bank Hol M. ⊖ 🅿 WC 🅰 🖪 🖢

Claremont House, Esher, Surrey (tel Esher 67841). 5 m SW of Kingston-upon-Thames on A244, turn W. TQ 1363 (OS 176). Palladian-style house built in 1760s by Henry Holland, Sir John Soane and Capability Brown for Robert Clive of India. The house is now used as a school. It is set in the earliest landscaped park in Britain. This was originally laid out by Vanbrugh and Bridgeman, then modified by William Kent before being reworked by Brown. There is a Gothick belvedere tower built by Vanbrugh in 1717. House open Feb to Nov, first S and Su in the month pm; gardens daily am and pm (exc Christmas). ⊖ 🅿 WC 🅰 ♠ 🖢

Clergy House, Alfriston, East Sussex (tel Alfriston [0323] 870001). 5 m N of Eastbourne on A22, turn W onto A27 for 4 m then turn S. TQ 5103 (OS 199). Timber-framed and thatched cottage of about 1350. It has a great hall, solar and store rooms. This was the first building to be acquired by the National Trust, in 1896; the house contains an exhibition of life in Chaucer's England. Open Apr to Oct daily am and pm. ⊖ ♠

Cobham Hall, Cobham, Kent (tel Shorne [047 482] 3371). 4 m W of Rochester, off A2. TQ 6868 (OS 178). House built in the late Elizabethan period, with the central portion completed in the 1660s. Inigo Jones and James Wyatt were both associated with it. The interior contains Elizabethan fireplaces, and the dramatic 17th-century gilt room. The grounds were laid out by Humphry Repton, and the house is now a girls' public school. Open mid Apr, daily; Aug, W, Th and S and Bank Hol M pm. ⊖ 🅿 WC 🅰 (by appt) ♠ 🖢

Danny, Hurstpierpoint, West Sussex (tel Hurstpierpoint [0273] 833000). 6 m N of Brighton on A23, turn W onto B2116 for 1 m then S. TQ 2814 (OS 198). Elizabethan E-shaped house, with an early 18th-century façade. Open May to Sept W and Th pm. ⊖ 🅿 🅰

Dickens House Museum, 48 Doughty St, Bloomsbury, London WC1 (tel 01-405 2127). TQ 3082 (OS 176). Georgian brick town house, the home where he wrote *Oliver Twist*, *Nicholas Nickelby* and finished *Pickwick Papers*. The house contains many personal and literary relics, and the reception rooms are preserved as they were in his day. Open M-S am and pm (exc Bank Hols). ⊖ 🅰

Down House, Downe, Kent (tel Farnborough [0689] 59119). 5½ m S of Bromley, on A233, turn E. TQ 4361 (OS 176). Early 19th-century house, the home of Charles Darwin for 40 years. It contains many objects associated with Darwin's career, and the Darwin memorial gardens. Open March to Jan T-Th, S and Su pm (also Bank Hols). ⊖ 🅿 🅰 ♠

Eastbridge Hospital, High St, Canterbury, Kent (tel Canterbury [0227] 62395). In city centre. TR 1457 (OS 189). One of the oldest buildings in Canterbury, dating back to the 12th century, and used as an almshouse since the 16th century. Open daily am and pm (exc Christmas and Good Friday). ⊖ 🅿 ★

Eltham Palace, Eltham, London SE9 (tel 01-859 2112). 9 m SE of central London on A20, turn S. TQ 4274 (OS 177). Medieval royal palace extended in the 15th and 16th centuries but little used from the time of Elizabeth I. There is a 15th-century brick great hall with hammerbeam roof built for Edward IV, and other timber-framed buildings. The palace is the headquarters of the Institute of Army Education. The moat is crossed by a medieval bridge. Open Th and Su am and pm. ⊖ 🅿 🅰 ★

Eynsford Castle, Eynsford, Kent. 9 m N of Sevenoaks on A225, turn W. TQ 5465 (OS 177). One of the earliest stone enclosure castles in England, with the walls built in the 1080s and 1090s on an artificial mound. The tower and other buildings are mainly 12th-century; there is a ruined gatehouse and a moat. Open daily am and pm (Su pm only, Oct to Apr). ⊖ 🅿

Farnham Castle, Castle Hill, Farnham, Surrey. In town centre off A287. SU 8347 (OS 186). Castle first built for the Bishop of Winchester in the 1130s, but with the original buildings replaced by a shell keep in the late 12th century. There is a 13th-century gatehouse. The castle was slighted in the Civil War, but continued to be used as a residence for the bishop. The great hall was rebuilt after the Restoration. Open Apr to Sept am and pm (Su pm only). ⊖ 🅿

Fenton House, Windmill Hill, Hampstead, London NW3 (tel 01-435 3471). On W side of Hampstead Grove, 4 m N of London centre. TQ 2686 (OS 176). Late 17th-century house set in a walled garden built for a London merchant. It contains a collection of 18th-century porcelain and the Benton Fletcher collection of early keyboard musical instruments, demonstrations of which may be heard. Open Apr to Oct S-W pm; March S and Su only pm. ⊖ WC 🅰 ♠

Finchcocks, Goudhurst, Kent (tel Goudhurst [0580] 211702). 12 m E of Tunbridge Wells on A262, turn S. TQ 7036 (OS 188). Medium-sized brick house built in 1725 for Edward Bathurst, and containing a collection of historic keyboard musical instruments, including early pianos. Open Easter to Sept Su; also Bank Hols and Aug W-S pm. 🅿 WC ♠ 🖢

Forty Hall, Forty Hill, Enfield, Greater London (tel 01-363 8196). 11 m N of central London off A10; 1 m N of Enfield. TQ 3398 (OS 176). Mansion built in 1629 for Sir Nicholas Raynton, with 17th- and 18th-century decoration. The house contains an art gallery and furniture museum. It is set in a wooded park. Open daily (exc M) am and pm. ⊖ 🅿 WC 🅰 ♠ 🖢 🅰 ★

Gad's Hill Place, Rochester, Kent. 3 m NW of Rochester, on A226. TQ 7170 (OS 178). Late Georgian house, the home of Charles Dickens from 1858 to 1870, now used as a school. The garden extends through a tunnel under the road. Open by appt only. ⊖ 🅿 ★

Glynde Place, near Lewes, East Sussex (tel Glynde [079 159] 248). 6 m SE of Lewes on A27, turn N. TQ 4509 (OS 198). Large 16th-century house, with bow windows and gables, and built arund a courtyard. The interior was modified in the mid-18th century, and there are many paintings, including portraits by Lely, Kneller and Zoffany of members of the Brand family. The rose garden is open on connoisseurs' day, last W of each month. Otherwise, open June to Sept W and Th pm; also Easter Su and M and Bank Hols. ⊖ 🅿 WC 🅰 (by appt) ♠ 🖢

Godington Park, Ashford, Kent (tel Ashford [0233] 20773). 1½ m W of Ashford on A20, turn S. TR 9843 (OS 189). Jacobean house, with a 15th-century great hall and much fine carving and panelling, especially on the main staircase. The rooms contain interesting portraits, china and furniture. There is a formal garden with topiary, laid out in the late 19th century. Open Easter, June to Sept Su and Bank Hols pm; other times by appt. ⊖ 🅿 WC 🅰 🅰 ♠

Great Dixter, Northiam, East Sussex (tel Northiam [07974] 3160). 8 m W of Rye, off A28. TQ 8125 (OS 199). 15th-century half-timbered hall manor house, modified by Sir Edwin Lutyens in 1910, attaching another hall to the main body of the house. The great hall has an unusual roof, combining hammerbeams with crown post construction. The gardens were laid out by Lutyens, with a wide range of plants and flowers. Open Apr to mid-Oct daily (exc M) pm; gardens also open am on Spring Bank Hol S, Su and M, and Aug Su. ⊖ 🅿 WC 🅰 (by appt) ♠

Great Maytham Hall, Rolvenden, Kent (tel Rolvenden [058 084] 346). 4½ m W of Tenterden on A28, turn E. TQ 8430 (OS 188). Georgian-style house designed in 1910 by Sir Edwin Lutyens for the Tennants family. It has now mostly been converted into flats. Open May to Sept W and Th pm. ⊖ 🅿 WC

Guildford Castle, Castle St, Guildford, Surrey (tel Guildford [0483] 505050). To the S of town centre, off A281. SU 9949 (OS 186). Early 12th-century castle with a virtually square tower on the site of an old motte. Until 1600 the castle was used as a local prison. The castle ditch is now a flower garden. Grounds open daily am and pm; buildings open Apr to Sept am and pm. ⊖ 🅿 🅰 ♠

Guildford House, 155 High St, Guildford, Surrey (tel Guildford [0483] 505050 ext 3531). In town centre. SU 9950 (OS 186). Timber-framed Restoration period house with fine carved staircase, ironwork and plasterwork. The house now contains a series of temporary exhibitions. Open M-S am and pm. ⊖ 🅰 ★

Hammerwood Park, near East Grinstead, East Sussex (tel Cowden [034 286] 594). 4 m E of East Grinstead on A264, turn S. TQ 4438 (OS 187). House built in 1792 by Latrobe, the architect of the White House and Capitol, Washington, and restored since 1982. The house contains displays of furniture and costume, and an account of its own varied fortunes. Open Easter to end Sept W, S, Su and Bank Hol M pm; also Th pm in Aug. ⊖ 🅿 WC 🅰 (by appt) ♠ 🖢 🅰

Haremere Hall, Etchingham, East Sussex (tel Etchingham [058 081] 245). 8 m N of Battle, off A265. TQ 7226 (OS 199). Early 17th-century manor house, with panelled great hall and period furniture. There is a collection of oriental *objets d'art*. The grounds include terraced gardens, and a shire horse farm, with daily demonstrations. Grounds open Easter to end Sept daily am and pm; house open Bank Hol weekends pm, other times by appt. ⊖ 🅿 WC 🅰 (by appt) ♠ 🖢

Haseley Manor, Hazeley Combe, Arreton, Isle of Wight (tel Arreton [098 377] 420). 3 m SE of Newport on A3056. SZ 5285 (OS 196). 16th-century house modified in the late 18th century. The dining room has a mid-Tudor fireplace. There is a small museum of rural life, pottery demonstrations, and children's play area. Open Easter to Oct daily am and pm; in winter M-F am and pm. 🅿 WC ♠ 🖢 🅰

Hastings Castle, Castle Hill, Hastings, East Sussex (tel Hastings [0424] 424242). In town centre. TQ 8209 (OS 199). A Norman castle built by William the Conqueror immediately after landing at Pevensey. A stone keep was erected in the 12th century, but has left no traces. Remains of 11th- and 12th-century walls and the 13th-century gatehouse can be seen. Open Easter to Sept daily am and pm. ⊖ 🅿

Hatchlands, East Clandon, Surrey (tel Guildford [0483] 222787). 5 m NE of Guildford, on A246. TQ 0652 (OS 187). Mid 18th-century brick house built for Admiral Boscawen. The interiors are an early example of the work of Robert Adam, with later modifications. There is an attractive garden. Open Apr to mid-Oct W, Th and Su pm. ⊖ 🅿 🅰 🅰 (by appt) ♠ 🖢

Hogarth's House, Chiswick, London W4 (01-994 6757). 6 m W of central London, off A4. TQ 2177 (OS 176). Brick-built country house residence of the painter William Hogarth from 1749 to 1764, now housing a Hogarth museum including prints of his best-known works. Open daily am and pm (Su pm only); closed first two weeks in Sept, three weeks over Christmas and New Year. ✆ ▯ ▣

Hurst Castle, near Milford, Hampshire. 3 m S of Lymington on A337, turn S. SZ 3189 (OS 196). Coastal fort built by Henry VIII in the 1540s, on a spit of land guarding the entrance to the Solent. It was designed with a series of low cylindrical towers arranged in trefoil pattern around a central tower. The castle was restored in the 19th century. It is reached by a lengthy walk, or by boat. Open daily am and pm (Oct to March Su pm only). ✆ WC ⊟ D ♠ ▰

Dr Johnson's House, 17 Gough Square, London EC4 (tel 01-353 3745). Off Fleet St. TQ 3181 (OS 176). Large late 17th-century house, the home of Dr Johnson from 1748 to 1759. He compiled his *English Dictionary* and other works in the attic. There is a collection of objects, letters, books and paintings connected with Dr Johnson. Open daily am and pm (exc Su). ✆

Keats' House, Well Walk, Hampstead, London NW3 (tel 01-435 2062). S end of Hampstead Heath. TQ 2785 (OS 176). Early 19th-century house, the home of John Keats from 1818 to 1820. It was restored in the 1970s and contains a collection of objects and papers connected with the poet and his fiancée Fanny Brawne. Open exc Christmas, New Year and Good Fri and Spring Bank Hol daily am and pm (Su and Bank Hols pm only). ✆ ▯ ▣ ★

Lamb House, West St, Rye, East Sussex. In town centre. TQ 9220 (OS 189). Early 18th-century red-brick house built for James Lamb, and the home of writer Henry James from 1898 to 1916. The study where many of his greatest novels were written was destroyed during the Second World War, but the house remains furnished in the style of his day. The gardens are attractive. ✆ ⊟ (by appt) ♠

Legh Manor, Ansty, West Sussex (tel Lewes [07916] 4379). 4 m W of Haywards Heath, off A272. TQ 2923 (OS 198). Architecturally interesting Elizabethan manor house, with a garden laid out in around 1900 by Gertrude Jekyll. Open Apr to Oct second and third W and second S in month pm. ✆ ▯

Linley Sambourne House, 18 Stafford Terrace, London W8 (tel 01-994 1019). N of Kensington High St. TQ 2579 (OS 176). 19th-century house, the home of Linley Sambourne, political cartoonist for *Punch* magazine in the late 19th century. It is decorated in the style of the period, and contains paintings and drawings by many artists of that time. Open March to Oct W am and pm, and Su pm only. ✆ ⊟ (by appt)

Little Holland House, Beeches Avenue, Carshalton, South London. 3 m E of Sutton, on

B278. TQ 2763 (OS 176). The home of Arts and Crafts designer Frank Dickinson, built to his own design and featuring his interior decor, painting, handmade furniture and other craft objects expressing his philosophy and theories. Open March to Oct 1st Su in month and Bank Holo Su and M pm. ✆ ▯ ★

Marlborough House, Pall Mall, London SW1 (tel 01-930 9249). W of Trafalgar Square. TQ 2980 (OS 176). House built for Sarah, Duchess of Marlborough in 1709-11 by Sir Christopher Wren, and decorated with heroic paintings of Marlborough's battles by Louis Laguerre. It was used as a royal residence from 1817 to 1953, and in the 1960s it became a Commonwealth conference and research centre. Open M-F when not in use for conferences, by appointment only. ✆

Monk's House, Rodmell, East Sussex. 4 m SE of Lewes, TQ 4105 (OS 198). Small 17th-century village house, the home of Virginia and Leonard Woolf from 1919 until his death in 1969. Open Apr to Oct W and S pm. ▯ ♠

Morton Manor, Brading, Isle of Wight (tel Sandown [0983] 406168). 1½ m N of Sandown off 3055. SZ 6085 (OS 196). Restoration house, built in 1680, and with period furniture. The gardens are attractively terraced and landscaped. Open Easter to Sept daily (exc S) am and pm. ✆ ▯ WC ▣ ♠ ▰

Mottisfont Abbey, Mottisfont, Hampshire (tel Lockerley [0794] 40757). 4½ m NW of Romsey off A3057. SU 3226 (OS 185). Founded as an Augustinian priory in the 12th century, it was converted into a private house by Lord Sandys in the 1540s and altered again in the 18th century when the south front was added. There is a room with Rex Whistler *trompe l'oeil* murals, a walled garden with a collection of old roses, and a large and beautiful park. The stable block contains a local history museum. House open Apr to end Sept W and S pm; grounds open T-S pm. ✆ ▯ WC ⊟ (by appt) ♠

Newtimber Place, Newtimber, West Sussex (tel Hurstpierpoint [0273] 833104). 11 m N of Brighton on A23, turn W. TQ 2613 (OS 198). 17th-century house with a moat and Etruscan-style wall-paintings. Open May to Aug Th pm. ✆ ▯

Norris Castle, East Cowes, Isle of Wight (tel Cowes [0983] 293434). ½ m E of East Cowes off A3021, on coast. SZ 5296 (OS 196). Fantasy castle built in 1799 by James Wyatt, a childhood resort of Queen Victoria (who later had Osborne House built nearby).The central tower houses the ballroom. The castle contains 18th- and 19th-century furniture. Open Easter, mid-May to mid-Sept S-M am and pm. ▯ WC ▣ ▰

Nunwell House, Brading, Isle of Wight (tel Brading [098 372] 240). 3 m S of Ryde on A3055, turn W. SZ 5987 (OS 196). Tudor and Jacobean house, with later additions. It contains period furniture in the Jacobean and Georgian wings, and houses a unique collection of family militaria. Open Easter to Sept Su-Th pm. ✆ ▯ WC ⊟ (by appt) ♠ ▰

Odiham Castle, Odiham, Hampshire. 7 m E of Basingstoke off A32. SU 7251 (OS 186). Ruined early 13th-century castle built by King John and expanded later. The shell of the polygonal great tower still stands. Open daily am and pm. ✆ ▯ ★

Orleans House, Riverside, Twickenham, Middlesex (tel 01-892 0221). 11 m W of central London, ½ m E of Twickenham. TQ 1673 (OS 176). 18th-century house, of which the only original surviving part is the octagon, built by James Gibbs in 1720, with exquisite decorative plasterwork. The house was the residence of Louis Philippe, Duc d'Orleans, during his period of exile, from 1830 to 1848. There is an art gallery in the house, which is set in woods. Open daily (exc M) pm. ✆ ▯ ▣ ♠ ★

Owletts, Cobham, Kent (tel Meopham [0474] 814260). 4 m W of Rochester on A2, turn S onto B2009. TQ 6668 (OS 177). Modest red-brick house built in the 1680s with richly-decorated plasterwork over the stairs. There are small, attractive gardens. Open Apr to Sept W and Th pm. ✆ ▣ ♠

Owl House, Lamberhurst, Kent (tel 01-235 1432). 7 m E of Tunbridge Wells on A21, turn S. TQ 6636 (OS 188). 16th-century half-timbered and tile-hung cottage with extensive gardens including azaleas, rhododendrons, shrubs and lakes; the setting for a book about 16th-century wool smugglers or 'Owlers'. Gardens only open M, W, F, Su and Bank Hols am and pm. ✆ ▯ ▣ ♠

Pevensey Castle, Pevensey, East Sussex. 6 m NE of Eastbourne on A259. TQ 6404 (OS 199). The Romans built the first fort on the site, as part of their Saxon Shore defences; William the Conqueror sheltered in its ruins and defended the site after landing. A stone great tower was erected in the 12th century, and the Roman walls were improved once more. Open daily am and pm (Oct to March Su pm only). ✆ ▯

Port Lympne, Lympne, Hythe, Kent (tel Hythe [0303] 64646). 3 m W of Hythe. TR 1234 (OS 169). Early 20th-century house designed by Sir Herbert Baker in Dutch colonial style, and with a number of original features including a tent room by Rex Whistler and a Moroccan patio. There is a wildlife art gallery, gardens, and a zoo park. Open all year daily am and pm (closed 25 Dec). ✆ ▯ WC ⊟ ♠ ▰

Preston Manor, Preston Park, Brighton, East Sussex (tel Brighton [0273] 55101). 2 m N of town centre on A23. TQ 3006 (OS 198). House built in the 1730s in the Classical style, and extended in the early 20th century. The house contains the Macquoid collection of 16th- and 17th-century furniture. Open W-S am and pm, Su pm only (closed Christmas and Good Fri). ✆ ▯ WC ⊟ (by appt) ♠

Quebec House, Westerham, Kent (tel Westerham [0959] 62206). 5 m W of Sevenoaks on A25. TQ 4454 (OS 187). Gabled 16th- and 17th-century red-brick house, the childhood home of General James Wolfe who captured Quebec from the French in 1759. The house and coach house contain an exhibition of pictures and objects related to Wolfe. Open Apr to Oct M-W, F, Su pm; March Su pm only. ✆ WC ♠

Quex Park, Birchington, Kent (tel Thanet [0843] 42168). 5 m W of Margate on A28, turn S onto B2048. TR 3168 (OS 179). 19th-century house containing Major Percy Powell-Cotton's ethnographic and natural historical objects from Africa and Asia, collected between 1887 and 1938. These include dioramas, stuffed animals, firearms, *objets d'art*, costumes etc. There are other rooms with 18th-century furniture, and an extensive park. Open Apr and May, Th and Su pm; June to Sept, W, Th and Su pm; also F in Aug and Bank Hols. ✆ ▯ WC ▣ ⊟ (by appt) ♠

Ranger's House, Blackheath, London SE10 (tel 01-853 0035). On S side of Blackheath, 6 m SE of central London on A2, turn N. TQ 3876 (OS 177). Red-brick late 17th-century house, the home in the mid-18th century of the Earl of Chesterfield, who added the bow-windowed gallery. The house is now an art gallery, with a collection of musical instruments. Open daily am and pm. ✆ ▰ WC ★

Mottisfont Abbey, Hampshire

Sir John Soane Museum, London

Riverhill House, Sevenoaks, Kent (tel Sevenoaks [0732] 452557). 3 m S of Sevenoaks on A225, turn E. TQ 5452 (OS 188). Small country house, with a notable and varied garden, including terraces, rhododendrons and azaleas. Garden open Apr to Aug Su and M pm; house by appt only. P ⊟ (by appt) ♠ ☕ ⊼

Roydon Hall, near Maidstone, Kent (tel Maidstone [0622] 813243). 10 m SW of Maidstone on A26, turn S. TQ 6651 (OS 188). 19th-century rebuilding of a Tudor manor house overlooking the Weald. The house is now a residential centre for Transcendental Meditation, and exhibitions and lectures are available. Open March to Oct W, Su and Bank Hols pm. P WC ⊟ (by appt) ♠ ☕

Sackville College, High St, East Grinstead, West Sussex (tel East Grinstead [0342] 21639). In town centre. TQ 3938 (OS 187). Quadrangular Jacobean almshouses, founded in 1609 by Robert Sackville, 2nd Earl of Dorset. The common rooms and hall have their original oak furniture. Open May to end Sept daily pm. ⊖ P ♿

Saltwood Castle, Saltwood, Kent (tel Hythe [0303] 67190). 2 m NW of Hythe. TR 1635 (OS 179). Mid 12th-century castle, the property of the Archbishops of Canterbury. It was the centre of a dispute between Henry II and Thomas à Becket in the 12th century. It was built in the form of an oval enclosure and was enlarged in the 14th century with a twin-cylinder tower gatehouse. It was converted into a house in the late 19th century. Open by appt, for parties only. ⊖ P WC ♿

Smallhythe Place, Tenterden, Kent (tel Tenterden [05806] 2334). 3 m S of Tenterden on B2082. TQ 8930 (OS 189). Half-timbered 16th-century yeoman's house in a medieval shipping village; it was the home of actress Ellen Terry from 1899 to 1928, and contains an extensive collection of memorabilia and objects associated with the theatre in the early 20th century. Open March S and Su pm; Apr to Oct daily (exc T and F) pm. ⊖ P ⊟ (by appt

Sir John Soane Museum, 13 Lincoln's Inn Fields, London WC2 (tel 01-405 2107). ½ m N of Aldwych. TQ 3081 (OS 176). The home of architect Sir John Soane, builder of the Bank of England. He designed it in 1812, and it now houses his extensive and varied collection of antiquities and paintings, as well as his own architectural drawings.Open T-S am and pm. ⊖ ★

Standen, East Grinstead, West Sussex (tel East Grinstead [0342] 23029). 1½ m S of East Grinstead off B2110. TQ 3935 (OS 187). Large house built in the 1890s by Philip Webb, adding to an existing farmhouse. The interior retains its original furnishings, including fabrics and wallpaper by William Morris, and other products of the Arts and Crafts movement. The gardens, also laid out by Webb, have fine views across the Medway valley. Open Apr to Oct W, Th, S and Su pm. ⊖ P WC ♿ ⊟ ♠

Stoneacre, Otham, near Maidstone, Kent. 3 m SE of Maidstone on A20, turn S. TQ 8053 (OS 183). Small half-timbered 15th-century manor house, restored in the 1920s, and with a crown post roof. The small gardens are attractive. Open Apr to Sept W and S pm. ⊖ P WC ⊟ ♠

Swallowfield Park, Swallowfield, Berkshire. 5 m SE of Reading on A33, turn SW onto B3349 for 4 m, then turn E. SU 7365 (OS 175). House built c. 1690 for the 2nd Earl of Clarendon by William Talman, architect of Chatsworth, and reworked in the 1820s. Features include the original Baroque doorway, now moved from its original position, and a fine four-acre walled garden. Open W and Th pm, May to Sept. ⊖ P WC ♿ ♠

Temple Manor, Knight Road, Strood, Rochester, Kent. ½m S of Strood centre. TQ 7368 (OS 179). 13th-century house built for the officers of the Knights Templar, with 17th-century extensions. The house is now empty of furnishings, but has a fine hall and vaulted undercroft. Open Apr to Sept M-F am and pm; Su pm only. ⊖ P

Titchfield Abbey, Titchfield, Hampshire. 3 m W of Fareham on A27, turn N. SU 5306 (OS 196). 13th-century abbey converted into a mansion in the 1540s after the Dissolution of the Monasteries by Thomas Wriothesley, the future Earl of Southampton. Much of the Tudor house was destroyed in the 1780s, but the gatehouse remains and the plan of the abbey can be traced in the ruins. Open daily am and pm (Su pm only). ⊖ P ♿

Tonbridge Castle, Tonbridge, Kent (tel West Malling [0732] 844522 ext 432). In town centre off High St. TQ 5846 (OS 188). Norman motte-and-bailey castle overlooking the River Medway, with a massive 13th-century gatehouse, containing unusually comfortable residential accommodation. A mid 18th-century house was built alongside the castle. The castle grounds have been laid out as gardens. Open Apr to mid-July S, Su and Bank Hols; July to Sept daily am and pm. Other times by appt for parties. ⊖ P ⊟ ♠

Tudor House, King Street, Margate, Kent (tel Thanet [0843] 25511 ext 217). In town centre. TR 3570 (OS 179). Timber-framed house of the early Tudor period, restored in 1951. The plaster ceilings and exposed timberwork of the interior are notable, and the house also contains a local history museum and a collection of sea shells. Open May to Sept M-S am and pm. ⊖ P

Walmer Castle, Walmer, Kent. In town centre, 2 m S of Deal on B2057. TR 3750 (OS 179). One of the castles built in the late 1530s (with Sandown and Deal) to defend this part of Kent. It is built on a quatrefoil plan with a cylindrical central tower. Walmer Castle has been the official home of the Warden of the Cinque Ports since the early 18th century, and has been modified for residential use. The house is furnished as it was in the 1830s and 1840s, when the Duke of Wellington was Warden, and contains a collection of memorabilia relating to him. Open T-F am and pm, Su pm only; closed when the Lord Warden is in residence. ⊖ P WC ♠

Wesley's House, 47 City Road, London EC1 (tel 01-253 2262). 1 m NE of St Paul's. TQ 3282 (OS 176). Late 18th-century town house, the home of John Wesley at the time of his death in 1791. It contains an extensive collection of objects and papers related to him. Next door is John Wesley's Chapel, opened in 1778 and restored in 1978. It houses a library on the history of Methodism. Wesley is buried in the graveyard. Open daily am and pm. ⊖ ♿

Winchester Castle, Winchester, Hampshire (tel Winchester [0962] 54411 ext 366). In city centre. SU 4729 (OS 185). A castle was built here by William the Conqueror and extended in the 13th century by Henry III; all that remains is the great hall of 1222-35. This contains clustered columns of Purbeck marble and the 'Round Table of King Arthur', probably dating from the 14th century. Open Apr to Sept daily am and pm (Su pm only); Oct to March M-F am and pm, S and Su pm only. ⊖ P ♿ ★

Yarmouth Castle, Yarmouth, Isle of Wight. In centre of Yarmouth. SZ 3589 (OS 196). One of Henry VIII's chain of castles built along the south coast, with repairs and additions made in the early 17th century. Open Apr to Sept daily am and pm. ⊖ P WC ⊟

Blickling Hall, Norfolk

Eastern Counties

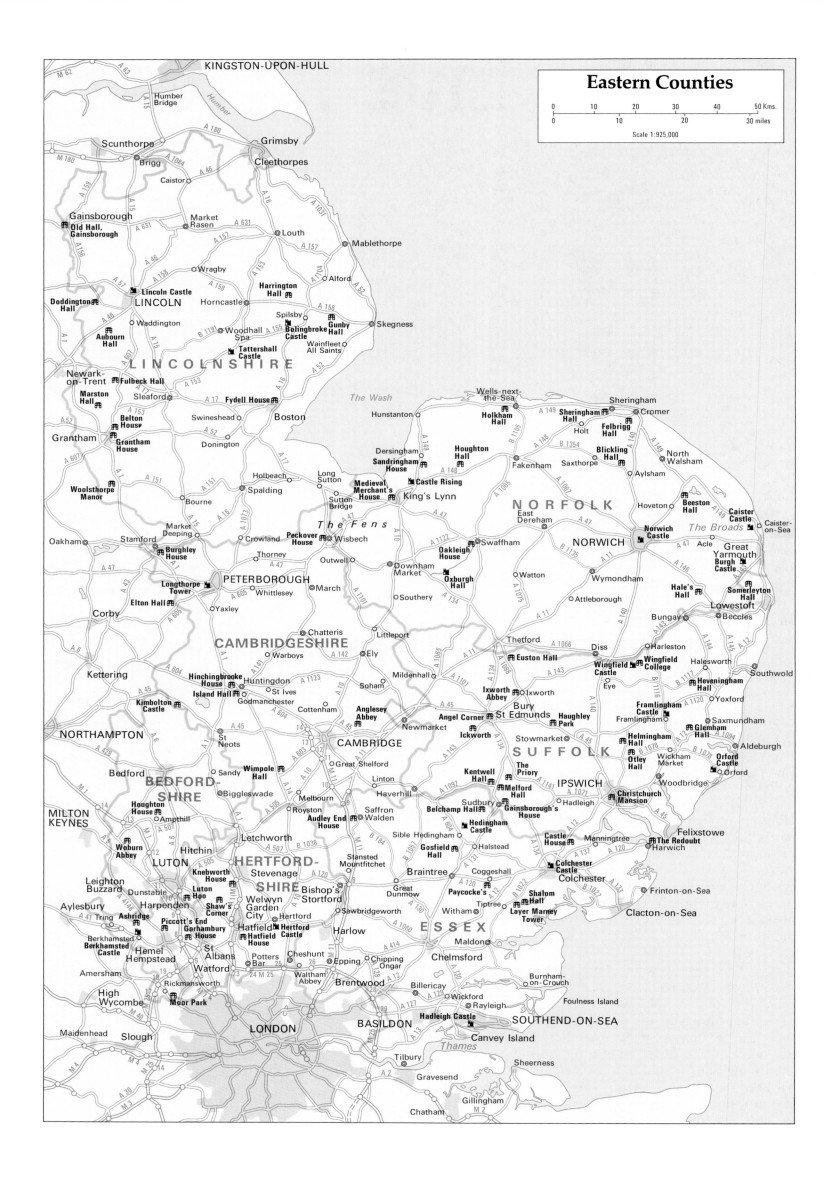

Audley End
Saffron Walden, Essex

Sir Thomas Audley, Lord Chancellor and a devoted servant of Henry VIII, was granted the Benedictine Abbey of Walden in Essex in 1538 and created Baron Audley of Walden in the same year. His new estate lay forty miles from London in the gentle valley where the river Cam flows north to Cambridge. Lord Audley adapted the abbey buildings for domestic use and gave the house his own name. No trace of the abbey buildings remains above ground but excavation has shown that the present house is built round three sides of the medieval cloisters.

After Lord Audley's death the estate passed to the Howard family and in 1572 to Thomas Howard, second son of the 4th Duke of Norfolk. In 1588 he was to distinguish himself in the running fight against the Armada and subsequently in the long war against Spain, becoming Baron Howard de Walden and later the 1st Earl of Suffolk. Between 1605 and 1614, in which year he was appointed Lord Treasurer to James I, he built a mansion at Audley End on the site of the old abbey buildings.

Four wings of brick and limestone, faced with hard chalk that would require much repairing and re-facing later, rose to three storeys round an inner court. The scale can be judged from the long gallery, about 240 feet in length, which occupied the whole first floor of the east wing. On the west side three longer ranges were then added to form a huge outer court with a separate kitchen block to the north and stables beyond the river. It was the largest building to be erected solely in the Jacobean period.

Top and detail above, the magnificent screen in the great hall of Audley End, a late example of the medieval screen, covered in decoration drawing freely on Classical imagery and carved by Italian craftsmen in about 1605.

The Earl had spent a fortune and in 1618 charges of embezzlement led to his resignation as Lord Treasurer and brought him a spell in the Tower of London. He was released on his promise to pay a large fine. He retired in disgrace to Audley End and died there in 1625, leaving to his successors an enormous house and enormous debts.

The debts continued to accumulate. In 1666 Charles II, attracted by a palace in all but name and situated conveniently close to Newmarket racecourse, purchased the estate from James Howard, the 3rd Earl. But Charles' successors did not use Audley End and in 1701 it was granted back to the Howards. For forty years they gradually reduced the house to a more manageable size. The north and south wings of the outer court were demolished, also the kitchen block. When the last Howard died without issue in 1745 the furnishings were sold and the remaining buildings seemed destined for destruction. They were saved by Elizabeth, Countess of Portsmouth, a great-granddaughter of the 3rd Earl of Suffolk and proud of her Howard ancestry. She purchased the estate and brought to the house furniture, pictures and books to form the nucleus of today's collections. The last vestiges of the outer court were cleared away and the east wing of the inner court demolished, much of the material being sold to help pay for renovations to the rest of the house. The truncated north and south wings were rounded off by single storey pavilions later raised to three storeys. By the 1780s the house had assumed its present size and three-block plan. It was a fragment of the 1st Earl's mansion yet still a very large building.

Lady Portsmouth's heir was her nephew, Sir John Griffin, 4th Lord Howard de Walden, created Lord Braybrooke in 1788. He employed Capability Brown to landscape the park and Robert Adam to reorganise and decorate the interior. A column in memory of Lady Portsmouth was set up in the park, a fine Palladian bridge built across the Cam and a cascade contrived. In 1786 Audley End was ready to receive George III but the intended visit was cancelled owing to the King's illness. Lord Braybrooke and his second wife also added significantly to the furnishings, pictures and library.

Lord Braybrooke's heir was a Neville, a great-nephew of Lady Portsmouth's first husband. He extended the park but made only minor alterations to the house. His son, the 3rd Lord Braybrooke, carried out the last substantial alterations. Both he and his wife, a Cornwallis, brought many possessions from their family homes to complete the collections at the house.

The west front is a fine example of the Jacobean style. Two ornate porches contrast with the simple lines of the rest of the façade. The ends of the north and south wings are of the original three storeys with tall windows and broad, rectangular bays. A parapet runs the whole length of the front only interrupted by turrets with cupolas and weather-vanes.

The visitor enters by the northern porch. To the right the Jacobean great hall was extensively restored by the 3rd Earl. The oak screen and most of the ceiling are Jacobean, the open stone screen at the south end early 18th-century, the rest mostly 19th-century.

At the top of the great stairs the attractive saloon combines Jacobean and late-18th-century features. Sea

monsters and ships decorate the ceiling panels, no doubt modelled to remind Thomas Howard of his days at sea. The frieze and wall panels were brought from the Jacobean long gallery when the east wing was pulled down. Adam turned the saloon into a breakfast room, raising the floor of the large bay window facing west so that people at table could see down to the river and beyond to his Temple of Victory on Ring Hill.

The important library on the first floor of the south wing was created by the 3rd Lord Braybrooke after the Adam library on the floor below was destroyed in 1825. The smaller south library adjoining contains portraits of the 1st Lord and his two wives by the American-born Benjamin West, who painted both ladies as sibyls of Classical legend to discourage comparisons. The room also contains a rare 16th-century walnut table that once belonged to Alexander Pope.

In the Second World War the house was requisitioned and used during 1942-44 for training the Polish section of Special Operations Executive. A memorial to those who did not return from their hazardous missions stands beside the drive south-west of the house.

The 7th Lord Braybrooke died in 1941 leaving two sons. Tragically the younger was killed on active service later in the year at the age of 21 and his brother, the 8th Lord, was killed in action in 1943 at the age of 25. The estate passed to his cousin, Henry Seymour Neville, who in 1948 sold the house, gardens and a hundred acres of park to the Ministry of Works. They are now looked after by the Historic Buildings and Monuments Commission. The family continues to live on the estate and to farm it.

☎ Cambridge (0223) 358911 ext 2245

1½ m W of Saffron Walden at Audley End

TL 5238 (OS 154)

Open Apr to Sept daily exc M (but inc Bank Hol M exc May Day) 1300-1830

♿ 🅿 WC ♿ (limited access) 🚼 D ♣ 🍽 ⛱ ◆ ❀ ⚘ Miniature railway

Above, the Palladian bridge, built by Robert Adam as a feature in the landscape design.

Opposite, Audley End remains impressive though now no more than a third of its original size.

Below, the 'Last Supper' window, designed by Biagio Rebecca in the chapel of Audley End, which was built in the 18th century in 'Gothick' style.

Burghley House

Stamford, Cambridgeshire

No provincial building commemorates the power and prosperity of Elizabethan England better than Burghley House. Three storeys of mullioned and transomed windows surround a courtyard and are surmounted by a single spire and many cupolas and tall, coupled chimneys. Clearly the Renaissance mansion incorporated Italian, French and Flemish features, but glimpsed now across the artificial lake or from the west across lawns the weathered stones express English qualities: restraint, endurance and firmly based aspirations. It serves as a fitting memorial to William Cecil (1520-98), chief minister to Elizabeth I for forty years.

The site was monastic, dating back to the 12th century. After the dissolution of the religious houses the Cecils purchased it. By 1589 the great house was completed and remained the seat of the senior branch of the family. William Cecil, despite all the demands of high office, seems to have been his own architect and attended to every detail of the construction. Created Lord Burghley in 1571, it is said that he subsequently refused the Queen's offer of an Earldom. However, after his death in 1598 the property passed to his eldest son, who was created Earl of Exeter in 1605.

John Cecil, the 5th Earl, was a lover of painting and architecture and especially of Italian art. He carried out a comprehensive reorganisation and decoration of the interior, in the latest style, between 1681 and 1700. From that time the Tudor exterior contained some of the finest Baroque rooms in England.

The state apartments on the first floor are vast and numerous; no wonder William III (r. 1689-1702) when he visited Burghley is reputed to have observed that the house was 'too large for a mere subject'. They are filled with fine furniture, pictures, tapestries, ceramics, carving. The painted ceilings and walls of many of the rooms are an outstanding feature. Most of these are by Antonio Verrio (d. 1707) whose portrait by Kneller hangs in the billiard room, but the walls of the painted stairs were the work of Stothard a hundred years later and the old ballroom was decorated by one of Verrio's assistants, Louis Laguerre (1663-1721). Alexander Pope satirised both these 17th-century artists:
On painted ceilings you devoutly stare,
Where sprawl the works of Verrio and Laguerre
but their styles were not the same. Laguerre did not paint the whirling, scantily clad figures that fascinated Verrio. His murals, telling the story of Antony and Cleopatra, seem formal and restrained in comparison to Verrio's. The figures are placed firmly on the ground in contrast to the flamboyant style of his master.

Verrio came to Burghley after covering acres of walls and ceilings at Windsor Castle and worked on the George Rooms in the south range. The 5th Earl found him intolerable. He demanded comfortable quarters for himself and his hangers-on and Italian food had to be imported specially for him. After ten years the Earl was glad to get rid of him.

Left, and above, Burghley House was one of the great Elizabethan prodigy houses, completed by the 1580s. Its exterior combines a unified plan and elevation with an exotic skyline. The house was enhanced by Capability Brown's gardens and lake.

A riot of naked gods and goddesses covers the ceiling of the state bedroom in Verrio's version of *Romulus Received on Olympus*. Mars, distinguished by a helmet and red cloak, presents his wolf-suckled son to Jupiter. Detached in space, the figures stand or sit or fly or fall. A gorgeous peacock has found its way to the home of the gods and is fondled by naked boys, the *putti* beloved of many Italian artists before Verrio. Queen Victoria and Prince Albert used the room on a visit in 1844 but it is not recorded what they thought of all those fleshy, voluptuous bodies.

The great dining room is panelled in Norwegian oak and the exuberance of Verrio's *Feast of the Gods* on the ceiling makes a dazzling contrast. The gods sit or sprawl at a long, cloud-borne table while Mercury swoops down on winged feet with a message and another splendid peacock poses among the clouds. Guards and servants surround the feasters, bare-thighed maidens fly in bearing garlands. From a painted balustrade spectators seem to avert their eyes from the orgy. It is all insubstantial and luxurious.

Those ceilings are preliminaries to the spectacle of the great saloon known as the 'heaven room'. Verrio covered not only the vast ceiling but the 24-foot high walls with an ambitious display of his skills as a decorative artist. The gods look down from the ceiling on a hall of painted columns among which Verrio's figures disport themselves. Theatrical effects abound: a bare-headed Verrio sits among the Cyclops while they fashion the armour of Achilles; a shaft of painted sunlight strikes polished shields; a horseman in a red cloak plunges down from the ceiling. Verrio's work at Burghley is considered his best, and the heaven room his masterpiece.

Three Cecils after the 5th Earl contributed to the fascination of Burghley, each in his own way. The 9th Earl carried out essential repairs to preserve the George rooms and commissioned Capability Brown to landscape the park, noted for its fine trees. The 10th Earl brought a touch of romance to the house. Ignoring his ancestor William Cecil's advice on choosing a wife – 'let her not be poor' – he married Sarah Hoggins, a village girl from Shropshire. Their romance and Sarah's early death inspired Tennyson's ballad 'The Earl of Burleigh':

> . . . *Three fair children first she bore him*
> *Then before her time she died.*
> *Weeping, weeping late and early,*
> *Walking up and pacing down,*
> *Deeply mourned the Lord of Burleigh,*
> *Burleigh House by Stamford-town.*

A fine portrait by Sir Thomas Lawrence of the Earl, Sarah and their daughter Sophia hangs in the billiard room. The Earl grieved sincerely for his wife. In 1801 he was raised to the dignity of Marquis and when he died three years later Sarah's son became the 2nd Marquis.

The 6th Marquis, who inherited in 1956, will always be best remembered by his previous title of Lord Burghley. In 1928 at the Amsterdam Olympics he won the 400 metres hurdles and four years later at Los Angeles a silver medal in the 400 metres relay. His Olympic medals and many other trophies of championships and races at home and abroad are displayed in the house. His devoted work for national and international athletics continued up to his death in 1981.

Top, the black and yellow bedchamber.

Opposite, the famous 'heaven room', the most spectacular of Verrio's decorative schemes.

Above, the kitchen at Burghley, complete with the bizarre animals that provided an essential inspiration for Victorian cookery!

☎ Stamford (0780) 52451

½ m S of Stamford, to E of A1, or on A43 turn onto B1081 and then E

TF 0406 (OS 141)

Open Apr to early Oct T, W, Th, S and Bank Hols 1100-1700; Good Fri and Su 1400-1700

♿ (limited) 🅿 WC 🚻 D (on lead) ♣ ● 🛤 ★
🔊 (available in foreign languages)

Hatfield House

Hatfield, Hertfordshire

At Hatfield in 1558 the twenty-five-year-old Princess Elizabeth Tudor received the news of the death of her half-sister, Queen Mary. When the messengers arrived from London she was reading under a tree in the Park; the stump of the tree is preserved in the present house. Elizabeth held her first Council of State in the great hall of old Hatfield Palace and here she appointed an able and experienced civil servant, William Cecil, to be her chief minister.

The Palace had been built about 1497 by the Bishop of Ely. A mansion of some splendour, to judge from the part that survives, it consisted of four blocks enclosing a courtyard, typical of the new age. When the possessions of the Church passed into Henry VIII's hands, to be distributed among the new nobility, the King retained Hatfield and used it mainly as a residence for his daughters Mary and Elizabeth.

The Palace remained in royal hands throughout Elizabeth's reign though it is doubtful if she spent much time there. William Cecil, created Lord Burghley, served Elizabeth loyally for forty years. After his death his second son, Robert, became chief minister to the ageing Queen, a task for which he had been groomed. In 1603 he presided over the smooth succession of James I and continued as chief minister. A few years later the King expressed a lack of interest in Hatfield and his preference for the estate which Robert Cecil had inherited from his father at Theobalds, near Waltham Cross. He proposed an exchange. The dutiful Robert, created Earl of Salisbury by the King, had little choice but to agree, whatever his private feelings may have been. The Act of Parliament granting Hatfield to him is preserved in the house.

In 1608 the Earl began to demolish three wings of the Tudor Palace and to build a new mansion. The surviving wing of the old Palace was used as stables for three centuries and was only restored to its former state fifty years ago. It is a remarkable 15th-century building, particularly the great hall where, beneath a splendid roof of oak and chestnut beams, 'Tudor banquets' are now held.

The site chosen for the new house was a little to the east and on slightly higher ground. Over the next five years rose the great mansion that stands today. Although a thoroughly Jacobean building, bricks from the Tudor palace were used and the E-shaped plan commemorated the Queen to whose trust and patronage the Cecil family owed much. Stone quoins and parapets, the large mullioned and transomed windows, serve to break up the mass of brickwork. A soaring white clocktower rises in three stages over the central block and the massed chimneys of the two wings. Unfortunately the visitor now enters by what was the back door and can only glimpse the main entrance and

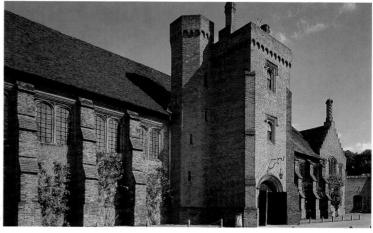

Left, the South façade at Hatfield, with its innovative Classical loggia, is dominated by the vast brick wings.

Above, the old Palace is a fine example of the brick architecture of the 15th century.

the noble south front from the west gardens or the park.

Robert did not live to enjoy his fine house, dying in 1612 as the work neared completion. But the junior branch of the Cecils has occupied Hatfield by direct descent to the present day. The 7th Earl was raised to the rank of Marquis in 1789.

Hatfield has at times been a political and social place of some importance but the power and eminence associated with the 1st Earl was not repeated until the 19th century. The 3rd Marquis, by coincidence another Robert and a second son, became a distinguished diplomat and politician, holding many high offices and serving three terms as Prime Minister. The political tradition was carried on by the 4th and 5th Marquises, the latter for a time a member of Churchill's War Cabinet.

The marble hall at Hatfield, occupying two floors, is comparable to the great hall of the old palace but the contrast is total. The black-and-white marble squares of the floor, which give the room its name; the wood and plaster ceiling and its broad coving; the Brussels tapestries above robust wainscoting; and the screened, wooden gallery – all these are unmistakably of the 17th century. They form the setting for the outstanding treasures of Hatfield, two portraits of Elizabeth I.

The *Ermine* portrait is by her court painter and miniaturist, Nicholas Hilliard. Sitting stiffly in a sumptuous dress, the Queen looks well aware of her heavy responsibilities and has the cool gaze of one able to fulfil them. The ermine standing on her sleeve, from which the picture is named, wears a gold crown for a collar and represents her purity.

The *Rainbow* portrait is attributed to Hilliard's pupil, Isaac Oliver. A magnificently clothed and jewelled Queen grasps a rainbow in her right hand, a symbol of peace. On her left sleeve a writhing serpent represents wisdom, a quality stressed by her self-assured and penetrating eyes. Her rich cloak is decorated with eyes and ears to indicate that she knows everything that is going on among her subjects. Both pictures are as confident and exquisite in detail as any portrait by an Italian master.

The grand staircase leading to the state apartments in the east wing is a masterpiece of Jacobean carving. The majestic stone flights of an Italian palace are here transformed into a smaller, English version in oak. Even the gates to prevent dogs going upstairs are a fretwork of fleurs-de-lis.

All great houses of the period boasted a long gallery where, in bad weather, the ladies could promenade without spoiling their elegant clothes. The one at Hatfield is a memorable example. It runs the whole length of the south front, connecting the state apartments in the two wings. Sixty yards in length, the windows looking out on what was the main approach to the house, it was meant to impress visitors and it still does.

In the long gallery a parchment roll is displayed tracing Elizabeth I's ancestors back to Adam, also her garden hat, a pair of gloves, and a pair of silk stockings. The library contains many of her letters. A picture on the grand staircase portrays the white horse she rode at Tilbury in 1588 when she spoke to the army mustered against the Armada. In the armoury in the closed-in arcade below the long gallery the main exhibits are accoutrements captured from Spanish soldiers who sailed with the Armada. They were presented to Lord Burghley as one of the architects of the victory.

Although actually built after the death of the Queen, the association with her inescapably permeates the whole house.

☎ Hatfield (30) 62055

21 m N of London on A1, opposite Hatfield BR station

TL 2308 (OS 166)

Open late Mar to mid Oct daily exc M and Good Fri but inc Bank Hol M

⊖ P WC ♿ 🚻 D ♣ 🍴 ⛩ ◆ ⚑ ♨ (available in foreign languages) ● (not in house) ⚔ (compulsory)

Above, the 17th-century gardens at Hatfield were stocked with many new plants brought to England by John Tradescant.

Below, the hall of the main house has a magnificent carved screen.

Opposite, the grand staircase, made of oak with lavishly ornamented newels, a classic example of the intricate and confident staircase design of the Jacobean era.

Holkham Hall
Wells, Norfolk

Opposite and right, Holkham Hall sits severe and somewhat daunting in the centre of a vast park, displaying a cold Palladian perfection. The house is built of a brick made on the estate itself of local materials. The north front is no less than 340 feet in length.

Below right, the column in the park erected to 'Coke of Norfolk' by his grateful tenants in 1845.

In 1712 a remarkable young man set out on the customary Grand Tour on the Continent. Thomas Coke's parents had died five years earlier leaving large estates, in Norfolk and elsewhere, which he would inherit on attaining his majority. Meanwhile he travelled and, drawn by a real interest in Classical literature and art, spent most of his time in Italy. He acquired many books, sculptures and other works of art, choosing them with exceptional judgement. In Italy he met Richard Boyle, 3rd Earl of Burlington (1694-1753), and his protégé William Kent (c. 1685-1748), landcape gardener, furniture designer and architect-to-be. These circumstances led in due course to the creation, amid an area of marsh and heathland on the West Norfolk coast, of Holkham Hall.

Influenced by Lord Burlington, the doyen of architectural taste at the time, Coke chose William Kent to prepare plans for a mansion in the Palladian or Neo-Classical style. He himself attended to every detail before approving the plans. Matthew Brettingham, a pupil of Kent, assisted and continued the work after Kent's death. The work began in 1734 and as it proceeded Coke's acquisitions were moved in and at last unpacked. He was created Earl of Leicester in 1744. Sadly he died before Holkham was finished and his widow pushed his life work through to completion.

The hall consisted of a central block and four wings built in yellowy-brown bricks made from local clay. It remains practically unaltered, one of the outstanding Neo-Classical buildings in England. The exterior is severe, the north aspect even forbidding, but approached from the south over the low hill where the obelisk stands, its grandeur matches the encircling park and the expanses of the North Sea beyond. The park extends to nearly 3000 acres and is surrounded by a stone wall nine miles long. Such is the scale of Holkham.

After Lady Leicester's death the estate (though not the title) passed to a nephew of the Earl, Wenham Roberts, who adopted the name of Coke. He was succeeded in 1776 by his son, Thomas William Coke (1752-1842). He was to become as famous as his renowned ancestor, Sir Edward Coke, the great 17th-century lawyer and defender of the Common Law, though in a very different field. Made Earl of Leicester of the second creation in 1837, he is known to history

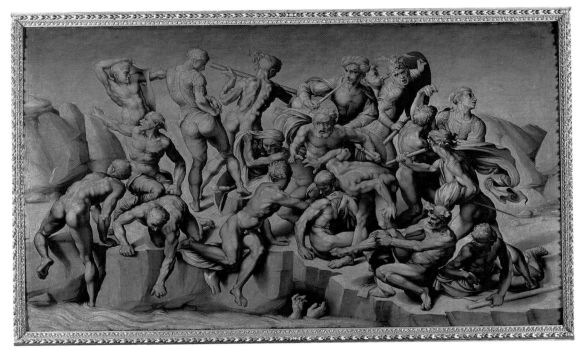

Left, the copy of Michelangelo's cartoon for the Battle of Cascina, *drawn by Bastiano di Sangallo.*

Opposite, the marble hall, based on a Roman temple, emulates the scale of the exterior but introduces a new opulence and complexity never hinted at in the façade.

simply as 'Coke of Norfolk', a paragon among land-owners and one of the greatest of agricultural innovators. He turned the land round Holkham from a sheep-walk into the rich arable of today and carried out extensive experiments with livestock. His annual 'Sheep-shearings' held in the Great Barn in the park were gatherings of hundreds of experts from all over Europe who came to see how land should be farmed and animals reared. By granting long leases with the provision that cultivation should be in accordance with his ideas, he made fortunes for many of his tenants. They contributed when a monument to him was put up in the park in 1845, two years after Nelson's column was erected in Trafalgar Square. Coke's column is surmounted by a wheatsheaf, not a statue; at the corners of the pedestal are not guardian lions but a plough and seed-drill, a Southdown sheep, a Devon ox, symbols of the improvements he made.

Not only farmers should be grateful to 'Coke of Norfolk'. While other landowners summoned Robert Adam to remodel their mansions or hankered after Gothick 'improvements', he left Holkham alone.

He died at the age of 88 in 1842, and the 2nd Earl added the north porch and built the orangery on the south-east side. He laid out the terraces and balustrades of the south front with the striking fountain of Perseus rescuing Andromeda from the sea-monster. He also reclaimed hundreds of acres from the sea and planted the belt of Corsican pines that stretches for four miles west of Wells to protect the reclaimed land. None of these improvements spoilt the original building.

All the Earls of Leicester down to the present have continued to cherish Holkham and to maintain high standards of agriculture and forestry. Partridge- and pheasant-shooting are traditional activities on the estate but the lake has been a 'nature reserve' for more than a hundred years, a safe wintering place for thousands of wild geese and ducks.

Inside the 19th-century porch and unassuming north door, the marble hall is rightly famous. It is Coke's and Kent's idea of a Roman temple set down in the English countryside but the design is so grand, the decoration so rich, that it is more like a vestibule to an emperor's palace. Under a magnificent ceiling that rises to the full height of the building, marble stairs lead to a peristyle of fluted Ionic columns of Derbyshire alabaster. Beyond it the saloon has another magnificent, complex ceiling and the walls are hung with their original Genoa velvet. Among the pictures are a restrained Rubens, *The Holy Family*, and Gainsborough's masterly portrait of *Coke of Norfolk* dressed in his country clothes, ramming a charge into his gun, his dogs around him. The furniture, as elsewhere in the house, was designed by Kent for the room. It is rare to find so many furnishings and decorations unaltered after two hundred years.

Strangely, Holkham's unique artistic possession is a mere copy on a reduced scale of a cartoon. When Michelangelo was invited to paint a large mural for the council chamber in the Palazzo Vecchio in Florence, he made a cartoon of an incident at the battle of Cascina. Soliders bathing in the Arno, surprised by the approach of the enemy, hurriedly scrambled to the bank to dress. The painting was never completed and Michelangelo's cartoon was destroyed. His design is best known from the cartoon at Holkham, a copy made from Michelangelo's own before its destruction.

In half a dozen rooms the pictures are mainly of Thomas Coke's collection. The statue gallery was built specifically for the busts and statues he brought back from Italy. The long library contains his famous collection of books. But though Thomas Coke remains the presiding genius of the Hall, the memory of 'Coke of Norfolk' pervades the surroundings. Livestock which he did much to improve graze on the reclaimed land, rich arable fields edge up to his wall round the park. His home farm and great barn are of no less historical significance than the Hall.

☎ Fakenham (0328) 710227

2 m W of Wells-next-the-Sea on A149 turn S at Holkham

TF 8842 (OS 132)

Open Jun to end Sept Su, M, Th also W in July and Aug 1330-1700; Bank Hols 1130-1700

⊖ (limited; 1 m walk) 🅿 WC
♿ (limited access) ⌂ D ♣ ☂
⛱ ◆ ⊞ ※ ● (not in house)

Anglesey Abbey

Lode, Cambridgeshire

The name of this house (formerly a priory of Augustinian canons, founded 1135) has nothing to do with the island of Anglesey, but comes from Angerhale, a fenland hamlet in the neighbourhood. The great attraction of the place lies not so much in the house – a comfortable residence built around the old priory chapter-house and day-room – as in the richness and variety of the art collection displayed within, and the generously laid out 20th-century park and gardens. A very rich owner, Huttleston Broughton, 1st Lord Fairhaven (1896-1966), was able to lavish a fortune on the collection and its setting. He built a library wing and a picture galleries block, adding a connecting bridge as late as 1955. To enjoy the furniture, *objets d'art*, paintings, engravings, tapestries and books and their extremely tasteful arrangement properly, visitors should allow themselves plenty of time and make use of the National Trust room-by-room guide. Lord Fairhaven's taste was catholic, ranging from the late Middle Ages to the 19th century, and cosmopolitan. A special interest of his was topographical views of Windsor Castle (the collection is now happy in the upper gallery). In the lower gallery are two paintings by Claude, and a selection from some twenty paintings by William Etty hang in the library corridor. The grounds are the other showpiece of Anglesey Abbey – an area of level fen entirely transformed with a breadth of conception that is almost unique in the 20th century.

☎ Cambridge (0223) 811200
4 m E of Cambridge on A1303 turn onto B1102 to Lode
TL 5362 (OS 154)

Open Apr S, Su and Easter M; end Apr to mid Oct W-Su and Bank Hol M 1400-1800

♿ ⓟ WC ♿ (limited access) ⏚ (W, Th and F, by appt) ♣ ⛟ ⛱ ★ ⚘ ● (by permit in house)

Ashridge

Berkhamsted, Hertfordshire

The history of Ashridge spans some 700 years, but the house owes its character to a major rebuilding between 1808 and 1814 by James Wyatt in the 'Gothick' style. After the Dissolution of the Monasteries, Ashridge passed to the Crown, and was one of the residences to which Henry VIII's children were frequently sent. Elizabeth I disposed of it in 1575, and in 1604 it was acquired by Thomas Egerton. He made many improvements to the old monastic building, and it was his descendant the 7th Earl of Bridgwater who carried out the 18th-century rebuilding. James Wyatt died before the work was completed, and it was finished by his nephew Sir Jeffry Wyattville. Another member of the Wyatt family, Matthew Digby Wyatt, remodelled all the interiors in the Italian style between 1855 and 1863. In the late 19th century Lady Brownlow, a talented hostess, turned the house into a setting worthy of her glittering hospitality, and royalty, distinguished politicians, artists and men of letters were entertained here. Ashridge was sold, under the terms of the 3rd Earl Brownlow's will, in 1923, and a large part of the enormous park was bought by the National Trust, though the pleasure gardens, designed by Humphry Repton, still belong to the house. Only the library is still used for its original purpose, but the opulent decorations throughout are unchanged. The showpiece of the 19th-century work is the conference room with its marble fireplaces and pillars and painted ceiling, while the lovely chapel is an outstanding example of Wyatt's romantic style.

☎ Little Gaddesden (044284) 3491
5 m N of Berkhamsted on B4506, turn E to Ashridge Park
SP 9912 (OS 165)

Open few weekends during summer, phone for detailed information

ⓟ WC ⏚ (by appt only) D ♣ ⚘

Belton House

near Grantham, Lincolnshire

This house of 1684-88 arouses little gasps of pleasure from architectural writers, and really does deserve its label as a 'perfect house from the age of Wren'. Relatively little altered from the time when it was built at the turn of the reigns of Charles II and James II, its sombre panelled and carved interiors and formal garden layout preserve the feeling of that period. The Brownlow family have lived on this site since about 1640, and the present Lord Brownlow lives in part of the house still. Some changes were made by James Wyatt and Sir Jeffry Wyattville for successive owners, but the overall impression of a home of a wealthy gentleman of late Stuart England remains intact. The paintings – many of them hung on panels framed by carved swags of high craftsmanship in the style of Grinling Gibbons – are in keeping with the original period. A family chapel of no mean size is part of the house, and it contains a richly decorated reredos which would not look out of place in St Paul's Cathedral. The main floor of the chapel is fitted with contemporary pews for the servants and grooms, while an upper gallery, garlanded with carved fruit and flowers, accommodated the owner's family on armchairs.

☎ Grantham (0476) 66116
3½ m N of Grantham on A607 turn E
SK 9239 (OS 130)

Open Apr to end Oct W-Su and Bank Hol M 1400-1800; parties at other times by appt

♿ (1 m walk) ⓟ ♿ ⏚ (by appt only)
D ♣ ⛟ ◆ ⚜ ⚘ ⚔

Blickling Hall

Blickling, Norwich, Norfolk

The Cecils' Hatfield House spawned Blickling: Robert Lyminge built both, and both buildings were status symbols of new men of the Jacobean age – one the Lord Treasurer, Robert Cecil, 1st Earl of Salisbury, the other the Lord Chief Justice, Sir Henry Hobart. Blickling was built between 1616 and 1625, and the entrance front, with its flanking, gabled outbuildings, is still as it was when finished in that year – a perfectly preserved forecourt of the early Stuart period. The other side of the house was rebuilt in the 1770s but as a scheme that harmonised with the features of the earlier parts (unusual for that time of sweeping 'modernisation' in the Palladian mood), and by using the same red brick established continuity on all four fronts of the building. Changes were made at the same time indoors, but much of Robert Lyminge's work survives – in particular the 120-foot-long gallery with its original plasterwork ceiling of allegories and armorials. The main staircase was moved to a different position and enlarged into a double-flight, but the original material was re-used for much of it, and some extra figures were carved to make up the full number needed – one of the intriguing features of Lyminge's staircase having been these soldiers and other characters standing on the newel-posts. The later work was done for the 2nd Earl of Buckinghamshire, who had brought back from serving as ambassador at St Petersburg a large tapestry of Tsar Peter the Great at the Battle of Poltava, for which hanging space on a wall of appropriate size was to be provided.

☎ Aylsham (0263) 733084
15 m N of Norwich on A140 continue onto B1354 for 3 m
TG 1728 (OS 133)

Phone for information on opening hours; reduced rates for parties of 15 or over by appt

🄵 WC 🗗 🖫 D ♣
🍺 ⋔ ◆ ⚘

Caister Castle

Caister-on-Sea, Norfolk

Caister is a spectacular ruin, with a single round tower rising some 90 foot above the River Bure and an accompanying stair turret almost 100 foot high. The builder was Sir John Fastolf, who is known to have been the original of Shakespeare's fat, comically cowardly knight, Sir John Falstaff. In reality Fastolf was a tough character who made his fortune in the French wars and built Caister out of the proceeds. It was one of the earliest English brick castles, built between 1432 and 1435, and was even more unusual in being defended by an elaborate system of moats; as a travelled man, Fastolf may have been influenced by the contemporary German *Wasserburg* (water-castle). The main castle at Caister consisted of a rectangular building round a courtyard; it had gatehouses in the east and west walls, and the tall, slender tower in the west corner. There was a forecourt to the east of the main block; its equivalent on the west side, which had access to a canal linked to the Bure, has been replaced by later buildings. In 1469 the Duke of Norfolk claimed Caister and successfully laid siege to it – supported (according to the Pastons) by 3000 men against their 30. The Pastons later regained Caister and lived there until 1599. It is now mainly ruinous, but it is still possible to climb the great tower, and the hall has been converted into a well-known motor museum.

☎ Wymondham (057 284) 251
2 m W of Caister-on-Sea on A1064, turn S
TG 5112 (OS 134)

Open throughout year; M-S Mar to Oct 0930-1830, Su 1400-1830; Oct to Mar 0930-1600, Su 1400-1600

⊖ 🗗 🖫 D ♣ ⚘

Castle Rising

Castle Rising, Norfolk

Castle Rising stands in a large area of grassy banks and ditches which form an unusually well-preserved example of Norman earthwork fortifications. The huge keep in the centre, which rivals Norwich in size and splendour, was built about 1138 by William de Albini, Earl of Lincoln, who had in the same year married Queen Alice, the widow of Henry I. The magnificent rooms in the keep proudly proclaimed to the world the owner's new wealth and position, and are impressive even in ruins (roof and floors have gone); and the forebuilding, which rises almost as high as the tower and has survived more or less complete, has a very fine staircase and the remains of decorative interlacing arches. The tower itself is rectangular and squat, with horizontal dimensions greater than its height. It is 50 feet high, though it would originally have been several feet higher with its parapet and the roofs to the corner turrets, and its length and width are approximately 78 by 68 feet. The other castle buildings are the remains of a Norman church built before the keep, and a Norman gatehouse built at about the same time, a rectangular tower with a room above the entrance passage. For some years Castle Rising was the home of Edward III's mother Isabella, who in collusion with her lover Roger Mortimer had caused the murder of Edward II in 1327 and virtually ruled England. Edward III seized power in 1330, Mortimer was executed and Isabella forced into 'retirement'.

5½ m NE of King's Lynn on A149 turn W
TF 6624 (OS 132)

Open daily throughout year; Mar to Oct 0930-1830 Oct to Mar 0930-1600 (Su 1400-1600)

⊖ (limited) WC 🗗 (limited access) 🖫 D ♣ 🍺 ⚘

Christchurch Mansion

Soane St, Ipswich, Suffolk

This delightful red-brick Elizabethan house, now a museum, was built on the site of an Augustinian priory in 1548 for Edmund Withipoll, a successful merchant with cultural leanings. The original plan was the usual Tudor E-shape, and the diamond pattern of burnt blue bricks is a feature of several East Anglian houses. Additions were made to the west wing before 1600, and a fire in the 17th century necessitated further improvements. The dormers with Dutch gables in the attic storey date from this period, and the hall was repanelled in the later Stuart style. Christchurch has been lived in by three successive families. Edmund Withipoll's granddaughter married Colonel Leicester Devereux, and the house passed into his family in 1645. Nearly a century later it was sold to Claude Fonnereau, whose family lived here until 1894. Demolition was threatened, but Felix Cobbold, a banker, bought it and presented it to Ipswich Corporation. It has been a museum since 1896, entirely due to his generosity and foresight. From 1929 new galleries were built attached to the main building, including the Wolsey Art Gallery, where the best of the Ipswich Museum's art collections are shown. The Wingfield Room, with panelling from the town house of the Wingfield family, and the two Tudor rooms, have been entirely reconstructed from local timber-framed houses. The other rooms are furnished in a variety of period styles, and contain a fascinating and diverse collection of furniture and fittings from Tudor times to the 19th century.

☎ Ipswich (0473) 53246

In Christchurch Park, in centre of Ipswich

TM 1645 (OS 169)

Open daily throughout year exc some Bank Hols 1000-1700 (dusk if earlier)

♿ 🅿 (by appt) ♣ ★ ◆ ⚘
✗ (in foreign languages by appt) ⚕

Elton Hall

Elton, near Peterborough, Cambridgeshire

Elton Hall is a large house, built in a mixture of architectural styles which are best seen in the south, or garden front. This incorporates the oldest part of the building, the 15th-century tower and chapel built by the Sapcotes. This family lived here until 1600, and the tower bears their coat-of-arms. The Proby family, who own the house today, acquired it in the 17th century and Sir Thomas Proby built a relatively modest new dwelling, adding the north wing. The next major building campaign was in the period 1780-1815, when the gatehouse was joined to the house by a two-storey block, and the west front stuccoed and given a castellated Gothic look. Much of this work, however, was undone by the architect Henry Ashton who removed the Gothic parts of the west front, though he left them on the south front which still has a picturesque pseudo-medieval look. Finally, in the 1870s the 4th Earl of Carysfort built the central tower, a billiards room and new kitchen. The entrance hall has fine 17th-century panelling which may originally have come from the old Antwerp Town Hall; the marble hall and main staircase, designed by Ashton, are in the mid-Victorian 18th-century revival style; the chapel has 15th-century fan vaulting from the old chapel. The upper octagon room is a fine example of the Strawberry Hill 'Gothick' style, and the drawing room has an 18th-century ceiling. The library contains an exceptional collection of early bibles and prayer books, and there are some excellent paintings by Constable, Hobbema, Millais and Alma-Tadema.

☎ Elton (08324) 223

10 m SW of Peterborough on A605

TL 0892 (OS 142)

Open May to July: W; Aug: W and Su; May and Aug Bank Hol weekends 1400-1700

♿ 🅿 WC 🅿 ♣ 🍴 ⌂ ⚘ ✗ (compulsory exc Bank Hol weekends) ● (not in house)

Framlingham Castle

Framlingham, Suffolk

The great curtain walls of this late 12th-century castle, all that remains, present a fine sight. The castle was built by Roger Bigod, 2nd Earl of Norfolk, on the site of his father's castle. It was built without a keep, its defences being a series of towers and a gatehouse linked by a ring of walls, approached by a drawbridge over a moat (the present bridge is 16th century). The Bigod family were rebels against royal authority and, although the castle was besieged and taken by King John in 1216, they were not finally crushed until the reign of Edward I, when their estates were received by the Crown and the castle became the seat of the Mowbrays, followed by the Howards, the new Earls of Norfolk. From time to time it was forfeit to the Crown, and on one such occasion (1553) Princess Mary was staying here when the Earl of Arundel arrived to tell her she had become Queen of England. The Earls of Norfolk made little use of Framlingham as they had more appealing properties elsewhere, and it played no part in the Civil War. The demolition of the domestic buildings which once stood inside the walls was due to other and more peaceful causes. In 1636 it was bequeathed to Pembroke College, Oxford, with the proviso that a poorhouse was built here, and 'all the Castle, saving the stone building, be pulled down'. The poorhouse still stands, the south wing, dated 1636, being the home of the curator, while the rest is empty. The ground floor is open to the public, and there is a wall-walk round the castle walls.

☎ Framlingham (0728) 723330

In centre of Framlingham off B1077 in Christchurch Park

TM 2863 (OS 156)

Open daily throughout year; Mar to Oct 0930-1830, Oct to Mar 0930-1600 (Su 1400-1600)

♿ 🅿 WC 🅿 (limited access) 🅿 D ♣ ⚘

Gainsborough's House

Sudbury, Suffolk

In 1723 John Gainsborough, the father of the painter Thomas Gainsborough (1727-88), bought two small, old-fashioned houses and united them, adding an elegant Georgian façade. The house remained in the Gainsborough family for many years, and only underwent one major alteration, in the 1790s, when the whole of the back of the house was remodelled in the 'Gothick' style. It was bought by the Gainsborough House Society in 1958, after having been a hotel for some considerable time, and it was opened to the public as a museum in 1961, restored as far as possible to its appearance of 150 years ago. By 1971 it had become established with a good permanent loan collection of Gainsborough's paintings, 18th-century furniture and some of the artist's personal possessions, but the rooms are also interesting in themselves, as they show clearly the different periods of architecture and decoration. The entrance room, part of the 15th-century house, has some of its original timbering, though the fireplace and alcove date from about 1600. The parlour is 16th century with fittings of this date, and here there are drawings and watercolours by Constable as well as three of Gainsborough's Bath portraits. The bedroom, like the entrance room, is part of the Tudor house, and a panel of wattle-and-daub has been exposed to show the construction. The room contains a fine 18th-century tallboy and portraits of three of the artist's contemporaries. The exhibition rooms, at the back of the house are used for temporary exhibitions of work by modern artists.

☎ Sudbury (0787) 72958
In Gainsborough St, in centre of Sudbury
TL 8741 (OS 155)

Open Easter to end Sept Tu to S 1000-1700, Su 1400-1700. Oct to Easter closes 1600; closed Good Fri and 24 Dec to 1 Jan
⊖ WC ⊟ (by appt) ♿ ☀ ● (not in house)

Gorhambury

near St Albans, Hertfordshire

This large Palladian villa built for the Viscount Grimston in 1777-84 by Robert Taylor has recently been refaced in Portland stone. Gorhambury, a former property of St Alban's Abbey, was bought by Sir Nicholas Bacon in 1561, and the ruins of the house he built here can still be seen in the park. It passed to his younger son, the famous Sir Francis Bacon, and the library of the present house contains many of his books. Bacon had no heirs, and the old house was bought by Sir Harbottle Grimston in 1652. The architect of the new house is best known for his relatively small villas, but at Gorhambury everything is very large; a massive stair leading to a vast portico and then to the great cube of the hall. Here two stained-glass windows of about 1620 showing plants and exotic scenes give an idea of the decoration of the old house. There is also an extremely fine carpet of 1570, and the walls are hung with portraits of 17th-century figures. In the dining room there are portraits of Sir Francis Bacon and Sir Harbottle Grimston, and the ballroom contains several lovely portraits and still-lifes by Sir Nathaniel Bacon, nephew of Sir Francis. In the yellow drawing room, where everything is 18th century, there is a portrait by Reynolds, and a fine chimneypiece designed by Piranesi and bought in Rome. The library contains three mid-16th-century heads in painted terracotta of Sir Nicholas Bacon, his wife and son. Also in the library are photocopies of some of the earliest printed editions of Shakespeare's plays, which were found here and are now in the Bodleian Library, Oxford.

☎ St Albans (0727) 54051
In W outskirts of St Albans on the A414 turn NW to Gorhambury
TL 1107 (OS 166)

Open May to Sept Th 1400-1700; reduced rates for parties by appt
⊖ P ⊟ (by appt) ☀ (compulsory)

Harrington Hall

Spilsby, Lincolnshire

A charming 17th-century house, long and well proportioned, built in a lovely mellow pinkish brick. In the 14th century the manor belonged to the Coppeldykes, who rebuilt the medieval house in 1535; the Elizabethan porch of the present house is a survival from this period. In 1673 the Tudor house was bought by Vincent Amcott, who entirely rebuilt the main part of it, leaving only the porch tower with its curious pilasters dating from about 1660. He also inserted most of the panelling. Despite its length it is, rather surprisingly, only one room thick, and only the ground-floor rooms are shown to visitors. The hall is part of the Tudor building, but was remodelled in the 1720s, the low, wide, elliptical arch taking the place of the former screen. The fine Doric panelling was also brought in at this time, and there is a William and Mary clock made by John Blundell in a lovely inlaid case. The oak staircase, carved with hops and wheat-ears, is also of the 1720s, but was rebuilt in 1951 owing to dry rot; fortunately the carving was not harmed. Most of the rooms are panelled, with the drawing-room panelling, put in before 1700, being the oldest. This room also contains the best furniture – some fine mainly 18th-century pieces – though there is good furniture in the other rooms too. The panelling in the dining room is 18th century, and has recently been painted Indian red. The delightful semi-formal walled garden is believed to be the original of Maud's garden in Tennyson's poem. The poet lived nearby and was in love with Rosa Baring of Harrington Hall.

☎ Spilsby (0790) 52281
8 m E of Horncastle on A158 turn N after Hagworthingham
TF 3671 (OS 122)

Open Easter tu end Sept Th and some Su 1200-2000 (dusk if earlier); other times by appt
P WC ♿ ⊟ (by appt) D ♣ ☕ (limited opening) ⊼ ◆ ❀ ☀

☎ Halstead (0787) 6084/60261

3½ m N of Halstead turn NE onto B1058 and N at Castle Hedingham

TL 7835 (OS 155)

Open Easter weekend and May to end Oct daily 1000-1700; parties throughout year by appt

🅿 WC 🍴 ♣ 🍽 🎪 ◆ ≈ 𝑘

Hedingham Castle

Castle Hedingham, near Halstead, Essex

Hedingham Castle was built by Aubrey de Vere, 1st Earl of Oxford, in about 1140, and the magnificent and well-preserved keep is a monument to his once-illustrious family. It stands alone in the grassy enclosure which was the inner bailey, once also containing the hall, chapel and other principal castle buildings; the original outer bailey is now occupied by a red-brick Queen Anne house (not open to the public). The stone great tower still has all its exterior walls, though two of its corner towers are gone. Access is at first-floor level via a flight of steps and a forebuilding, of which only the lower walls remain. A fine doorway with Norman chevron ornamentation leads into the single room which fills the whole of the first floor, with walls some 12 feet thick. A spiral staircase leads to the second-floor banqueting hall, the most splendid room in the keep, with a timbered ceiling supported by a great central arch 28 feet wide. The smaller arches and the windows are richly decorated with chevron moulding in different patterns. This room would have been used for entertaining, giving audience and so on, and 12 feet above floor level a gallery runs right round the room, tunnelled within the thickness of the walls and with its own set of windows, where minstrels or troubadours played during a banquet. The lovely Tudor bridge spanning the dry moat on the castle's eastern approach was built in 1496 and is the only survivor of several buildings put up by the 13th Earl of Oxford, an important supporter of the Lancastrians and Tudors in the Wars of the Roses.

☎ Ubbeston (098 683) 355

5 m SW of Halesworth on B117

TM 3573 (OS 156)

Open Aug only; telephone for details

🅿 WC 🍴 ♣ 🍽 🎪 ◆ ≈ 𝑘 ● (not in house)

Heveningham Hall

Stowmarket, Suffolk

Sir Gerald Vanneck inherited the estate in 1777 and immediately decided to demolish the existing small 18th-century house and build a grand mansion. His architect for this extremely fine Palladian house, one of the best in the country, was Sir Robert Taylor, who had started his career as a sculptor. The house consists of a central block with pillars, rising from an arcaded basement and with wings on each side, also pillared. The park, with its fine lake, was laid out by Capability Brown in 1780. Heveningham's greatest glory is its interior, by James Wyatt. Taylor had begun his designs for the interior before the building was finished, so he cannot have been pleased to hear that a much younger man was to be entrusted with the whole of the interior (Wyatt was then thirty-four and Taylor sixty-six). But whatever ill-feeling there may have been, the rooms, all in Wyatt's own version of the Adam style, lighter and airier than Adam's, are a triumph, and he cleverly transformed the empty, box-like rooms into gentle, curving spaces by means of apses, semi-domes, niches and coves. The hall at Heveningham is one of the most beautiful rooms in England, pale blue, with a screen of golden-yellow *scagliola* (imitation marble) columns at either end, a vaulted ceiling with white plaster roundels and a patterned marble floor. The other rooms are scarcely less fine, and the saloon has painted decoration by Biagio Rebecca. The interior is perfectly preserved, and the entrance hall, Etruscan room and library still have their original furnishings.

☎ East Rudham (048522) 569

16 m NE of King's Lynn on A148 turn N at Harpley

TF 7928 (OS 132)

Open Easter Su to end Sept Su, Th, Bank Hols 1230-1730; reduced rates for parties

♿ (1 m walk) 🅿 WC 🚼 🍴 (by appt)
D ♣ 🍽 ◆ ≈ 𝑘

Houghton Hall

Houghton, King's Lynn, Norfolk

Houghton Hall, one of the most splendid Palladian houses in Britain, was built by Sir Robert Walpole on the site of a Jacobean house, and completed in 1735. The original designs were prepared by Colen Campbell in 1721 but revised by Thomas Ripley, who added the four domes, and chose the attractive and hard-wearing Aislaby sandstone, which was brought by sea from Whitby. For the interior Walpole engaged a third architect, William Kent, which proved a masterstroke as he was responsible for everything – the marble fireplaces, the carved woodwork, most of the murals and a large part of the furniture. The state rooms are on the first floor, up the great mahogany staircase lined with mural paintings by Kent. The centrepiece of the state rooms is the 'stone hall', a perfect 40-foot cube in which all the decoration is on the grandest possible scale. The lovely carved ceiling frieze is by Atari; the reliefs over the fireplace and door are by Rysbrack; the chairs were made for the house (the green velvet upholstery is original); there is a 16th-century Persian carpet and an Aubusson of the Louis XV period. The other state rooms are equally splendid: the cabinet room has 18th-century Chinese hand-painted wallpaper; the tapestry drawing room was designed around a set of Mortlake tapestries depicting the Stuart kings and queens; the green velvet bedchamber has a state bed designed by Kent. The most sumptuous room of all is the saloon, with its luxurious furniture, walls covered in crimson Genoa silk velvet, and its carved and gilded ceiling.

Ickworth

Horringer, Bury St Edmunds, Suffolk

The extraordinary building, modelled on an earlier circular house, Belle Isle on Lake Windermere, was the creation of the enormously rich traveller and art collector Frederick Hervey, Bishop of Derry and 4th Earl of Bristol. Sadly he did not live to see his masterpiece; begun in 1795, it was not completed until 1830. The Earl-Bishop died in Italy in 1803 when the house was only half built. The original design was by an Italian architect, Mario Asprucci, but the work was carried out by the Sandys brothers, Francis and the Rev. Joseph. Ickworth is a huge house, with the great central domed rotunda linked to the two wings by long, curving passages intended as art galleries. When the Earl-Bishop died, his son, who became the 1st Marquess of Bristol, wanted to demolish it as it was so impractical, but in the end he completed it, reversing the original scheme so that the east wing became the living quarters and the great rotunda rooms were used for art displays and receptions. The last major alterations were made in the 1900s, when Reginald Blomfield was employed to remodel the east wing and make improvements to the rotunda, and the interior of the ground floor, with three vast reception rooms grouped round a top-lit staircase-well, owes its appearance to his alterations. The rooms contain good 18th-century furniture acquired by the 1st Marquess and a few of the Earl-Bishop's own treasures, including John Flaxman's sculpture *Fury of Athemas* in the hall. The Pompeian Room, decorated by J. D. Crace in 1879, contains the original architect's model of the house.

☎ Horringer (028 488) 270
2½ m SW of Bury St Edmunds on A143 at Horringer
TL 8161 (OS 155)

Open Apr to end Aug daily exc M; Sept to mid-Oct, daily exc M and F, also Bank Hol M 1400-1800

🅿 WC ♿ ⊟ (by appt) D ♥ ♥ ⊓ ◆ 🕮 ⚹ ⚐ ⚘

Island Hall

Godmanchester, Cambridgeshire

Looking at this stylish 18th-century mansion today it is hard to believe that in the late 1970s its owner could stand in the cellar and see daylight through the roof. The house was the home of the Baumgartner family (they later changed their name to Percy) from 1810 until 1943. Then it was requisitioned by the RAF, and later became the property of the local council and was converted into flatlets. It was allowed to become derelict, and then in 1977 a fire destroyed the south wing. The house seemed doomed, but amazingly many of the furnishings, including lovely carved fireplaces, survived intact, and when Simon Herrtage and his mother bought it in 1978 they were able to restore it to its 18th-century design. In 1983, their work complete, they put the house on the market, and it was reclaimed for the family by Christopher Vane Percy and his wife, who are continuing the work of restoration and refurnishing. The house had been built in 1750 by a gentleman with the unusual name of Original Jackson as a twenty-first birthday present for his son. The architect is not recorded, but the symmetry of the house suggests a professional hand, as do the well-balanced interiors, particularly the staircase hall with its soaring fluted columns. The muniments room, to the right of the entrance, has a collection of early photographs of the house and two family trees, both drawn up by ancestors of the owner, but one rather more truthful than the other.

1 m SE of Huntingdon on A604 at Godmanchester
TL 2470 (OS 153)

Open June to end Sept: Su, T and Th also May and Aug Bank Hol weekends 1430-1730

⊖ 🅿 WC ⊟ ♥ ♥ ⚹ ⚐ occasional concerts

Knebworth House

Knebworth, Hertfordshire

The theatrically romantic exterior of Knebworth House, with its turrets and pinnacles and its gargoyles silhouetted against the sky, was the creation of the Victorian novelist Edward Bulwer-Lytton, 1st Lord Lytton. But the 19th-century decoration conceals a house dating back to Tudor times. Sir Robert Lytton began building at the end of the 15th century, and successive generations added, subtracted, altered and redecorated. The visitor enters on the west side, the only remaining Tudor wing, into an entrance hall given its present form in the early part of this century by Sir Edwin Lutyens. The banqueting hall, the great hall of the Tudor building, ranks as one of the most beautiful rooms in England. It is now entirely 17th century, the oak decoration of the ceiling hiding the Tudor open-timber roof. Sir Rowland Lytton's great oak screen is a perfect example of the native Jacobean style, while the other walls show Classical influences from Italy. The library was Bulwer-Lytton's and his novels still fill the shelves. The mid-19th-century Jacobean-style staircase leads to his study. The state drawing room, originally the presence chamber leading to the long gallery (now demolished) is a superb example of Victorian High Gothic decoration, the work of John Crace. The Gothic furniture is similar to that which Crace made for Pugin; walls and ceiling are painted with heraldry, and the window contains a stained-glass portrait of Henry VII.

☎ Stevenage (0438) 812661
3½ m S of Stevenage on B197 turn W at Knebworth for Old Knebworth
TL 2320 (OS 166)

Open Apr and May Su, Bank and school hols; late May to mid Sept daily exc M 1200-1700

⊖ 🅿 WC ♿ (limited access) ⊟ D ♥ ♥ ⊓ ◆ ⚹ ⚐ (compulsory T-F) ● ⚘

Layer Marney Tower

Colchester, Essex

No one could forget the first sight of the enormous Tudor gatehouse at Layer Marney; it is quite simply astonishing. Although there are several such gatehouses in East Anglia, none other is on this scale. It was begun in 1520 by Henry Marney, who rose to wealth under Henry VIII, but he died in 1523 and his son two years later, so the huge, ambitious, Renaissance brick house of which the tower is the gatehouse was never completed. There is an east and a west wing, and an isolated south range, but no courtyard. The gatehouse itself is three storeys high, and the pairs of towers flanking the central part, with their seven tiers of windows, rise clear above the roofline and finish in terracotta crests. Visitors are admitted inside the tower, but not into the adjoining wing, where the present owners live. On the second floor there are some interesting documents relating to the house and its former occupants, and here the windows are of terracotta with winged cherubs' heads at the apex. Continuing up the west staircase, the visitor can ascend to the roof, where decorations on top of the tower can be viewed clearly. On one side of the garden is a long brick range which was originally stables, but has now been converted into a long gallery. This can be visited, as can the parish church, containing Marney tombs, on the other side of the garden.

☎ Colchester (0206) 330202
7 m SW of Colchester on B1022 turn S to Layer Marney
TL 9217 (OS 168)

Open Apr to end Sept Su and Th, also July and Aug T 1400-1800; Bank Hol M 1100-1800
🅿 WC ♿ 🍴 (by appt) ◆

Luton Hoo

Park St, Luton, Bedfordshire

Luton Hoo is a museum first and a country house second. The house has many virtues, but only a true architectural gem could rival the marvellous collection of works of art within. The house as it is today dates from 1903, although there had been a house at Luton Hoo for 700 years before this. In the 1760s Robert Adam was employed by the Earl of Bute to rebuild the existing house, and further alterations were made by Robert Smirke in about 1800. The large park was landscaped by Capability Brown. However, very little of the architecture of this period survives, as the house was gutted by fire in 1843. Sir Julius Wernher, South African diamond magnate, bought it in 1903, and employed the firm of Mewès and Davies, architects of London's Ritz Hotel, to remodel it and give it a new roof. They were responsible for its splendid Edwardian appearance: the fine white marble staircase gives an idea of the quality of their work, but their *pièce de résistance* is the dining room, with its polychrome marble and opulent gilded cornice framing the superb Beauvais tapestries. Half the house is now the family's private residence, while the rest houses the art collections. There are fine pieces of furniture, French tapestries and important paintings, including a late work by Altdorfer, but the real stars are the objects. The ivories, enamels, Renaissance bronzes and jewellery cannot be equalled by any other private collection. One of the most fascinating is a display of Imperial Russian objects, including several by Fabergé.

☎ Luton [0582] 22955
3 m SE of Luton on A6129 turn S to Luton Hoo Park
TL 1018 (OS 166)

Open Apr to Mid Oct: M, W, Th, S and Good Fri 1100-1745; Su 1400-1745
♿ 🅿 WC ♿ 🍴 ♣ 🍴 ㍿
★ ❀ ● (not in house)

Moor Park

Moor Park Golf Club, Rickmansworth, Hertfordshire

The splendid 18th-century mansion of Moor Park is now a golf club, but the house is still open to the public. In the 1680s a brick house was built for the Duke of Monmouth, which was much admired by contemporaries, but in the 1720s it was completely restyled by Benjamin Styles. The painter Sir James Thornhill apparently had a hand in the design until he quarrelled with Styles, but the principal architect was Giacomo Leoni, who was responsible for the magnificent Corinthian portico on the west front. The huge and perfectly proportioned entrance hall has a painted and gilded ceiling with a painted dome in imitation of that in St Peter's, Rome, and is the work of Thornhill, while the wall paintings of mythological subjects were done by the Italian artist Amiconi. The elaborate plaster decoration is probably also of Italian workmanship, and the staircase leading to the gallery is decorated with more mythological paintings by Sleker. The lounge at the back of the house is known as the Thornhill room because its superb painted ceiling was believed to have been done by Thornhill, but some experts now think it was painted by Verrio, in which case it must have formed part of the decorations of the older house, since Verrio returned to Italy in 1707. The room also has two carved fireplaces and fine panelling, both pre-Georgian, and the dining room has a coffered ceiling with painted decoration by Cipriani, part of a programme of 'beautification' carried out by Sir Lawrence Dundas, who bought the property in 1763.

☎ Rickmansworth (0923) 776611
2 m SE of Rickmansworth on A404 turn NE to Moor Park
SU 0793 (OS 176)

Open throughout year M-F 1000-1600, S 1000-1200; visitors must report to reception
♿ 🅿 ♿ 🍴 (by appt) ♣ 🍴 (by appt)
★ ❀ ⚹

Oakleigh House

Swaffham, Norfolk

Oakleigh House, standing in the north corner of Swaffham market place, has no pretensions to grandeur; it was built as a comfortable farmhouse, and remains so today. It was built on the site of a dwelling occupied by John Chapman, the 'Swaffham Pedlar', who is reputed to have found buried treasure following a prophetic dream. The house was probably begun in the late 16th century and continued in the 17th, and the imposing façade dates from the mid-18th century. The estate was evidently still in the hands of the Chapman family in 1658, as in 1893 a carved oak door-head was discovered with the inscription 'J.C. 1658 E.C.' (John and Edward Chapman), but since that time it has passed through many hands, becoming the home of the Grammar School headmaster in 1949 and a sixth-form centre in 1975. In 1982, after remaining empty for two years, it was auctioned and is now once again a home. The house is interesting as, being a humbler dwelling than the grand country houses, it gives an idea of ordinary middle-class life. The stone-flagged floor in the attractive reception hall is original, and there is an attractive dado of carved pine of the 18th century. The fine Jacobean staircase, built in 1620, is similar to that at Blickling Hall, though simpler, and there are 17th-century doors and door jambs at the top of the house. The massive fireplace in the living room, three times filled in, and plastered over before restoration, is now a working fireplace again.

☎ Swaffham (0760) 24280

In Swaffham on Market Place

TF 8209 (OS 132)

Open Apr to end Sept Th and Su 1400-1700; parties by appt at other times

⊖ 🅿 WC 🚽 D ♣ 🍴 ♨
● (permission required)

Oxburgh Hall

Oxborough, near King's Lynn, Norfolk

At first sight more of a castle than a house, Oxburgh was begun by Sir Edmund Bedingfeld in 1482, just before the Wars of the Roses came to an end. The house, with its wide moat and great central fortified gatehouse, has all the features of a medieval castle, but it was clearly intended primarily as a dwelling – the large windows would have had no place in a real castle, and the machicolations on the south side are sealed by stone. The Bedingfeld family, who still live here, have made various changes over the generations, not all of them good. In 1775 Sir Richard Bedingfeld pulled down the Tudor great hall and great chamber; in the 18th and 19th centuries respectively two low towers were built; and in 1880 external corridors were built round the courtyard. The oldest interiors are the King's and Queen's rooms in the gatehouse tower which, although their furnishings are 17th century, have not been altered since the 15th century. The spiral staircase that links them is also of the 15th century, and is a masterpiece of intricate bricklaying. The rooms seen by visitors are Sir Richard's saloon of 1778 and three rooms decorated in the Victorian Gothic style, richly patterned and with decorated ceilings. Pugin was possibly responsible for these; the fireplace in the library and the small chapel in the grounds are his work. Both staircases are hung with 17th-century embossed Spanish leather, and one of the upstairs rooms contains Oxburgh's greatest single treasure, a set of bed-hangings and a coverlet embroidered by Mary Queen of Scots and Bess of Hardwick.

☎ Gooderstone (036 621) 258

9½ m SW of Swaffham on road to Cockley Cley and Oxburgh

TF 7401 (OS 143)

Open Apr to mid Oct M, T, W, S, Su 1400-1800

🅿 WC ♣ 🍴 ◆ ♨ 🐾

Paycocke's

West St, Great Coggeshall, Essex

The house, completed about 1505, is named after its original owner, Thomas Paycocke, one of the town's leading clothiers, whose family is represented by four tombstones in the church. It is an outstanding example of the type of half-timbered house built in some profusion in this part of the world by successful tradesmen and merchants. The house has been much restored, and the fabric between the timbers is now brick, but originally it would have been wattle and daub, woven slats of wood covered in mud or plaster. Paycocke's is famous for its lovely carved decoration, and the frieze on the horizontal beam at the base of the upper storey is particularly interesting, and contains the initials of Thomas Paycocke and his trade sign as well as two reclining figures, a head growing out of a flower and a baby diving into a lily. There are five oriel windows in the upper storey. The interior contains more carving, that on the ceiling joists of the hall being especially good. The over-mantel, which incorporates the arms of the Buxton family, who succeeded the Paycockes at the house, was made up in the 1920s from old timbers and is a composite piece. The house is let to National Trust tenants, and some of the furniture is theirs, but the large oak pieces have been lent to the house. The attractive garden, which is full of interesting and unusual plants, is also open to the public, and provides a good view of the buildings at the back of the house, some of which are very old.

6 m E of Braintree on A120 turn S to Coggeshall for 1 m

TL 8422 (OS 168)

Open Apr to mid Oct W, Th, Su and Bank Hol M 1400-1730; parties of 6 and over by appt

⊖ WC ♿ 🚽 (by appt only)

☎ King's Lynn (0553) 772675

8½ m NE of King's Lynn on A149 turn E

TF 6928 (OS 132)

Open Apr to late Sept M-Th 1100-1645, Su 1200-1645. Closed late July to early Aug

☉ 🅿 WC ♿ 🏠 ♣ ♥ ◆ ⚙ ※

Sandringham House

Sandringham, Norfolk

The Sandringham estate was bought by the Royal Family in 1861 when the future Edward VII came of age, but by the time of his marriage to Princess Alexandra the old house had already become inadequate, and today's sprawling scarlet-brick house was built in 1870. The architect was A. J. Humbert, who had built Prince Albert's Mausoleum at Windsor, and the style is solidly neo-Jacobean. Visitors are shown five main rooms, and the front door opens directly into the saloon, built on the pattern of a Jacobean great hall, with a minstrels' gallery at one end and the walls hung with 17th-century tapestries. The main drawing room, in the French style, has plaster and carved panelling, and is all in white with a painted ceiling. The paintings on the walls, both here and in the saloon, are mainly Victorian, with many portraits, and the atmosphere of the rooms is Edwardian, although they are used by the Royal Family today. The tapestries in the dining room, two of which were woven from Goya cartoons, were given by the King of Spain in 1876, and there are many other treasures. The sporting pictures and trophies on show in the lobby and ballroom corridor reflect the particular feature of life at Sandringham – Edward VII developed the estate into one of the finest game reserves in the country. In his day the beaters wore special uniforms, which are sometimes shown in the old stable block. This also contains gifts presented to Her Majesty the Queen, big game trophies, vintage royal cars and a vintage fire engine. The Victorian gardens are still very attractive.

☎ Lowestoft (0502) 730224

8 m NW of Lowestoft on B1074

TM 4997 (OS 134)

Open Easter Su to end Sept Th, Su and Bank Hols, also Tu and W in July and Aug 0900-1730

☉ (1½ m walk) 🅿 WC ♿ 🏠 ♣ ♥ 🍴 ◆
※ 🐎 ● (not in house) 🌳 🐕

Somerleyton Hall

near Lowestoft, Suffolk

This splendid and imposing Victorian palace was the creation of Sir Morgan Peto, a clever ex-bricklayer turned railway contractor. He was only thirty-three in 1844 when he bought the existing 17th-century house and proceeded to bring it up to date. The original house was meant to provide the inspiration for the rebuilding, and Peto employed the sculptor John Thomas to turn it into a 'Jacobean mansion'. What they produced, however, is the purest red-brick Victorian, albeit with hints of Italian and French styles. There is a very Italian tower on one side, and the French look comes partly through the use of the soft, pale Caen stone, which Thomas favoured because it was easy to carve. There is a great deal of carved ornament on the building, and the stone connecting screen between the wings in the French Renaissance style, is most elaborately carved. The main rooms with their oak panelling seem rather sombre in contrast to the bright exterior. In the oak parlour the 17th-century panelling survives, and the staircase hall and dining room have some of the original features. But the Victorian rooms are the most impressive, particularly the entrance hall, which has dark oak woodwork relieved by marble panels, Minton floor tiles, a painted stained-glass dome and stuffed polar bears. Sadly, Sir Morgan's business failed and he had to sell the house in 1863. It was bought by the Crossleys, later Lords of Somerleyton. They recently redecorated and refurnished the dining room, for which a carpet was woven by John Crossley and Sons, the family firm.

☎ Conningsby (0526) 42543

15 m S of Horncastle on A153 at Tattershall

TF 2157 (OS 122)

Open throughout year M-S 1100-1830, Su 1300-1830 (dusk if earlier)

☉ (exc Su) 🅿 WC ♿ 🏠 D ♣ 🍴 ◆ ※

Tattershall Castle

Tattershall, Lincolnshire

The huge red-brick keep, perched on the highest point for many miles around, is all that remains of Tattershall Castle, and it is entirely thanks to Lord Curzon (1859-1925) that anything remains at all. He bought the ruin in 1911, when it had already been sold to speculators and the carved stone chimneypieces were on the way to America, and in the following years he carried out extensive restoration work including tracing and reinstating the chimneypieces. The original castle was built in 1231, but almost nothing now remains, and the keep itself is part of the new building campaign carried out by Ralph Cromwell, Lord Treasurer of England, in 1450. The plan followed that of castles built in earlier times, but although certainly fortified, it was clearly more of a country house than a fortress: for example, the windows are relatively large – and thus vulnerable – and there is a decorative roof gallery which serves no functional purpose at all. Cromwell's new tower, which was linked to the old hall by a first-floor passage, contained the state rooms, each storey having one large chamber, with smaller rooms and passages in the turrets. Lord Curzon, as well as replacing the chimneypieces, restored the top two storeys, constructed new floors and replaced tracery in the lower windows, but otherwise the tower is just as it was when built, and provides an excellent example of a 15th-century fortified house. Lord Cromwell had no children, and the castle passed through various hands before being finally abandoned – it was a ruin by about 1700.

Wimpole Hall

Arrington, near Royston, Cambridgeshire

This huge house, the largest in Cambridgeshire, set in an equally huge park, is notable for the astonishing number of architects and landscape gardeners it gave employment to during the course of its building. The original house, some of whose internal walls survive, was built between 1640 and 1670, the formal gardens were laid out at the end of the century, and the east and west wings were added by the architect James Gibbs for Edward Harley between 1713 and 1721. The library, also by Gibbs, was built in 1730 to house the famous Harleian collection. In 1740 Wimpole was sold to the 1st Earl of Hardwicke, for whom some further alterations were done; Sir John Soane made improvements to the interior for the 3rd Earl, and the 4th Earl employed the architect H. E. Kendall to build a new service wing and stables. The 5th Earl, nicknamed 'Champagne Charlie', sold the estate, and some time later it was bought by Captain Bambridge and his wife Elsie, daughter of Rudyard Kipling, who removed some of the less pleasing Victorian additions. The interiors are enormously rich and varied, Soane's yellow drawing room, and the south drawing room, which is a combination of Flitcroft and Gibbs, being two of the loveliest rooms. The great library, containing over 50,000 volumes, is most impressive, and the Baroque chapel, which fills the whole of the east wing, is entirely covered with painted decorations by Sir James Thornhill. The house contains excellent 18th-century furniture and paintings collected by Mrs Bambridge.

☎ Cambridge (0233) 207257
11 m SW of Cambridge on A603 turn NW to Old Wimpole
TL 3351 (OS 153)

Open end Mar to early Nov daily exc F 1400-1800; reduced rates for parties by appt
♿ (limited) 🅿 WC ♿ 🚻 (M-Th only) D
♣ 🍴 ⊓ ★ ✳ ✗

Wingfield Castle

Wingfield, Eye, Suffolk

In medieval times Wingfield was the home of one of England's most powerful families, the de la Poles, Earls and Dukes of Suffolk, and in 1384 Michael de la Pole, Lord Chancellor, was given licence to crenellate and fortify his manor house. The de la Poles intermarried with the Wingfields, another prestigious old family, soon after, and the castle remained in the same family until 1510, when it came to Anne, daughter of Edward IV and wife of Lord Thomas Howard. The greater part of the house we see today dates from this period, when the old fortified house was transformed into a more comfortable Tudor residence. Parts of the fortifications were dismantled, and the old manor house was replaced by the Tudor house constructed about 1540 within the remaining fortifications. Most of the great medieval outer walls and towers still remain, however, and the bridge to the entrance gateway still bears the grooves of the former gate, drawbridge and portcullis. The two main towers, dating from about 1384, rise to nearly 60 feet above the moat, with the corner towers only slightly lower, and the south-facing battlement wall is over four feet thick. The visitor can explore the gatehouse towers and the barbican room which straddles the entrance, and there is access to the top of one of the towers, which gives a fine view of the countryside. The courtyard, entered through the lovely arched gatehouse, is now an attractive garden with an impressive backdrop of medieval and Tudor flint and brickwork.

☎ Stradbrooke (037 984) 393
6 m S of Harleston on B1116 turn W at Fressingfield
TM 2277 (OS 156)

Open Easter to end Oct S, Su, Bank Hol M 1400-1800; parties by appt at other times
🅿 WC ♿ (limited access) 🚻 ♣ 🍴 ⊓ ◆ ✳

Woburn Abbey

Woburn, near Leighton Buzzard, Bedfordshire

The present Duke of Bedford, whose family has lived at Woburn since the 17th century, was the founder of the 'stately home business'; Woburn opened its gates to the throng in 1955, and has since become a thoroughly professional entertainment centre. The house, often ignored in favour of baboons and hippos, was built on the site of the cloister of the original Cistercian abbey, but it was not really lived in until Francis Russell took possession in 1619. Rebuilding began soon after, and the north wing became the private apartments. The west side, with its central pediment, was added by Henry Flitcroft between 1747 and 1761, and at the end of the century Henry Holland built the south and east sides. Until 1950 the house kept its original Cistercian quadrangular form, but sadly the entire eastern half, including Holland's east wing, had to be demolished because of dry rot. However, the house still retains an impressive and dignified appearance, and the lavish interior contains many treasures. The state rooms, designed by Flitcroft, include a Chinese room with a superb wallpaper brought from China in the 18th century, and most of the rooms have fine plaster ceilings. More of Flitcroft's work can be seen in his skilful remodelling of the long gallery. The house contains a superb collection of paintings, including works by Van Dyck, Velasquez and Reynolds as well as the famous Armada Portrait of Elizabeth I. The library is the finest of the Holland rooms, and Holland's pretty 'Chinese Dairy' can still be seen in the grounds.

☎ Woburn (052 525) 666
9 m SE of Newport Pagnell on A5130 turn E at Woburn
SP 9632 (OS 152)

Open Apr to end Oct daily 1100-1700; Jan to end Mar S, Su 1030-1545
♿ (1½ m walk) 🅿 WC 🚻 D (guide dogs only in house) ♣ 🍴 ⊓ ★ 🎫 ✳ ✗ ● (not in house) 🐾

Angel Corner, Angel Hill, Bury St Edmunds, Suffolk (tel Bury St Edmunds [0284] 63233 ext 227). In town centre. TL 8564 (OS 155). Queen Anne house, containing a large collection of clocks and watches of many styles and dates. Open daily (exc Su) am and pm; closed Christmas, Easter, May Bank Hol. ⊖ 🅿 ★

Aubourn Hall, near Lincoln, Lincolnshire (tel Bassingham [052 285] 270). 9 m S of Lincoln on A46, turn SE. SK 9262 (OS 121). 16th-century house attributed to the Smythson family, with a notable Jacobean carved staircase and panelled rooms. Open July to Aug W pm; other times by appt. ⊖ 🅿

Beeston Hall, Beeston St Lawrence, near Wroxham, Norfolk (tel Horning [0692] 630771). 14 m NE of Norwich on A1151. TG 3324 (OS 134). 18th-century house built by William Wilkins, with fantasy Gothick exterior and a mixture of Gothick and Classical Georgian interiors. It is set in a picturesque landscaped park. Open daily am and pm (Su pm only). ⊖ 🅿 WC ♣ 🐾

Belchamp Hall, Belchamp Walter, Sudbury, Essex (tel Sudbury [0787] 72744). 5 m SW of Sudbury. TL 8240 (OS 155). Queen Anne brick-built house with furniture and family portraits of the 17th and 18th centuries. Open by appt only, May to Sept T, Th and Bank Hols pm. 🅿 🚻 (by appt) ♣

Berkhampsted Castle, Berkhampsted, Hertfordshire. Near town centre on A41. SP 9908 (OS 166). Ruins of a typical motte-and-bailey castle of the 11th century, surrounded by a restored moat. Thomas à Becket probably built the shell keep, and King John added further walls. The castle was used as a place of confinement for the French king John after the battle of Poitiers (1356). Open daily am and pm. ⊖ 🅿 ★

Bolingbroke Castle, Old Bolingbroke, Lincolnshire. 7 m SE of Horncastle. TF 3464 (OS 122). Ruined site, recently excavated, of a 13th-century castle built by Ranulf, Earl of Chester. It was made up of a hexagonal enclosure with a twin-towered gatehouse. The castle was defended by the Royalists in the Civil War, and later slighted. Open daily am and pm (Su pm only). ⊖ 🅿

Burgh Castle, near Great Yarmouth, Norfolk. 3 m W of Great Yarmouth off A143. TG 4704 (OS 134). A Roman fort of about AD 300, one of the Saxon Shore camps built to keep out Saxon raiders. A small Norman motte-and-bailey castle was built, but little trace of it now remains, though the surviving Roman walls are impressive. Open daily am and pm (Su pm only). 🅿

Castle House, Dedham, Essex (tel Colchester [0206] 322127). 7 m NE of Colchester on A137, turn N. TM 0632 (OS 168). Georgian house, from 1919 to 1959 the home of Alfred Munnings, former President of the Royal Academy. There is a large collection of his paintings and sketches on many subjects, notably of horses. Open mid-May to mid-Oct W, Su and Bank Hols pm; also Aug Th and S pm. ⊖ 🅿 WC 🔲 ♣

Colchester Castle, Colchester, Essex (tel Colchester [0206] 577475). In town centre, N of High St. TL 9925 (OS 168). The largest, and one of the earliest, great tower in England, built c. 1075-80 with a plan similar to that of the White Tower in London. It is built on the site of a Roman temple, and uses Roman bricks. The castle now houses a museum of Roman and other antiquities. Open M-S, am and pm, also Apr to Sept Su pm. ⊖ 🅿 WC

Doddington Hall, Doddington, Lincolnshire (tel Lincoln [0522] 694308). 3 m S of Lincoln on A1180, turn NW onto B1190. SK 8970 (OS 121). Large Elizabethan house built in about 1600 by Robert Smythson, with a gabled Tudor gatehouse. The interior has been redecorated to a Georgian taste, and contains a rich variety of furniture and porcelain. There is a large park and walled rose garden. Open Easter M, May to Sept W, Su and Bank Hols pm. 🅿 WC 🔲 🚻 (by appt) ♣ 🐾

Euston Hall, Euston, Thetford, Suffolk (tel Thetford [0842] 3281). 4 m SE of Thetford on A1088. TL 8978 (OS 144). House built in the Restoration period and altered in the 1750s. Much of the house was destroyed in the 20th century. What remains contains a fine collection of 17th-century portraits. There is a landscaped park, the work of William Kent and John Evelyn. Open June to end Sept Th pm. ⊖ 🅿 WC 🔲 ♣ 🐾 🞖

Felbrigg Hall, near Cromer, Norfolk (tel West Runton [026 375] 444). 2 m SW of Cromer on A148, turn W. TG 1939 (OS 133). Jacobean house built in about 1620, with the west front added in the William-and-Mary style. The interiors are mainly 18th and 19th century, and there is a fine library, with books from Dr Johnson's collection. There is a walled garden, orangery and landscaped park. Open Apr to Nov T-Th, S, Su and Bank Hols pm. ⊖ 🅿 WC 🔲 🚻 (by appt) ♣ 🐾

Fulbeck Hall, near Grantham, Lincolnshire (tel Loveden [0400] 72205). 14 m S of Lincoln on A607. SK 9450. A mainly 18th-century house in a large park, the home of the Fane family for 350 years. The interiors are decorated in 18th- and 19th-century styles. Open Aug daily pm; also Bank Hol Apr and May pm. ⊖ 🅿 🔲 ♣ 🐾

Fydell House, South St, Boston, Lincolnshire (tel Boston [0205] 51520). In town centre. TF 3343 (OS 121). House built in 1726 for William Fydell, three times mayor of Boston. It is now used as a college. It has notable plasterwork, panelling and a fine carved staircase. Open M-F am and pm, other times by appt. ⊖ 🅿 WC ★

Glemham Hall, Woodbridge, Suffolk (tel Wickham Market [0728] 746 219). 13 m NE of Woodbridge on A12. TM 3459 (OS 156). Elizabethan house remodelled in the early 18th century in a severe manner. There is a staircase of oak inlaid with walnut, and much 18th-century panelling. There is some notable japanned furniture, and pieces by Hepplewhite and Sheraton.The walled garden is attractive. Open Easter to end Sept Su, W and Bank Hol M pm. ⊖ 🅿 WC 🔲 ♣ 🐾

Gosfield Hall, Halstead, Essex (tel Halstead [078 74] 2914). 4 m NE of Braintree on A1017, turn W. TL 7729 (OS 167). Unusual house built in the mid-16th century and with 18th-century additions and façades. The Tudor long gallery has notable panelling. Open May to Sept, W and Th pm. ⊖ 🅿 ♣

Grantham House, Castlegate, Grantham, Lincolnshire. In town centre. SK 9136 (OS 130). House dating from the 14th century and much altered over the centuries. The grounds run down to the River Witham. Open Apr to Sept W and Th pm. ⊖

Gunby Hall, Burgh-le-Marsh, Lincolnshire (tel Scremby [075 485] 212). 10 m NW of Skegness on A158. TF 4666 (OS 122). House built in about 1700 in the style of Sir Christopher Wren, the home of the Massingberd family. There is some fine 17th-century furniture, and portraits by Joshua Reynolds. The garden is formal and walled. Open Apr to Sept Th pm; other times by appt. ⊖ 🅿 WC 🔲 (garden only) 🚻 ♣

Hadleigh Castle, near Leigh on Sea, Essex. 6 m W of Southend-on-Sea, on A13, turn S. TQ 8186 (OS 178). 13th-century castle built by Hubert de Burgh and converted by Edward III in the 1360s, as both a military building and a royal residence. Two original towers remain standing. Open daily am and pm. ⊖ 🅿 ★

Hale's Hall, Loddon, Norfolk (tel Raveningham [050 846] 395). 12 m SE of Norwich on A146. TM 3798 (OS 134). Fortified medieval manor house, with a great hall of the 1470s restored in the 1970s. The ruins and moat have ben excavated, and there are demonstrations of East Anglian crafts. Open June to Aug F, Su, Bank Hols pm (Easter to May, Sept Su only). 🅿 🔲 ♣ 🐾 🞖

Haughley Park, near Wetherden, Suffolk (tel Elmswell [0359] 40205). 4 m NW of Stowmarket on A45, turn NW. TM 0062 (OS 155). Jacobean manor house, built on the E-plan and gabled. The garden front dates from 1800. The interior has been accurately reconstructed in the 1960s. The gardens include woods and rhododendron walks. Open May to Sept T pm. ⊖ 🅿 WC 🔲 ♣

Helmingham Hall, Helmingham, near Ipswich, Suffolk (tel Helmingham [047 339] 363). 9 m N of Ipswich on B1077. TM 1857 (OS 156). Moated house built in 1510 by the Tollemache family; its drawbridges are raised nightly. The large park contains herds of deer and Highland cattle, and the gardens have fine herbaceous borders. The house is not open to visitors. Gardens open Easter to end Sept Su pm. 🅿 WC ♣ 🐾 🞖

Hertford Castle, Hertfordshire (tel Hertford [0992] 54977). In town centre. TL 3212 (OS 166). Motte-and-bailey castle built by William the Conqueror, on which stone walls and towers were built from the late 12th century. The late 15th-century gatehouse survives, with part of the curtain walls and other more modern wings. Open May to Sept first Su in the month pm. ⊖ 🅿 ★

Hinchingbrooke House, Huntingdon, Cambridgeshire (tel Huntingdon [0480] 51121). ½ m W of Huntingdon on A604. TL 2271 (OS 153). 13th-century Benedictine nunnery dissolved in 1538; the house was acquired by the Cromwell family and was extended in the 16th century, then passed to the Montagu family in 1627. It was again extended in the 1660s, and restored in the 1820s. The house is now a comprehensive school. Open Apr to Aug, Su pm; also Bank Hols. ⊖ 🅿 WC 🔲 🚻 (by appt) 🐾

Houghton House, Ampthill, Bedfordshire. 9 m S of Bedford, to E of A418. TL 0339 (OS 153). Ruined red-brick mansion built for the Dowager Countess of Pembroke 1615-21, with heavily decorated stone centrepieces on the north and west fronts. Inigo Jones has been attributed as the architect, and John Bunyan is said to have been inspired by it. The house was dismantled in the 1790s; only the outside walls remain. Open daily am and pm. 🅿 🔲 🚻 D ★

Ixworth Abbey, near Bury St Edmunds, Suffolk (tel Pakenham [0359] 30374). 8 m NE of Bury St Edmunds, on A143. TL 9370 (OS 155). 12th-century Augustinian priory, with some 13th-century cloisters surviving. There is a timber-framed prior's lodging of the late 15th century, and a private house mainly dating from the 17th century was built on the site of the abbey. Open May to end Aug T, Su and Bank Hols pm. ⊖ 🅿

Kentwell Hall, Long Melford, Suffolk (tel Long Melford [078 725] 207). 5 m N of Sudbury on A134, turn NW. TL 8647 (OS 155). Red-brick Tudor house with a moat, and approached by an avenue of limes planted in the 1670s. The interior was reworked in the 1820s, and is being refurbished. The restoration works may be viewed. Open July to Sept W-Su pm; Apr to June W, Th and Su; also Bank Hol weekends. ⊖ 🅿 WC 🚻 ♣ 🐾

Kimbolton Castle, Kimbolton, Cambridgeshire. 9 m NW of St Neots on A45. TL 1067. Tudor manor house, the home of Katherine of Aragon in the 1530s, and mostly remodelled in the early 18th century by Vanbrugh, with murals by Pellegrini and a gatehouse by Robert Adam. Open Easter, Spring and Summer Bank Hol Su and M pm; also late July to early Sept Su pm. 🅿

Lincoln Castle, Castle Hill, Lincoln, Lincolnshire (tel Lincoln [0522] 25951). In city centre. SK 9771 (OS 121). Norman motte-and-bailey castle with two mottes. One carries a shell keep of the 12th century, the other a 19th-century observatory tower. There is a parapet walk around the walls, and a fine eastern gateway. Open M-S am and pm; Apr to Oct Su pm. ⊖ 🅿 🔲

Longthorpe Tower, Peterborough, Cambridgeshire. 2 m SW of town centre on A47. TL 1698 (OS 142). 13th- and 14th-century great tower, built as a family defence against the possibility of raids along the River Nene. There are remarkable 14th-century religious and allegorical frescos on the walls of the great chamber. Open daily am and pm (Su pm only). ⊖ 🅿

Marston Hall, Grantham, Lincolnshire (tel Loveden [0400] 50225). 6 m NW of Grantham on A1, turn NE. SK 8943 (OS 130). 16th-century manor house modified in the 1720s. There is an ancient garden and an 18th-century Gothick gazebo. Open on occasional Su; other times by appt. 🅿

Medieval Merchant's House, King St, King's Lynn, Norfolk. In town centre. TF 6120 (OS 132). Medieval house of the 14th century, now with a Georgian façade. Open some weekends Apr to July; Aug T, F-Su am and pm. ⊖ 🚻 (by appt)

Melford Hall, Long Melford, Suffolk. 4 m N of Sudbury on A134. TL 8746 (OS 155). Turreted brick house begun in 1554, built for Sir William Cordell. There is an 18th-century drawing room, and the interior was partly reworked in the 1810s, with a fine library. The contents include Chinese porcelain, 18th- and 19th-century naval paintings, and a collection of objects relating to Beatrix Potter, who was a regular visitor to the house. There is a Tudor pavilion in the garden. Open Apr to end Sept W, Th, Su, and Bank Hols pm. ⊖ 🅿 WC ♿ 🚻 (by appt) ♣

Norwich Castle, Castle Meadow, Norwich, Norfolk (tel Norwich [0603] 611277 ext 279). In city centre. TG 2308 (OS 134). Vast Norman motte-and-bailey castle, with unusual blind arcading on the restored keep of 1120-30, which was used as a gaol until 1839. The castle now houses a museum, with important collections of paintings and silver, as well as armour and social history displays. Open daily am and pm (Su pm only); closed Christmas, New Year and Good Fri. ⊖ WC 🐾

Old Hall, Gainsborough, Lincolnshire (tel Gainsborough [0427] 2669). In town centre. SK 8190 (OS 112). Excellent 15th- and 16th-century brick and timber manor house with medieval kitchens and associated rooms (perhaps the best survivng in England), and a huge great hall with original oriel window and roof. The Pilgrim Fathers used to meet here and John Wesley preached several times at Old Hall. There is a small museum of archaeological finds from the locality. Open daily am and pm (Su pm only) ⊖ 🅿 WC ♿ 🚻 (by appt)

Orford Castle, Orford, Suffolk. 8 m E of Woodbridge, on B1084. TM 4149 (OS 169). Castle built by Henry II in the 1160s to guard Orford harbour and assert royal supremacy over the county. All that remains is the unique 90-foot high, 21-sided great tower, which incorporates three buttress-turrets, and contains a circular room on each floor. The rest of the castle has since collapsed. Open daily am and pm (Oct to March, Su pm only). ⊖ 🅿

Otley Hall, Otley, near Ipswich, Suffolk. 9 m N of Woodbridge on B1079, turn NE. TM 2055 (OS 156). Moated 15th-century hall, the home of the Gosnold family for 250 years. It has fine timbers, herring-bone brickwork, panelling and frescos. Open Easter, Spring and Summer Bank Hol Su and M. ⊖ 🅿 🚻 (by appt) 🐾

Peckover House, North Brink, Wisbech, Cambridgeshire (Wisbech [0945] 3463). Close to town centre, on river bank. TF 4509 (OS 143). Town house built in 1722, with a fine interior, displaying rich Rococo carvings, plasterwork and many other details. There is a notable Victorian garden, containing many rare and exotic trees (including fruit-bearing orange trees), and 18th-century stables. Open mid-Apr to mid-Oct, S to W pm; early to mid Apr, S and Su pm only. ⊖ 🅿 WC ♿ (garden only) ♣ 🐾

68 Piccott's End, near Hemel Hempstead, Hertfordshire (tel Hemel Hempstead [0442] 56729). 2 m N of Hemel Hempstead on A4146, turn E. TL 0509 (OS 166). Medieval cottage once used as a hostel for pilgrims, and with a remarkable 15th-century religious wall-painting. The house contains interesting early kitchens, and in 1826 became the first cottage hospital in Britain. It now houses a collection of early medical instruments. Open March to Nov daily am and pm; Dec-Feb parties only by appt. ⊖ 🅿 🚻 (by appt)

Priory, The, Water St, Lavenham, Suffolk (tel Lavenham [0787] 247417). In town centre, 6 m NE of Sudbury. TL 9149 (OS 155). Complex timber-framed building of the 13th to 16th century, with Jacobean staircase and fireplaces. The building has recently been restored, and contains a collection of photographs showing the progress of this work. Open Apr to Sept daily pm. ⊖

Redoubt, Harwich, Essex (tel Harwich [025 55] 3429). In town centre. TM 2732 (OS 168). Circular fort built in the early 18th century as part of the coastal defences against invasion by Napoleon. 180ft in diameter and surrounded by a dry moat, the fort now houses historical museums. Open Easter to Oct Su am and pm. ⊖ 🅿 🚻 (by appt) 🐾

Shalom Hall, Layer Breton, near Colchester, Essex. 6 m SW of Colchester on B1022, turn S. TL 9418 (OS 168). Victorian house containing a collection of 17th- and 18th-century French furniture and porcelain, and several notable 18th-century portraits. Open Aug M-F am and pm. 🅿 ★

Shaw's Corner, Ayot St Lawrence, Hertfordshire (tel Stevenage [0438] 820307). 1 m NE of Wheat-hampstead. TL 1916 (OS 166). Early 20th-century small house, the home of George Bernard Shaw from 1906 to his death in 1950. It has been preserved as it was during his lifetime, and contains a large collection of his belongings; his plays are produced in the grounds. Open Apr to end Oct W-Su and Bank Hols am and pm; March and Nov S and Su only. ⊖ 🅿 WC ♿ ♣ 🐾

Sheringham Hall, Sheringham, Norfolk (tel Sheringham [0263] 823074). ¼ m W of town centre on A149, turn S. TG 1342 (OS 133). Early 19th-century house and garden designed by Sir Humphry Repton and his son. The grounds include a long rhododendron drive. Open May to Sept F pm, by appt only. 🅿 ♿ ♣

Wingfield College, Eye, Suffolk (tel Stradbroke [037 984] 505). 7 m SE of Diss. TM 2277 (OS 156). 14th-century hall, the home of the Wingfield family for over 700 years. It contains a medieval cloister, gallery and lodgings range, with Elizabethan and Georgian interiors and an 18th-century façade. Open Easter to end Sept S, Su and Bank Hols pm. 🅿 🚻 (by appt) ♣ 🐾

Woolsthorpe Manor, near Grantham, Lincolnshire (tel Grantham [0476] 860338). 11 m S of Grantham on A1, turn W to B6403 for ¼ m then W. SK 9224 (OS 130). Small farmhouse of about 1620, the birthplace of Sir Isaac Newton in 1642. It was here that he returned during the plague years of 1665-66 and according to legend conceived the Theory of Gravitation in the orchard. Open Apr to Oct S-Th pm. ⊖ 🅿 WC ♿ 🚻

Melford Hall, Suffolk

Central England

Broughton Castle, Oxfordshire

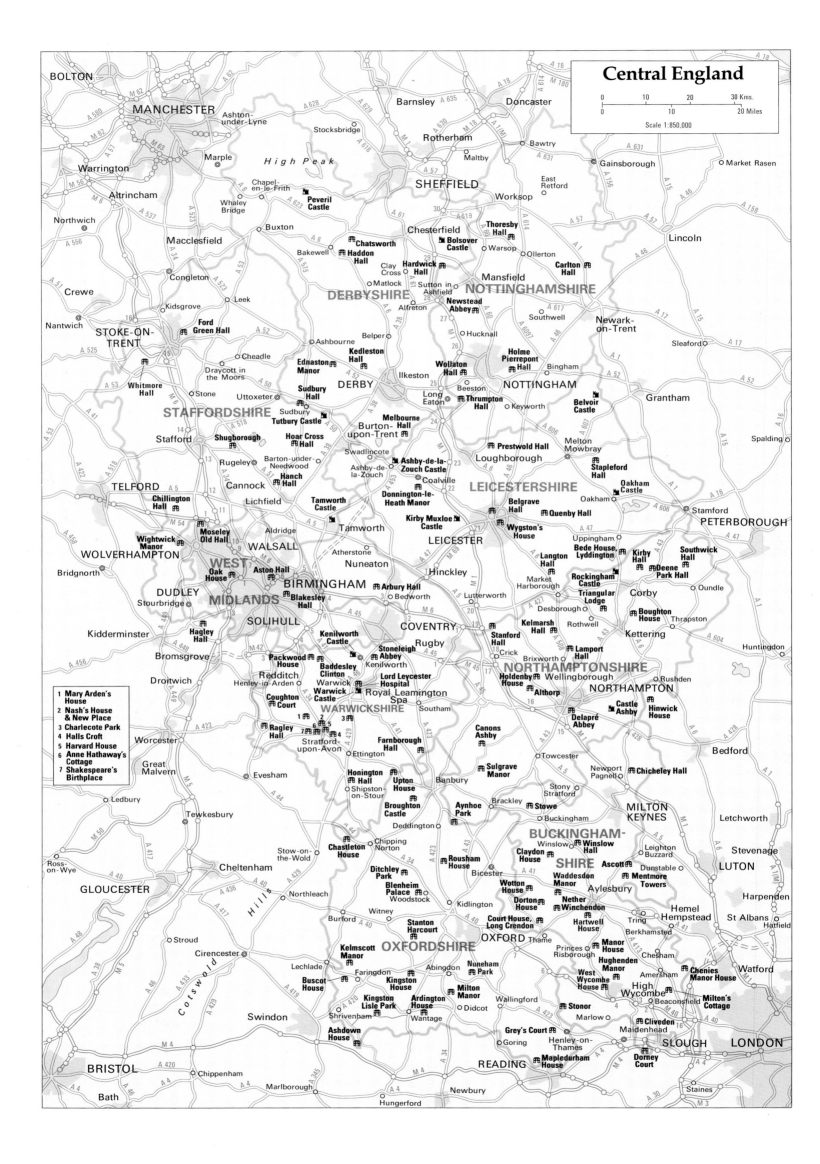

Central England

Scale 1:850,000

| 0 | 10 | 20 | 30 Kms. |
| 0 | 10 | 20 Miles |

BOLTON

MANCHESTER
Ashton-under-Lyne

Warrington
Altrincham
Northwich

Marple
High Peak

Macclesfield
Buxton
Chapel-en-le-Frith
Peveril Castle
Whaley Bridge

Stocksbridge

SHEFFIELD

Barnsley
Rotherham
Maltby

Doncaster

Bawtry
Gainsborough
Market Rasen

Worksop
East Retford
Lincoln

Crewe
Nantwich

Congleton
Kidsgrove
Leek

STOKE-ON-TRENT
Ford Green Hall

Cheadle
Draycott in the Moors

Ashbourne
Belper

DERBYSHIRE
Chatsworth
Haddon Hall
Bakewell
Clay Cross
Matlock

Chesterfield
Bolsover Castle
Warsop
Ollerton

Thoresby Hall

Carlton Hall

Hardwick Hall
Sutton in Ashfield
Alfreton

Mansfield
NOTTINGHAMSHIRE

Newark-on-Trent
Sleaford

Whitmore Hall
Stone

Uttoxeter
Sudbury

Kedleston Hall
Ednaston Manor

Sudbury Hall

DERBY
Ilkeston

Newstead Abbey
Hucknall

Southwell
Bingham

Holme Pierrepont Hall

Belvoir Castle
Grantham

Spalding

STAFFORDSHIRE
Stafford
Shugborough

Rugeley
Barton-under-Needwood

Tutbury Castle
Hoar Cross Hall
Hanch Hall

Burton-upon-Trent
Swadlincote
Ashby-de-la-Zouch

Melbourne Hall

Long Eaton
Thrumpton Hall

Wollaton Hall

NOTTINGHAM
Beeston
Keyworth

Prestwold Hall
Loughborough

Melton Mowbray

Stapleford Hall
Oakham Castle
Oakham

Stamford

PETERBOROUGH

TELFORD
Cannock
Lichfield

Ashby-de-la-Zouch Castle
Coalville

Donnington-le-Heath Manor

LEICESTERSHIRE

Belgrave Hall
Quenby Hall

Chillington Hall

Tamworth Castle
Tamworth

Kirby Muxloe Castle

Wygston's House

Bede House, Lyddington
Uppingham

Kirby Hall
Deene Park Hall
Southwick Hall

Bridgnorth
WOLVERHAMPTON

Wightwick Manor
Moseley Old Hall
WALSALL
Aldridge
Atherstone
Nuneaton

LEICESTER
Langton Hall

Market Harborough
Rockingham Castle
Triangular Lodge

Corby
Oundle

DUDLEY
Stourbridge
WEST MIDLANDS
Oak House
Aston Hall
BIRMINGHAM
Blakesley Hall

Arbury Hall
Bedworth

Hinckley
Lutterworth

Kelmarsh Hall
Rothwell

Boughton House
Kettering
Thrapston
Huntingdon

Kiddermister
Bromsgrove

Hagley Hall
SOLIHULL

Kenilworth Castle
Rugby

Stanford Hall
Crick

Lamport Hall

NORTHAMPTONSHIRE

Droitwich

Packwood House
Redditch
Henley-in-Arden

Stoneleigh Abbey
Kenilworth

Baddesley Clinton
Warwick
Warwick Castle

Lord Leycester Hospital
Royal Leamington Spa

Southam

Holdenby House
Wellingborough
Rushden

Worcester

Coughton Court

Ragley Hall

WARWICKSHIRE
Stratford-upon-Avon
Ettington

Farnborough Hall

Canons Ashby

Althorp
NORTHAMPTON

Castle Ashby
Delapré Abbey
Towcester

Hinwick House

Bedford

Great Malvern
Evesham

Honington Hall
Shipston-on-Stour
Upton House

Banbury

Sulgrave Manor

Newport Pagnell

Chicheley Hall

Ledbury
Tewkesbury

Broughton Castle
Deddington

Aynhoe Park
Brackley
Buckingham

Stowe

Stony Stratford

MILTON KEYNES
Letchworth

Ross-on-Wye

Chastleton House
Chipping Norton

Rousham House
Bicester

BUCKINGHAM-SHIRE
Winslow
Winslow Hall

Leighton Buzzard
Stevenage

Cheltenham

Ditchley Park
Blenheim Palace
Woodstock

Kidlington

Claydon House
Ascott
Dunstable
LUTON

GLOUCESTER
Northleach
Witney
Burford

Stanton Harcourt

Waddesdon Manor
Mentmore Towers

Wotton House
Dorton House
Nether Winchendon

Aylesbury

Harpenden

Hemel Hempstead
St Albans
Hatfield

Stroud
Cirencester

Kelmscott Manor
Lechlade

Faringdon

Abingdon
Nuneham Park

Court House, Long Crendon
OXFORD
Thame

Hartwell House
Princes Risborough

Berkhamsted
Tring

Manor House
Hughenden Manor

Chesham
Amersham

Chenies Manor House
Watford

OXFORDSHIRE

Buscot House
Kingston House

Kingston Lisle Park
Ardington House
Shrivenham
Wantage

Milton Manor
Didcot

Wallingford

West Wycombe House
High Wycombe

Stonor
Marlow

Beaconsfield
Milton's Cottage

Cliveden
Maidenhead

SLOUGH
LONDON

Swindon

Ashdown House

Grey's Court
Goring

Henley-on-Thames

Dorney Court

BRISTOL
Chippenham
Marlborough

READING
Mapledurham House

Newbury
Hungerford

Staines

Bath

Cotswold Hills

1	Mary Arden's House
2	Nash's House & New Place
3	Charlecote Park
4	Halls Croft
5	Harvard House
6	Anne Hathaway's Cottage
7	Shakespeare's Birthplace

Blenheim Palace

Woodstock, Oxfordshire

In her *Memoirs* Consuelo Vanderbilt, the American-born wife of the 9th Duke of Marlborough, deprecated the domestic arrangements at Blenheim. She claimed to dislike the small bedrooms, the airless closets, the dark dining rooms situated hundreds of yards from the kitchens. She thought the marble mantelpiece in her bedroom looked like a tomb. But the Palace was not primarily conceived as a home. Sir John Vanbrugh planned it on a vast scale, regardless of cost, to be a tribute to John Churchill, Duke of Marlborough (1650-1722), a celebration of his triumphs as soldier and diplomatist. Comfort and convenience were low down on the list of Vanbrugh's priorities. And in seeking to improve on his previous work at Castle Howard, he did succeed in creating the greatest Baroque mansion in England. Planted square and massive in the valley of the River Glyme eight miles north of Oxford, it is not even overawed by its enormous park.

Top, the grand banqueting hall at Blenheim, where painted spectators look down onto the diners seated at table.

Above, Blenheim, the palatial gift of the nation to its conquering hero.

In gratitude for the Duke's victory in 1704, Queen Anne granted him the Royal Manor of Woodstock and money for the building of a hero's mansion. Work on the foundations began in the following year. The grand design was pushed forward by Vanbrugh with the assistance of the experienced Nicholas Hawksmoor and other leading artists and craftsmen. From the start Vanbrugh was hampered by the enmity of the Duchess, the redoubtable Sarah Jennings (1660-1744). She would have preferred Sir Christopher Wren to build her a comfortable residence, at far less expense. She continually quarrelled with Vanbrugh and by 1716, when the Duke suffered a stroke and all control passed to her, he decided he had had enough. He resigned, leaving his assistants to complete the design. By this time the Marlboroughs were having to finish the Palace at their own expense. The work dragged on and, though practically completed when the Duke died six years later, the chapel was not finished for another ten years. The Duke and Duchess are buried in the chapel, which is dominated by a flamboyant memorial to the Duke commissioned by the Duchess. Executed by Rysbrack after a design of William Kent, this memorial is considered a masterpiece of Baroque sculpture.

A distant view of the Palace across the park reveals something of Vanbrugh's grand design. An array of towers breaks the skyline above the massive bulk of the buildings. The 30-foot high finials of the towers are both ducal and martial: flaming grenades each surmounted by a coronet.

Entering the great court and approaching the entrance, with the huge stable- and service-blocks set back on either side, the sheer size of the main façade is overwhelming. From the driveway two broad flights of steps lead to a towering portico. Corinthian columns and pillars support a pediment where a helmeted Minerva, representing both victory and wisdom, marshalls chained captives as though for a Roman triumph. To right and left curving arcades across the corners of the court enhance the straight lines and height of the portico.

This grand entrance leads to a hall where the highest in the land could be received with fitting splendour. The oval painting in the ceiling, 67 feet above the floor, is by Sir John Thornhill. The Duke, in the guise of a Roman general, points to a plan of the battle of Blenheim while Britannia presents him with the laurel wreath of victory. The hall is lit by windows towards the portico, and by a tall clerestory above two arcades of stone arcades. It has the majestic lines of a cathedral transept.

Across the hall, double doors, surmounted by a bust of Marlborough and two battle standards, a portrait of Queen Anne above, lead to the banqueting hall. The walls and ceiling of this great room were painted by Louis Laguerre who also worked at Chatsworth and other great houses. The ceiling is another celebration of victory, the Duke riding through the heavens in a chariot. The lower part of the walls have painted columns with balustrades between them. Over the

balustrades spectators, among them Laguerre himself, have stared at ducal banquets for more than two-and-a-half centuries. The huge marble doorways bear the Duke's coat of arms superimposed on the double-headed eagle of the Holy Roman Empire, of which he was a Prince. On either side of the hall are the former state apartments, their walls covered by the famous Brussels tapestries of scenes from the Duke's many campaigns.

The gallery on the west side of the Palace, 180 feet long with a fine bay window looking over terraced gardens to the lake, maintains the grand theme. But today the visitor will be eager to see the modest bedroom where Sir Winston Churchill was born in 1874 and the exhibition commemorating his association with the Palace. Heir-presumptive to the 9th Duke until Consuelo Vanderbilt gave birth to a son, he retained a warm affection for his birthplace throughout his long life and was a frequent visitor.

Among the many treasures of the Palace, three paintings in the family apartments summarise its history. A portrait of the 1st Duke by Godfrey Kneller (c. 1646-1723) shows him as he should be remembered, at the height of his fame and before the loss of royal favour and the paralysing stroke that brought senility. In the red drawing room two large family groups continue the story: on the east wall the 4th Duke with his wife and six children, painted by the master of 18th-century portraiture, Sir Joshua Reynolds, and on the opposite wall John Singer Sargent's imitative portrait of the 9th Duke with the beautiful Consuelo Vanderbilt and their two sons. The 4th Duke employed Capability Brown to landscape the park and the 9th Duke did much to restore the Palace, after a long period of neglect, in the first decades of this century.

The gardens and park were included in Vanbrugh's design and the former were laid out by Queen Anne's gardener, Henry Wise, while building was in progress. Vanbrugh built a noble bridge over the river but the park remained unfinished until Capability Brown came to complete the landscaping in 1784. He did this on a suitably grand scale and many consider it his greatest achievement. He dammed the River Glyme to form two natural-seeming lakes, and planted battalions of trees to supplement the wide avenue that already stretched northwards beyond the river to a point two miles from the Palace. Long belts of trees were also planted round much of the park's boundary.

The present formal gardens were planned by Duchêne at the instigation of the 9th Duke. East of the Palace a flower garden centres on a fountain and to the west are the lovely terraced water gardens completed some sixty years ago.

The Palace, set in its man-made landscape, is a monument to the aspirations of the early 18th century.

Above, the austere entrance hall is crowned with a great arch, within which resides a bust of the Duke of Marlborough beneath a portrait of Queen Anne.

Top, the façade of Blenheim, with its complex planes and rhythms, emphasises the heroic intentions of the building; the chimneys, once the glory of English architecture, are here grouped and discreetly disguised beneath columns and finials.

Left, though originally intended to be surrounded by formal gardens, Blenheim now owes much to the lake constructed by Capability Brown below the house, with the fine bridge designed by Vanbrugh.

☎ Woodstock (0993) 811325

11 m NW of Oxford on A34

SP 4416 (OS 164)

Open mid Mar to end Oct daily 1100-1800; reduced rates for parties

⊖ 🅿 WC ♿ (preferably by appt) 🚻 D ♣ 🛍 ⊓ ◆ ❀ ✄ 🏃 ● (no flash in house) ✦ Butterfly House

Chatsworth Bakewell, Derbyshire

It is doubtful if any great house in the country has a finer setting than Chatsworth. The River Derwent winds through clumps of trees and pastures, the house and garden stand on a terrace above the left bank. Behind the house the ground rises steeply to plantations and moorland. The spectacle is a result of centuries of labour and care by dukes and duchesses, architects, gardeners and craftsmen of all kinds. A wild valley of the Peak District has been tamed for human delight.

In 1547 that formidable Derbyshire widow Bess of Hardwick (1518-1608) married Sir William Cavendish. She persuaded him to forsake his rich Suffolk lands for remote and rugged Derbyshire. Five years later they began to build a mansion at Chatsworth on the Tudor plan of four blocks round a courtyard.

Bess and William were succeeded by their son William, who became Earl of Devonshire in 1618. The 4th Earl, yet another William, was created Duke in 1694 for his services in helping William of Orange to the throne. He started to rebuild Chatsworth in a rather haphazard fashion, first replacing the south front with a façade in the latest style. When this was finished he realised how odd it looked beside the older work. He then set about the east wing and so on, piecemeal, until by his death in 1707 only a few interior walls of the Tudor building remained and the house had a new and fashionable face of classical grandeur, the yellow stone embellished by restrained carving. During the same period avenues and flower beds were laid out to complement the new building and a water supply from

the moors was harnessed to fill the gardens with ponds and fountains. The Duke removed an inconvenient hillock to the south of the house to make way for the long, rectangular stretch of water known as the canal pond. Above all, he commissioned the Frenchman Grillet to devise the world-famous cascade, still the most spectacular feature of the grounds.

Except for the building of new stables and a kitchen wing on the north side, the house remained little changed for a hundred years. Not so the grounds. In the mid-18th century Capability Brown cleared away most of the 1st Duke's formal gardens and all his waterworks except for the sea-horse fountain, the canal pond and the cascade. The moors were driven back from the east hill by plantations and the valley landscaped into the beautiful parkland that so enhances Chatsworth today. The park came right up to the west front of the house. Brown gave the river its serpentine course below the house and James Paine, the architect of the new stables, erected the fine bridge over it.

The 6th Duke, a bachelor, inherited in 1811. For forty years he devoted much of his energies to the alteration and enlargement of Chatsworth and its gardens, at the cost of nearly a million pounds. His architect was Jeffry Wyattville (1766-1840), later knighted for his work at Windsor Castle. He had learnt his profession under his uncle James Wyatt, instigator of the Gothic revival.

The state apartments were on the second floor, an inconvenient arrangement when it came to entertaining, and the 6th Duke was a great host. Wyattville built a new set of rooms for him in two of the wings and extending into a new north wing almost as large as the original house. The work included alterations to the family apartments on the first floor and to the impressive painted hall. The hall was altered again in 1912 but still has its original ceiling painted by Louis Laguerre in the 1690s. Wyattville also created a new library for the Duke's magnificent collection of books and manuscripts, a sculpture gallery for the works of contemporary artists such as Canova, Thorwaldsen and John Gibson acquired after much travelling and bargaining by the Duke, and a theatre. When Wyattville departed, Chatsworth boasted 175 rooms and the roof covered an area of about one and a third acres.

The outstanding survival from the time of the 1st Duke is the chapel, a little masterpiece of Baroque art. Laguerre painted the walls and ceiling, Verrio the altarpiece. The carved reredos, the cedar panelling and the high-backed chairs facing each other across the aisle are all originals.

Opposite, Chatsworth is a house for all seasons, growing organically from its lush valley.

Below, the cascade, in which a stream rises in a temple and pours down a sequence of steps.

Chatsworth, as seen from the south-east, with the library and hall shown in cutaway. The south front, which looks out on the canal pond, carries the Cavendish family motto.

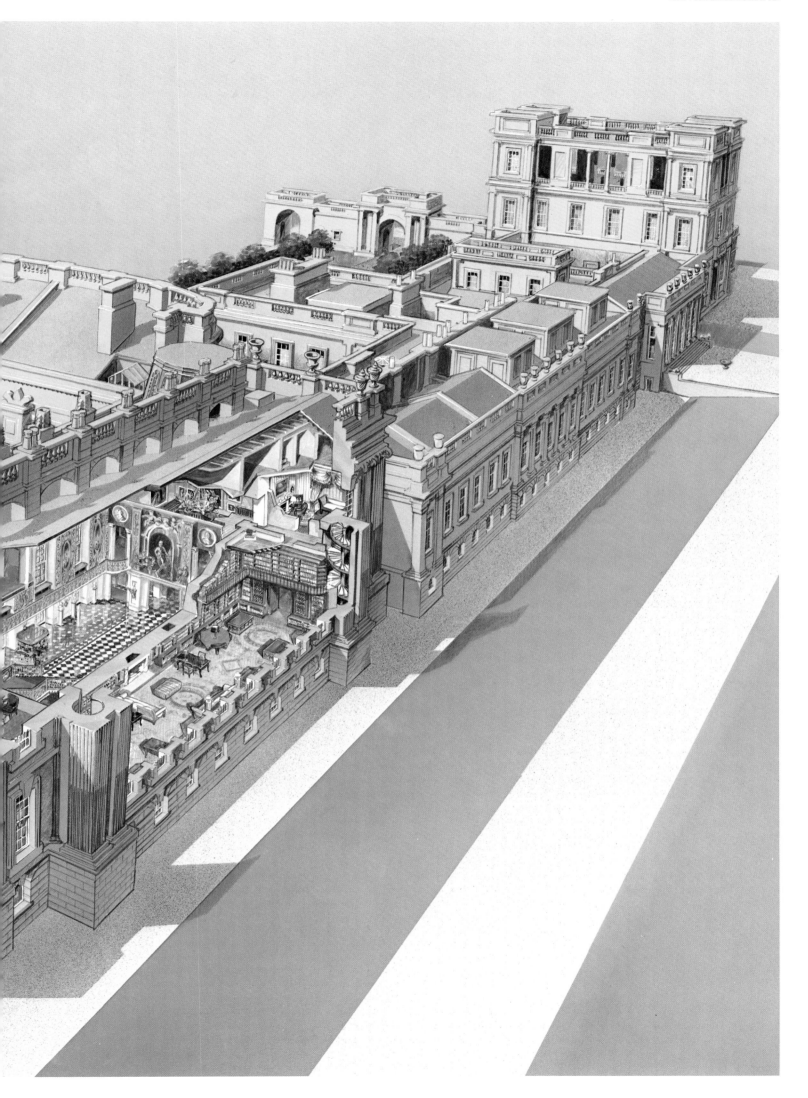

During the Second World War the house proved large enough to accommodate three hundred schoolgirls and their teachers. After six years and more of compulsory neglect a great deal of work was necessary before the house could be re-opened to the public at Easter 1949. Visitors have always been welcome at Chatsworth from the days of the 1st Duke. He entertained such famous late 17th-century travellers as Celia Fiennes and Daniel Defoe. Tourists in a modern sense began to arrive in large numbers when the railway reached Rowsley, three miles away, in 1849. Soon 80,000 people were visiting each summer. No entrance fee was charged until 1908, and then only to pay the guides, any surplus going to charities.

In 1826 the 6th Duke employed Joseph Paxton, then a youth of twenty-two, as his gardener. He married the housekeeper's niece in the following year and became an intimate, life-long friend of the Duke. He later earned fame and a knighthood by designing the Crystal Palace for the Great Exhibition in Hyde Park in 1851. Meanwhile at Chatsworth he founded the superb gardens seen today. Vegetables, fruit and flowers reached perfection under his hand. He created the arboretum, the pinetum and the amazing rock gardens. His great 'emperor fountain' in the canal pond still throws a jet 290 feet in the air. Rare trees and plants were brought from all over the world and nurtured in special houses and in the great conservatory which foreshadowed the Crystal Palace. When the conservatory was demolished in 1920, two tennis courts barely covered the foundations of the middle section. Later this became the site of the yew maze planted by the present Duke and Duchess. They have made many other improvements to the gardens during their twenty-five years of occupancy. In 1970 a big new greenhouse was built for exotic flowers and fruit. The western parterre has been planted with yew hedges and thousands of golden box shrubs, better able to withstand the winds than the former flower beds. They also planted the winding beech hedges that lead to and embrace the bronze bust of the 6th Duke, placed by him on a pedestal of ancient marble blocks shipped from Greece. The gardens extend to more than a hundred acres. Planning and planting go on all the time to maintain them to the standard set by Paxton. Notwithstanding the fabulous treasures of the house, many people visit Chatsworth solely for its gardens and graceful park.

☎ Baslow (024688) 2204

10 m W of Chesterfield on A619 turn S at junction with A621; ½ m E of Edensor

SK 2670 (OS 119)

Open late Mar to end Oct daily 1130-1630

♿ (limited) 🅿 WC 🚻 🚻
D ♣ 🍴 🏕 ◆ 🐕 ♒ (available in foreign languages) 🎿
● (no video cameras in house) 🎯 (adventure playground) Special events throughout year

Above right, James Paine and Capability Brown added the bridge and the parkland which help give Chatsworth its special serenity.

Right, the state bedroom.

Opposite below, the drawing room was decorated in the late 17th century and hung with Mortlake tapestries which follow Raphael's designs of the Acts of the Apostles.

Warwick Castle Warwick, Warwickshire

On a sandstone bluff above the River Avon, the castle is an impressive survivor. Through all the mischances of civil war and royal displeasure, which meant abandonment or destruction for many castles, it has continued in use with few breaks for more than nine centuries. For most of the time it was held by the Earls of Warwick. In 1978 the present Earl sold the castle and a hundred acres of parkland to Madame Tussaud's who maintain it as an historic home open to the public. More than half a million people visit it each year.

The site was fortified by the Saxons against marauding Danes in the 10th century but the Normans erected the first castle in 1068. In the south-west angle of the present walls the motte or mound has survived and on it are fragments of an octagonal shell-keep. Eastward from the mound the oblong bailey or courtyard is defined on three sides by a deep, dry moat and on the fourth by the cliff falling to the river. The area enclosed is about two acres in extent.

Today the castle is mainly a 14th-century reconstruction, with later alterations that mark the change from medieval fortress to great house. Thomas Beauchamp (1315-69) began the rebuilding on a grand scale and his son, another Thomas, completed the work. Their memorial is the north curtain wall with its two fine towers, and the splendid barbican and gatehouse which constitute a late masterpiece of castle-building. After the last Beauchamp Earl died without male heir in 1445 the title and estates passed by marriage to Richard Neville, the famous 'Kingmaker' of the Wars of the Roses. When he was killed at the battle of Barnet in 1471 the title again passed through the female line to his son-in-law, Shakespeare's 'false, fleeting perjured Clarence' – put to death in the Tower of London only seven years later. His son, too, was executed in the Tower and the title lapsed for sixty years.

Entrance to the castle is through the formidable gatehouse of the Beauchamps. A graded driveway up to it, cut through the rock in the 18th century, replaces the steep slope of medieval times, and a stone bridge replaces the former drawbridge over the moat. At the river end of the north curtain the Beauchamps' masterwork, called Caesar's Tower, is one of the most remarkable wall-towers in Britain. It rises nearly 150 feet from the base of a massive plinth outside the curtain wall. Its size and lobed shape, the machicolations and double-tiered battlements, show the last refinements in medieval castle-building. The interior consists of a dungeon inside the plinth, below the level of the courtyard, and over it three vaulted storeys for more fortunate prisoners. Each floor has a large rectangular room with a bedchamber and latrine in the thickness of the walls. Two upper storeys provided a guardroom and a store for arms and ammunition. Today a collection of instruments of torture is on view in the tower.

Left, Warwick Castle, one of the finest and most popular castles in all Europe, sits on a small bluff above the River Avon.

Above, Caesar's Tower, built in the mid-14th century, is unusual for its double parapet.

The domestic block along the east curtain, above the steep fall to the river, was included in the Beauchamps' grand design but has been much extended and rebuilt since. When James I granted the castle to Sir Fulke Greville in 1604 it was in a ruinous condition. He spent £20,000 on the house and grounds, a fortune in those days. He was a cousin and biographer of Sir Philip Sidney and portraits of them both can be seen in the Watergate tower which Sir Fulke occupied while restoration of the house was being carried out. The Grevilles were to remain at Warwick for 374 years, acquiring the dignities of Baron Brooke in 1621, Earl Brooke in 1746 and Earl of Warwick thirteen years later.

A dozen rooms formerly occupied by the family have been laid out to represent a factual week-end party in 1898. Much of the furniture and fittings were in the rooms ninety years ago and care has been taken to make every detail of the tableaux authentic. The elegantly dressed wax figures include the principal guest, the Prince of Wales, shortly to be Edward VII.

The state apartments remain much as the Grevilles left them. The 14th-century great hall, 62 foot long, was almost totally refurbished after damage by fire in 1871. Under the supervision of Anthony Salvin a new roof was erected, the clerestorey re-opened and a thin cladding of new stone placed over the old walls. The striking red-and-white marble squares of the floor predate the fire but were relaid after it.

In the hall weapons and suits of armour from the renowned Warwick collection are exhibited to good effect, among them the armour of the 2nd Baron Brooke who held the castle for Parliament during the Civil War until killed in action at Lichfield in 1643. The remainder of the collection is shown in what was once a brew house at the north end of the domestic block. Nearly a thousand items range from a rare two-handed medieval sword to Brown Bess muskets.

The other state apartments have fared better than the hall and are exceptionally well maintained by the new owners. The cedar dining room has panelling carved by local craftsmen about 1670 and an ornate plaster ceiling of the same period. Most of the furniture, the five chandeliers and the remarkable Adam fireplace of Carrara marble are 18th-century. The beautiful carpet was woven in one piece at the Aubusson factory in France in the 19th century.

Red lacquer panelling of the late 17th century distinguishes the red drawing room. The state dining room, with its white and gold panelling, was created in the 1760s. Above the fireplace, instead of the more usual portrait or mirror, hangs a painting of two lions by Frans Snyder. He collaborated with Rubens and this is thought to be a study for part of one of Rubens' large pictures. All the state rooms have portraits of quality and the small room known as the blue boudoir a formidable study of Henry VIII. The solid figure in stiff clothes, the stubby hands and square face in which the eyes are rather small and utterly ruthless – the sheer physical presence – comes as something of a shock. He seems out of place in this small, charming room overlooking the river, though the painting is an integral part of the 17th-century decoration.

No more Earls of Warwick will live at the castle. But Madame Tussaud's own history goes back nearly two hundred years and this historic place – one of the most visited in the country – is in experienced hands.

Above, the cedar saloon, one of the fine range of state apartments of the 18th century.

Opposite, the gatehouse, built by Thomas Beauchamp on his winnings in the Hundred Years War.

Top, the great hall was rebuilt after being gutted by fire in 1871, but still contains a fine carved Elizabethan oak sideboard, and a small part of Warwick's extensive collection of arms and armour.

☎ Warwick (0926) 495421

In centre of Warwick

SP 2864 (OS 151)

Open daily throughout year;
Mar to end Oct 100-1730;
Nov to end Feb 1000-1630

⊖ P WC ☐ ♣ ☞ 🛆 ◆
❋ (available in foreign
languages) ⚔ ● (no use of
flash)

Althorp

Northampton, Northamptonshire

Home of the Spencer family, the house was originally built by Sir John Spencer soon after 1508. His red-brick house surrounded by a moat and formal gardens was remodelled in 1650 by Dorothy, wife of the 1st Earl of Sunderland, and the inner courtyard became the saloon and great staircase. The house owes most of its character to the architect Henry Holland, who in 1786 was called in to remodel it again. He refaced it in the fashionable grey-white brick tiles baked at Ipswich, filled in the moat and improved the gardens with the help of Samuel Lapidge, Capability Brown's chief assistant. The grand stable block was designed by Roger Morris and built in 1732. Morris was also responsible, with Colen Campbell, for the splendid lofty Palladian entrance hall with its lovely plaster ceiling. This room is known as the Wootton hall as it was designed for equestrian paintings by John Wootton, which exactly fit the walls. The rooms at Althorp house one of the finest private collections of art in England, which was begun by Robert Spencer, 2nd Earl, and enlarged and improved by successive generations. The Marlborough room contains particularly fine portraits by Gainsborough and Reynolds; there are portraits by Rubens and many Old Masters; the picture gallery has works by Van Dyck, Lely and others, while the staircase is hung with portraits of the Spencer family since the time of Elizabeth I. The porcelain and furniture are equally fine, and there is some marvellous 18th-century furniture.

Arbury Hall

Nuneaton, Warwickshire

One of the best examples in the country of the 18th-century 'Gothick' style, Arbury, originally an Elizabethan courtyard house, was largely the creation of Sir Roger Newdigate from 1748, using a variety of architects. Mary Ann Evans, later known as George Eliot, was born on the estate, and described it in one of her early books, writing of the 'transformation from plain brick into the model of a Gothic manor-house'. In the 1670s Sir Richard Newdigate had built the impressive stables (partly to a design by Wren) and employed a plasterer who had worked on Wren's City churches to redecorate the chapel; but the character of the house comes from the 18th-century work. The 'Gothicking' continued gradually up to Sir Roger's death in 1806, the earlier parts being contemporary with Horace Walpole's Strawberry Hill, and the architects included Sanderson Miller, Henry Keene and Thomas Crouchman. Miller also advised on the gardens, which were landscaped by Sir Roger. The style of the house is a light and exuberant version of the true Perpendicular Gothic, and the lovely, delicate vaults are not of stone but of plaster. The tour covers most of the finest rooms, and it is interesting to see the changes in style as the work progressed. The drawing room, of 1762, has a very pretty plaster ceiling, while the dining room, designed by Keene ten years later, has a fine fan vault, but the plasterwork vaulting really reaches its height in the spectacular saloon ceiling, with its pendant drops and lace-like tracery; the inspiration was Henry VII's chapel in Westminster Abbey.

Aston Hall

Trinity Road, Aston, Birmingham, West Midlands

This fine Jacobean mansion was begun in 1618 for Sir Thomas Holte, 1st Baronet, and completed about 1635. The architect is not known, but it may have been John Thorpe, as there are two manuscript plans for it in his *The Book of Architecture*. It has been little altered, though it underwent some remodelling in the late 17th and early 18th centuries. It remained in the hands of the Holte family until 1817, when it was rented by James Watt, son of the famous engineer, who lived here to his death in 1848. He worked his family crest into the decorations in many places, and some of the upstairs rooms are decorated in the 19th-century taste – he was one of the first to commission furniture in the neo-Jacobean style. The house was empty for some years, and was then acquired by a private company, on whose behalf Queen Victoria opened it to the public in 1858 as a museum and place of public entertainment. It is now a branch of the Birmingham Museums and Art Gallery. The house contains some fine plaster ceilings, notably in the long gallery and the dining room, dating from about 1630, and several rooms have their original panelling. Although the Holte furniture and the other contents of the house were dispersed by sale in 1817 and 1849, it has now been furnished as far as possible in accordance with inventories of the 17th and 18th centuries, its contents being drawn from museums and private collections, and most of the rooms are open to the public. The house has recently been closed for restoration work, and was re-opened in April 1984.

Belgrave Hall

Church Road, Leicester, Leicestershire

This modest red-brick house, standing on the edge of the suburbs of Leicester, was built in 1709-10 for Edmund Cradock, 'gent', son of a local innkeeper whose family was prominent in local affairs. In spite of its very splendid iron gateway, the exterior of the house is very plain, though not actually ugly. It has passed through various hands since the Cradocks' time, and in 1936 was acquired by the Leicester Museums Service, who have furnished each of the rooms in the style of a particular period from the late 17th century to the 1870s. Although none of the furniture is that which belonged to the actual occupants of the house, the rooms give a very good idea of the lifestyles of moderately well-to-do familes in the 18th and 19th centuries, in contrast to the great country houses, where everything is for show rather than for use. The most outstanding furniture is a set of early 18th-century mahogany chairs with embroidered covers, and there is also a fine red lacquer bureau. These are in the drawing and dining rooms respectively. Other rooms on show are bedrooms, a workroom, a music room, a Victorian nursery and a large kitchen of the early 19th century. There is an attractive garden at the back of the house, and the stables contain an interesting collection of farm implements and harnesses as well as an 18th-century coach.

☎ Leicester (0533) 554100

2 m N of Leicester city centre on A6

SK 5806 (OS 140)

Open throughout year M-S exc F 100-1730, Su 1400-1730. Closed 25,26 Dec

⊖ 🅕 🅔 (limited access) 🚻 (by appt) D
♣ ★ ◆ ❀ ✄

Belvoir Castle

Grantham, Lincolnshire

The battlements of Belvoir (pronounced 'beaver') are all too obviously the product of early 19th-century 'Gothick' fantasy – to a large extent that of Elizabeth, 5th Duchess of Rutland, aided by the family's domestic chaplain and some help from the more professionally qualified James Wyatt, from 1801 onwards. The core of their romantic castle, which was equipped with the civilised comforts expected by Regency nobility, is a medieval fortress raised soon after the Conquest, and later ruined in the Wars of the Roses. A second castle was demolished by the Parliamentarians in 1649, but rebuilding began during Cromwell's lifetime. About a century later, this in turn was demolished to make way for something grander, which is the castle we see today. The family of de Ros held Belvoir from 1247, and it passed by marriage to the Manners family in the reign of Henry VII. Raised to the earldom of Rutland (1526) and then to the dukedom (1703), the Manners can claim one of their members – under the title of Marquis of Granby (d. 1770) – as perhaps the most popular soldier ever to be honoured by English pubs. The entrance and guardroom contain a small arsenal of old firearms, and the military note is reinforced by the regimental museum of the 17th/21st Lancers. The rest of the interior is decorated in a variety of 19th-century revival styles, and contains, apart from Dutch and Flemish paintings and English portraits, a set of the five sacraments by Poussin and a series of Gobelin tapestries with a rose-pink ground with illustrations of some adventures of Don Quixote.

☎ Grantham (0476) 870262

4½ m SW of Grantham on A607 turn N to Denton

SK 8133 (OS 130)

Open mid Mar to late Sept T, W, Th, S 1200-1900

⊖ (limited; 1 m walk) 🅕 WC 🅔 (by appt)
🚻 (by appt) ♣ 🐾 ⍾ ◆ ❀ ✄ 🦌 (by appt)
🎯 (not in castle) Jousting tournaments

Boughton House

Kettering, Northamptonshire

Ralph, 3rd Lord Montagu of Boughton, was sent on several ambassadorial missions to the court of Louis XIV, and so great a taste did he acquire there for French style that he transplanted the idea for this palatial country seat to England. Not only would the exterior look as if it would be at home in the main square of a 17th-century French provincial town, but the friezes and ceilings inside were painted by a French artist, Louis Cheron. Begun in the late 1680s to absorb a straggling Tudor manor built on land bought by an ancestor in 1528, Boughton was left almost finished by Ralph (Duke of Montagu since 1705) when he died in 1709. The dukedom dying out before the end of the 18th century, Boughton passed by marriage into the possession of the Dukes of Buccleuch and since they had seats elsewhere this house was left alone without later 'improvements'. Complete with its original furnishings, it is as if preserved in amber: visiting its stately panelled and moulded rooms is like walking into a stage set for a play by Molière. Neither the gilt-and-brocade richness of the late Stuart and William-and-Mary furniture, nor the splendour of the tapestries and wall paintings soften the formality of its spaces and uncovered floors (part of which introduced the new fashion of 'Versailles' parquet to England). The finest rooms are in the state apartments. The abundance of Mortlake tapestries there is not unconnected with Lord Montagu having bought the management of the factory in 1674.

☎ Kettering (0536) 82248

3 m NE of Kettering on A43 turn E to Boughton Park

SP 9081 (OS 141)

Open frequently between spring and autumn, phone for details

⊖ 🅕 WC 🅔 (separate access by appt)
🚻 D ♣ 🐾 ⍾ ◆ ❀ ✄ 🦌

☎ Banbury (0295) 62624

3 m SW of Banbury on B4035

SP 4138 (OS 151)

Open mid May to mid Sept W, Su, Bank Hol M also
Th in Jul and Aug 1400-1700

⊖ (1½ m walk)

🅿 WC 🍴 D ♣ 🍴 ◆ ☀ ⚔ ● (not in house)

Broughton Castle

Broughton, near Banbury, Oxfordshire

More by courtesy a castle than by virtue of its moat, Broughton is a fine example of a late medieval mansion enhanced by Tudor architects and happily unspoiled by later alterations. In fact, the spendthrift Regency owner, the 15th baron of Saye and Sele, could not afford to keep it up, and so Broughton Castle was spared the enthusiastic 'restoration' imposed on so many country houses in the 19th century. The buildings as left in 1554 (at the start of Mary's reign), gracefully blend the Middle Ages with the English Renaissance in the continuity of their warm yellow stone. The interior was finished in 1599. One can therefore see, all in one house, the 14th-century carved corbel-heads in the groined passage, the private chapel with its untouched altar stone, the exuberant Elizabethan plasterwork ceiling in the white room, and the splendid Jacobean panelling of the oak room. There are also two important chimneypieces: the English-made marble one of not later than 1551, and the stone-and-stucco one in the Fontainebleau style. The only major legacy of the 18th century are the 'Gothick' ceiling pendants in the great hall which, although fanciful, do not offend the bare 14th-century masonry below them. The Fiennes family, whose title of Lords of Saye & Sele is borne today by the 21st Baron, had strong Puritan and Parliamentary associations, and the house was the scene of important meetings of like-minded politicians in the 17th century.

☎ Yardley Hastings (060 129) 234

7½ m SE of Northampton on A428, ½ m E
of Denton turn N

SP 8659 (OS 152)

Open few days each year, phone for details;
parties by appt throughout year

🅿 WC 🍴 (by appt) D ♣ 🍴 ⊼ ◆ ☀
⚔ (compulsory) ● (not in house) ⚕

Castle Ashby

near Northampton, Northamptonshire

The two main periods of building activity at Castle Ashby are explicit in the entrance front: two sides of the Elizabethan house begun in 1574 are linked by a Classical screen of 1635 (possibly by Inigo Jones). Other 17th-century elements are the lettered roof balustrade with texts from Psalm 127 (begun 1624) and the reconstruction of the inside of the east side (from about 1675). The interiors are decorated and furnished mainly of that period, with magnificent carved wooden foliage, plaster ceilings (one surviving from 1620) and Mortlake tapestries. The gilded, inlaid and lacquered cabinets and the high-backed chairs are all in keeping. The Compton family, who have been the owners throughout, made alterations in the 1880s to reinstate the Jacobean-century appearance of part of the house – having previously, from the 1860s, reversed the garden scheme of Capability Brown on the north and east sides, and laid out a formal, Italianate garden with terraces. (Brown's landscaped park, with its two long grassy rides dating from the reign of William III, was left alone.) An important collection of Greek vases is on display in the long gallery (the upper part of the 1635 courtyard screen). The paintings are of high quality. There is the Antonis Mor portrait of Queen Mary I and Van Dyck's study of Charles I's favourite, the Duke of Buckingham, done after his assassination. There are fine examples by Dobson, Ramsay and Reynolds, some good Dutch pieces, and a Giovanni Bellini *Madonna* and a Mantegna *Adoration*.

☎ Stratford-upon-Avon (0789) 840277

5 m E of Stratford on B4086

SP 2656 (OS 151)

Open Apr and Oct S, Su, Bank Hol M and T 1100-
1700 (dusk if earlier); May to end Sept daily exc M
and Th but inc Bank Hol M 1100-1800

⊖ 🅿 WC ♿ 🍴 (by appt) ♣ 🍴 ⊼ ◆ ☀ ⚔

Charlecote Park

Wellesbourne, Warwickshire

Charlecote was built in the 1550s for Sir Thomas Lucy. The house belonged to the Lucy family from the 12th century until 1948, but only the gatehouse survives intact from the Elizabethan building, as George and Mary Elizabeth Lucy made extensive alterations in the 1820s and 1850s. Their avowed intention was to restore the house to its former Elizabethan splendour rather than to alter it, and they made it their life's work, scouring the Continent for suitable fireplaces, paintings and marble pavings, and using only the very best in craftsmen and materials. Thomas Willement, a fashionable designer best known for his stained glass, advised on the decoration, and John Gibson, a pupil of Barry, was employed to design the church as well as some of the interiors. Inside the house there is no hint of the building Elizabeth I would have seen; the rooms are all 19th century and all arranged to look just as they would have done in the 1860s. The richly coloured decorations in the library, dining room and great hall are the work of Willement, while John Gibson's hand can be seen in the ebony bedroom and the drawing room in the north wing, dating from the 1850s. The hall contains an interesting collection of family portraits as well as a huge table bought from Fonthill Abbey in 1823 by George, who had much admired William Beckford. More of the Fonthill furniture can be seen in the tapestry bedroom. The spectacular carved and ornamented sideboard in the dining room, made by George Willcox in 1858, was bought by Mrs Lucy for £2000.

Chastleton House

near Moreton-in-Marsh, Oxfordshire

Chastleton has been scarcely touched by changing fashions – it looks now as it did in the opening years of the 17th century, when it was built for Walter Jones, a successful wool merchant. The architect is not known – it may have been mainly Jones himself – but the front, of golden Cotswold stone, is a sophisticated design, with projections and recessions, windows set at different levels, and towers containing staircases on each side. The house is built round a courtyard, and the front door, which is set sideways, opens into the screens passage and thence into the great hall. This hall has an ornately carved screen and a long oak refectory table. The inside of the house is complex and bewildering, with a great many rooms, but the finest is the great chamber on the first floor, with its painted and carved panelling, vast ornate chimneypiece bearing the arms of the Joneses, and equally ornate plaster ceiling. Several of the other rooms also have plaster ceilings and good fireplaces, and much of the furniture in the house, like the refectory table in the hall, has been there since the house was built. Later additions, such as early lacquer cabinets, blend well, and there are some fine tapestries and hangings, including crewel-work made in the house. Both staircases, east and west, lead up to the great tunnel of the long gallery, which runs right across the top of the house and has a splendid barrel-vaulted ceiling decorated with strapwork and flowers.

☎ Barton-on-the-Heath (060 874) 355
5½ m NW of Chipping Norton on A44 turn SW
SP 2429 (OS 163)

Open throughout year M, T, Th, F 1030-1300 and 1400-1730 S and Su 1400-1700 (or dusk if earlier)
🅿 WC ♿ (limited access) 🚻 D ♣
♣ (limited opening) 🍴 ✸ ✗

Chenies Manor House

Chenies, near Rickmansworth, Buckinghamshire

Chenies, owned by the Russells until the 1950s, was originally a brick manor house built about 1460 by the Cheyne family, and the central part of today's house, with the tower, is of that date. In 1523 John Russell, 1st Earl of Bedford, married the owner of the manor, and the additions he made, the main one being the long brick range set at right-angles to the old gabled one, gave the house its present appearance. A feature of the house is its ornamental chimneys, very similar to those at Hampton Court, and the two buildings shared some of the same workmen. In the 18th century the north wing became a ruin, and the inner courtyard now has walls on two sides where the domestic buildings once were. The 1st Earl made his extensions primarily to entertain Henry VIII and his Court, and the King made two visits. On the second of these, in 1542, Catherine Howard, the current wife, committed adultery with Thomas Culpeper. It is said that the slow steps of a lame man are sometimes heard leading to Catherine's room – the King was at the time in pain from an ulcerated leg. After 1627 Woburn Abbey became the Russells' main seat, though they preserved Chenies as a relic of the past. The interiors are a mixture of styles: Queen Elizabeth's room contains 16th- and 17th-century furniture, while the dining room was modernised in the early 19th century and contains furniture of that period. Among the Tudor survivals are the privy in a closet off the library, and the small dark closets opening off each of the upstairs rooms.

☎ Little Chalfont (02404) 2888
3 m E of Amersham on A404 turn N on B485
TQ 0198 (OS 176)

Open Apr to Oct: W and Th 1400-1700; parties at other times by appt
♿ 🅿 WC 🚻 ♣ ♣ ★ 🍴 ✸ ✗ ● (not in house)

Chicheley Hall

Newport Pagnell, Buckinghamshire

Chicheley was built between 1719 and 1723 by Francis Smith of Warwick, a well-known Midlands architect, and its main front, with a projecting and elevated central bay and giant pilasters, is a fine example of the English Baroque style. It is thought that the owner, Sir John Chester, and his friend Burrell Massingberd also had a hand in the design, and contemporary letters suggest that they did not always see eye to eye. Each side of the house is different, and both the highly Baroque doors (which were criticised by Massingberd) and the windows, many of which still have their original glass and thick glazing bars, are important features of the building. The front door, modelled on Bernini's Chapel of the Holy Crucifix in the Vatican, opens directly into an elegant entrance hall designed by Henry Flitcroft in the Palladian style. The early-18th-century staircase, made of oak but with handrail and treads inlaid with walnut, is particularly fine, and was the combined effort of several craftsmen. The main rooms give a comfortable and intimate feeling, and many contain fine panelling and ceilings. A curious feature of the house is Sir John Chester's library, in which the books are entirely hidden behind ingeniously hinged panelling. The present occupants of the house are the descendants of the First World War naval commander Admiral Beatty, and there are many relics of his career in the study, as well as a naval museum on the second floor.

☎ North Crawley [023065] 252
7½ m NE of Milton Keynes on A422
SP 9145 (OS 153)

Open Apr to late Sept Su, Bank Hols also W in Aug 1430-1800; parties at other times by appt
♿ 🅿 WC ♿ 🚻 (by appt)
♣ ♣ 🍴 ★ ✸ ✗ (compulsory)

☎ Brewood (0902) 850236
6½ m N of Wolverhampton on A449 turn NW to
Brewood for 3 m then SW
SJ 8606 (OS 127)

Open May to mid Sept Th, Su of Bank Hol
weekends and Su in Aug 1430-1730; parties at
other times by appt

🅿 🍴 (by appt) D ♣ ⌁ ⚔

Chillington Hall

near Wolverhampton, Staffordshire

Chillington, home of the Giffard family, has had one of the longest family successions in the country, having passed down directly from father to son since 1178. The house itself, however, is almost entirely 18th century, though a Tudor house certainly existed, and the plan of the 18th-century building was dictated by the original layout. The south side was rebuilt for Peter Giffard in 1724, but the main front is part of a major building campaign carried out in the 1780s by Thomas Giffard. The latter, fresh from his obligatory travels in Italy, engaged the Classical architect John Soane to rebuild the house, and it is an interesting example of Soane's earlier work. The remaining Tudor buildings were demolished, but Soane was forced to retain the 1724 range, and had to alter his design to accommodate them. The columned entrance hall and the three tall ground-floor rooms with their huge windows show the fine quality of his work. The saloon, which is built within the Tudor great hall, is more typical of his work: it is lit by means of a domed roof, an experiment in overhead lighting that he was to develop in the Bank of England. A small drawing room is shown in the largely private 1724 range, and the fine oak staircase with Italian-style plasterwork and the family's crest carved into each bracket. This leads to an elegant arched and vaulted corridor by Soane, and thence to the state bedroom, where there is a splendid painted bed. The park, with its huge lake and ornamental bridges, is one of the finest examples of Capability Brown's work.

☎ Bulwick (078 085) 278/361/223
7 m NE of Corby on A43 turn W
SP 9592 (OS 141)

Open Jun to Aug Su also Bank Hols Easter to Aug
1400-1700; by appt at other times

🅿 WC ♿ 🍴 ♣ 🍽 (for parties by appt)
⌁ ♦ ⚘ (occasional) ⚙ ⚔ (by appt)

Deene Park

near Corby, Northamptonshire

Deene Park, a house that has been built over six centuries, has been the home of the Brudenell family since Sir Robert acquired it in 1514. An Elizabethan house was built here on earlier foundations, and each generation has made alterations and additions. Considerable building was done in the 18th century, so that the house has grown into a part Tudor and part Georgian mansion. The old part of the house, which includes the large block projecting towards the lake, stands round a courtyard, and the first great hall, on the left, dates from 1540. This was later turned into a billiards room, and a 13th-century doorway was found in one of the walls. The Renaissance oriel window bears the initials 'EA' for Edmund and his wife Agnes, whose fortune paid for the building of another and larger great hall in 1571. The main front, facing across the lake, has a central part of about 1810 in a simple Gothick style. The visitor enters the house through a door in the east range, the old part of the house, forming the old hall. This once rose through three storeys to an open roof, but when Sir Edmund built the new great hall he divided it horizontally into three rooms. Sir Edmund's hall has some fine panelling and a complex hammerbeam roof as well as a refectory table and matching seat of about 1560. The stained glass was put in in the 17th century by Sir Thomas Brudenell, later 1st Earl of Cardigan. The dining room has portraits of the horses of Lord Cardigan, hero of Balaclava, and a painting showing him leading the Charge of the Light Brigade.

☎ Burnham (06286) 4638
1 m N of Windsor on B022 turn W onto B3026, after
3 m turn SW at Dorney
SU 9279 (OS 175)

Open Easter to mid Oct Su and Bank Hol M; June to
Sept Su, M and T 1400-1730

🅿 WC ♿ (limited access) 🍴 (by appt) ♣ 🍽
⌁ ★ ⚙ ⚔ (for parties by appt)

Dorney Court

Dorney, near Windsor, Buckinghamshire

This delightful, rambling house, of mellow red brick, dates from 1500, but Dorney Court has always been the manor house of the village, and a house on the site was first recorded after the Norman Conquest. The building, with its irregular roofs and gables, set in a traditional English garden with box hedges, seems at first sight to be entirely medieval, but in fact some of the exterior is a Victorian reconstruction. It has been the home of the Palmer family since the late 16th century, and there is a legend that the first English pineapple was grown here by Rose, the gardener, and presented to Charles II in 1661. The interior layout of the house – the relationship of hall to kitchens, buttery, cellar, courtyard and so on – is similar to many medieval houses, and is little changed from 1500. The oldest part of the house is the panelled parlour with its low-beamed ceiling, which sits beneath the great chamber on the floor above (now a bedroom). This room, with its barrel-vaulted ceiling, contains fine furniture, as do the other rooms on display. The great hall, which contains an impressive collection of family portraits and some superb linenfold panelling brought from Faversham Abbey, was at one time used to hold the Manor Court. The only room of a later date from the rest is the dining room, an elegant panelled interior in the William and Mary style.

Haddon Hall

Bakewell, Derbyshire

Perched on a limestone slope above the Derbyshire River Wye, the grey walls, battlements and towers of Haddon Hall look like an illustration from a book of medieval history. The Hall was abandoned by its owners, the Manners family, in 1700, but from 1912 was lovingly restored to its former condition by the 9th Duke of Rutland, whose life's work it was. There are two courtyards, divided by the 14th-century range containing the banqueting hall, kitchen and dining room, and the gatehouse leads into the lower court, with a small museum to the left. The chapel contains a remarkable series of medieval wallpaintings, and the roof and woodwork all date from 1624. The roof of the banqueting hall is part of the 1920 restorations, but the screen is of 1450, and the kitchens beyond still contain many of their original fittings. The dining room, completed about 1545, has interesting heraldic panelling, carved medallions in the alcove and heraldic ceiling paintings. Above the dining room, and almost identical in shape, is the great chamber, with its lovely Elizabethan plaster frieze and fine timber roof. The long gallery, a splendidly light and airy room lit by large bay windows, has panelling later in style than the other rooms, with interesting heraldic details. A feature of the bay windows is that some of the leaded lights bulge outwards. This was designed to produce a pretty effect, and was preserved when the gallery was restored. The effect can be seen best from the delightful gardens, which were laid out in terraces in the 17th century, and are now planted with a variety of flowers.

☎ Bakewell (062981) 2855

2½ m SE of Bakewell on A6 turn N

SK 2366 (OS 119)

Open Apr, May Jun, Sept daily exc M; Jul, Aug daily exc Su and M 100-1800; also Bank Hol weekends; reduced rates for parties

Hagley Hall

Hagley, near Stourbridge, West Midlands

The Palladian house and its park were created for Sir George, 1st Lord Lyttleton, in the 1750s. The Lyttletons had owned Hagley since 1564, but the old family home had by this time become rather dilapidated. The new house was designed by the 'gentleman' architect Sanderson Miller, who produced a plain building at the request of his patrons: Sir George wrote to him that 'we are pretty indifferent about the outside, it is enough if it is nothing offensive to the eye', and Lady Lyttleton, who had stronger views, vetoed anything 'Gothick'. The interiors, however, are superb, and show where their real preoccupations lay. The lovely plasterwork, the delight of the formal rooms, shows English Rococo at its height, and since a fire in 1925 all the decorations have been restored with great skill. Some furniture and paintings were destroyed, but many remain, including a pair of elaborate pier-glasses in the columned gallery, attributed to the famous carver Thomas Johnson. The finest of the rooms is undoubtedly the tapestry drawing room, which was unharmed by the fire. It was designed around a set of beautiful Soho arabesque tapestries woven in 1720, and the entire room is in the most delicate Rococo style, with carved mirror- and door-frames complementing the plasterwork, a painted ceiling, and French 17th-century chairs covered with tapestry. The park contains some fine garden buildings, the best being the Rotunda of 1747, Miller's 'Gothick' castle and the Temple of Theseus designed in the Greek style by 'Athenian' Stuart.

☎ Hagley (0562) 882408

7½ m NE of Kidderminster on A456, turn E at junction with A491

SO 9180 (OS 139)

Open Easter to end May Bank Hol Su and M, July to end Aug daily exc S 1230-1700

⊖ 🅿 WC ♿ (by appt) 🚻 D ♣ 🍽 ⊼ ◆ ✂ ⟨ ● (not in house)

Hanch Hall

Lichfield, Staffordshire

Hanch Hall has associations going back to the 13th century, when the Aston family built a dwelling here, but very little is known about the early history of the house. There was clearly some building in Tudor times – 16th-century timbers can be seen in one room, and the cellars are Elizabethan, but little else remains. The fine red-brick and stone range facing the garden is 18th century, and the rest of the exterior seems to date from around the early Victorian period. The guided tours, which take in eighteen rooms, are conducted by members of the family, who bought the house in 1975 and are restoring it themselves. One of the best features is a splendid early Victorian oak staircase with carved decoration in the 'Elizabethan' style, and the windows above it have armorial glass recording the families who have lived here. Most of the downstairs rooms have old panelling, and there is some good 18th-century furniture, including a fine Georgian four-poster bed supposed to have been used by the poet Shelley. There are also some *boulle* and marquetry pieces, and the 19th-century ballroom contains a stool of the 1920s made of stuffed leopards' feet. The upstairs rooms, which are arranged to illustrate different periods, display various collections: dolls, needlework, porcelain, teapots, costume, christening gowns and even one called 'Postmen through the Ages'. The grounds, which are open to visitors, contain free-roaming peacocks, pheasants and other wildfowl.

☎ Armitage (0543) 490308

4 m N of Lichfield on A515, turn N onto B5014 for ¾ m

SK 1013 (OS 128)

Open Apr to end Sept Su, Bank Hol M and following T; June to Sept T-F, S 1400-1800

🅿 WC ♿ 🚻 ♣ 🍽 ⟨ (candlelit tours by appt)

Hardwick Hall

Doe Lea, Chesterfield, Derbyshire

Hardwick Hall, glittering with the glass of its great mullioned windows, and bearing the initials and coronets of its builder on its six towers, is one of the most beautiful Elizabethan houses. It was built by 'Bess of Hardwick', who was born in 1518 in the manor house nearby. She married four times, becoming richer with each new marriage, and Hardwick Hall was built after the death of her last husband, the Earl of Shrewsbury, in 1590. She had already rebuilt her father's old house, which now stands in ruins a stone's throw away. Her architect was Robert Smythson – though she probably made most of the decisions herself – and the building is innovatory in many ways, with the great hall at right-angles to the façade instead of parallel to it, and the state rooms at the top of the house. The private family apartments were on the first floor; the ground floor, apart from the great hall, was mainly used by servants, and the windows become progressively taller to suit this interior arrangement. The hall, which contains pieces of 16th-century appliqué work, leads to the tapestry-hung staircase which ascends past the first-floor drawing room to the showpiece of the house, the high great chamber. It was designed for the tapestries which still line the walls, and above them is a painted plaster frieze by Abraham Smith. Behind this room is the long gallery, in which family portraits are hung over more tapestries. The other second-floor rooms also have rich decoration and fine furniture. The back staircase is hung with more examples of excellent embroidery.

☎ Hoar Cross (028 375) 224

12 m W of Burton-on-Trent on B5234, turn S

SK 1223 (OS 128)

Telephone for details of opening hours

🅿 WC ♿ (by appt) 🚌 D ♠
♣ (parties by appt) 🚻 ⚘ 🍴 (parties by appt) ⚘

Hoar Cross Hall

Hoar Cross, near Burton-on-Trent, Staffordshire

This huge seventy-roomed Elizabethan-style mansion, set in twenty acres of woodland and gardens, was built at the height of Victorian prosperity for Hugo and Emily Meynell, to replace the old Elizabethan house which stands nearby. Hugo died in a hunting accident in 1871, the year the house was completed, and his widow built the adjoining Church of the Holy Angels in his memory. The architect of this fine Victorian building was G. F. Bradley, who was also responsible for some of the interior work in the house. The house itself was designed by Henry Clutton, and is large and imposing if not adventurous. The interiors are safely Elizabethan in style, with oak panelling and richly moulded plaster ceilings. That in the long gallery is the work of Bodley, and so is the fine carved screen in the hall, standing astride a short flight of steps. The best of Bodley's work, however, is the chapel, built in 1897, with a richly decorated ceiling, much gilding and carving, stained glass, and panelled walls in the Henry VII style. Between the Second World War and 1970, when the property finally passed out of the Meynell family, the house and gardens fell into a state of some decay. Much restoration work has been done on the house since then, and the grounds are now also being restored. There are some fine and rare trees, and a pair of wrought-iron gates attributed to the famous Robert Bakewell of Derby. Hoar Cross Hall is well known for its medieval banquets, which are held throughout the season.

☎ Radcliffe-on-Trent (06073) 2371

2 m S of Nottingham on A52 take 1st turning E after River Trent to Abbleton

SK 6239 (OS129)

Open Easter and May Bank Hol weekends Su-T; June to Aug Su, T, Th, F 1400-1800

♿ (1 m walk) 🅿 WC ♿ (limited access) 🚌
♠ ♣ 🚻 ◆ ⚘ ⚘ 🍴

Holme Pierrepont Hall

Nottingham, Nottinghamshire

Holme Pierrepont, one of the earliest brick buildings in the county, and originally a courtyard house, shows the work of three centuries. The brickwork of the Tudor front range dates from about 1490, and behind this survives intact a timber roof whose beams run the whole length of the house. Considerable enlargements were made in the 17th century, but apart from one range, most of this Jacobean work was demolished in the 1730s, and a Victorian range was added in the 1870s. The three ranges are grouped round a courtyard garden, which has been laid out by the present owners to the original plan of 1875, with a formal box parterre, rose beds and a huge herbaceous border. Visitors are free to walk through the house at will. The grand staircase, which has elaborately carved floral panels, probably came from the demolished Jacobean hall range, as it dates from the time of Charles II; and the 'big room' has a lovely plaster ceiling of the 1660s recently brought from another house, and 18th-century walnut furniture. Some of the other rooms have Tudor fireplaces and doorways, and all are lived in by the family, who are carrying out extensive restoration work. The early Tudor 'lodgings' range, which still has its original garderobes (lavatories), has been fully restored, with the ornamental timber roof beams exposed and the rooms well furnished with pieces collected by the family over the last 250 years. Holme Pierrepont is also the setting for the authentic productions of Baroque operas staged by the Holme Pierrepont Opera Trust.

Hughenden Manor

High Wycombe, Buckinghamshire

The house, home of Benjamin Disraeli, Earl of Beaconsfield, for the last thirty-three years of his life, is more interesting from a historical point of view than from an architectural one, and makes an interesting contrast with the nearby Waddesdon Manor, owned by Baron Ferdinand de Rothschild. The owners, both Jewish and both married but childless, were friends but their houses could not be more different, Hughenden being as unassuming as Waddesdon is breathtaking. When Disraeli bought the house in 1847, it was of plain white stucco, dating mainly from the 18th century. In 1862 he and his wife brought in the architect Edward Buckton Lamb to remodel the house in 19th-century Gothic style. Disraeli believed it was 'being restored to what it was before the Civil War', but in fact it simply looks thoroughly Victorian: Lamb faced the outside with red brick and a great many pinnacles and arches, while inside he put in some simple, vaguely Gothic-looking ceilings and chimneypieces. The Disraelis loved Hughenden and spent all the time they could here. Some of the rooms still contain their furniture and pictures, and are arranged as though they still lived in the house, but it is mainly a museum of Disraeli's political career, with letters, mementoes and pictures of all the people he had known during his long life, including Queen Victoria. The Queen was very fond of Disraeli; on one occasion, in 1877, she lunched with him at Hughenden, and when he died she sent a wreath of primroses, 'his favourite flower from Osborne'.

☎ High Wycombe (0494) 32580
1½ m N of High Wycombe W of A4128
SU 8695 (OS 165)

Open Apr to Oct W-S and Bank Hol M 1400-1800; Mar S and Su 1400-1800
⊖ (½ m walk) F WC ⚿ (limited access)
⊟ ♣ ♥ ⊼ ★ ⚘

Kedleston Hall

Derby, Derbyshire

Kedleston Hall, home of the Curzons for nearly 900 years, is one of the masterpieces of Robert Adam. It is a vast building, with the great pedimented central block flanked by pavilions big enough to be houses in themselves; but it seems curiously unostentatious. It was built for Sir Nathanial Curzon, 1st Lord Scarsdale, and work began in 1759. The original architect was Matthew Brettingham, who produced the design; James Paine took over in 1760 but was almost immediately replaced by Adam, who designed a completely new south front and modified the entrance front. This south front, with its centre in the form of a Roman triumphal arch and its curving dome and staircase, shows all of Adam's genius, but was never realised, for the money finally ran out. The great portico leads into the marble hall, a stately room which owes more to Brettingham than to Adam. The other rooms were all decorated to Adam's designs, and three rooms on the left of the hall, which were devoted to music, painting and literature, have fine Adam ceilings. The Italian and Dutch paintings here, most of which were bought by Sir Nathaniel, are still arranged as he and Adam placed them. At the centre of the house is the saloon, a circular room based on a Roman temple and designed to display sculpture. Of the four state rooms on the other side of the building, the dining room is the most recognisably 'Adam' in style, and the great apartment is notable for its state bed with posts carved to resemble palm trees.

☎ Derby (0332) 842191
4 m NW of Derby on A52, turn N at Kirk Langley
SK 3140 (OS 128)

Open Easter weekend then May to end Aug Su, Bank Hol M and T 1300-1730; parties at other times by appt
⊖ F WC ⊟ D ♣ ♥ ⊼ ◆ ⚘

Kenilworth Castle

Kenilworth, Warwickshire

Kenilworth Castle, proud and romantic, was built in the 12th century by Geoffrey de Clinton, Treasurer to Henry I, and was appropriated for the Crown by Henry II. In 1266 it was held by the son of the rebel Simon de Montfort and was the scene of a famous siege by Henry III. In those days its water-defences consisted of a vast lake 100 acres in area, and the building was virtually impregnable. The garrison held out for six months and only surrendered in the end because they were starving. The oldest part of the castle is the great Norman keep with its square corner turrets, built about 1180; the outer walls date from about 1205, and the group of buildings to the west and south of the keep was erected by John of Gaunt, the castle's most illustrious owner, who completely remodelled it in the 1370s. He spent a great deal of money on turning it into a palatial residence, and although all his buildings are now ruins, the remains of the great hall, with its lovely decorated oriel widows, give some idea of its past magnificence. The last of the builders of Kenilworth was Robert Dudley, Earl of Leicester, Elizabeth I's favourite. The buildings next to John of Gaunt's, still known as the Leicester Buildings, are his work, as is the gatehouse (now a private residence) and the stable block with its ornamented timberwork. In 1575 Elizabeth I was entertained here in a magnificent round of festivities lasting nineteen days and costing, it is estimated, £1,000 per day. These are vividly depicted in Walter Scott's novel *Kenilworth*.

☎ Kenilworth (0926) 52078
In W outskirts of Kenilworth off B4103
SP 2772 (OS 140)

Open daily throughout year; Mar to Oct 0930-1830, Oct to Mar 0930-1600 (Su 1400-1600)
⊖ F WC ⚿ ⊟ D ♣ ⊼ ◆ ⚘

☎ Uffington (036 782) 223
W of Wantage on B4507
SU 3287 (OS 176)

Open Apr to Aug Th and Bank Hol weekends 1400-1700; parties at other times by appt

🅿 WC 🚪 D ♣ 🍴 ⚹ ✗
◆ (compulsory) ● (not in house)

Kingstone Lisle Park

near Wantage, Oxfordshire

This fine house with its Classical proportions is very much in the style of Sir John Soane, and owes its character to the extensive alterations made in about 1812 by either Cockerell or Basevi, both of whom had been apprenticed to Soane. The two wings were added at this date, though the central part of the house dates from 1677, and one of the wings, that housing the billiards room, has dummy windows on the approach side, making the house appear larger than it actually is. The interior is noted particularly for its superb 'flying staircase', one of the finest in the country, though the designer is not known. The drawing room contains some good late-18th-century furniture and two unusual carpets, modern, though in traditional Morris designs, and made by hand, using the embroidery techniques of gros- and petit-point. There is much exceptional needlework throughout the house, and the card table, stools and firescreen were all worked by the mother of Mrs Lonsdale, the present owner. The room also contains a collection of glass made by Captain Lonsdale, several pieces of miniature furniture and an interesting portrait by Marc Gheeraerts of Elizabeth Throckmorton, the wife of Sir Walter Raleigh. The morning room has several good paintings, including an unusual view of Whitehall by Hogarth, a small Constable and a Norfolk landscape by John Crome. The furniture here is mainly Queen Anne, and the tapestries were worked by Mrs Lonsdale, as was the splendid carpet in the sitting room, which was designed for the room and took seven years to complete.

☎ Longworth (0865) 820259
7 m W of Abingdon on A415 at Kingston Bagpuize
SU 4097 (OS 163)

Open Apr to end Jun S, Su, Bank Hol m 1430-1730; parties by appt at other times; no children under 5

♿ (limited) 🅿 (limited) WC 🚪 (by appt)
♣ 🍴 🎋 ◆ ⚿ ⚹ ✗ ● (not in house)

Kingston House

Kingston Bagpuize, Oxfordshire

There is some doubt about the date of this compact red-brick manor house, nor is the architect known. Its Baroque feeling, and its similarity to some of the work of Wren and Gibbs, have led some experts to claim that it was built about 1710, but the family have found deeds that show it was in existence by 1670, when John Latton sold it to Edmund Fettiplace. Tours, which are conducted by members of the family, start in the staircase hall. The staircase, magnificently cantilevered and with no supporting pillars, is one of the important features of the house. The saloon, which was originally the entrance to the house, is a good vantage point from which to appreciate the lovely proportions of the house, with its symmetry of design, high rooms and fine architectural detail. The rooms are all of a similar character, with Queen Anne fireplaces and panelling in some cases. There are some good paintings, though no major works, and the furniture is mainly 18th century, a mixture of French and English. The library contains a longcase clock showing the phases of the moon and has an intricately carved chimneypiece in the style of Grinling Gibbons. The charming small morning room, which may have been a bedroom, has panelling of an earlier type than the other rooms. Some of this was removed fifty years ago and found in the stables by Miss Raphael, the previous owner, who replaced it. Miss Raphael also laid out the English garden, which is kept up by her niece Lady Tweedsmuir, the present owner.

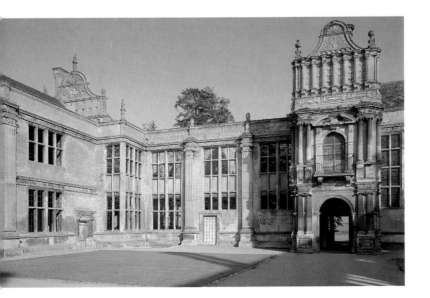

7 m NE of Corby on A43 turn W to Deene, continue for 3 m then turn N
SP 9292 (OS 141)

Open daily throughout year, mid Mar to mid Oct 0930-1830, mid Oct to mid Mar 0930-1600

🅿 WC ♿ (limited access) 🚪 D
♣ 🍴 ⚹

Kirby Hall

Deene, near Corby, Northamptonshire

Kirby Hall is an uninhabited ruin, lacking the greater part of its roof, but it is still one of the most beautiful Elizabethan buildings in the country. It was begun in 1570 by Sir Humphrey Stafford and completed after his death by Sir Christopher Hatton, who bought the property in 1575. Important alterations were made in 1638-40 for Christopher Hatton III, and the Hattons owned and occupied the Hall until 1764. It then passed down the female line to the Finch-Hattons, whose descendants still retain the estate. The buildings are arranged round a central courtyard, and the visitor enters through the porch in the north range, which was almost certainly altered by Inigo Jones. The main south range containing the great hall is opposite, while the ranges at the sides contained the 'lodgings' or guest rooms. The courtyard itself is essentially Sir Humphrey Stafford's building, and all four elevations are decorated with Giant Orders of pilasters which ascend the whole height of the building, the first known use of such a device in England. The great hall is entered through the lovely decorated two-storey porch, French in inspiration, and dated 1572 at the base of the gable (the carved plaster ceiling was added in the 17th century). The hall still has its original timber roof, with corbels decorated with carved devices of the Staffords, while the gallery dates from about 1660. The great staircase was built by Christopher Hatton, as was the south-west wing, the two main rooms of which are lit by great bay windows, among the earliest known in the country.

Kirby Muxloe Castle

Kirby Muxloe, Leicestershire

Kirby Muxloe was begun in 1480, unusually late for a castle, and also unusually, it was built of brick. The building, an ambitious project begun for Lord Hastings, was never completed: Lord Hastings, a rich and respected nobleman, was a supporter of the Yorkist King Edward IV, and in 1483 he was executed by Richard III for suspected treason. All that remains now is the gatehouse and one corner tower standing within the broad moat; the building records, which still survive, indicate that the roofs of the towers were never built, although they may have been thatched to give some protection from the weather. Like other castles built at about this time, Kirby Muxloe seems to have been intended more as a fortified manor house than a serious fortress, and the use of the red brick with black-and-white patterning instead of stone may show a preoccupation with aesthetic rather than military values. However, the military aspect was not entirely neglected: the building records show that the gatehouse would have had machicolations (arched openings through which boiling oil and so on was poured), and there are references to murder holes, which probably mean the openings for cannon in the walls of the gatehouse. The plan of the building is typical of a 15th-century castle: a rectangular outer wall with corner towers, towers in the middle of three sides, and the gatehouse on the fourth side. The main living quarters were built against the walls on the inside.

5½ m W of Leicester on A47 turn NW onto B5380 turn N at Kirkby Muxloe for 1 m

SK 5204 (OS 140)

Open throughout year; M-F Mar to Oct 0930- 1830, Su 1400-1830; Oct to Mar 0930-1600, Su 1400-1600

⊖ P ⅏ ⊟ D ⊟ ◆ ⚹

Lamport Hall

Lamport, Northampton, Northamptonshire

The Isham family held the manor of Isham from the Norman Conquest, and possibly before, but although there was rebuilding in the Elizabethan era, very little now survives. The oldest part of the house is the 'Italian palace' of 1655, built for Sir Justinian Isham by John Webb. This now forms the centre of the main front; the wings were built by Francis Smith of Warwick between 1732 and 1738, improvements being made to the interior at the same time. A new staircase was built, and much of Webb's Classical decoration in the high room, now called the music room, was replaced with exuberant ornamental plasterwork. Webb's fine chimneypiece, however, carved by Cibber with the Isham swans, survives. Further alterations and rebuilding took place in the first part of the 19th century, and the north entrance front was built for Sir Charles Isham in 1861 to designs of William Burn. The house contains fine furnishings, including two large 17th-century cabinets with mythological scenes painted on glass and some excellent 17th- and 18th-century Chinese porcelain. An unusually complete collection of family portraits gives an unbroken record of 400 years of Ishams, and there is a huge painting of Queen Anne of Denmark, who visited Pytchley Hall, residence of another branch of the family, in 1605. The gardens were the main interest of Sir Charles Isham, who appears to have invented the garden gnome – his alpine rockery was once alive with tiny figures, all made in Nuremburg. Only one of these now survives, and is shown in the hall.

☎ Maidwell (060 128) 272

10 m N of Northampton on A508

SP 7574 (OS 141)

Open Easter to end Sept Su and Bank Hol M also Th in July and Aug 1415-1715

⊖ P WC ⊟ (by appt) ♣ ⬤ (limited opening) ⊟ ⚹ ⚿

Lord Leycester Hospital

Warwick, Warwickshire

The hospital is formed of a group of buildings, the oldest of which is the Chapel of St James, built over the archway of the town's west gate in the late 14th century. The chapel became the property of the Guild of St George, which was granted its charter in 1383 and later merged with two other guilds to become the United Guilds of Warwick, and the great hall was built by them soon after this (it still has its original timber ceiling). This was the United Guilds' public room, for such functions as assemblies and feasts, while the Guildhall, built by Neville, Earl of Warwick, about 1450, was the private meeting chamber, where the public was not admitted. The hospital itself was founded in 1571 as a haven for aged and infirm retainers and their wives by Robert Dudley, Earl of Leicester (Leycester), and the Guildhall was divided up into living quarters which, although fairly primitive, continued in use until 1956. The building was then found to be in a dangerous condition, and the original Corporation of the Master and Brethren, which had been in existence since the charter from Elizabeth I, was replaced by a Board of Governors. The extensive restoration work was completed in 1966; eight ex-servicemen and their wives now live here in modernised flats and help with the running of the hospital. The buildings, in spite of some necessary alterations, retain a genuinely medieval feeling: the Master's House has been in continuous occupation since 1400, and the delightful courtyard bears the arms and devices of Lord Leycester and the Sidney family.

☎ Warwick (0926) 492797

In centre of Warwick by the west gate

SP 2865 (OS 151)

Open daily exc Su, Good Fri and 25 Dec; summer 1000-1730, winter 1000-1600

⊖ P WC ⅏ (limited access) ⊟ D ⬤ ◆ ⚹ ⚿

☎ Reading (0734) 723350
4 m NW of Reading on A4074 turn SW to Trench Green
SU 6776 (OS 175)

Open Easter to end Sept S, Su and Bank Hols 1430-1700

☉ P WC ♿ (limited access) ⊟ D ♣ ☞
Ā ◆ ⚹ ✗ (parties by appt)

Mapledurham House

near Reading, Oxfordshire

The house, an attractive Elizabethan building of patterned red brick, was built between 1581 and 1612 by Sir Michael Blount, whose family have lived here ever since. Built on an H-plan, with the central range containing the main rooms, it was altered in the 18th century, when battlements were added to replace the old roof gables. At the same time a small chapel was built in the 'Gothick' style, the great hall was divided up and also 'Gothicked', and sash windows were put in instead of the original mullions. In the 1830s, however, the front was changed back again to more or less its original appearance and a porch was added. The tour of the house starts in the entrance hall, part of the 18th-century alterations. The bleached oak panelling, from another house, was installed in 1863, and there is an interesting and unusual collection of 17th- and 18th-century carved wooden animal heads – such as the wolf in sheep's clothing – which apparently symbolise virtues and vices. The elaborate main staircase is the original Tudor work, and there is still some 17th-century plaster decoration to be seen. The house contains good collections of 17th- and 18th-century furniture and paintings, including a portrait by Sir Godfrey Kneller of Alexander Pope. The latter came frequently to the house between 1707 and 1715 to visit Martha and Teresa Blount, and when he died in 1744 he left his possessions to Martha. The state bedroom has a fine four-poster bed dated 1760, covered with a marvellous 19th-century patchwork quilt containing 15,700 pieces.

☎ Melbourne (03316) 2502
6 m S of Derby on A5132 turn S onto A514 for 1½ m then onto B587
SK 3925 (OS 128)

Open June to Oct Su 1400-1700; parties of 20 or more throughout year by appt

☉ P (limited) WC ♿ (limited access) ⊟ D ♣ ☞
◆ ⚇ ⚹ ✗ (parties only) ● (not in house) ⚘

Melbourne Hall

Melbourne, near Derby, Derbyshire

The parsonage of Melbourne, a small country town, was leased to Sir John Coke in about 1620, and the 17th- and 18th-century Hall, which stands very near the church, may conceal a medieval parsonage. The house is very mixed in style both outside and in, as Sir John, instead of rebuilding, as was usual at the time, merely made some additions to the old house. His son Thomas, who owned the house in the early 18th century, was more interested in the garden and only later considered building a new house. In fact he only remodelled the courtyard and built a new east wing facing the garden. The designer of this garden wing, built in 1725, was the master-builder Francis Smith, but its Palladian front was added by his son William in 1744. The staircase inside, hung with paintings, is a fine example of carved joinery. The original great hall is now a dark-panelled dining room, and most of the other rooms have simple 18th-century decoration. Some of the furniture is very good, and there are some interesting paintings, including several of Stuart courtiers who were friends of Thomas Coke. A fine double portrait by Lely shows Thomas' parents-in-law, Lord and Lady Chesterfield, and there are charming, rather primitive Jacobean portraits of the Cokes' maternal family, the Leventhorpes. The formal gardens have been very little changed since Thomas Coke laid them out with Henry Wise in 1704. The focal point, the wrought-iron arbour or 'birdcage' painted in bright colours and gilded, is an early work by Robert Bakewell of Derby.

☎ Cheddington (0296) 661881
4 m S of Leighton Buzzard on B488 turn W to Mentmore
SP 9019 (OS 166)

Open throughout year Su and Bank Hol; Apr to late Oct 1300-1700; Oct to Apr 1300-1600

☉ (1 m walk) P WC ♿ (by appt) ⊟ D ♣ Ā ★
⚹ ✗ Seasonal festivals; banquets

Mentmore Towers

Mentmore, near Leighton Buzzard, Buckinghamshire

The splendid Victorian mansion was built for Baron Meyer Amschel de Rothschild in 1855 by Joseph Paxton, the designer of the Crystal Palace. The style is Jacobean, and the house is closely based on Wollaton Hall in Nottinghamshire, using the same stone, and with the same corner towers and decorative features. Mentmore has had an eventful history. In 1878 it became the home of the 5th Earl of Rosebery, and over the next hundred years saw many distinguished guests including Napoleon III, Czar Nicholas II, Winston Churchill and Her Majesty Queen Elizabeth II. In 1977 its entire contents were sold in a much publicised auction, raising £6½ million, and a year later it was purchased by the Maharishi Mahesh Yogi and is now the headquarters of the Maharishi University of Natural Law. The palatial interiors, a reminder of the wealth and power of the Rothschild family, are a mixture of the 'Versailles' and the 'Italian palazzo' styles, with much use of carving and gilding. The rooms are all arranged round a huge central hall surrounded by plate-glass doors and windows, which express Paxton's love of glass and light. The fireplace, of black-and-white marble, was imported from Rubens' house at Antwerp, while the dining room contains ornament from the Hôtel de Villars in Paris. The rooms have recently been redecorated, and the tours, which are conducted by a member of the university, end with a visit to the old servants' wing, now laboratories where research is being conducted into higher states of consciousness.

Milton Manor

Abingdon, Oxfordshire

This graceful red-brick house, built in 1663 for Thomas Calton, presents something of a mystery, as tradition says it was designed by Inigo Jones, and it is referred to by Bryant Barrett, a later owner, as 'the Manor House built on a design of Inigo Jones'. Jones had, in fact, been dead for eleven years, but Barrett's words are probably quite literal – Jones's designs continued to be used for some time, and in any case his ideas were still much in vogue. The house, a simple square three storeys high, has an unusual feature in that the front and back are identical, and all four roof elevations are precisely equal. In 1764, Bryant Barrett, a London lacemaker and devout convert to Roman Catholicism, bought the house (his descendants live here still), and with the help of his architect Stephen Wright, added the two Georgian wings and all the outhouses, including stables, a bakery and a brewery. He also landscaped the garden, keeping detailed notes of all his plantings. The new wings, quite plain outside, are far from plain inside. The hall has a marvellous 17th-century carved fireplace and a 16th-century monk's settle said to have belonged to the abbots of Abingdon; the charming drawing room still has its original carved ceiling, and most of the rooms have fine Georgian panelling. But the high spot is undoubtedly the library in the Strawberry Hill 'Gothick' style, on which the well-known carver Richard Lawrence worked with Stephen Wright. The room contains a portrait of Barrett and his family, and a telescope belonging to Admiral Benbow.

☎ Abingdon (0235) 831287/831871
16 m N of Newbury on A34 turn NE at junction with A4130
SU 4892 (OS 164)

Open Easter to end Oct S, Su, Bank Hols 1400-1730; parties at other times by appt
WC ⑤ ☐ (appt only) D ♣ ♥ ☐
☆ ✗ (compulsory) ● (not in house)

Ragley Hall

Alcester, Warwickshire

This large and imposing house, in its lovely park laid out by Capability Brown, was built between 1679 and 1683 for Sir Edward Seymour, ancestor of the Marquess of Hertford, whose home it is today. The original architect was the scientist Robert Hooke, contemporary of Wren, and it is the only surviving example of his building work. In 1750 James Gibbs made improvements to the interior, notably the fine Baroque entrance hall with Rococo plasterwork by Atari, and the stately portico was added by James Wyatt, who also redesigned several of the state rooms in anticipation of a visit from George III. One of his rooms is the red saloon, with delicate Adam-style plasterwork and walls hung with crimson silk, and it is still almost exactly as he left it. Wyatt also designed the stable block, which still houses horses and carriages. During the Second World War the house was used as a hospital, and thereafter became almost derelict, but many of the rooms have since been redecorated in colours similar to the original ones, and the owners are still in the process of restoring and improving. Apart from its lovely interiors, Ragley is full of treasures. There are good paintings, including a landscape by Vernet, *The Raising of Lazarus* by Cornelis van Haarlem and many family portraits; the furniture is outstanding, and there is a fine collection of silver including a cruet set made by Paul Storr in 1804. The Prince Regent's bedroom contains a bed made in 1796. The mural in the south staircase hall, completed in 1983, was painted by Graham Rust.

☎ Alcester (0789) 762090/762455
11 m S of Redditch pn A435, turn W after junction with A422
SP 0755 (OS 150)

Open Apr to end Sept daily exc M and F in Apr, May, June and Sept 1330-1730
⊖ (1 m walk) ℙ WC ⑤ ☐ D ♣ ♥ ☐ ◆
☆ (available in foreign languages)

Rockingham Castle

Rockingham, near Market Harborough, Northamptonshire

The site, a high hill overlooking Rockingham Forest, was a Saxon stronghold of long standing, but William I built the castle, and it was enlarged by subsequent kings, notably Edward I, who made many improvements. By 1530 it had become decayed, and was leased to Edward Watson, ancestor of the present owner, who set about converting it into a comfortable Tudor residence, a task which took him thirty years. His grandson, Sir Lewis Watson, who bought the castle from James I, rebuilt the gallery wing in 1631, but the whole building was so badly damaged in the Civil War that he spent the rest of his life restoring it, a process completed by his son. By 1669 all was complete, though some remodelling was done by Anthony Salvin in 1850, including the addition of a tower. The visitor enters through the servants' hall, past the delightful cobbled 'street', with its bakehouses and breweries, and through the kitchen. The great hall, which was once much larger, was given a lower ceiling by Edward Watson and divided in two to make a hall and parlour (now the panel room). The hall, which is now used as the main dining room, contains an iron-bound chest believed to have been left by King John, another with the painted arms of Henry V, and some interesting 16th-century paintings. The panel room displays a fine collection of Post-Impressionist and 20th-century paintings. The finest room of all is the 17th-century long gallery, which contains some good 18th-century furniture and fine paintings by Angelica Kauffmann, Reynolds and Zoffany.

☎ Rockingham (0536) 770240
3¼ m NW of Corby on A6003 turn S just before Rockingham
SP 8691 (OS 141)

Open Easter Su to end Sept Su, Th, Bank Hol M and T, also T in Aug 1400-1800
ℙ WC ☐ D ♣ ♥ ☐ ◆ ☆ ✗
● (not in house)

☎ Steeple Aston (0869) 47110

14 m N of Oxford on A423 turn E to Rousham

SP 4724 (OS 164)

Open Apr to Sept W, Su and Bank Hols 1400-1630

⊖ (exc Su) 🅿 WC ⊟ ♣ ♥ (limited opening) 🎪 🅰 (occasional) ⚹ 🗡 ● (not in house) No children under 15 admitted even if accompanied

Rousham Park

Rousham, Steeple Aston, Oxfordshire

Rousham, together with its garden, is one of the finest examples of the work of the great 18th-century architect William Kent, and the garden, one of the first landscape designs in the country, is almost as he left it. The house itself, built around 1635 for Sir Robert Dormer, was on the common Tudor H-plan with mullioned windows and gables. Kent, who was called in by General James Dormer in 1738 to make improvements to both house and garden, turned it into a sort of Tudor palace with Gothic overtones. He gave it a straight battlemented parapet instead of the gables, glazed the windows with octagonal panes and built two low wings, that on the garden side having Gothic ogee niches containing Classical statuary. The south front has been little altered, but unfortunately Kent's windows were replaced with sash windows. Kent improved most of the rooms by inserting new fireplaces and doors, but left untouched the original Jacobean staircase and one small room, which retains its 17th-century panelling. Two of the rooms he created are particularly memorable, the painted parlour and the great parlour. The former is purely Palladian, with a marvellous marble chimneypiece, richly carved, as is every other architectural detail. Kent supervised every detail, designed the furniture, and painted the mythological scene on the ceiling himself. The great parlour, more romantic in feeling, has an extraordinary ribbed and vaulted ceiling. It was originally the library, but in 1764 the bookshelves were replaced by the Rococo frames that now adorn the walls.

☎ Little Haywood (0889) 881388

6 m SE of Stafford on A513, turn NE

SJ 9922 (OS 127)

Open mid Mar to late Oct T-F and Bank Hol M 1030-1730, S and Su 1400-1730. Closed Good Fri

⊖ (1 m walk) 🅿 WC 🦽 ⊟ D ♣ ♥ (limited opening) 🎪 ◆ ⚹ 🗡 (parties by appt)

Shugborough

Milford, near Stafford, Staffordshire

This elegant house, set in its lovely 18th-century park, has been the home of the Anson family since 1624. The three-storey central block was built for William Anson in 1693, and in the 1740s Thomas Anson added the pavilions on either side, with their domed bow windows. He later commissioned the architect 'Athenian' Stuart to make further alterations and to design the buildings in the park. These monuments, temples and pavilions which are superb examples of the Greek Revival style and are more famous than the house itself, were financed by Thomas' younger brother, Admiral Lord Anson. The last important additions were made between 1790 and 1806 and the architect was Samuel Wyatt who added the huge colonnaded portico on the main front. He also cased the whole exterior in slates painted to resemble stone, but most of these were later replaced with stucco. The oval shape of the hall was Wyatt's creation, and he introduced a ring of *scagliola* (imitation marble) columns with Doric capitals based on those found at Delos. The plasterwork frieze by Joseph Rose incorporates the Anson crest. Most of the rest of the interior is Wyatt's work, though the library and dining room have kept their original 1740s decoration. The most impressive room is the red drawing room. The coved ceiling with its Neo-Classical ornament is one of the finest works of the famous plasterer Joseph Rose, and there is an elegant white marble chimneypiece with ormolu mounts. The house contains some excellent French furniture, family portraits and sporting paintings.

☎ Oundle (0832) 74013/74064

8 m NE of Corby on A43 turn E just before Bullwick

TL 0292 (OS 141)

Open Apr to end Aug Bank Hol Su and M also w 1430-1700; parties by appt at other times

🅿 WC 🦽 ⊟ D ♣ ♥ ⚹ 🗡

Southwick Hall

near Oundle, Northamptonshire

Southwick Hall, a manor house built over the centuries, has been the home of three inter-related families, the Knyvetts, the Lynns and the Caprons, who still live here today. The Knyvetts built the medieval house, parts of which still remain, notably the two towers. The Lynns, who owned the manor from 1441 to 1840, rebuilt in Tudor times and again in the 18th century, when George Lynn, a cultured man with antiquarian and scientific interests, extended the house on the west side and 'Georgianised' a large part of the interior. The Caprons, who bought the house in 1841, later rebuilt the east wing, built the stable block, and in 1909 altered the entrance through the undercroft. The interiors of the main rooms, particularly the hall, clearly illustrate the three main periods of building. The hall, originally the great hall built about 1300 by John Knyvett, was rebuilt in 1571 to become a ground-floor room with two bedrooms above; in the 18th century it was stripped of its wainscotting and given Georgian details. The oldest part of the house is the vaulted room and circular stair turret built about 1300, while the undercroft, or crypt, was part of the extension built about twenty years later by John's son Richard, as was the Gothic room, which was apparently used as both a living room and a chapel. The middle room, once the solar, was rebuilt by George Lynn in 1580; the Elizabethan windows still remain, and one of the Elizabethan bedrooms over the hall has its original panelling. The bed, made in about 1640, is still in use.

Stanford Hall

Lutterworth, Leicestershire

This large and dignified William and Mary house was designed by the well-known Midlands architect William Smith of Warwick for Sir Roger Cave, whose descendants still live here. It was begun in the 1690s as a replacement for an older house, but both Sir Roger and William Smith died during the building, and it was completed by Smith's sons, William the younger and Francis, for Sir Thomas Cave. The stable block and courtyard were added in the early 18th century by Francis Smith, who was also responsible for many of the interiors. Most of the ground-floor rooms and two of the upstairs are open to visitors, and there is much to see, including a unique collection of Stuart portraits and religious relics. These, which are displayed in the ballroom, were part of the collecton of Cardinal Henry Stuart, and were bought by Baroness Braye after 1807. Most rooms have their original panelling and fireplaces, and there is very good furniture, including Hepplewhite and Queen Anne pieces and a particularly fine 17th-century marquetry clock. The green drawing room has 17th-century portraits, and the marble passage and the stairs are both hung with family portraits. The bedrooms contain 17th-century Flemish tapestries as well as tapestry curtains and bed-hangings, and the old dining room has some furniture from the old house, including an old refectory table and Charles II chairs. The aviation museum in the stables was set up in memory of Percy Pilcher, a pioneer of aviation, who was killed when his machine crashed in the park.

☎ Rugby (0788) 860250
8 m NE of Rugby on B5414 turn E for 1½ m at Swinford
SP 5879 (OS 140)

Open Easter to end Sept Th, S, Su, Bank Hol M and following T; reduced rates for parties
P WC ♿ (by appt) 🚌 (by appt) D 🌳 ☕
⛩ ◆ ☀ 🚶 ● (not in house) 🏃 🚶

Stoneleigh Abbey

Kenilworth, Warwickshire

Originally a Cistercian abbey and then an Elizabethan house, Stoneleigh was transformed during the early 18th century, and turned into an Italianate mansion by the 3rd Lord Leigh. The only part of the monastic building to survive is the 14th-century gatehouse; the rest was in ruins by 1561, and the site had to be cleared before Sir Thomas Leigh could begin to build the house where he and his descendants were to live. Until 1710 Stoneleigh remained an Elizabethan building, but three years earlier Edward Leigh had married an heiress, and now he began to plan a new house that would reflect the spirit of the age. His architect was Francis Smith of Warwick, who also planned and built the interior and designed the panelling of the ground-floor rooms. This now survives only in two rooms, the silk drawing room and the velvet drawing room, but the exterior remains virtually unchanged. The elaborate plaster work in the saloon was carried out in the 1780s, possibly to the designs of Cipriani, but no further alterations were made until 1836, when the long gallery was destroyed and replaced by the present ground-floor porch and entrance corridor. The house contains exceptionally fine furniture, much of it made for the house during Francis Smith's building, which took twelve years. There is also an excellent collection of paintings, mainly portraits, including one of Henry VIII and a small painting of Prince Charles Edward, the Young Pretender, who (legend claims) was smuggled out of the house in a beer cask in the guise of a mysterious 'Mr Fox'.

☎ Kenilworth (0926) 52116
4 m N of Royal Leamington Spa on A444, turn NW to National Agricultural Centre
SP 3171 (OS 140)

Open Easter to end Sept Su, M, Th 1300-1730
P WC ♿ 🚌 D 🌳 ☕ ⛩ ◆ ☀ 🚶
● (not in abbey)

Stonor

Henley-on-Thames, Oxfordshire

The house, hidden in a fold of the Chilterns and surrounded by beechwoods, is largely 18th-century in appearance, but its long, low, red-brick Georgian façade fronts the greater part of a large medieval house. The Stonor family, who have always been Roman Catholics, have lived here since the 12th century, and the heavy penalties they had to pay after the Reformation for their beliefs prevented them from doing much new building. The house is still, in its core, a group of medieval buildings, the first recorded ones being the old hall, buttery, solar and flint-and-stone chapel all built between 1280 and 1331. For the next two hundred years there was constant building and renovation, and in the 16th century Sir Walter Stonor joined the buildings to make a formal E-shaped Tudor house and built a many-gabled brick front. The house was altered again in the 1750s by the architect John Aitkins, who removed all but the central gable, put in sash windows and added the present roof with its heavy cornice. He also redecorated the hall in the 'Gothick' style – the same style was later used for the chapel. There are some attractive and well furnished rooms, and several have been redecorated. The dining room has early-19th-century wallpaper showing the buildings of Paris; there is a bedroom with an 18th-century French bed and chairs shaped like seashells, and the house contains important Renaissance bronzes and good tapestries. The library holds a large collection of books relating to secret Roman Catholicism.

☎ Turville Heath (049 163) 587
6 m N of Henley-on-Thames on B480 turn E after Stonor
SU 7489 (OS 175)

Open Apr to end Sept W, Th, Su 1400-1730; on T by appt
P WC ♿ (by appt) 🚌 D 🌳 ☕
⛩ ◆ ☀ 🚶 ● (not in house)

☎ Sulgrave (029 576) 205
8 m NE of Banbury on B4525 turn E after Thorpe Mandeville
SP 5645 (OS 152)

Open Feb to end Dec daily exc W; Apr to end Sept 1030-1300, 1400-1730; Oct to end Mar closes 1600

🅿 WC 🚌 ♣ 🍴 ◆ ⚘
🏃 ● (not in house)

Sulgrave Manor

Sulgrave, near Banbury, Oxfordshire

The fame of this charming 16th-century manor house rests on its historical associations, as it was the home of the ancestors of George Washington. His great grandfather, John, emigrated in 1657. The land came into the Washington family when Lawrence Washington bought it in 1539 – for the sum of £324 14s 10d. Lawrence was at the time Lord Mayor of Northampton and reasonably prosperous. He also had four sons and seven daughters, which presumably necessitated a larger dwelling. The house he built, a modest one of the local stone, was completed in 1560, but there have been several alterations, and it passed through many hands and became quite dilapidated before being purchased by subscription in 1914 and restored as a memorial to Anglo-American friendship. The most valuable item is a fine portrait of George Washington by the famous American painter Gilbert Stuart (1755-1828), but there are many other relics of the great man, and two small rooms are used as a Washington museum. The manor has been very carefully restored, and there are some fine fittings and pieces of furniture, including an Elizabethan four-poster bed with an embroidered coverlet from the reign of William and Mary. During work on the great hall an Elizabethan sixpence and a baby shoe were found, together with a knife case which evidently belonged to Lawrence Washington himself. The kitchen is particularly interesting as it contains a 200-year-old kitchen bought, complete with all its fittings, from a manor house in Hampshire.

☎ Aylesbury (0296) 651211/651282
7 m W of Aylesbury on A41
SP 7316 (OS 165)

Open late Mar to end Oct W-Su (exc W following Bank Hol also Good Fri and Bank Hol M) 1400-1800

⊖ (limited) 🅿 WC ♿ 🚌 (by appt) D ♣ 🍴
★ ⚘ 🏃 (by appt) ● (not in house) Aviary

Waddesdon Manor

Aylesbury, Buckinghamshire

Waddesdon is a French château in the heart of the English countryside, but it was built by Baron Ferdinand de Rothschild, who was in love with French 18th-century art. The house was designed in the Renaissance style by Gabriel-Hippolyte Destailleur, and built between 1874 and 1889. It was no small operation, as before building could begin the ground had to be levelled and woods planted on the bare hillside. To speed things up, half-grown trees were dragged to the hilltop site by teams of horses, and a railway was constructed to carry stone to the bottom of the hill. The exterior is surprising but the interior is incredible, illustrating the lifelong passion of this rich and cultured collector. Baron Ferdinand not only had a deep love and understanding of French 18th-century art, he was also a collector of English 18th-century portraits and paintings of the Dutch and Flemish schools, so there are many fine paintings, while rooms upstairs contain more specialised collections of china, musical instruments and costume. Miss Alice de Rothschild, the Baron's sister, was also a keen collector, and added Sèvres and Meissen as well as arms and armour. The best features of the house are the ground-floor rooms, where there are interiors matched only in the great French houses, with incomparable collections of 18th-century furniture, carpets, porcelain and sculpture. Many of these richly decorated rooms contain carved wooden panels (*boiseries*) brought from houses in France.

☎ High Wycombe (0494) 24411
3 m W of High Wycombe on A40
SU 8294 (OS 175)

Open June M-F, July and Aug daily exc S 1400-1800; reduced rates for parties of 15 or over by appt

⊖ 🅿 WC 🚌 (by appt) ♣ ⚘ 🏃 (exc Su)
● (not in house) ♿

West Wycombe Park

West Wycombe, Buckinghamshire

The Dashwood family bought the estate in 1698, and the original brick house was built by Sir Francis soon after, but the 18th-century house we see today owes its character entirely to his son, the second Sir Francis Dashwood, founder member of both the Society of Dilettanti and the Hell Fire Club. From 1769, when he returned from travelling in Italy, he began to alter the house, but it is impossible to fit it into any architectural pigeon-hole as it accurately reflects his ever-changing tastes and sudden enthusiasms. He employed several different architects and artists as well as having a good many ideas of his own, so that the house is a patchwork – albeit a charming one – of 18th-century styles. The Palladian north front, the first to be completed, the south façade with its two-storey colonnade, and the east front with its Doric portico are all the work of a little-known architect, John Donowell. The west front, in contrast, is by Nicholas Revett and has a Greek portico. The interiors are equally mixed in style: the hall and dining room are Neo-Classical, and painted to imitate coloured marbles; the staircase landing, the undersides of the stairs and the ceilings of library and study have delightful Rococo plasterwork, while several of the other rooms have Baroque painted ceilings by an Italian artist, Guiseppe Borgnis. The park, to which Sir Francis devoted as much attention as the house, is attractively laid out and contains several 18th-century 'garden temples'.

Whitmore Hall

near Newcastle-under-Lyme, Staffordshire

Although no more than three or four miles from the Potteries, Whitmore Hall is charmingly manorial and rural in setting. It forms a unit with the estate village and the little medieval church, and is shielded from the industrial scene by the woods of Swynnerton Old Park. The visitor passes down a broad avenue of limes from the churchyard to the south front of rich red brickwork with stone dressings and a stone balustrade at the top; behind the façade, the house is actually a four-storey structure. The entrance hall, with its twin Corinthian columns, dates from the Georgian period, and the porch is mid 19th-century. However, within its 17th-century casing of brick lies a much older, timber-framed house. The history of the estate can be traced back to John de Whitmore, who held it in the late 12th century. Over the centuries it was always passed down by inheritance. Towards the end of the 14th century Elizabeth de Whitmore brought it to the de Boghays by marriage. Then in 1546 Alice de Boghay married Edward Mainwearing; and there have been Mainwearings at Whitmore ever since. The stables at Whitmore are particularly admired, since they provide an unusual example of early 17th-century craftsmanship in wood; the interior fitments – including the horses' stalls, with their turned columns and arches – are wonderfully well preserved. Among the other attractions of Whitmore are the elegantly landscaped park and lake behind the house.

☎ Whitmore (0782) 680235

4 m SW of Newcastle-under-Lyme on A53

SJ 8040 (OS 118)

Open May to Aug T and W 1400-1730

🅿 WC 🚻 ♣

Wightwick Manor

Wolverhampton, West Midlands

At first glance Wightwick (pronounced Witick) looks like one of the black-and-white timber-framed houses so common in Lancashire and Cheshire, but in fact it is late Victorian, and its main importance lies in its superb decorations by William Morris and other artists and craftsmen influenced by Ruskin and the Pre-Raphaelites. In 1887 Samuel Theodore Mander, a wealthy paint manufacturer, bought the old manor and employed the architect Edward Ould, a specialist in timber-framed buildings, to design a new house near the old one. The earlier buildings were given dressings of shiny red Ruabon brick, which was also used for the first stage of the new house. Six years later the more elaborate east wing was begun, with architectural details from Little Moreton Hall, spiral Tudor chimneys and intricate carving. The interior displays examples of all aspects of Morris' own designs – wallpaper, fabrics, carpets and tiles – as well as the work of other artists and craftsmen supplied by the firm – metalwork by W. A. S. Benson, tiles by William de Morgan and stained glass by C. E. Kempe. The house also contains paintings and drawings by Burne-Jones and other Pre-Raphaelites, and Morris' designs, as he intended, provide a setting for Jacobean furniture, Persian rugs and Chinese porcelain. The collection has been enlarged by the late Sir Geoffrey Mander and Lady Mander, who still lives in the house and is an expert on the period. The gardens, contemporary with the house and conceived as part of it, were laid out by Alfred Parsons.

☎ Wolverhampton (0902) 761108

3 m W of Wolverhampton on A454

SO 8698 (OS 139)

Open Mar to end Jan Th, S, Bank Hol Su and M 1430-1730; no children under 10

⊖ 🅿 WC 🦽 (limited access) 🚻 (by appt) D ♣

◆ ⁂ ✗ (exc Bank Hols) ● (not in house)

Winslow Hall

Winslow, Buckinghamshire

This red-brick house, modest in scale for a country house, was almost certainly the work of the great architect Sir Christopher Wren, who built a great many churches but few domestic buildings. It was built between 1699 and 1702 for William Lowndes, Secretary to the Treasury, whose family had lived in Winslow since the early 16th century, and several very well-known craftsmen were employed on the brickwork and carpentry. The building of the house is well documented, and the owners show visitors the original accounts which mention all the craftsmen by name, itemise the various expenses and give a total for the whole work – £6,585. 10s. 2¼d. The exterior is quite simple, with two tall main fronts which are made to look even taller by the four huge chimneys and the pointed central pediment. Originally the flanking buildings for kitchens, servants' accommodation and so on were detached, but in 1901 they were rather clumsily joined to the main house. The interiors are well proportioned, and most of the rooms have their original oak panelling and fireplaces, but with one exception the decoration is pleasant rather than spectacular. The exception is the Painted Room, where four wide spaces on the walls are filled with paintings in heavily ornate frames with scrolls, cartouches and drapery. The artist is unknown, but the paintings were apparently based on a well-known series of tapestries. The gardens were laid out in 1695 but nothing remains of their formal layout, though the present gardens are charming and well kept.

☎ Winslow (029 671) 3433

On NW outskirts of Winslow on A413

SP 7628 (OS 165)

Open May and June Su 1400-1700; July to mid Sept daily exc M 1430-1730

⊖ 🅿 WC 🚻 🛉 ☕ ⁂ ✗

● (by permission in house)

Anne Hathaway's Cottage, Hewlands Farm, Shottery, near Stratford-upon-Avon, Warwickshire (tel Stratford-upon-Avon [0789] 292100). 1 m W of Stratford. SP 1854 (OS 151). Half-timbered, thatched farmhouse, the home of Anne Hathaway before her marriage to William Shakespeare. There is an attractive cottage garden. One of the most popular sites in Britain. Open daily am and pm (Nov to March Su pm only). ⊖ 🅿 wc 🚻

Ardington House, near Wantage, Oxfordshire (tel East Hendred [023 588] 244). 2½ m E of Wantage, off A417. SU 4388 (OS 174). Classical house of about 1720, built of grey stone and red brick. The hall is notable, and there is an Imperial staircase and panelled dining room with painted ceiling. The grounds contain fine cedar trees. Open May to Sept Th, F and Bank Hols pm. ⊖ 🅿 wc 🚻 (by appt) ♣ 🐾

Ascott, Wing, Buckinghamshire (tel Wing [029 668] 242). 2 m SW of Leighton Buzzard on A418. SP 8922 (OS 165). Small 17th-century farmhouse extended in the 1870s and 1930s, when the house was in the possession of the Rothschild family. It contains Anthony de Rothschild's collection of paintings (notably 17th-century Dutch, and 18th- and 19th-century English), Chinese porcelain and French furniture. The 19th-century garden has many rare trees and attractive flower borders. Open Apr to end Sept W and Th pm; also S in Aug and Sept, and Summer Bank Hol M. ⊖ 🅿 wc 🚻 (by appt) ♣

Ashby-de-la-Zouche Castle, Ashby-de-la-Zouche, Leicestershire. On E outskirts of town. SK 3616 (OS 128). Mainly 15th-century fortified manor with the massive 'Hastings tower', built on a rectangular plan during the Wars of the Roses. The castle was a Royalist base during the Civil War, and besieged in 1644-46. Open am and pm daily (Su pm only). ⊖

Ashdown House, Ashbury, near Lambourn, Oxfordshire. 3½ m N of Lambourn, off B4000. SU 2882 (OS 174). Restoration period house built alone on the Downs, in the tall Dutch style, by William Winde. There is a carved four-storey staircase, hung with family portraits; the grounds are laid out to late 17th-century taste. Open May to Sept W and alternate S pm; Apr W pm only. ⊖ 🅿 wc D (grounds only) ♣

Aynhoe Park, Aynho, Northamptonshire (tel Croughton [0869] 810659). 7 m SE of Banbury on A41. SP 5233 (OS 151). Jacobean mansion, partly rebuilt in the 1680s and again between 1707 and 1714. Sir John Soane made further alterations in the early 19th century, inside and out. The house has now been partially converted into flats. Open May to Sept W and Th pm. ⊖ 🅿 wc 🚻 ♣

Baddesley Clinton, Solihull, West Midlands (tel Lapworth [056 43] 3294). 9 m NW of Warwick on A41, turn W. SP 2071 (OS 141). Moated medieval manor house dating in part to the early 14th century, and little changed since Jacobean times. There are 120 acres of grounds. Open Apr to Sept W-Su and Bank Hols pm; Oct, S and Su pm only. 🅿 🚻 🚻 (by appt) ♣ 🐾

Bede House, Lyddington, Leicestershire. 7 m S of Oakham on A6003, turn E. SP 8797 (OS 141). Mid-15th century palace for the Bishop of Lincoln, converted into a bedehouse or almshouse by Lord Burghley in 1602. It retains its 15th- and 16th-century decorations and painted glass in the bishop's apartment. Open Apr to Sept daily am and pm (Su pm only). ⊖ 🅿

Blakesley Hall, Yardley, Birmingham, West Midlands (tel 021-783 2193). 3 m E of city centre. SP 1285 (OS 139). Large, ornate timber-framed yeoman's cottage of 1575, with 18th-century outhouses. Several rooms are furnished as period settings, and have displays of local history and crafts. There is an attractive formal garden. Open daily am and pm (Su pm only); closed Christmas, New Year and Good Fri. ⊖ 🅿 wc 🚻 🚻 ♣

Bolsover Castle, Derbyshire (tel Bolsover [0246] 823349). In town centre. SK 4770 (OS 120). Ruined house built for the Cavendish family on the site of a 12th- and 13th-century castle. The mock keep was built by Robert Smythson in the 1610s, and his son John was responsible for much of the rest before 1640. The castle was slighted in the Civil

War. There is a riding school with a fine timber roof, probably dating from the 1660s, and still in use. Open daily am and pm. ⊖ 🅿 wc

Buscot House, near Faringdon, Oxfordshire (tel Faringdon [0367] 20786). 3 m SE of Lechlade on A417. SU 2496 (OS 163). House of the 1780s, restored to its original condition in the 1930s. Its contents include paintings (including works by Rembrandt and Burne-Jones) and fine furniture. The grounds include an Italian water-garden designed in the early 20th century. Open Apr to Sept W-F and alternate S and Su pm. 🅿 wc 🚻 ♣ 🐾

Canon's Ashby House, Canon's Ashby, Northamptonshire (tel Blakesley [0327] 86004). 18 m SW of Northampton, on B4525. SP 8659 (OS 152). A small manor house, with restored garden including 18th-century terraces and walls. The house was originally part of an Augustinian priory, and was converted in the 16th century by the Dryden family. There are Elizabethan wall-paintings, and Jacobean plasterwork. Open Apr to end Oct W-Su and Bank Hols pm. 🅿 🚻 (by appt)

Carlton Hall, Carlton-on-Trent, Nottinghamshire. 7 m N of Newark on A1, turn E. SK 7964 (OS 129). Georgian house built by Carr of York in 1765, set in attractive grounds. There is a large and magnificent drawing-room, with elaborate plaster decoration. Open by appt, Apr to Oct. 🅿

Claydon House, Middle Claydon, Buckinghamshire (Steeple Claydon [029 673] 349). 3½ m SE of Buckingham on A413, turn SW. SP 7225 (OS 165). House built by the 2nd Earl Verney in 1754, of which only the west end survives. The interior has lavish Rococo woodcarvings by Luke Lightfoot, including a unique Chinese room and parquetry and wrought-iron staircase. A Florence Nightingale museum is found on the upper floor. Open S and M to W pm, Apr to end Oct. ⊖ 🅿 wc 🚻 🚻 ♣

Cliveden, Maidenhead, Buckinghamshire (tel Burnham [062 86] 5069). 1½ m E of Maidenhead. SU 9185 (OS 178). House in the style of an Italian Renaissance palace, built in the 1850s by Charles Barry for the Duke of Sunderland; the third house on the site since the Restoration. It has been owned by the Astor family, and the Duke of Westminster; it is now used as a college. The magnificent formal gardens reach down to the River Thames, with statuary and water gardens. House open Apr to end Oct S and Su pm; gardens open all year daily am and pm. ⊖ 🅿 wc 🚻 🚻 (by appt) ♣ 🐾

Coughton Court, Alcester, Warwickshire (tel Alcester [0789] 762435). 7 m S of Redditch, on A435. SP 0860 (OS 150). 15th- and 16th-century house with an early 19th-century façade, the home of the Throckmorton family. Through the succeeding centuries they were one of the leading

Catholic families in Britain, and the house contains relics of the history of British Catholicism, including those relating to Mary, Queen of Scots, the Gunpowder Plot and the Jacobites. The main gatehouse dates from 1509. Open May to Sept W-Su and Bank Hols pm; Apr and Oct S and Su pm; also Easter week to Th. ⊖ 🅿 wc 🚻 (by appt) ♣ 🐾

Courthouse, Long Crendon, Buckinghamshire. 2 m N of Thame via B4011. SP 6909 (OS 165). 14th-century building, with two storeys and half-timbered, probably built as a wool-store, but used for manorial courts from the 15th century until recent times. Open S and Su and Bank Hols am and pm, W pm only, Apr to Sept. 🅿 🚻

Delapré Abbey, Northampton, Northamptonshire (tel Northampton [0604] 62297). 1 m S of town centre, off A508. SP 7559 (OS 152). A 12th-century Benedictine nunnery, converted into a private house in 1538. Most of the house dates from the 17th-18th centuries, and it is used as the Northamptonshire Record Office and Library. There is an attractive park. House open Th pm; park open daily am and pm. ⊖ 🅿 wc 🚻 ♣ ★

Ditchley Park, Enstone, Oxfordshire (tel Enstone [060 872] 346). 9 m NW of Oxford on A34, turn W. SP 3921 (OS 164). The third great 18th-century mansion in Oxfordshire, designed by James Gibbs and with interior decoration by William Kent and Henry Flitcroft. It was the weekend headquarters of Sir Winston Churchill during the Second World War, and is now used as an Anglo-American Conference Centre. Open late July to early Aug daily pm. 🅿 🚻

Donnington-le-Heath Manor House, near Coalville, Leicestershire (tel Coalville [0530] 31259). 13 m NW of Leicester, off A447. SK 4212 (OS 129). Small manor house of about 1280, now restored. It contains a kitchen with medieval equipment below the great hall. There is a medieval herb garden, and a medieval barn in the grounds. Open Easter to Oct W-Su pm, and Bank Hol M and T pm. ⊖ 🅿 wc 🚻 ♣ 🐾 ★

Dorton House, Dorton, Buckinghamshire (Brill [0844] 238237). 6 m N of Thame off A4011. SP 6713 (OS 165). Jacobean red-brick house built in 1626, now used as a school. The interior includes the original great hall with screens passage; other notable features include the ceilings, fireplaces and staircases. Open May to July and Sept pm; other times by appt. 🅿 wc 🚻 🐾 (in school terms)

Ednaston Manor, Ednaston, Derbyshire (tel Ashbourne [0335] 60325). 6 m NE of Derby, off A52. SK 2442 (OS 129). House built by Sir Edwin Lutyens in Arts and Crafts style; the garden is of particular interest, with a large collection of shrubs and unusual plants. Open Easter to Sept, daily (exc S) pm. 🅿 wc 🚻 ♣ 🐾 ★

Claydon House, Buckinghamshire

Farnborough Hall, near Banbury, Warwickshire (tel Farnborough [029589] 202). 8 m N of Banbury off A423. SP 4349 (OS 151). 17th- and 18th-century house, mostly rebuilt in the mid-18th century, with fine Rococo plasterwork. There is a terraced garden with wide views and garden temples. Open Apr to end Sept W, S and Bank Hol M, pm. ⊖ 🅿 WC 🔊 D (grounds only) ♣

Ford Green Hall, Smallthorne, Stoke-on-Trent, Staffordshire (tel Stoke-on-Trent [0782] 534771). SJ 8850 (OS 118). 4 m N of city centre, off A53. Timber-framed yeoman's cottage of the 16th century, with furniture of the 16th to 18th centuries. Open M, W, Th, S am and pm, Su pm only. ⊖ 🅿 ★

Greys Court, Henley-on-Thames, Oxfordshire (tel Rotherfield Greys [049 17] 529). 3 m W of Henley-on-Thames. SU 7283 (OS 175). Jacobean house set in the 14th-century walls of a medieval manor. There is a Tudor donkey wheel for raising well water, and the house contains some excellent Rococo plasterwork. The very extensive gardens include a recently opened maze. Open Apr to Sept; house M, W, F pm, garden M-S pm. ⊖ 🅿 WC 🔊 (by appt) 🚻 (by appt) ♣ 🐾

Farnborough Hall, Warwickshire

Halls Croft, Old Town, Stratford-upon-Avon, Warwickshire (tel Stratford-upon-Avon [0789] 292107). In town centre. SP 2055 (OS 151). Fine Tudor house with walled garden, the home of William Shakespeare's daughter Susanna and her husband Dr John Hall. There is an exhibition of 17th-century medicine in the house. Open Apr to Oct daily am and pm (Su pm only); Nov to March M-S am and pm. ⊖ WC 🔊 ♣ 🐾

Hanch Hall, Lichfield, Staffordshire (tel Armitage [0543] 490308). 5 m N of Lichfield off A515 turn NW. SK 1013 (OS 128). House made up of varied elements ranging from the Tudor to the Victorian. Most of the exterior is early 19th-century, apart from the Georgian garden front. There is a Victorian oak staircase in the Elizabethan manner. The upstairs rooms contain a doll collection, a needlework display, and a collection of early teapots and porcelain. Open June to end Sept T-Th, S pm; Apr to end May Su, Bank Hol M and following T only. Parties at other times by appt. ⊖ 🅿 WC 🚻 (by appt) ♣ 🐾 🍴

Hartwell House, Hartwell, Buckinghamshire (tel Aylesbury [0296] 748355). 1½ m W of Aylesbury off A418. SP 7913 (OS 165). Jacobean mansion with original staircase and façade remodelled in mid-18th century. Louis XVIII lived here from 1808 to 1814. The house is now used as a college. Open mid-May to mid-July, W pm. 🅿 🔊

Harvard House, High St, Stratford-upon-Avon, Warwickshire. In town centre. SP 2055 (OS 151). Heavily decorated half-timbered town house of the last years of the 16th century, the home of the mother of John Harvard, founder of the American University. Open Apr to Oct, M-S am and pm, Su pm only; Nov to March Th, F and S am and pm (closed Christmas and New Year). ⊖ 🅿 🔊

Hinwick House, near Wellingborough, Northamptonshire (tel Rushden [093 34] 53624). 5 m SE of Wellingborough on A509 turn W. SP 9362 (OS 153). Attractive Queen Anne house, with notable 17th-century paintings, including works by Van Dyck, Lely and Kneller. There are displays of lace and tapestries, and of fashion from 1840 to 1940. Open Easter Spring and Summer Bank Hols; other times by appt. 🅿 🚻 🐾

Holdenby House, Holdenby, Northamptonshire (tel Northampton [0604] 770786). 4 m NW of Northampton on A50 turn NW. SP 6967 (OS 152). The largest private house in England in Elizabeth I's reign, built by Christopher Hatton. The original garden and park can be seen, including fragrant and silver borders, and rare breeds of cattle and sheep. House open only by arrangement for parties; gardens open Apr to Sept Su and Bank Hol M pm (also July and Aug Th pm). 🅿 WC 🔊 🚻 (by appt) ♣ 🐾

Honington Hall, Shipston-on-Stour, Warwickshire (tel Shipston-on-Stour [0608] 61434). 15 m SE of Stratford-upon-Avon off A34. SP 2642 (OS 151). Elegant house built in 1682 for the merchant Henry Parker, remodelled inside in the 1740s by John Freeman in elaborate Rococo style, with fine plasterwork. Open May to Sept W and Bank Hol M pm. ⊖ 🅿 WC 🔊 🚻 (by appt) ♣

Kelmarsh Hall, near Market Harborough, Northamptonshire (tel Maidwell [060 128] 276). 7 m S of Market Harborough on A508. SP 7379 (OS 141). Neo-Classical house built by James Gibbs around 1730, set in attractive grounds, and now restored to its original appearance. The interior contains exceptional stucco plasterwork, and fine 18th-century furniture. Open Easter to Aug S, Su and Bank Hols pm. ⊖ 🅿 WC 🔊 ♣ 🐾

Kelmscott Manor, Kelmscot, near Lechlade, Oxfordshire. 4½ m W of Faringdon. SU 2163 (OS 163). Large Cotswold manor house that was the home of Arts and Crafts reformer and socialist William Morris from 1871 to 1896. Morris directed the restoration of the house. The contents include examples of his work. Open Apr to Sept, first W in the month, am and pm. ⊖ 🅿 ♣

Langton Hall, near Market Harborough, Leicestershire (tel East Langton [085 884] 240). 3½ m N of Market Harborough on A6, turn N. SP 7193 (OS 141). Late medieval country house, enhanced in the late 17th and 18th centuries, and redecorated in 19th-century neo-Gothic style. It contains fine 18th-century French furniture and the drawing room is covered in Venetian lace. There is a collection of exquisite Chinese furniture. There are extensive gardens in the French style, with a centre for breeding and demonstrating birds of prey. Open Easter to Oct Th, S, Su and Bank Hols pm. ⊖ 🅿 WC 🔊 🚻 (by appt) ♣ 🐾

Manor House, Princes Risborough, Buckinghamshire. In town centre, opposite church off market square. SP 8003 (OS 165). Jacobean red-brick, hip-roofed house with original oak staircase. Two rooms open for show in interior. Open W pm by appt. ⊖ 🅿 🔊

Mary Arden's House, Wilmcote, near Stratford-upon-Avon, Warwickshire (tel Stratford-upon-Avon [0789] 293455). 4 m NW of Stratford, off A34. SP 1658 (OS 151). Early 16th-century timber-framed farmhouse, the home of Shakespeare's mother Mary Arden. It contains a range of 16th- and 17th-century furniture. There are outbuildings of the Tudor period, including a dovecote, and a collection of objects connected with old farming techniques. Open Apr to Oct daily am and pm (Su pm only); Nov to March M-S am and pm. ⊖ 🅿 WC 🔊 🚻 ♣

Milton's Cottage, Buckinghamshire

Milton's Cottage, Chalfont St Giles, Buckinghamshire (tel Chalfont St Giles [024 07] 2313). 4 m SE of Amersham on A413, turn SW. SU 9893 (OS 176). Half-timbered 16th-century cottage, the home of John Milton in 1665-66, where he wrote *Paradise Lost* and part of *Paradise Regained*. The house contains Milton relics and a library of early books. Open T to S am and pm, Su pm, Feb-Oct, also Spring and Summer Bank Hols. ⊖ 🅿 WC ⊟ ♣

Moseley Old Hall, near Wolverhampton, West Midlands (tel Wolverhampton [0902] 782808). 5 m N of Wolverhampton on A449, turn E. SJ 9304 (OS 139). Small brick-clad timber-framed manor house of the early 17th century, refuge of the defeated future Charles II after the battle of Worcester (1651). The house contains 17th-century furniture, and a display about the Whitgrave family, the owners at that time. There is a formal 17th-century-style garden. Open Apr to Oct, W, Th, S, Su and Bank Hols pm; March and Nov W and Su pm. ⊖ 🅿 WC 🅰 ⊟ (by appt) ♣ 🐾

New Place and Nash's House, Chapel St, Stratford-upon-Avon, Warwickshire (tel Stratford-upon-Avon [0789] 292325). In town centre. SP 2055 (OS 151). Foundations of New Place, Shakespeare's last home, bought by him in 1597 as the second largest house in Stratford, and to which he retired in 1612. The house itself was destroyed in 1759, but an Elizabethan knot garden remains. Nash's House next door contains a display of furniture and local history. Open Apr to Oct daily am and pm (Su pm only); Nov to March M-S am and pm. ⊖ WC 🅰 ♣

Nether Winchendon House, near Aylesbury, Buckinghamshire (tel Haddenham [0844] 290101). 7 m SW of Aylesbury, on A418, turn N. SP 7311 (OS 165). Medieval and Tudor manor house, reworked and given a Gothick façade in the late 18th century by Scrope Bernard. The house contains Tudor and later furniture and decorations, and a collection of objects relating to the Bernard family. Open May to Aug Th pm; also May and Aug Bank Hol weekends; parties at other times by appt. ⊖ 🅿 🅰 ⊟ (by appt) 🐾

Newstead Abbey, Linby, Nottinghamshire (tel Bidworth [062 34] 3557). 9 m N of Nottingham on A60, turn E. SK 5353 (OS 120). 13th-century abbey, converted into a private house in the 1540s by the Byron family, and restored in the 1820s by John Shaw. The original cloisters, and the west front of the church, survive. The house contains a Jacobean saloon, a fine 19th-century hall, and rooms containing relics of the 6th Lord Byron (the poet) and other family treasures. There is an extensive and beautiful park. House open Easter to end Sept daily pm; gardens open all year daily am and pm. ⊖ 🅿 WC 🅰 🐾

Nuneham Park, Nuneham Courtenay, near Oxford, Oxfordshire. 7 m SE of Oxford on A423, turn W. SU 5497 (OS 164). 18th-century Palladian villa in a landscaped park by the River Thames. There is a temple in the grounds. The house is now a conference centre. Open end Aug and early Sept S and Su pm. ⊖ 🅿 WC ♣ 🐾 ⌂

Oakham Castle, off Market Place, Oakham, Leicestershire (tel Oakham [0572] 3654). In town centre. SK 8609 (OS 141). Norman castle with the best surviving example of a free-standing 12th-century castle hall. It contains a unique collection of presentation horseshoes, given by peers of the realm. The castle is used as a magistrates' courthouse on Mondays. Open Apr to Oct T-S and Bank Hols am and pm; Su and other M pm only. Grounds open daily am and pm. ⊖ 🅿 🅰 ★

Oak House, Oak Road, West Bromwich, West Midlands (tel 021-553 0759). ¼m W of town centre, off A41. SP 0092 (OS 139). Gabled 16th-century timber-framed house with a unique lantern-tower. The interior has much original panelling and wood carvings, and contains 16th-pnd 17th-century furniture. Open Apr to Sept daily am and pm (Th am only, Su pm only); Oct to March M-S am and pm only. ⊖ 🅿 WC 🅰 🏵 ★

Packwood House, Hockley Heath, Warwickshire (tel Lapworth [056 43] 2024). 11 m NE of Stratford-upon-Avon on A34, turn NE to Lapworth. SP 1772 (OS 139). Timber-framed mid-Tudor house with 17th-century additions. The house was altered in the 19th century, and restored to its original form in the 1920s and 30s. It contains fine 16th- and 17th-century furniture and tapestries, and the grounds are well known for their topiary, with a formal Carolean garden and a yew garden representing the Sermon on the Mount. Open Apr to end Sept W-Su and Bank Hol M pm.; Oct S and Su pm only. ⊖ 🅿 WC 🅰 ⊟ (by appt) ♣

Peveril Castle, or Peak Castle, Castleton, Derbyshire. 20 m W of Sheffield, on A625. SK 1482 (OS 110). Ruins of castle on a steep ridge. The great tower was erected by Henry II in the 12th century; there is also an earlier curtain wall. Open daily am and pm. ⊖ 🅿

Prestwold Hall, Loughborough, Leicestershire. 2½ m SE of Loughborough. SK 5721 (OS 141). 19th-century Classical house set in extensive gardens, designed by William Burn for the Packe family. It contains interesting plasterwork and a collection of 18th-century English and European furniture. Open by appointment for parties.

Quenby Hall, Hungarton, Leicestershire (tel Hungarton [053 750] 224). 6 m E of Leicester, turn N SK 7006 (OS 141). Fine Jacobean house built in 1620 for George Ashby on an H-plan, restored in the 19th century to its original appearance. It contains notable panelling, plasterwork, and fireplaces. The hall is set in an extensive park. Open June to Sept Su pm; also Apr to Aug Bank Hol M and T pm. 🅿 WC 🅰 ♣ 🐾

Shakespeare's Birthplace, Henley St, Stratford-upon-Avon, Warwickshire (tel Stratford-upon-Avon [0789] 204016). In town centre. SP 2055 (OS 151). Half-timbered house in which the poet was born in April 1564. The supposed room in which he was born can be seen, and the house contains an exhibition of rare Elizabethan items, and a BBC costume display. Open Apr to Oct daily am and pm; Nov to March daily am and pm (Su pm only). ⊖ WC

Stanton Harcourt Manor, Stanton Harcourt, Oxfordshire. 5 m SE of Witney on A415, turn E. SP 4105 (OS 164). Unusually well-preserved medieval buildings, including the 'Pope's tower', old kitchen and domestic chapel. There is a fine collection of paintings, furniture, silver and porcelain. Open Apr to Sept, alternate Th and S, also Bank Hol weekends pm. ⊖ 🅿 ♣

New Place and Nash's House, Warwickshire

Stapleford Park, near Melton Mowbray, Leicestershire (tel Wymondham [057 284] 245). 5 m E of Melton Mowbray on B676, turn S. SK 8118 (OS 130). Country house set in a large park, and built between 1500 and the late 19th century for the Sherard family. Most of the house dates from the Restoration period, with decorative carving of that date. There are varied paintings and tapestries, and a collection of Staffordshire figurines. The church in the park was built in 1783 in the Gothick style. There is a miniature railway round the park. Open Easter, May Bank Hol weekends, June to Aug T-Th, Su and Bank Hols pm; Sept W, Th, Su pm. 🄿 WC ♿ ♣ 🐾

Stowe House, Stowe, Buckinghamshire (tel Buckingham [0280] 813650). 3 m NW of Buckingham on A422, turn NE. SP 6737 (OS 152). Fine 18th-century house, formerly home of the Duke of Buckingham, now a public school. The 18th-century garden and garden buildings, which include temples and statuary, were designed by Bridgeman, Kent, Gibbs, Vanbrugh and Brown. Grounds open S and Su, mid-July to early Sept pm, also Easter and Summer Bank Hol; other times by appt. No admission to the house. ⊖ 🄿 WC 🄳 D ♣ ⛺

Sudbury Hall, near Derby, Derbyshire (tel Sudbury [028 378] 305). At Sudbury, 6½ m SE of Uttoxeter on A50, turn S. SK 1532 (OS 128). Early 17th-century house built for the Lords Vernon, with exceptionally fine Restoration interiors, including woodcarvings by Grinling Gibbons, a richly decorated staircase by Edward Pierce and murals by Laguerre. There is also a museum of childhood. Open Apr to Oct W-Su and Bank Hols pm. ⊖ 🄿 WC ♣ 🐾

Tamworth Castle, Tamworth, Staffordshire (tel Tamworth [0827] 3563). In town centre. SK 2003 (OS 139). Early Norman motte-and-bailey castle, with the 12th-century stone shell keep still surviving. A 17th-century house was built inside the walls for the Ferrers family. The castle is now a museum of local history, with many Anglo-Saxon coins. Open M-Th, S am and pm; Su pm only (exc Christmas). ⊖ 🄿 WC ♣

Thoresby Hall, Ollerton, Nottinghamshire (tel Mansfield [0623] 823210). 9 m SE of Worksop on A6005, turn E. SK 6471 (OS 120). 19th-century house in the Elizabethan style, designed by Anthony Salvin. It replaced a Georgian house of the 1760s. The interior is decorated in Tudor fashion, but contains 18th-century furniture. The park is set in Sherwood Forest, and has woodland walks. Open Easter, Spring and Summer Bank Hol weekends and June to Aug S, park am and pm, house pm only. ⊖ 🄿 WC ♣ 🐾

Thrumpton Hall, Nottinghamshire (tel Nottingham [0602] 830333). 9 m SW of Nottingham on A453, turn W. SK 5031 (OS 129). Jacobean house of 1607 built by Gervase Pigot, with a Restoration period staircase and carved and panelled saloon. There is a formal garden and extensive park. Open by appointment only, for parties of 20 or more. 🄿

Triangular Lodge, Rushton, Northamptonshire. 4 m NW of Kettering on A6003, turn E. SP 8383 (OS 141). Three-sided house built by Thomas Tresham in 1593-96, incorporating the symbolic number three as a consistent architectural motif (three sides, three storeys, three windows, etc.). Open daily am and pm (Su pm only). 🄿

Tutbury Castle, Tutbury, Staffordshire (tel Burton on Trent [0283] 812129). 3 m NW of Burton on Trent on A50. SK 2029 (OS 128). Early motte-and-bailey castle, dismantled in the 1170s and rebuilt in the early 14th century, with a curtain wall added in the 15th century. Mary, Queen of Scots was imprisoned here. The castle was slighted in the Civil War. A folly tower was built in the 1760s as was a small house. Open daily am and pm (exc Christmas). ⊖ 🄿 WC 🄳 ♣ 🐾 🅿

Upton House, Edge Hill, Warwickshire (tel Edge Hill [029 587] 266). 11 m NW of Banbury off A422. SP 3645 (OS 151). Late 17th-century house, heavily reworked in the 1920s, containing a fine collection of *objets d'art* (including furniture, Brussels tapestries and porcelain) and paintings, including works by Bosch, El Greco, Rembrandt, and Hogarth. There are attractive terraced gardens with several lakes. Open Apr to end Sept M-Th pm, and occasional S and Su. ⊖ 🄿 WC 🄳 🅿 (by appt) ♣

Wollaton Hall, Wollaton, Nottinghamshire (tel Nottingham [0602] 281333). 2½ m W of Nottingham on A609. SK 5339 (OS 129). Exceptional Elizabethan house, built by Robert Smythson for Sir Francis Willoughby in the 1580s. The façade is heavily ornamented and served as the model for Mentmore Towers in the 19th century. The house is now used as a museum of natural history, covering botany, geology, zoology and a herbarium, with special emphasis on the natural history of Nottinghamshire. The grounds contain a 19th-century iron-and-glass camellia house, and an industrial museum in the stable block. Open daily am and pm (Su pm only). ⊖ 🄿 WC ♣ 🐾

Wotton House, near Aylesbury, Buckinghamshire. 6 m N of Thame, in the village of Wotton Underwood. SP 6816 (OS 165). House built in 1704 on the plan of Buckingham House (which was to become Buckingham Palace), with interior remodelled in 1820 by Sir John Soane, containing fine wrought-ironwork. The gardens were laid out by Capability Brown. Open W pm, Aug and Sept. ⊖ 🄿 🅿 (by appt) ♣

Wygston's House, Applegate St, Leicester, Leicestershire (tel Leicester [0533] 554100). In city centre, near St Nicholas' Circle. SK 5804 (OS 140). Medieval timber-framed house with an 18th-century brick façade, originally the home of the merchant Roger Wygston. It contains a museum of historical costumes, and a sequence of period interiors and 1920s shop reconstructions. Open M-Th am and pm, Su pm only. Closed Christmas and Good Fri. ⊖ WC 🄳 ★

Wollaton Hall, Nottinghamshire

Penrhyn Castle, Gwynedd

Wales and Western Counties

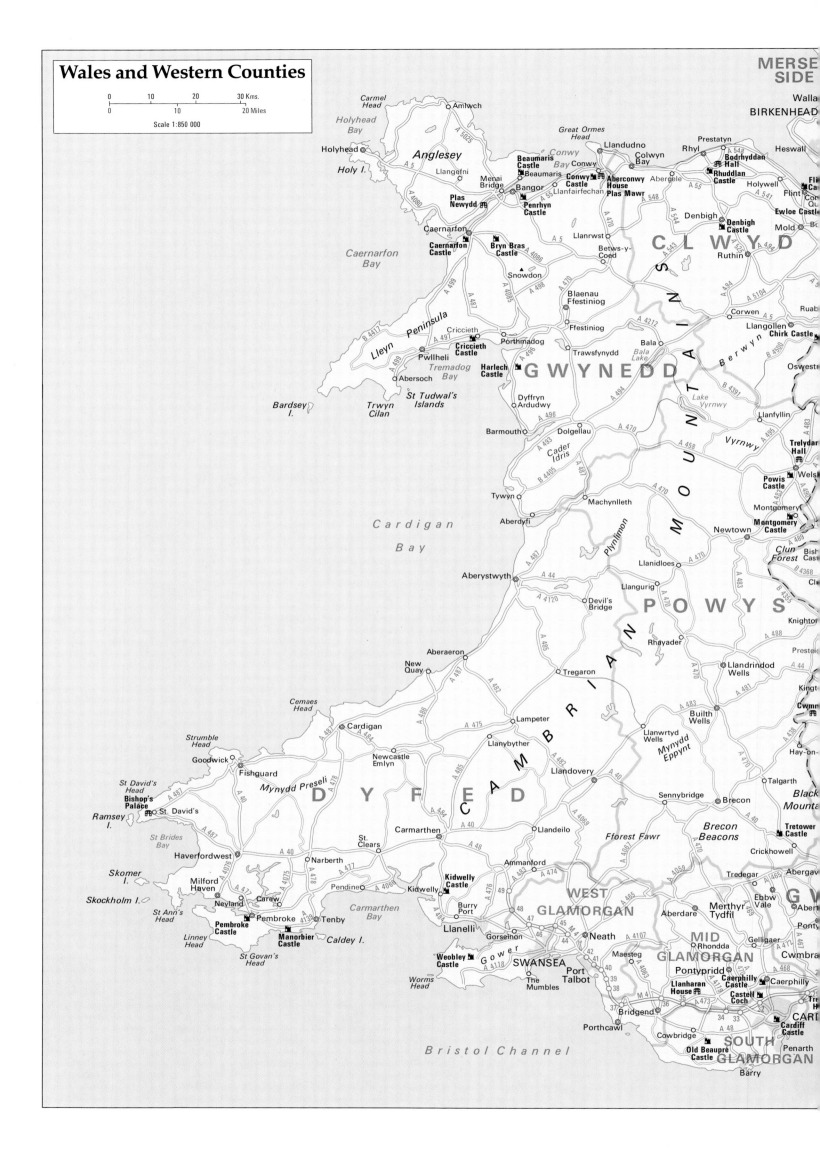

Wales and Western Counties

Scale 1:850 000

0 10 20 30 Kms.
0 10 20 Miles

MERSEY SIDE

BIRKENHEAD
Walla

Carmel Head
Holyhead Bay
Amlwch
Anglesey
Holyhead
Holy I.
Llangefni
A 5025
A 5
A 4080
Menai Bridge
Bangor
Plas Newydd
Penrhyn Castle
Caernarfon
Caernarfon Castle
Bryn Bras Castle
Snowdon

Great Ormes Head
Llandudno
Conwy Bay
Beaumaris Castle
Beaumaris
Conwy
Conwy Castle
Aberconwy House
Plas Mawr
Colwyn Bay
Llanfairfechan
Abergele
Prestatyn
Rhyl
Bodrhyddan Hall
Rhuddlan Castle
Holywell
Heswall

CLWYD
Denbigh
Denbigh Castle
Mold
Ewloe Castle
Flint
Corn Qu

Llanrwst
Betws-y-Coed
A 470
A 5
A 543
A 544
Ruthin
A 525
A 494
A 5104
Corwen
A 5
Ruab

Blaenau Ffestiniog
Ffestiniog
A 4212
Llangollen
Chirk Castle
B 4500
Oswestr
Berwyn

Criccieth
Criccieth Castle
Porthmadog
A 496
Trawsfynydd
Bala
Bala Lake
GWYNEDD
B 4391
Llanfyllin
A 483

Lleyn Peninsula
B 4417
A 499
A 497
Pwllheli
Abersoch
Tremadog Bay
St Tudwal's Islands
Harlech Castle
Dyffryn Ardudwy
A 496
Lake Vyrnwy

Bardsey I.
Trwyn Cilan
Barmouth
A 493
Dolgellau
Cader Idris
A 470
Vyrnwy
A 495
A 458
Trelydan Hall

Cardigan Bay
A 4405
A 487
Tywyn
Machynlleth
A 470
Powis Castle
Wels

Aberdyfi
Plynlimon
A 470
Montgomery
Montgomery Castle
Newtown
A 489

Aberystwyth
A 44
A 4120
Devil's Bridge
A 485
POWYS
Clun Forest
Bish Cas
B 4368
Cl

Llangurig
A 483
A 4355

Llanidloes
A 470
Knighton

Rhayader
A 488
Presteig

Aberaeron
New Quay
A 487
A 482
Tregaron
Llandrindod Wells
A 44
Kingt

A 483
A 481
Cwmn

Cemaes Head
Cardigan
A 487
A 484
A 475
Lampeter
Llanwrtyd Wells
Builth Wells
A 483
Hay-on-
A 438

Strumble Head
Goodwick
Fishguard
A 487
Newcastle Emlyn
Llanybyther
A 482
Mynydd Eppynt
A 470

St David's Head
Bishop's Palace
Ramsey I.
St David's
Mynydd Preseli
A 478
A 40
DYFED
CAMBRIAN
Llandovery
A 40
Talgarth
Black Mountain

St Brides Bay
Goodwick
A 487
A 40
A 484
Llandeilo
A 4069
Sennybridge
Brecon
A 40

Skomer I.
Haverfordwest
A 4076
Narberth
A 477
St Clears
Carmarthen
A 48
Fforest Fawr
Brecon Beacons
Tretower Castle

Skockholm I.
Milford Haven
A 477
Carew
Pendine
A 4075
A 178
Kidwelly
Kidwelly Castle
Ammanford
A 483
A 474
Crickhowell
Abergav

St Ann's Head
Neyland
Pembroke
Pembroke Castle
A 4139
Tenby
Caldey I.
Burry Port
49
48
WEST GLAMORGAN
A 465
A 4069
Tredegar
A 465

Linney Head
Manorbier Castle
Carmarthen Bay
Llanelli
Gorseinon
47
46
45
44
M4
Neath
A 4107
Aberdare
Merthyr Tydfil
Ebbw Vale
G

St Govan's Head
Weobley Castle
Gower
Worms Head
A 4118
SWANSEA
The Mumbles
Port Talbot
42
41
40
39
38
Maesteg
MID GLAMORGAN
Rhondda
Pontypridd
Gelligaer
Caerphilly
Caerphilly Castle
Cwmbra
A 468

Bridgend
37
36
35
M4
34 33
A 473
Llanharan House
Castell Coch
CARD
Cardiff Castle

Porthcawl
Cowbridge
A 48
SOUTH GLAMORGAN
Penarth

Bristol Channel
Old Beaupré Castle
Barry

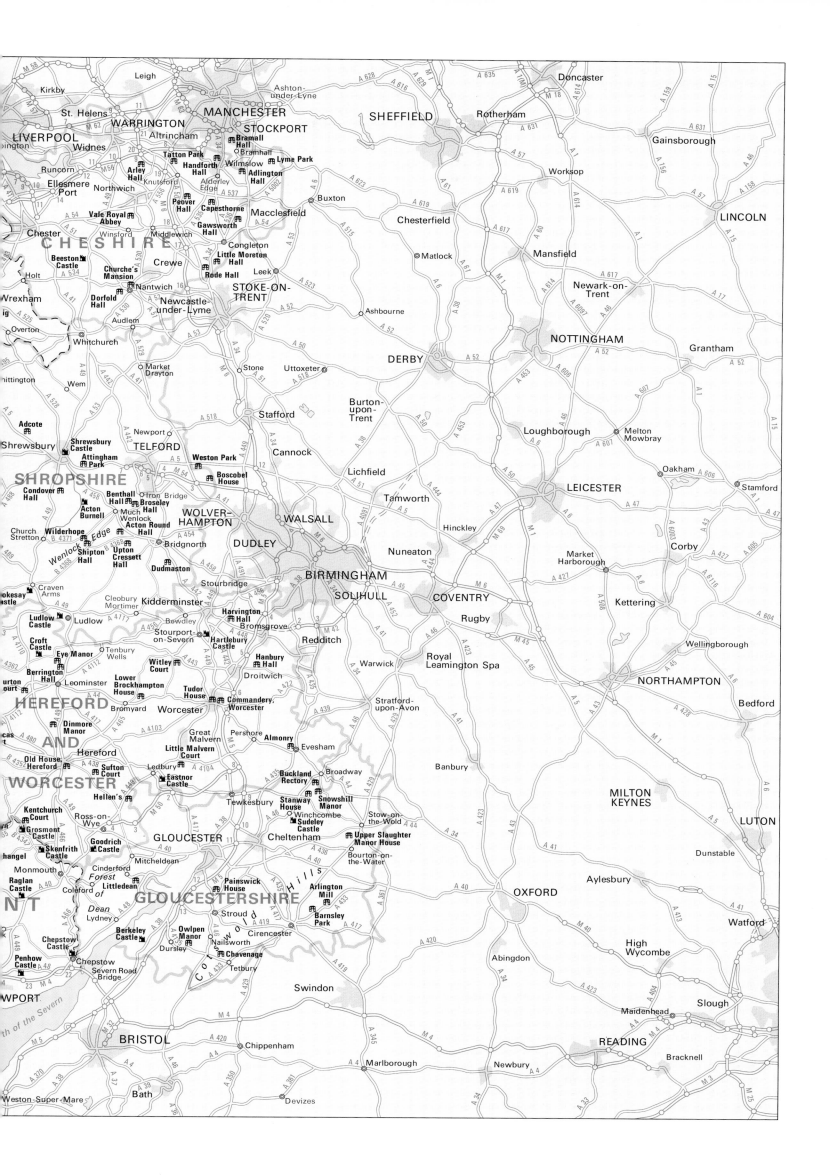

Caernarfon Castle Caernarfon, Gwynedd

At the southern end of the Menai Strait stands one of the greatest examples of medieval military architecture anywhere. The evolution of castles from the simple motte-and-bailey type reached its culmination in Britain in the chain of fortresses built by Edward I (r. 1272-1307) to hold down the conquered Welsh. Among these, the castle at Caernarfon, with its majesty and sophistication, holds pride of place.

The site was first used by the Normans. On the peninsula, almost an island, formed by the River Seoint and the Cadnant brook flowing into the Strait, a motte-and-bailey castle was constructed about 1090 with a timbered keep and palisades. Long before the English came, the Welsh princes would have constructed stone buildings, as they did not far away at Dolbadarn, to provide a safe refuge in the uneasy conditions of the 12th and 13th centuries.

All the northern Welsh castles fell to Edward I in 1283 and work on new fortresses at Conwy, Harlech and Caernarfon began at once. In 1284 Edward's wife Eleanor gave birth at Caernarfon to the Prince Edward who was to become the first English Prince of Wales, a title now hereditary to the sovereign's eldest son.

At the same time as the castle took shape, walls were built out from it to enclose a new town where English settlers could rely on the castle garrison for protection. With wall towers, fortified gateways and straight streets running at right-angles to each other, the town is one of the few examples of a 'bastide' in Britain. For two hundred and fifty years Caernarfon was to serve as the administrative centre for its own shire and for Anglesey and Merioneth.

In 1294 the Welsh rose against their oppressors, parts of the town wall were thrown down and entry to the castle gained through the weaker northern defences facing the town. The English soon returned to repair the damage and to strengthen the castle, particularly the northern wall. Although several features of the design were left incomplete, work finally came to a halt in 1330.

The castle consists of two baileys narrowing at their junction to form a ground plan roughly like an hour-glass. The Norman motte was incorporated in the eastern bailey and controlled its rounded shape. By contrast, the long straight walls of the lower or western bailey enclose a five-sided space.

The distinction of Caernarfon lies in the bulk and height of the curtain walls, the thirteen multi-angular towers astride them and the elaborate defensive devices. The foundations were cut from rock and the walls are 20 foot thick in places at the base. The towers all differ in size and design and, except for those at the ruined castle at Denbigh, are the only multi-angular towers in Wales. Many have turrets that rise high above their battlements. Seen from across the River Seoint the southern towers and lofty curtain wall are magnificent. Decorative courses of a darker stone break the expanse of limestone masonry and two lines of arrow slits below the ramparts reveal additional firing positions in the thickness of the wall.

Left and above, Caernarfon Castle was built as the administrative centre for Edward I's dominions in north Wales. The eagle tower, on the western tip of the castle, at 124 feet high is one of the highest ever built in the Middle Ages.

Above, the castle is a ring of strong towers around two baileys; the gatehouse served as the royal residential area, and was fortified for defence against attack from within, as well as beyond, the castle walls.

Opposite, the Investiture of the Prince of Wales in 1969, probably the most glorious moment in the castle's history.

Left, the night-time lighting of the castle walls accentuates its presence looming over the Menai Strait.

The entrance from the town through the King's gate still shows what a formidable task awaited an assailant. A drawbridge over the deep ditch dividing town from castle, now a fixed bridge, led to a vaulted passage between two strong towers. Narrow at the first door and portcullis, the passage broadens slightly as it passes through two more doorways and three portcullises to a right-angle turn into another narrow passage. In this two doors and portcullises had to be negotiated to reach the western bailey. At all stages an intruder was covered by arrow slits at different levels and by so-called 'murder holes' in the vault, holes not only for casting down missiles on the heads of attackers but for pouring water if fire was used against the doors. The upper part of the gatehouse could only be reached by a narrow, easily defensible stair leading off the second passage.

The entrance to the eastern bailey, the Queen's gate, was another strong point. Built on the slope of the Norman motte, it stands high above the original ditch with no apparent approach to it. A ramp from the vanished outer bank of the ditch would have led up to meet a drawbridge pivoting under the soaring arch of the gatehouse. The deep pit into which the inner portion of the drawbridge descended when it was raised can be seen dug into the motte and faced with masonry.

Caernarfon has no keep but the great Eagle tower at the western end of the curtain is an early and remarkable example of the tower-houses then beginning to come into vogue. It rises from a basement through three storeys to battlements and three tall, six-sided turrets. Steps from the western bailey go down to a door below ground level and another flight in the thickness of the wall leads to the basement. This is a ten-sided room measuring about 30 by 35 foot. From it a postern gate

barred by a portcullis and double doors gives access to the waterside. Fighting men could assemble in the basement for a sally or to escape by boat. More importantly, water-borne supplies could be brought into the castle if it was invested by land. The three upper storeys of the tower are similar in size and shape to the basement but have many chambers for domestic amenities built in the massive walls. The whole is designed for the comfort and security of the Constable of the castle.

In 1911 the first recorded Investiture of a Prince of Wales in the setting of the castle took place. The idea of making the Investiture a Welsh event seems to have originated with Lloyd George, Member of Parliament for the constituency and Constable of the castle. The ceremony took place on a blazing summer day with all the dignified pageantry that the British have come to do so well. The Home Secretary, Winston Churchill, read out the Letters Patent of Appointment of the seventeen-year-old Prince Edward, afterwards Edward VIII. To conclude the ceremony King George V presented his son, from a platform erected beneath the lofty arch of the Queen's gate, to the Welsh people thronging the open spaces below, perhaps numbering a few thousand. Fifty-eight years later many millions watched on television, with enjoyment and pride, the Investiture at Caernarfon of the present Prince of Wales.

☎ Caernarfon (0286) 3096

In centre of Caernarfon

SH 4762 (OS 115)

Open daily throughout year; Mar to Oct 0930-1830, Oct to Mar 0930-1600 (Su 1400-1600). Closed 24, 25, 26 Dec and 1 Jan

⊖ P WC ⊟ D ◆ ⚘ Royal Welsh Fusiliers Museum

Cardiff Castle

Left, Cardiff Castle presents a façade that unites the medieval remains with some of the wilder inventions of 19th-century Gothic.

Opposite, the summer smoking room in the Clock tower is probably the most energetic of all Burges's designs at Cardiff, with figures climbing oddly out of the tops of the columns.

The Romans were the first to occupy the site of Cardiff Castle, two miles up the River Taff from the Bristol Channel. A fort was erected and subsequently rebuilt in the 1st century AD, and about two hundred years later another and stronger fort, of which remains can be seen today in the castle walls, was constructed. It served as a base for the Bristol Channel fleet and was similar to the 'forts of the Saxon Shore' erected by the Romans in East Anglia and south-east England. A broad ditch and high, massive walls enclosed a rectangle eight acres in extent. Semi-octagonal towers projected at the corners and at intervals along the sides. Narrow entrances in the north and south walls were closed by heavy, barred doors.

After the Romans abandoned Britain nothing is heard of the site until the coming of the Normans six centuries later. They took over the remains of the fort, throwing up a 40-foot mound surrounded by a ditch in the north-west corner and dividing the rest into an inner and an outer bailey. They broadened and deepened the silted-up ditch round the fort, covered the remains of the Roman walls with excavated soil and built a wall on top so that the ancient fortifications lay hidden for nearly eight centuries.

Early in the 12th century the twelve-sided shell-keep was built on the mound, the walls 30-foot high and an entrance on the south side. The octagonal tower in front of the entrance is a later, probably 15th-century, addition.

Cardiff Castle as seen from the castle courtyard, with the library and banqueting hall shown in cutaway. The Clock Tower is on the left, the Octagon tower carries the fleche, and the Bute tower is on the right.

The medieval domestic quarters were established against the western curtain and some of their foundations are incorporated in the existing range of buildings. The entrance to the castle was through the Black tower in the south wall (where the Welch Regiment Museum is housed), and from this a wall led to the mound, dividing the two baileys.

Many of the most powerful families in Britain held the castle at various times down to the 18th century: the Clares, the Despensers – notorious for their association with Edward II – the Beauchamp and Neville Earls of Warwick, the Tudors and the Herberts. Each made some alteration or addition to the living quarters. In 1766 the castle passed to John Stuart, husband of the last Herbert heiress. He came from an ancient Scottish family and was afterwards the 4th Earl and 1st Marquis of Bute. His family continued to hold the castle until it came into the care of the City of Cardiff in 1947.

At the beginning of the 19th century the town had less than two thousand inhabitants. The Bute family built the docks and changed it from a village into a great coal-exporting city. From 1778 onwards they carried out work at the castle but the present towers and apartments along the western curtain are mainly the result of reconstruction in the second half of the 19th century. An interesting partnership was responsible. In 1865 the 3rd Marquis of Bute, a shy, wealthy aristocrat of eighteen, asked William Burges, twenty years his senior and an established architect and man of the world, to make plans for a grand restoration and improvement of the living quarters. The work began in 1867 and was still going on when Burges died in 1881.

Burges gathered round him sculptors, glass- and tile-makers and decorative artists of all kinds. The Marquis set up workshops to deal with every aspect of the rebuilding and decoration. Only the superb skills of Victorian craftsmen could translate the far-ranging ideas of the Marquis and Burges into reality. Only Victorian power and wealth could bring about the mingling of so many styles in one great extravaganza.

The chapel is a colourful riot of Gothic, dedicated to the memory of the Marquis' father. His bust by John Evans Thomas makes him look like a Roman emperor. In the so-called Arab room, the stalactite ceiling, the cedar and marble linings imitate – without achieving the requisite delicacy – Islamic decoration. The Chaucer room commemorates, incongruously in Cardiff, the father of English literature. Perhaps the banqueting hall, built above medieval foundations and intended to

Above left, detail of the roof decorations of the banqueting hall, built by Burges with a great deal of original material.

Above, the roof garden on the Bute tower, above the Marquis's private apartments.

be a Tudor or medieval great hall, serves best to show the lavish self-indulgence of the whole conception. An elaborate timbered roof with carved angels is supported on fan vaults springing from slender half-columns. Murals influenced by the Pre-Raphaelites cover the large spaces between the half-columns and the panelled wainscot. Ogee mouldings with leafy finials enclose flat-pointed mouldings over rectangular doorways. The stained-glass windows depict the owners of the castle down the centuries. The chimneypiece is a castle gatehouse, trumpeters sounding from the battlements and the lady in an embrasure bidding goodbye to a mounted knight. This medley, with ecclesiastical overtones, is exuberant, eccentric and confusing.

Externally the castle is dominated by spectacular towers that form an exciting skyline. Burges seems to have relished his instructions to build upwards rather than expand into the bailey. He began with the clock tower at the south-west angle of the curtain, where a Roman bastion once stood. It is a fine modern tower, not so much a strong point but rather a detached residence suitable for a gentleman. The fantastically decorated rooms rise one above the other, connected by a newel staircase.

The Guest and Bute towers were also the work of Burges, the latter containing the Marquis' private apartments. The Herbert tower, of Tudor origin, was restored and heightened. Even the Octagon tower, the one surviving medieval tower apart from those on the south wall and the Norman mound, was not left alone. Burges, not content merely to restore it, added a timber spire which increased its height – though hardly its medieval dignity.

After Burges' death in 1881 the work went on under his assistant William Frame. During this period occurred the important discovery of sections of the 3rd-century Roman walling under the Norman curtain. Excavations in the 1970s and 1980s have revealed the existence of the earlier Roman forts. The castle's history has been pushed back a thousand years.

☎ Cardiff (0222) 31033 ext 725

In centre of Cardiff at junction of North Road and Duke Street

ST 1876 (OS 171)

Open daily: Mar, Apr Oct 1000-1700; May to end Sept 1000-1800; Nov to end Feb 1000-1600

♿ WC ♨ (by appt) ☕ (limited opening) ⚲ ● (not in castle) ◆ ⚹ (audio guide)

Above right, the lantern of the Chaucer room, which is incorporated in the medieval Octagon or Beauchamp tower.

Harlech Castle Harlech, Gwynedd

One of the nine fortresses planned by Edward I to consolidate his conquest of North Wales, Harlech was built on a rocky hill 200 feet above the shoreline of Tremadoc Bay in the years 1286-90. The King's master mason, James of St George, supervised the work and adapted the building to the precipitous site in a remarkable way.

Harlech is a good example of a 'concentric' castle, with two rectangles of fortifications, one within the other, forming an inner and a middle bailey. The fortifications are set squarely on top of the hill, and to the south and east a moat was hacked out of the rock to strengthen the defence. To the north and west the rock falls in precipitous steps to sea-level and is enclosed by a wall to form an outer bailey. Since medieval times the sea has receded and the castle's water gate in the outer bailey wall is now some distance from the shore. As originally planned the castle could be maintained from

the sea and a steep path for carrying up supplies led along the bailey wall from the water gate. At one point it was interrupted by a ditch with a drawbridge and covering gate. When it reached the south-west angle of the middle bailey the approach was commanded from the massive corner tower of the inner bailey.

The number of soldiers necessary to defend the castle would have varied according to conditions but records suggest that, apart from the Constable and his retinue, the permanent garrison of Harlech was probably about ten men-at-arms and thirty archers. The castle successfully withstood a siege during the Welsh uprising of 1294 but a century later, in the early 1400s, the Welsh again attacked under their hero Owain Glyndŵr, who had proclaimed himself Prince of Wales, and the castle fell. Within a few years the English returned under their Prince of Wales, the future Henry V. He regained the castle, took Glyndŵr's family prisoner and drove

Glyndŵr himself to seek refuge in Snowdonia.

Some fifty years later, during the Wars of the Roses, occurred the most famous episode in the castle's history. The last Lancastrian stronghold in North Wales to resist the Yorkists, it only surrendered after a seven-year siege. The traditional song 'Men of Harlech' was composed to celebrate the garrison's bravery. Among them was a young boy called Henry Tudor, afterwards Henry VII (r. 1485-1509) and founder of the Tudor dynasty.

The castle's active history came to an end during the Civil War. Far away from the main battles and sieges, it was the last Royalist stronghold in Wales. It withstood a siege by Cromwell's brother-in-law, Colonel John Jones, but shortly afterwards surrendered to other Parliamentary forces. Unlike many Royalist fortresses it was not battered down or blown up after capture. This may have been due to the peaceful surrender or simply

Above and opposite, the perfectly concentric plan of Harlech Castle, with a high inner wall and a lower outer one arranged in a near-square, is never compromised by the precipitous rock on which the castle is solidly perched.

to the absence of the Parliamentary siege train which had not made the long journey by sea or over the mountains to reduce such a remote place. The castle nevertheless fell into ruin, the domestic buildings, the battlements and the floors and roofs of the towers destroyed or collapsed. Fortunately sufficient of the main structure survived in its original form to testify to the architectural skills of James of St George. In 1914 the continuing decay was halted when the castle passed into the care of the Office of Works and Public Buildings, now the Historic Buildings and Monuments Commission.

Some foundations of the domestic buildings are

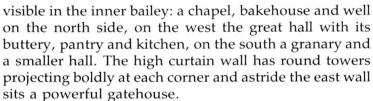

visible in the inner bailey: a chapel, bakehouse and well on the north side, on the west the great hall with its buttery, pantry and kitchen, on the south a granary and a smaller hall. The high curtain wall has round towers projecting boldly at each corner and astride the east wall sits a powerful gatehouse.

The middle bailey forms a narrow terrace round the inner bailey and has much lower walls. An attacker would come under fire from both sets of battlements. If the middle bailey was captured the attackers would find themselves in a narrow 'killing ground' dominated from the inner bailey ramparts and projecting towers.

The castle was most vulnerable on the east side, where it faced higher ground, and there the defences were strongest. The moat was crossed by a bridge (now a causeway) with a drawbridge at either end, the outer one protected by a barbican. On the bridge or in the moat below an assailant was vulnerable to fire from both ramparts and also from the outer bailey wall on the north flank. The great gatehouse controlled any further penetration. Two doors and three portcullises, arrow slits in the side walls and seven lines of machicolations at short intervals in the vault enabled an intruder to be assailed all through the passageway. A portcullis was usually lowered in front of a door but at the inner end the last portcullis was behind the door to guard against attack from *within* the bailey. The gatehouse blocked the wall walk and could only be entered from it or from the passageway. It was a self-contained fortress of its own, comparable to a keep of earlier times. The present stairs to the gatehouse inside the bailey are a much later

Above left, the gatehouse, here seen from inside the castle, was by far the most powerful feature and contained a lavish domestic suite; the large, unmilitary windows are an original feature.

Above, at Harlech, perhaps more than at any other Welsh castle, the sheer force of Edward I's impact on Wales and the enduring nature of the changes he brought, are inescapable.

Right, the steep approach to the Harlech gatehouse protected the castle from demolition by Cromwell's artillery in the Civil War.

addition. To complete the east-facing defences the curtain wall for some distance on either side of the gatehouse was made even thicker than the nine-foot walls of the remainder.

In some ways Harlech is a grim ruin, a symbol of unwelcome authority, a monument to old wars. The inner bailey, shut in by its high walls and towers, is no place for people who feel the cold or suffer from claustrophobia. Under siege conditions only resolute leadership would maintain resistance.

But the walls and towers observed from outside have an almost classical symmetry and at times, particularly when evening sunlight mellows them, a vigorous beauty. They seem to grow out of the crag on which they stand as though they have always been there.

From the lofty ramparts the whole plan of the castle can be understood and, on a clear day, the view is memorable. The western sea stretches up to the Lleyn peninsula and down to Cardigan Bay, the majestic peaks of the Snowdon range rise to the north-east and the eye is drawn southward down the flank of the Cambrian Mountains to the dark ridge of Cader Idris.

☎ Harlech (0766) 552

In centre of Harlech, W of A496

SH 5731 (OS 124)

Open daily throughout year; Mar to Oct 0930-1830, Oct to Mar 0930-1600 (Su 1400-1600). Closed 24, 25, 26 Dec and 1 Jan

⊖ P ⊟ D ❊

☎ Macclesfield (0625) 829206

9 m S of Stockport on A523 turn W at Adlington

SJ 9080 (OS 118)

Open Good Fri to end Sept Su and Bank Hols;
Aug W, S, Su and Bank Hol M 1400-1730

⊖ (1 m walk) ⒫ WC ⊟ D (strictly on lead)
🖝 ⊓ ★ ⚹ ⚔

Adlington Hall

Macclesfield, Cheshire

This small manor house, an attractive mixture of brick and the black-and-white timbering so common in Cheshire, has been the home of the Legh family since 1315, and additions and alterations have been carried out by successive generations. The timber parts of the building date mainly from the 16th century, and the north front seems to have been rebuilt in the mid-17th century. Extensive alterations were made after 1739 by Charles Legh, who added a west wing, several rooms in the north-west corner, and a Georgian south front connecting the new wing with the old Elizabethan east wing. In 1928 part of the west side was removed, the house having been found unmanageably large. Visitors see the Elizabethan front first, but enter through a door in the north front into a screens passage leading to the Elizabethan staircase. After passing through some charming small panelled rooms on the first floor of the north range, we see the attractive 18th-century drawing room and dining room, and then the lofty and impressive great hall, the centre from which the house grew. Completed in 1505, the hall was given new and bigger windows in 1581, and has a fine hammerbeam roof. Its most striking features, however, are the twin oak trees supporting the east end, all that remains of the original hunting lodge. These have been adze-carved into octagonal shape, and between them is one of the finest 17th-century organs in the country, which was built by 'Father' Bernard Smith in about 1670 and is richly ornamented.

☎ Upton Magna (074 377) 203

4½ m SE of Shrewsbury on A5 turn N for ½ m
at Atcham

SJ 5410 (OS 126)

Open Apr to end Sept M, W, S, Su; Oct S, Su 1400-1730; Bank Hol M 1130-1730

⊖ ⒫ WC ♿ ⊟ (by appt) D 🖝 🖝
⊓ ◆ ⚹ (available in braille)

Attingham Park

Shrewsbury, Shropshire

Looking rather like a Classical cube dumped in the featureless countryside that was the despair of the garden designer, Humphry Repton, Attingham has an interior of considerable elegance and distinction. The house was put up in 1783-85 to envelop a house of around 1700. The owner was the Whig magnate Noël Hill and the new place was to go with his title (1784) of Lord Berwick. It is the only surviving country house of the Scottish architect, George Steuart. The layout of the very fine rooms, and the delicately painted wall decorations, show the influence of French taste as was often the case with the houses of the Whig oligarchy in the years before the French Revolution. Opening off the hall on the left are the baron's apartments with the dining room, and on the right, Lady Berwick's with the drawing room. The painted and moulded ceilings recall the Adam style, and the octagon room and the round boudoir both display a variety of touches in the Neo-Classical manner. The second Lord Berwick, returning from a Grand Tour in his twenties, engaged Repton to improve the park, and then, in 1807, brought in John Nash to construct the picture gallery. This is one of the earliest structures in the country to be lit from above by a glass roof supported on a cast-iron framework. The collection of paintings is still hung there in close order all the way up the wall, as was usual in the 19th century. The contents of Attingham were sold in 1827, but the 3rd Baron was able to replenish the house with his own collection.

☎ Beaumaris (0248) 810361

5 m NE of Menai Bridge on A545 in Beaumaris

SH 6076 (OS 115)

⒫ WC ♿ ⊟ D 🖝 ⊓ ⚹

Beaumaris Castle

Beaumaris, Anglesey, Gwynedd

Beaumaris, strategically situated in flat, once-marshy land on the south side of Anglesey, was the last of the great Welsh castles built by Edward I in the early 14th century. It was designed by Edward's military engineer Master James of St George, and the flat land allowed him to build a castle which is almost perfectly symmetrical. It consists of two concentric rings of walls, an inner and an outer. The smaller and lower outer wall had sixteen towers defended by a broad moat, whose waters were fed by the Menai Strait, while the square inner ward, whose walls are some 16 feet thick, has cylindrical towers on the corners and two gatehouses. Beaumaris was never completed – even though the building took over thirty-five years and at one time 3,500 people were working on it – and the southern gatehouse lacks its rear portions. Both gatehouses contained suites of rooms for royalty, and other residential buildings once stood against the walls. By the 1330s the castle was as complete as it ever was to be, and it was considered impregnable. The southern gatehouse was protected by a barbican, and both rings of walls had arrow slits all round, providing maximum cover in the event of attack from any quarter. But the castle's defences were never put to the test, and within twenty years of the last building operations the stonework was apparently deteriorating and the timber rotting. One gatehouse and the walls now survive, and visitors can walk round the walls, through the passages and into the attractive chapel.

Berkeley Castle

Berkeley, Gloucestershire

A couple of miles inland from where the Severn begins to broaden out above Chepstow, Berkeley Castle hides the secret of King Edward II's murder on the orders of his Queen Isabella and her lover Roger Mortimer in 1327. 'Hides' because within some twenty years or so of that horrific crime, the whole castle had been gutted and rebuilt (1340-50) inside its old walls. Many of the buildings in the inner courtyard date from that time. The cost of such extensive works may well have been put against the price of total discretion on the part of the then Lord Berkeley and his family. The castle was started very soon after the Conquest by William FitzOsbern, one of William's closest supporters, who was rewarded with the earldom of Hereford. It continued to be extended, with masonry replacing timber, and in 1153 passed to a supporter of Henry II, Robert Fitzharding, in whose line it has remained to the present day. The chapel has a timber roof painted with 14th-century texts translated from the Book of Revelations. There are stone fireplaces and doorways in various positions which were acquired in France by the 8th Earl (died 1942). The gem of the rebuilding in 1340-50 is the great hall, with its fine saddle-beam timber roof and five-sided 'Berkeley arches', which was raised on the foundations of the old hall. The inner keep, one of the oldest parts of the castle, is unusual, being a circular wall over 60 feet high and empty inside, like a hollow stone drum (a 'shell keep'). The breach was made by the Parliamentarians after the siege of 1645 to prevent its further use for warfare.

☎ Dursley (0453) 810332
19 m SW of Gloucester on A38 turn W onto B4066 to Berkeley
ST 6899 (OS 162)

Open daily exc M; Apr and Oct 1000-1700; May to Sept 1100-1700
⊖ (limited) 🅿 WC ♿ (limited access) 🚻 (by appt) ♣ 🍴 ⅋ ◆ ✄ 🗡 ● (not in castle)

Berrington Hall

Leominster, Herefordshire

Berrington is a rectangular Classical mid-Georgian house, built of the local pinkish sandstone, with a large and graceful columned portico. It was built between 1778 and 1781 for Thomas Harley, then Lord Mayor of London, who chose the site with the help of Capability Brown, and the architect was Henry Holland. It is a perfectly proportioned building, its austerity enlivened by the unusual variety of window and door shapes on the front, and the servants' hall, kitchens and other offices are grouped round a courtyard at the back so that the symmetry is unbroken. If the exterior is rather severe for some tastes, the interior certainly is not: the decoration throughout is of an elaborate richness unparalleled in Holland's other work, and many of the colour-schemes and furnishings are original. The entrance hall, with polychrome marble paving echoing the pattern of the ceiling, leads to a magnificent staircase hall, a brilliant exercise in spatial design and still in its original clear, pale colours delicately picked out with gilding. The most splendid of the actual rooms is the drawing room, which has a marble chimneypiece, and one of the most elaborate ceilings Holland ever designed. The central part is probably the work of Biagio Rebecca, who was also responsible for some of the decoration in the library and business room. The boudoir, which opens out of the drawing room, is also very fine, with columns of lapis-lazuli blue and a ceiling picked out with pink, blue and gold. The outbuildings include a Victorian laundry and the original dairy.

☎ Leominster (0568) 5721
5 m NE of Leominster on A49 turn W to Moreton
SO 5163 (OS 149)

Open Apr, Oct S, Su, Bank Hol M 1400-1700; May to end Sept W-Su and Bank Hol M 1400-1800
⊖ 🅿 WC 🚻 D ♣ 🍴
● (by permission)

Bodrhyddan Hall

near Rhyl, Clwyd

This house is the very old home of the Conwy family who have held the hereditary office of Constable of Rhuddlan Castle, a few miles distant, since 1399. However, the feature which has stamped its character on the whole building dates from only 1874 – the spectacular three-storeyed 'Queen Anne revival' frontage (actually, it is at one side) built by W. E. Nesfield. Bodrhyddan comes at the beginning of an architectural fashion that was to fill the suburbs of Britain with red-brick, rather Dutch-looking, gabled houses, and to inspire some grand country houses down to the period of Edwin Lutyens in the late 1890s. The old house behind this frontage preserves an Elizabethan carved stone doorway as well as the former front door, dated 1696. In the current front hall, the owners display a collection of arms and armour. Another, smaller, room contains two mummy-cases brought back from Egypt in the 1830s by an intrepid lady traveller of the Conwy family, Mrs Rowley, whose portrait hangs in the big dining room. In one of the cases is the embalmed body of a young priest. Beyond the front hall is the old hall, which Nesfield clad in light oak panelling. Two portraits dated 1696 by Jean-François de Troy hang there. The white drawing room upstairs has been altered in colour for its present use from its former character of the library, dark with carved woodwork. The family portraits in the 18th-century big dining room include works by Hogarth, Reynolds and Ramsay.

3 m SE of Rhyl on A525 continue on A5151 for 1½ m
SJ 0478 (OS 116)

Open June-Sept T and Th 1400-1730
🅿 WC ♿ (limited access) 🚻 D ♣ 🍴 ⅋ ✄ 🗡

Bramall Hall

Bramhall Park, Bramhall, Stockport, Cheshire

This unusually large timber-framed house of the black-and-white Cheshire type was built mainly between 1500 and 1600 for the Davenport family. The buildings were originally arranged round a central courtyard, but one entire side was removed in the 18th century. The Industrial Revolution in the 19th century brought considerable wealth to the area through the cotton, steel and hatting industries, and a newly-rich Victorian owner, Charles Neville, carried out extensive repair and restoration work on the house. There are some extremely fine rooms, the ballroom in the south wing being particularly notable for its Tudor and Stuart wallpaintings depicting 16th- and 17th-century life. The withdrawing room has a lovely Tudor plaster ceiling and fireplace, and the walls are hung with family portraits. 'Dame Dorothy's bedroom', with its plaster frieze and secret 'hide', dates from the same period. The great hall has early stained glass, and there is more in the chapel, which also contains wallpaintings on the theme of the Reformation. The house, which is administered by Stockport Borough Council, is not lived in, and there is not a great deal of furniture, but there are some good early pieces, and the 'Chapel Room' contains some excellent furniture by A. W. N. Pugin. The park is landscaped, and extends to some 60 acres.

☎ (061) 485 3708

3 m S of Stockport on A5102 at Bramhall Park

SJ 8986 (OS 109)

Open Apr to Sept daily exc M 1200-1700; Oct to Mar (closed Dec) 1200-1600

⊖ 🅿 WC 🚽 D 🍴 🍽 🎪 ◆ (wheelchair users) ★ ♨ 🏹 ● (not in house) ⚲

Caerphilly Castle

Caerphilly, Mid-Glamorgan

Caerphilly is the largest castle in Wales, in a splendid state of preservation, and with enough of its artificial moats and lakes still in place to give a fair idea of its original majestic complexity. Among its other distinctions, Caerphilly was the first concentric castle, antedating Edward I's famous strongholds. In characteristic 'Edwardian' style, the heart of the castle consists of two roughly rectangular curtain walls; the outer is protected by two twin-towered gateways, and the inner is even stronger, with two more gateways and four massive drum towers at the corners. But few attackers could hope to get so far. The mighty concentric castle was protected by an outer defensive system that was, if anything, more formidable still. Beyond the outer curtain lay the lakes and moats, with a strong outwork to the west and, to the east, a notable piece of engineering – a 1000-foot-long screen or barrage that served both as a dam and as a crenellated stronghold, consisting of defensive platforms, gatehouses and walls bristling with towers. Caerphilly Castle was the creation of Gilbert de Clare, Earl of Gloucester, who began a castle in 1268 that was destroyed by Llywelyn, Prince of Wales. Gilbert started again in 1271. Edward's conquests removed the main Welsh threat, but Caerphilly was besieged twice during the troubled reign of Edward II (surrendering once) and was occupied for a time by Owain Glyndŵr in the early 1400s.

☎ Caerphilly (0222) 883143

In centre of Caerphilly

ST 1587 (OS 171)

Open daily throughout year; Mar to Oct 0930-1830, Oct to Mar 0930-1600 (Su 1400-1600)

⊖ 🅿 WC ♿ (limited access) 🚽 D 🍴 ♨

Castell Coch

Tongwynlais, South Glamorgan

Castell Coch is unique, a medieval fantasy created by the Victorian revivalist architect William Burges for John Crichton-Stuart, 3rd Marquis of Bute. Little is known of the original castle except that it was built of red sandstone (coch=red) and was probably destroyed in the 15th century, but its ruins prompted the rich, energetic and scholarly Marquis to commission his '13th-century' retreat. Work began in 1875, and Burges treated the commission extremely seriously, producing a building that could easily be a real medieval fortress. Its bold, round towers are 10 feet thick at the base, there is a dry moat, portcullis and drawbridge with winding mechanism, the walls are battlemented and the arrow slits fully operational. Inside, the castle is quite small, with the four main rooms, which Burges called the castellan rooms, grouped round a galleried courtyard. These rooms are wonderfully decorated with paintings and carvings in Burges's own 'medieval' style. The great fireplaces have almost life-size carved figures, while walls and ceilings are covered in murals, resembling one of the richer medieval manuscripts. The most lavishly decorated of all is the octagonal vaulted room in the keep, two storeys high, which has delicate flower paintings in panels round the lower part and illustrations from Aesop's *Fables* above. Birds and butterflies mingle with Aesop's creatures, and the ribs of the dome are decorated with more butterflies, carved in wood and painted in different colours. The furniture was also designed by Burges.

☎ Cardiff (0222) 810101

8 m NW of Cardiff on A470 turn SW onto B4262 and at roundabout turn NE under A470

ST 1382 (OS 171)

Open throughout year; M-S Mar to Oct 0930-1830, Su 1400-1830; Oct to Mar 0930-1600, Su 1400-1600

⊖ (1 m walk) 🅿 WC 🚽 ♨

Chavenage

Tetbury, Gloucestershire

Chavenage is mainly Elizabethan; the date 1576 is carved on the porch, although it may have been built on to an existing medieval house. It was built for the Stephens family, and it has always been, and still is, the centre of a working farm, with fine outbuildings. The house is on the common Tudor E-plan, though there have been several later additions, and the garden front is a mixture of every style of architecture from the 16th century to the 20th. The porch has 17th-century Dutch stained glass. The very fine great hall has part of its original screen, a splendid fireplace with the arms of Robert Stephens, who was here until about 1608, and some medieval stained glass in its two tall windows. This probably came from the old Horsley Priory nearby. The drawing room has interesting panelling, some of which is dated 1627, while some, carved with portrait heads or allegorical figures and gilded, is Renaissance in style and seems likely to be mid-16th century. This room also contains some good porcelain. Upstairs there are two 17th-century bedrooms with dark oak furniture and tapestry-hung walls. These are called Cromwell and Ireton after the two generals who stayed here in 1648. Nathaniel Stephens was a staunch Parliamentarian, and Chavenage had been a headquarters during the Civil War. The exit is through the back part of the house, which was enlarged in 1905 by John Mickelthwaite. The nearby chapel has carved figures set into 17th-century stonework.

☎ Tetbury (0666) 52329
2 m NW of Tetbury on B4014 turn W to Chavenage Green for 1 m
ST 8795 (OS 162)

Open Easter Su and M; May to Sept Th, Su and Bank Hol M 1400-1700; parties by appt, other times
🅿 (limited) WC 🍴 (by appt) D ♠
🐕 (by appt) ⚸ 🏃 (compulsory)

Chirk Castle

Chirk, Clwyd

The Welsh name for the castle is Castell y Waun, which means 'meadow castle'. The rather grim-looking building was built as one of the great Marcher (border) castles by Roger Mortimer, one of Edward I's generals (completed 1310). In 1595 it was bought by the merchant adventurer Sir Thomas Myddelton, who began to convert it into a country house. The Myddletons still live in the castle, which has examples of decoration from the 16th to the 19th centuries, though the exterior has been little changed, and the dungeon, portcullis gate, and stone steps leading to the watch tower remain exactly as originally built. Considerable interior remodelling was done in the 19th century by A. W. N. Pugin, and the entrance hall, in the Victorian Gothic style, is his work. The great staircase next to it, formed inside one of the towers, was designed by Joseph Turner in 1777, and the first-floor state rooms, with their elegant Adam-style decorations, are of the same period. They contain good furniture, portraits and tapestries, and both the saloon and the drawing room have delightful blue-and-gold coffered ceilings. The long gallery, with its boldly carved panelling and mullioned windows, was built about a century earlier. The garden has seen many changes since it was first laid out, but in the 1870s part of the original formal garden was recreated, with topiary work and a charming rose garden. The park, entered from the town, has superb wrought-iron gates made in 1721 by the Davies brothers.

☎ Chirk (0691) 777701
6 m N of Oswestry on A483 turn W onto B4500 for 2 m
SJ 2638 (OS 126)

Open May to end Sept Su, T, W, Th and Bank Hol M; Oct S and Su 1200-1700
⊖ 🅿 WC 🍴 ♠ 🐕 🍴 ♦ ⚸ ● (no use of flash)

Conwy Castle

Conwy, Gwynedd

Conwy Castle, together with the great town wall with its twenty-one towers, forms one of the most impressive medieval fortifications in the British Isles, and it was completed in the astonishingly short time of five years, from 1283 to 1288. It is one of Edward I's castles, and was built under the supervision of the great military engineer James of St George, Master of the Royal Works. Unlike Beaumaris and several other Welsh castles, it is not concentric, since its wall follows the oblong contours of the rock and there is no gatehouse, but the town itself is strongly fortified, and the castle forecourt was defended by two of the great towers. Although the inside of the castle is ruined, the walls are almost intact, and the great round towers still stand to their full height. The entrance is through the old main gate leading into the outer ward, with the old great hall on the right and a narrow gate to the inner ward opposite. The four corner towers of the inner ward held the royal apartments, while beyond this is the east barbican, giving access to the back gate. The castle began to fall into decay relatively early, and in 1628 it was sold to Viscount Conway for as little as £100. At the outbreak of the Civil War it was repaired by John Williams, Archbishop of York, an ardent Royalist, but was taken quite easily by Cromwell's forces, and in 1665 the 3rd Earl of Conway ordered all movables to be shipped to Ireland. Long after the castle's ruin its interest was enhanced by the building of the two bridges which stand side by side alongside it, Telford's of 1817 and Stephenson's of 1848.

☎ Conwy (049 263) 2358
In centre of Conwy S of Conwy estuary
SH 7877 (OS 115)

Open daily throughout year; Mar to Oct 0930-1830, Oct to Mar 0930-1600 (Su 1400-1600)
⊖ 🅿 ♿ (limited access) 🍴 D ♦ ⚸

Cwmmau Farmhouse

Brilley, Whitney-on-Wye, Herefordshire and Worcestershire

Cwmmau farmhouse is a notable case of the mixed blessing resulting from remoteness of setting. Situated in a peaceful rural landscape, it stands high on a ridge close to the Anglo-Welsh border, looking right out across the Wye Valley. Historic events and industrial developments have passed it by – so much so that very little is known about the history of this interesting old house. On the other hand, 'progress' has not spoiled it: despite its workaday character, Cwmmau has not been altered out of recognition, but remains a rare example of an early 17th-century farmhouse, with such original features as its two-storey porch and stone-tiled floors. It is still a family home, and still the centre of a small, self-supporting family farm. Cwmmau – pronounced 'cooma' – is a Welsh word meaning 'many dingles.'

☎ Clifford (04973) 251

3 m S of Kington on A4111, turn SW

SO 2851 (OS 137)

Open Easter to end Aug Bank Hol weekends S-M 1400-1800; by appt at other times

WC ● ⌖ (by appt) ✗ (compulsory) ● (not in house)

Eastnor Castle

Ledbury, Herefordshire

The massive, dramatic pile of Eastnor Castle was built between 1812 and 1815 for Lord Somers, whose family had owned the manor for 200 years but who now found his ancestral seat unworthy. The architect was Robert Smirke, who was later to design the British Museum. Eastnor is his early experiment in the Gothic style, and is sombrely medieval both outside and in. Only about half of Smirke's interiors remain, as extensive alterations were done in the later 19th century, notably by A. W. N. Pugin, but the great hall, an immense room 60 foot high, is his design, though the embellishments, the coloured marbles and painted walls, were done by George Fox in the 1860s. The room contains a collection of arms and armour made by the 3rd Earl. The dining room is also Smirke's, and has all its original furniture, but the drawing room, with its Gothic-style fan vault, is largely the work of Pugin, who was commissioned to redecorate it in 1849. He designed all the furniture as well as the great iron chandelier and the sumptuous chimneypiece. There are some fine Gobelin tapestries in this room, while most of the other rooms reflect the Italian taste of the 3rd Earl. In the library, which was designed by Fox, there is a set of bookcases and two chimneypieces carved in Verona. The frescos in the staircase hall, brought from Carlton House Terrace, are by G. F. Watts.

☎ Ledbury (0531) 2304

7 m SW of Great Malvern on A449 turn SE onto A438 for 2½ m then N to Bronsil

SO 7336 (OS 150)

Open Easter to early May, Bank Hol M; May to end Sept, Su also W and Th in July and Aug 1415-1730

WC ♿ (by appt) ⊟ D ● ● ⌖ ◆ ⚹ ✗

Erddig

near Wrexham, Clwyd

At Erddig all the workings of a large 18th- and 19th-century country estate can be seen in minute detail. The owners, the Yorkes, never threw anything away, and the National Trust, who now own the property, have put it all on show. The large plain, red-brick house was built in the 1680s by Thomas Webb for Joshua Edisbury, and the wings were added in 1724 by the next owner, John Mellor. The Yorke family inherited the property in 1733, and further improvements were made in the 1770s, including the stone facing of the west front. Visitors are shown into the house through the back yard and servants' rooms, and all the outbuildings and below-stairs rooms have their original fittings. They are arranged as though they were still in use, and the servants themselves are immortalised in a series of portraits which hang in the servants' hall and the corridor. These were all commissioned by the family, and some are accompanied by doggerel verses by the kindly but eccentric Philip Yorke II. The main rooms of the house are pleasant but not noteworthy, with the exception of a severe Neo-Classical dining room designed by Thomas Hopper in 1826. The furniture, however, is outstanding. Most of the best pieces were bought in London by John Mellor before he moved into the house in 1716. There are carved and gilded chairs, lacquered and japanned pieces, lovely pier glasses, Soho tapestries and a state bed with Chinese embroidered hangings. Apart from these treasures, the house is crammed with a medley of family possessions.

☎ Wrexham (0978) 355314

1 m SW of Wrexham on A483 turn S to Erddig Park

SJ 3248 (OS 117)

Open Apr to end Sept daily exc F but inc Good Fri 1200-1730; Oct W, S, Su 1200-1530

♿ WC ♿ ⊟ D (guide dogs only) ● ●
⚹ (braille guide available)

Gawsworth Hall

Macclesfield, Cheshire

A pretty half-timbered manor house with a fine three-storey bow window in its long show front. The Hall dates mainly from the 15th century, though additions were made later, and the south and east walls were rebuilt in brick in the 18th century. The rooms are relatively small and many contain fine furniture, paintings and sculpture. The library, a double cube room measuring 16 by 32 feet, has a lovely carved Tudor chimneypiece, and the bookcases were designed by A. W. N. Pugin. The chapel contains some stained glass by William Morris and Burne-Jones. The outbuildings house a collection of 19th-century vehicles, the centrepiece being three Victorian horse-drawn double-decker buses. The park, encompassed by its Tudor wall, remains much the same as in medieval times, when it was the scene of knightly tournaments. Gawsworth Hall, now the home of the Roper-Richards family, has seen many stirring events since the long tenure (1316-1662) of its original owners, the 'fighting Fittons'. Mary Fitton, the 'wayward maid of Gawsworth', and thought to have been Shakespeare's 'Dark Lady', lived here, and in 1701 a famous duel was fought here between Lord Mohun and the Duke of Hamilton. Both were killed. The last professional jester in England, 'Magotty Johnson', was dancing master to the children of the house, and lies buried in a nearby spinney.

☎ North Rode (026 03) 456
3½ m SW of Macclesfield on A536 turn E at Warren for Gawsworth
SJ 8969 (OS 118)

Open late Mar to end Oct daily 1400-1730
⊖ ▮WC ⊟ D ✦ ☛ ☖ ★ ⋇
● (general views of house only)

Littledean Hall

Littledean, Gloucestershire

The Hall has been built over centuries; the 'Jacobean' north front is a Victorian replacement of an early Georgian one, which in its turn was a conversion of a genuine Jacobean front. The remains of a Norman house are enclosed within the structure of the north front, and this stands on the walls of a Roman building, which was rebuilt as a church and became a house after the Norman Conquest. Gradually this Norman house grew into a manor house, with a great hall added in the 14th century and further additions made in the 15th. In 1612 Charles Bridgeman bought the house and completely overhauled it to provide a country squire's residence, and in 1664 he sold it to the Pyrke family, who retained it until 1896 and made considerable changes during this period. The interiors are mainly a mixture of the 17th and 18th centuries, but the old parlour, which houses a small museum, gives an idea of an Elizabethan parlour with its huge open fireplace. The overmantel in the library is a fine example of Flemish 16th-century craftsmanship, and the room also has fine 17th-century panelling, as do three of the other rooms. To the right of the fireplace there is a secret closet, and at one time there was a mechanism in the fireplace which allowed the overmantel to swing open, revealing a ladder. The gardens and grounds are open to the public; the Victorian ornamental garden is gradually being replaced by a new water garden with pools stocked with exotic fish.

☎ Dean (0594) 24213
13 m SW of Gloucester on A48 turn W onto A4151 to Littledean
SO 6713 (OS 162)

Open Apr to Sept daily; parties at other times by appt
⊖ ▮WC ♿ (limited access) ⊟ (by appt)
D ✦ ☛ ☖ ◆ ⋇ ⚹ ⚳

Little Moreton Hall

Congleton, Cheshire

Little Moreton Hall is probably the best-known example of timber-framed architecture in England. It is a delightful building and full of atmosphere, surrounded by a knot garden based on a design of 1688 and then by a water-filled moat. What strikes the visitor first is the charming crookedness of the house – it is hard to find a vertical or horizontal line anywhere. It was built by three successive generations of the Moreton family, who owned the property from about 1250 to the present century. The bridge over the moat leads to a gatehouse and then to the courtyard around which all the buildings are grouped, the main entrance to the great hall being across the yard. The hall is the oldest part of the house, and was 'modernised' in 1599 by William Moreton, who gave it a fireplace in the north wall and a first floor. This was removed before 1807, but the remains of the beam which supported it are still visible. The rooms on either side, completed in 1480, were improved in the 1550s by the addition of large bay windows. The other sides of the courtyard, including the long gallery at the top, with its crazily tilting floor and odd allegorical plasterwork, were completed about 1580, and the house has hardly been touched since. It is almost empty of furniture now, except for two pieces in the hall and the 'great Rounde table in the parlour', but there is painted decoration, some lovely early panelling and splendid decorated fireplaces in the drawing room and upper porch room. A major programme of restoration work has been going on since 1977.

☎ Congleton (02602) 272018
4 m SW of Congleton on A34
SJ 8358 (OS 118)

Open Mar and Oct S and Su; Apr to end Sept daily exc Tu and Good Fri 1400-1800 (or dusk if earlier)
⊖ ▮WC ♿ ⊟ ✦ ☛ (by appt for parties)
☖ ◆ ⋇ ⚹ Open-air play in July

Ludlow Castle

Ludlow, Shropshire

Ludlow Castle, perched on its rocky promontory over the river Teme, is one of the great Welsh border castles, and its extensive remains span the entire medieval period. It was begun about 1085 by Roger de Lacy, but the lovely round Norman chapel, one of the earliest castle chapels in the country, was built in the 1130s by a rival claimant, Sir Joyce de Dinan, who temporarily ousted the Lacys from their home. The outer defences were constructed about 1180, the round towers added a century later, and most of the other buildings within the enclosure – the great hall, great chamber, service rooms and so on – were built in the 14th century and embellished in the Tudor period. After the Lacy line died out in 1240 the castle was held by the villainous Roger Mortimer and five generations of his descendants, becoming royal property in 1461 when one of the line was crowned as Edward IV. The 'Princes' tower is so named because his two young sons lived here before their final imprisonment and death in the Tower of London, and 'Arthur's tower' takes its name from Henry VIII's elder brother, who died here in 1507. The castle then became the increasingly sumptuous residence of the Lords President of the Council of Wales, and extensive rebuilding, including the gatehouse on the north side (1581), was carried out by one of the holders of this office, Sir Henry Sidney, father of Sir Philip. In 1634, the castle had a last glorious fling with the performance of Milton's masque *Comus*, to celebrate the Earl of Bridgwater's presidency of Wales and the Marches.

☎ Disley (06632) 2023
8 m SE of Stockport on A6 turn S at Disley
SJ 9682 (OS 109)

Open Apr to Oct daily exc M 1400-1700
♿ (1½ m walk) 🅿 WC 🅿 🚌 (by appt only)
D ♣ ♥ (limited opening) 🏕 ◆ ⚲
● (permission required in house) 🕆

Lyme Park

Disley, Stockport, Cheshire

A large and imposing stone house set in a huge park, nine miles round. The house, home of the Legh family since Tudor times, and given to the National Trust in 1946, is partly of the 16th and partly of the 18th century. About 1550 Sir Piers Legh replaced an earlier hall with the fine courtyard, the main lines of which, with its early Renaissance gateway, can still be seen. From 1650 to 1720 further improvements and reconstructions were carried out, and in 1725 the architect Giacomo Leoni was brought to Lyme to modernise the house. He built the splendid west front facing the lake, made some alterations to the courtyard to give it its present Italianate look, and improved some of the rooms inside. Some further alterations were made in the early 19th century by Lewis Wyatt, who added the tower above the south front to house the servants. The showpiece of the house is the saloon, with its lovely carved wood decorations believed to be by Grinling Gibbons. This room forms part of Leoni's alterations, as does the fine entrance hall with its Mortlake tapestries. Hunting the stag was the traditional occupation at Lyme, so it is fitting that herds of deer still roam in the great park, which itself still retains much of its old forest character, being set in wild, open country. Various activities, such as nature trails, are suggested to the visitor, and the park is frequently the scene of events in the country calendar.

☎ Manorbier (083 482) 421
5½ m SW of Tenby on A4139 turn E onto B4585
to Manorbier
SS 0697 (OS 158)

Open Easter week and mid May to end Sept daily
1030-1730
♿ 🅿 (limited) 🚌 D ♣ ⚲

Manorbier Castle

near Pembroke, Dyfed

This small castle is a perfect model of a medieval nobleman's seat, although partly in ruins. It is best known as the birthplace and home of Gerald de Barry (Giraldus Cambrensis) who wrote vivid accounts of life in 12th-century Wales and Ireland. Gerald was also well known in his day for his unsuccessful struggle with Henry II to make the See of St David's independent from Canterbury, and his brothers played a prominent part in Henry's conquest of Ireland. The de Barrys held Manorbier from about 1130 until the mid-14th century, and nearly all the buildings and fortifications had been put up by 1300, with only minor alterations made since. In 1403 the castle was ordered to be put into a state of defence against Owain Glyndŵr, and during the Civil War it was held by the Royalists but captured by Cromwell's forces in 1646. The castle had a large outer ward, and the main feature of the inner ward was the stone-built hall block, with the hall itself at first-floor level and rising through two storeys. It was divided by a wall from the buttery, which was also on the first floor, though it once had another room above it – the solar, or withdrawing room. This structure and the gatehouse date from about 1140, while the defences, which would originally have been earth and timber, were rebuilt in stone about 1230, and the chapel was added about 1260. These buildings are all now ruined, but the castle is still occupied (some of the domestic buildings have been altered recently), and the inner ward has a very attractive flower garden.

Penhow Castle

Penhow, near Newport, Gwent

Penhow was one of a ring of Norman castles surrounding the great stronghold of Chepstow, seat of the Marcher lords. It was the seat of the St Maur family, who came from France in the wake of the Conqueror and founded the illustrious Seymour line. Sir Roger, who moved away from Penhow to Somerset in the 14th century, was the ancestor of the Dukes of Somerset and Marquesses of Hertford. The castle, which unlike most Welsh castles is still inhabited, is quite small, with the buildings grouped round a courtyard. The square stone battlemented keep was built in the 12th century, the curtain wall in the 13th, and the hall block, built in the 14th century, was enlarged in the 15th, when it was remodelled to make two halls, the one below for retainers, and the other, more splendid one above with a screen and minstrels' gallery, for the lord of the castle. Gradually the keep fell into disuse, and various additions and alterations continued to be made, including the building, in the Tudor period, of another hall wing. This was modernised in the late 17th century, and contains a delightful Restoration-style dining room and a fine oak staircase. In 1709 the castle was let as a farmhouse and only the Tudor wing occupied. It became derelict, and remained so until the present owner, Mr Stephen Weeks, bought it in 1973. He is now restoring it as his home. Excavations have shown that the present buildings are only the castle's inner bailey; most of the outer bailey has disappeared, but the outer defences included a moat.

☎ Penhow (0633) 400800

10 m SW of Chepstow on A48 at Penhow

ST 4290 (OS 172)

Open Good Fri to end Sept W-Su and Bank Hols 1000-1715; parties at other times by appt

⊖ ⓕ WC 🍴 ⮐ ⊼ ◆ ✴ (available in foreign languages) ☀ (evening candlelit tours by appt)

Penrhyn Castle

Bangor, Gwynedd

This great Victorian mock-medieval building was the result of a large fortune made by Richard Pennant from developing the slate quarries above Bethesda. George Hay Dawkins Pennant inherited both fortune and estate in 1808, and decided to rebuild the existing 'Gothick' house, designed by James Wyatt, as a huge Norman castle. His architect was Thomas Hopper, who was given responsibility for every detail as well as unlimited funds, and building began in 1825. The Norman style had to be rather freely interpreted, but Hopper succeeded in producing a fine Norman-looking building without sacrificing modern comfort, and he clearly enjoyed the challenge. The interiors, though a little overpowering, are undoubtedly spectacular, with arches and columns everywhere, and much elaborate carving and plaster-work. The front door leads into a low, vaulted corridor and thence to the vast great hall, a room more like a cathedral than a castle, rising up the whole height of the building, and lit by softly glowing stained-glass windows. The library has more Norman arches and ornament everywhere, and both rooms contain massive furniture designed by Hopper. Two of the tables in the hall are of carved slate, and there is a slate four-poster bed in one of the bedrooms in the keep. Another of the bedrooms contains a very large collection of dolls and toys. The main staircase is one of the strangest features of any interior in the country, with a profusion of nightmarish writhing ornament.

☎ Bangor (0248) 353084/353356

2 m S of Bangor on A5 turn NE

SH 6071 (OS 115)

Open Apr to late Oct daily exc T 1200-1700; reduced rates for parties by appt

⊖ ⓕ WC ♿ (limited access) 🍴 D ◆ ⮐ ⊼ ◆ ✴ (braille guide available)

Powis Castle

Welshpool, Powys

Powis Castle, continuously inhabited since medieval times, began as a stronghold of Welsh princes, and was built between 1200 and 1300. In 1587 it was bought by Sir Edward Herbert, who added the long gallery and did a great deal of remodelling; in the late 17th century a state bedroom was added, and further alterations were made in the 18th century. Most of the 18th-century work was lost, however, when the architect G. F. Bodley remodelled the interiors in the 1900s in the 'Jacobean' style. In 1784 the Herbert family married into the Clive family; the 2nd Lord Clive (son of Clive of India) was created Earl of Powis in 1804, and his son changed his name to Herbert. This alliance was financially important for the Herberts, and it also brought to Powis a fine collection of books, paintings and furniture as well as a collection of Indian works of art unequalled outside London. The interior of the castle is also interesting for its variety of architectural styles. Notable interiors are the Restoration-period state bedroom with silvered furniture and 17th-century Brussels tapestries; the lovely Elizabethan long gallery with its plaster ceiling and painted panelling; and the ballroom, originally built in the late 18th century to serve as a ballroom as well as a picture gallery, but altered in the 19th century. The dining room, which looks Elizabethan, is in fact the work of Bodley, as is the oak drawing room, though traces of Elizabethan decoration survive in both. The late 17th-century formal gardens are among the finest in Britain, and there is a huge deer park.

☎ Welshpool (0938) 4336

1 m S of Welshpool on A483 turn W for ½ m

SJ 2106 (OS 126)

Open few days in Apr then May to end Jun and Sept W-S 1300-1730; Jul and Aug T-Su 1300-1800; Bank Hol M 1130-1800

⊖ (1 m walk; exc Su) ⓕ WC 🍴 ◆ ⮐ ⊼ ◆ ✴

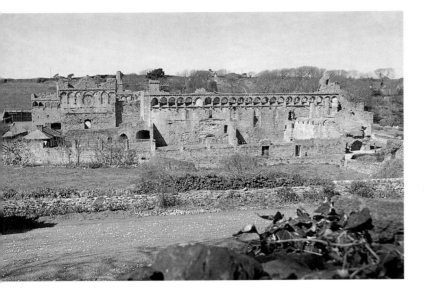

☎ St David's (0437) 720517

In centre of St David's off A487

SM 7525 (OS 157)

Open daily throughout year; Mar to Oct 0930
Oct to Mar 0930-1600 (Su 1400-1600)

⊖ P WC ⓦ (limited access) ⊟ ♠ ◆ ⚹ ⚔
● (on purchase of permit)

St David's, Bishop's Palace

Dyfed

Just inland from St David's Head – the westernmost point on the Welsh coastline – stands the village of St David's with its famous cathedral. The settlement grew up initially as a shrine to the patron saint of Wales, but in 1081 William the Conqueror visited it and resolved to incorporate it into the Anglo-Norman ecclesiastical system. As a result, St David's became an English see in 1115. The Bishop's Palace, built a few hundred yards away from the town and cathedral, is now a ruin of imposing proportions, and makes a considerable impact on first viewing. This is mainly thanks to the extraordinary arcading that runs along the parapets in place of the usual battlements of balustrades. The arcading was an idiosyncracy of Bishop Gower, who greatly extended the palace (1327-47), though much of the structure originated before his time. The gatehouse is late 13th century, and leads into a nearly square courtyard round which the buildings are arranged. One small but splendidly vaulted room dates back to c. 1200, but the bishop's hall and solar, chapel and gatehouse were all part of an ambitious building programme, undertaken after a royal visit in 1284 showed up the deficiencies of hospitality at St David's. Although the bishop's hall was a sizable building, Gower added a great hall; entertainment must have been lavish, for both halls evidently remained in use. The decline of the palace began when Bishop Barlow (1536-48) removed the lead from the roof (to provide dowries for his five daughters), and by the late 17th century it was uninhabitable.

☎ Stanton (038 673) 469

10½ m NE of Cheltenham on A46 turn E onto
B4077 to Stanway

SP 0632 (OS 150)

Open Jun, Jul, Aug T and Th 1400-1700; parties at
other times by appt

P WC ⓦ (limited access) ⊟ D ♠
🌢 ⚔ ● (no photography)

Stanway House

Stanway, Cheltenham, Gloucestershire

This delightful Jacobean manor house was built between 1580 and 1640 on the site of an abbey by the Tracys, a local landowning family. Its interest lies in its development as a typical squire's house, a gradual accumulation through the generations of buildings, furniture and paintings of local significance. The lovely gatehouse ascribed to Timothy Strong of Barrington, was built about 1630 and is adorned with scallop shells, the crest of the Tracys. The south front of the house, built about 1640, linked two existing but separate buildings, the great hall at the west end and the abbot's house at the east end; the curved 'broken pediment' in the middle was added in 1724. An arch to the left of the kitchen range leads past the brewhouse to the entrance porch, and visitors go into a corridor, through the dining room and the former lamp room, where the lamps were cleaned, and then into the audit room. This is where the rents were, and still are, collected from the tenants, and the special 'rent table' with a revolving top made about 1780 is still in use. The other rooms contain a fine collection of family portraits, several good tapestries and some interesting pieces of furniture, notable examples being a shuffleboard table in the hall, made about 1620, and a pair of Chinese Chippendale daybeds in the drawing room, which also contains two pianos by John Broadwood. The buildings outside the main house are equally varied: the tithe barn with its stone roof and oak timbers was built about 1370, and the Pyramid on the hill behind the house in 1750.

☎ Craven Arms (058 82) 2544

10 m NW of Ludlow on A49 turn W

SO 4381 (OS 137)

Open Mar and Oct daily exc T 1000-1700; Apr to
end Sept daily exc T 1000-1800; Nov S and Su
1000-dusk

⊖ P WC ⓦ (limited access) ⊟ ♠ ◆ ⚹

Stokesay Castle

Craven Arms, Shropshire

Despite its name, Stokesay is not a castle but a fortified manor house, picturesque and an authentic and unique medieval survival. Say was the name of the family who originally owned it, and Stoke means 'dairy farm', but of the de Says' early-13th-century house only the moat (once filled with water) and the base of the north tower remain. In 1281 it was bought by a wealthy wool merchant, Lawrence de Ludlow, who built the hall and solar and the top storey of the north tower, adding the battlemented south tower ten years later when he was given permission to fortify. The only addition since then was the Elizabethan gatehouse, built some time between 1570 and 1620. In 1620 Stokesay was bought by Dame Elizabeth Craven, mother of the ardent Royalist Lord Craven, but it was not built to resist cannon, and surrendered to Cromwell's troops in 1645. It was then leased to the Baldwyn family, and from 1728 to farmers, the hall becoming a coopers' workshop. In 1869 Lord Craven sold it to the grandfather of the present owners, who began its careful restoration. The rooms are empty, but are very atmospheric, particularly the great hall with its timber roof, central hearth and shuttered lower windows. The upper room has a fine 14th-century fireplace; the solar has oak panelling and a Flemish overmantel probably brought here in the 17th century. The south tower, once reached only by a drawbridge, is an irregular polygon of three storeys, with a staircase rising within the thickness of the walls, single lancet windows and garderobes.

Sudeley Castle

Winchcombe, Gloucestershire

Sudeley Castle, perched on its lofty hill, was largely built in 1442 by Ralph Boteler. In 1469 he was forced to sell to the future Yorkist king, Richard III, who rebuilt the east side as a sumptuous state apartment. The castle remained royal for nearly eighty years, but in 1547 it was granted to Sir Thomas Seymour, who married Henry VIII's ex-wife Catherine Parr. She died the following year and was buried in the chapel, but Seymour's ambitions led him to the Tower. The castle was then granted by Queen Mary to Lord Chandos, who rebuilt the outer courtyard about 1572 (Elizabeth I was entertained here several times). The 6th Lord Chandos, a Royalist, held the castle for Charles I during the Civil War, and although he later changed sides, the order to slight the castle was not revoked. The building became more or less a ruin, and remained so until 1837, when it was bought and restored by the brothers Dent, wealthy glovemakers from Worcester. This restoration was carried out with a care and attention to detail unusual at the time, and the exterior work is hard to tell from the original fabric. The rooms open to visitors are those on one side of the outer courtyard, and they are almost entirely 19th-century, though Catherine Parr's room has a 15th-century window. There are many excellent paintings including works by Rubens, Van Dyck, Poussin, Turner and Constable; a collection of lace is shown in the first-floor corridor, and the great dungeon tower contains one of the largest collections of dolls and toys in the country.

☎ Winchcombe (0242) 602308
9 m NE of Cheltenham on A46 turn SE at Winchcombe
SP 0327 (OS 163)

Open Apr to end Oct daily 1200-1900
⊖ 🅿 WC ♿ (limited access) 🍴 ♦ 🍽 ⏬
◆ 🎁 ☕ 𝄐 (by appt) ● (not in house) 🐕
Falconry display W, Th, Su May to end Aug

Tredegar House

Newport, Gwent

Now one of the finest late 17th-century houses in Britain, Tredegar House was the home of the Morgan family from the early 15th to the 17th centuries. The original medieval stone house was apparently quite substantial, and William Morgan completely rebuilt it between 1664 and 1672 in brick. The new house is very grand, and the stable block in front, built 1717-31, is no less so, while the wrought-iron gates at right-angles to the stable block, made between 1714 and 1718 by William and Simon Edney, are among the finest in the country. The Morgans left Tredegar in 1951 and most of the contents were sold, but it was bought by Newport Borough Council in 1974 and is now being restored and refurnished. Three of the ground-floor rooms, the side hall, dining room and morning room, which were altered in the 19th century, are being refurnished and decorated as Victorian rooms, while the state rooms, which occupy the main front, are 17th century. The best of these are the brown room, which has lavish carved panelling and a plaster ceiling in the 17th-century style, and the gilt room, with walls inset with paintings, gilt decoration gleaming from every surface and an elaborate 17th-century gilt and stucco ceiling. The carved and decorated 17th-century staircase leads to panelled bedchambers, after which a back staircase leads to the servants' quarters. The wine cellar has a 'bath' at one end for washing bottles and cooling wine, which is fed by a natural spring running beneath the house.

☎ Newport (0633) 62275
SW of Newport at junction of A48 and B4239
ST 2885 (OS 171)

Open Good Fri to end Sept W-Su and Bank Hols 1330-1700; other times by appt
⊖ 🅿 WC ♿ (by appt) 🍴 D
♦ 🍽 ◆ ☕ 𝄐 (compulsory) 🐕

Weston Park

Weston-under-Lizard, near Shifnal, Shropshire

This complex of red-brick and stone buildings – the house, home farm, stables and church – set in an enormous park, more or less forms a village. The large brick house, built in 1671 for Sir Thomas and Lady Wilbraham, is an early example of the Classical style designed by Lady Wilbraham herself, who was a follower of the ideas of the Palladians. In the 18th century the estate passed to the Bridgeman family, later Earls of Bradford, who made alterations and improvements to house and park, and inside the house nothing survives from the earlier period. Many of the rooms have 18th-century marble chimneypieces and plasterwork, but there have been three major remodellings, and the great dining room with its stuccoed ceiling was only completed in 1968, in time for the coming-of-age of Viscount Newport. Two rooms, however, remain entirely 18th century: the charming library with its grained woodwork and the tapestry room, hung with a set of 18th-century Gobelin tapestries. There is a very fine collection of paintings; as well as Dutch and Italian paintings and works by Gainsborough, Reynolds and Stubbs, there are some interesting small portraits, including one by Holbein of Sir George Carew, several recently cleaned Van Dycks and, perhaps most important, Jacopo Bassano's *Way to Golgotha*, which has pride of place in the hall. The park has several attractive buildings, including a Roman bridge and a Temple of Diana built by James Paine about 1760, and behind the temple is a large adventure playground.

☎ Weston-under-Lizard (095 276) 207/385
9 m E of Telford on A5 turn S at Weston-under-Lizard
SJ 8010 (OS 127)

Open Apr, May and Sept S, Su and Bank Hols; June to end Aug daily exc M and F but inc Bank Hols 1100-1700; reduced rates for parties
⊖ 🅿 WC ♿ 🍴 D ♦ 🍽 ⏬ ◆ ☕ 𝄐 🐕 🐾

Aberconwy House, Castle St, Conwy, Gwynedd (tel Conwy [0492 63] 2246). In town centre. SH 7877 (OS 115). 14th-century house, the oldest in Conwy. It contains the Conwy museum, covering the history of the town from Roman times. Open Apr to end Sept daily (exc T) am and pm; Oct S and Su only, am and pm. ⊖ 🅿 ⊟ (by appt)

Acton Burnell Castle, Acton Burnell, Shropshire. 7 m SE of Shrewsbury. SJ 5301 (OS 138). Ruins of fortified 13th-century house in the grounds of an 18th-century country house. Despite its battlements, the interior layout is more that of a manor house. Parliament is said to have met here in 1283. There are also ruins of a barn and church built by Bishop Robert Burnell, who was responsible for the house. Open daily am and pm. 🅿 ♿ ♣ ★

Acton Round Hall, Bridgnorth, Shropshire. 7 m NW of Bridgnorth on A458, turn W. SO 6495 (OS 138). Queen Anne period house built for Sir Whitmore Acton of red brick, preserved with its original decorations. The house was abandoned for 200 years to 1918, and now contains a varied collection of furniture belonging to the present owners. Open May to Sept Th pm. ⊖ 🅿 ♿ (by appt)

Adcote, Little Ness, near Shrewsbury, Shropshire (tel Baschurch [0939] 260202). 7 m NW of Shrewsbury off A5. SJ 4119 (OS 126). Victorian country house designed by Norman Shaw in the 1870s, in a style based on Elizabethan houses. There are several tiled fireplaces by William de Morgan, stained glass by William Morris and a large great hall. The house is now used as a school. Open end Apr to mid-July, mid to end Sept, daily pm. 🅿 ♣ ★

Almonry, Vine St, Evesham, Hereford and Worcester (tel Evesham [0386] 6944). In town centre. SP 0344 (OS 150). Stone and half-timbered house, once part of a 14th-century abbey, now containing a museum of local history for the Vale of Evesham. Open Easter to Sept T, Th-Su am and pm (Su pm only); also Bank Hols am and pm. ⊖ 🅿 ♿

Arley Hall, Northwich, Cheshire (tel Arley [056 585] 353). 5 m N of Northwich, turn SW. SJ 6780 (OS 109). Early-Victorian 'Jacobean' house and private chapel, with extensive and varied gardens, including walled garden, topiary, herbaceous borders, woodland walk and animals. The house has a collection of 19th-century watercolours of local great houses. Open Apr to Oct T to Su pm, and Bank Hols pm. 🅿 WC ⊟ (by appt) ♣ ☂

Arlington Mill, Bibury, Gloucestershire (tel Bibury [028 574] 368). 7 m NE of Cirencester on A433. SP 1106 (OS 163). 17th-century corn mill situated on River Coln. The interior contains a museum of working machinery, agricultural implements, Staffordshire pottery, Victorian costume etc. Open March to Oct daily am and pm; Oct to March S and Su am and pm only. ⊖ 🅿 ♿ ⌂

Barnsley House, Barnsley, near Cirencester, Gloucestershire (tel Bibury [028 574] 281). 5 m NE of Cirencester on A433, turn N. SP 0805 (OS 163). 18th- and 19th-century garden completey redesigned in the 1960s, and including many spring bulbs, a laburnum avenue, lime walk, knot garden and vegetable garden. There is an 18th-century summerhouse in the Gothick style, and a Classical temple. The house, which dates from 1697, is not open. Garden open W am and pm; also first Su, May to July. Other times by appt. 🅿 ♿ ♣

Beeston Castle, Beeston, Cheshire. In Beeston village, 9½ m SE of Chester on A51, turn SW onto A49 for 2 m then W. SJ 5359 (OS 117). Castle built in the 1220s by the Earl of Chester on an impregnable hill, and extended by Henry III and the future Edward II. There is an upper enclosure with a strong gatehouse, and a lower bailey, defended by circular towers. The castle was already ruined by the mid-16th century. Open M-S, am and pm, Su pm only. ♣

Benthall Hall, Much Wenlock, Shropshire (tel Telford [0952] 882254). 4 m NE of Much Wenlock on B4375, turn NE. SJ 6502 (OS 127). Stone-built 16th-century house with mullion windows. The interior has 16th-century panelling and 17th-century furniture; there is an intricately carved oak staircase put up in about 1610. Open Easter to Sept T, W, S and Bank Hols pm. ⊖ 🅿 WC ♿ ♣

Boscobel House, near Shifnal, Shropshire. 6 m NW of Wolverhampton on A41, turn N. SJ 8308 (OS 127).Small 17th-century timber-framed house in which the future King Charles II took refuge after his defeat at the battle of Worcester in 1651. The rooms that may have been used by him are on view. There is a formal 17th-century garden, and nearby is an oak tree on the site of the Royal Oak in which Charles is said to have hidden. Open daily am and pm (Su pm only). ⊖ 🅿 WC ♣

Broseley Hall, Broseley, Shropshire (tel Telford [0952] 882748). 4 m NE of Much Wenlock. SJ 6802 (OS 127). Small 18th-century house improved by T.F. Pritchard, architect of the bridge at Ironbridge, in 1767. The house contains the collection of the Wellington Society dedicated to the work of John Wilkinson, a late 18th-century iron master. Open May to Sept Th and Bank Hol M pm. ⊖ 🅿 ⊟ (by appt) ☂ (by appt)

Bryn Bras Castle, Llanrug, near Caernarfon, Gwynedd (tel Llanberis [0286] 870 210). 6 m E of Caernarfon off A4086, turn S. SH 5462 (OS 115). 18th-century country house reworked in the early Victorian period in the style of a medieval castle. The gardens are especially extensive and peaceful, with fine views. Open July and Aug daily exc S am and pm; Spring Bank Hol to mid July and Sept pm only. 🅿 WC ⊟ ♣ ☂ ⌂

Buckland Rectory, near Broadway, Gloucestershire (tel Broadway [0386] 852479). 2 m SW of Broadway on A46, turn SE. SP 0836 (OS 150). The oldest surviving rectory in the county, built in the late 15th century with 17th-century additions. The house has associations with John Wesley. The hall has a hammerbeam roof. Open May to Sept M am and pm; also Aug F am and pm. 🅿 ♿ ★

Burton Court, Eardisland, Hereford and Worcester (tel Pembridge [054 47] 231). 5 m W of Leominster on A4112, turn N onto B4457. SO 4257(OS 149). 18th-century house adapted in the Victorian period, but with a 14th-century great hall with a complicated sweet-chestnut timber roof. There is a collection of working period fairground amusements, and of European and oriental costumes. Open end May to mid-Sept W-Su and Bank Hols pm. ⊖ 🅿 WC ♿ ⊟ ☂

Acton Burnell Castle, Shropshire

Benthall Hall, Shropshire

Capesthorne, Macclesfield, Cheshire (tel Chelford [0625] 861221). 7 m S of Wilmslow on A34. SJ 8472 (OS 118). House built in the 1720s and rebuilt in the mid-19th century in the Jacobean style for the Davenport family, who have lived on the site since Norman times. The interior contains 18th- and 19th-century furniture, paintings, family muniments and Americana. The chapel of 1722 is the earliest known work of John Wood the Elder. There is an extensive park. Open July to Sept T, W, Th, S and Su pm; May and June, T, Th and Su pm; Apr Su pm only; also Bank Hol M. ⊖ 🅿 WC ♿ ⊟ (by appt) D (park only) ♣ ☕

Chepstow Castle, Chepstow, Gwent (tel Chepstow [029 12] 4065). 15 m E of Newport, on A48. ST 5394 (OS 172). One of the first stone castles in Britain, begun in 1068 on a ridge over the River Wye. The curtain walls are of the mid-13th century, and most of the other buildings, including the large Marten's tower, are of the following 50 years. It was besieged by the Parliamentarians in the Civil War but not slighted. Open daily am and pm (Oct to March Su pm only). ⊖ 🅿 ⊟ ♣

Churche's Mansion, Nantwich, Cheshire (Nantwich [0270] 625933). In town centre, at junction of A534 and A51. SJ 6552 (OS 118). Elaborately decorated half-timbered house built in the 1570s on the H-plan, for Richard Churche, a local merchant. Restored in the 1930s, and now housing a restaurant, with upper floor open for visitors, showing details of house construction. Open Apr to Oct am and pm. ⊖ 🅿 WC ☕

Commandery, Sidbury, Worcester, Hereford and Worcester (tel Worcester [0905] 355071). In city centre. SO 8555 (OS 150).An early medieval hospital for the poor, turned into a private house in 1540; the surviving buildings date from the mid-15th century. The great hall has some 15th-century painted glass. The house contains a display of local history, with particular reference to the Civil War; the house formed the local Royalist headquarters in 1651. Open T-S am and pm; also Apr-Sept Su and Bank Hols pm. ⊖ WC ♿ ♣ ☕

Condover Hall, Condover, Shropshire. 5 m SE of Shrewsbury on A49, turn SE. SJ 4904 (OS 126). Late 16th-century manor house, on the E-plan; a fine example of the art of the Elizabethan mason, Walter Hancock, with some 18th-century additions. The house is now owned by the Royal National Institute for the Blind. Open by appt only, Aug pm. ⊖ 🅿

Criccieth Castle, Criccieth, Gwynedd. 5 m W of Porthmadog. SH 4937 (OS 123). Early 13th-century castle built by the Welsh in the reign of Llywellyn the Great, on a high cliff, and with extensive views towards Snowdonia. There are two great towers within the curtain wall. After the conquest of Wales by Edward I, an inner enclosure was erected, with its own strong gatehouse and tower. Open daily am and pm (Oct to March Su pm only). ⊖ 🅿

Croft Castle, near Leominster, Hereford and Worcester (tel Yarpole [056 885] 246). 5 m NW of Leominster on B4362, turn N. SO 4565 (OS 137). Castle originating from the 14th century, built by the Croft family. The house was enriched with 18th-century Gothick features including a staircase by Thomas Pritchard. The interior decoration mixes Jacobean with 18th-century styles. There is a large park. Open May to Sept W-Su and Bank Hols, pm; Apr and Oct S, Su and Easter M, pm. ⊖ 🅿 WC ♿ ⊟ (by appt) ♣

Denbigh Castle, Denbigh, Clwyd. To the S of Denbigh on B4501. SJ 0565 (OS 116). Castle built by Henry de Lacy in 1282-1311, after Edward I's conquest of Wales. It originally had polygonal towers at each corner of the enclosure, and an elaborate and unusual gatehouse made up of three linked towers, with decorative stonework. The castle was besieged for six months by the Parliamentarians in the Civil War. Open daily am and pm (Oct to March Su pm only). ⊖ 🅿

Dinmore Manor, near Hereford, Hereford and Worcester (tel Hereford [0452] 71322). 6 m N of Hereford on A49, turn W. SU 4850 (OS 149). Originally a property of the Knights Hospitallers of St John of Jerusalem, whose 12th- to 14th-century chapel survives; the house, which includes a music room and cloisters, is mainly 20th-century 'medieval'. There is a fine rock garden. Open daily (exc Christmas and Boxing Day) am and pm. ⊖ 🅿 WC ♿ ♣

Dorfold Hall, near Nantwich, Cheshire (tel Nantwich [0270] 625245). 1 m W of Nantwich on A534. SJ 6352 (OS 118). Red-brick gabled Jacobean house with diaper-pattern decorations. The great chamber has fine original plasterwork and panelling; other rooms have 18th-century furniture and decorations. Open Apr to Oct, T and Bank Hols pm; other times by appt. ⊖ 🅿 ♣

Dudmaston, Quatt, Bridgnorth, Shropshire (tel Quatt [0746] 780866). 4 m SE of Bridgnorth on A442. SO 7488 (OS 138). Late 17th-century house built for the Wolryche family, containing fine contemporary furniture. There is a wide-ranging collection of art, particularly flower paintings (including some that belonged to Francis Darby of Coalbrookdale) and 20th-century paintings and sculpture. The house is set in extensive grounds. Open Apr to Sept W and Su pm; parties Th pm by appt. ⊖ 🅿 WC ♿ ⊟ (by appt) ♣ ☕

Eye Manor, near Leominster, Hereford and Worcester (tel Yarpole [056 885] 244). 4 m N of Leominster on A49, turn W. SO 4963 (OS 137). Small late 17th-century house richly decorated inside with abundant plasterwork and panelling. Open Apr to end Sept daily pm (exc F, Apr to June). ⊖ 🅿 WC ♿ ♣

Flint Castle, Flint, Clwyd. In town centre, 10 m NW of Chester. SJ 2473 (OS 117). The first castle built in Wales by Edward I, begun in 1277 and mostly finished by 1286. The round great tower, at the corner of the rectangular enclosure, had its own moat, and the enclosure was covered by three other towers and a complex system of outer defences. The castle was thoroughly slighted in the Civil War. Open daily am and pm. ⊖ 🅿 ★

Goodrich Castle, Goodrich, near Ross-on-Wye, Hereford and Worcester. 6 m NE of Monmouth on A40, turn E. SO 5719 (OS 162). Spectacular 13th- and 14th-century Marcher castle, built on a rock outcrop above the River Wye. The three-storey keep is rectangular; the castle was built on a symmetrical plan recalling Harlech. A barbican was added in the 14th century. The castle was slighted in the Civil War. Open daily am and pm (Su pm only). ⊖ 🅿 WC

Grosmont Castle, Grosmont, Gwent. 12 m NW of Monmouth, on B4347. SO 4024 (OS 161). Ruined Marcher castle, built by Hubert de Burgh in the 13th century, on a hill above the River Monnow. It was made up of a rectangular hall tower, with a curtain wall and several semi-circular towers let into it. Open daily am and pm. ⊖ 🅿 ★

Hanbury Hall, near Droitwich, Hereford and Worcester (tel Hanbury [052 784] 214). 3½ m E of Droitwich on B4090, turn N. SO 9463 (OS 150). Brick-built house of around 1700, in the style of Christopher Wren and following the model of the nearby Ragley Hall. The staircase and long room are painted by Thornhill; the furnishings are of the 18th century. There is a collection of English porcelain figures, and an orangery. Open May to Sept W-Su, and Bank Hol M and T, pm; Apr and Oct S, Su, Easter M and T pm. ⊖ 🅿 WC ♿ ♣ ☕

Lower Brockhampton House, Hereford and Worcester

Handforth Hall, Handforth, near Wilmslow, Cheshire. ½ m E of Handforth on B5358. SJ 8683 (OS 109). 16th-century half-timbered manor house built for the Brereton family, with fine Elizabethan oak staircase and furniture. Open June to Sept by appt. ⊖ 🅿

Hartlebury Castle, near Kidderminster, Hereford and Worcester (tel Hartlebury [0299] 250410 and 250416). 5 m S of Kidderminster on A449. SO 8371 (OS 139). The home of the bishops of Worcester for over 1000 years, destroyed in the Civil War and rebuilt in 18th-century Gothick style. The medieval great hall is intact. The north wing houses the county museum, including country crafts and industries, costumes, toys, forge, etc. Castle open late Apr to early Sept first S in the month and W pm; also Bank Hol weekends Su-T pm; parties by appt. Museum open March to Oct daily (exc S) pm; Bank Hols am and pm. ⊖ 🅿 WC ♿ 🚻

Harvington Hall, near Kidderminster, Hereford and Worcester (tel Chaddesley Corbett [056 283] 267). 4 m SE of Kidderminster off A448, turn N. SO 8774 (OS 139). Moated medieval hall modified in the 1570s and in the early 18th century. The house was owned by the Pakingtons, a Catholic family, and contains a chapel, seven priest holes, and fine Elizabethan murals. Open Easter to Sept daily (exc M) am and pm; Oct, Nov, Feb to Easter pm only. ⊖ 🅿 WC ♿ 🍴

Hellen's, Much Marcle, near Ledbury, Hereford and Worcester (tel Much Marcle [053 184] 608). 9 m NE of Ross-on-Wye off A449. SO 6633 (OS 149). Jacobean brick-built manor house with some older elements. There is a collection of 19th-century coaches and old cider presses. Open Easter to early Oct W, S, Su pm; other times by appt. ⊖ 🅿 🚻 (by appt) D ♦ 🍴 (by appt) 🚻

Kentchurch Court, Hereford, Hereford and Worcester (tel Golden Valley [0981] 240228). 12 m NW of Monmouth on B4347, turn E. SO 4225 (OS 161). Fortified manor house rebuilt by John Nash.

The original gateway survives, and there are distinctive wood-carvings by Grinling Gibbons. Open May to Sept, parties only, by appt. ⊖ 🅿

Kidwelly Castle, Kidwelly, Dyfed. In town centre, 7 m W of Llanelli. SN 4007 (OS 159). Well preserved 13th-century concentric castle on an early Norman defensive site. The castle consists of a square inner bailey with four round corner towers, and an outer curtain wall in a semi-circle with a substantial gatehouse. There are remarkable ovens, and the castle chapel can be seen. Open daily am and pm (Oct to March Su pm only). ⊖ 🅿

Little Malvern Court, Little Malvern, Hereford and Worcester (tel Malvern [068 45] 4580). 5 m S of Great Malvern on A449. SO 7640 (OS 150). Part of the 12th-century priory of Little Malvern, with Elizabethan and 19th-century elements. The prior's hall is a fine 14th-century room, with exposed timber roof. There is a collection of early needlework. Open May to Sept, by appt only.

Llanfihangel Court, Abergavenny, Gwent. 6½ m NE of Abergavenny on A465, turn E. SO 3220 (OS 161). Stone-built medieval manor house rebuilt in the 16th and 17th centuries. There is fine mid 16th-century panelling and plasterwork, and an exceptional mid 17th-century yew staircase. There are various outbuildings of similar date. Open Aug Su pm; also Easter and Summer Bank Hol Su and M pm. ⊖ 🅿 🚻 (by appt) 🍴

Llanharan House, Llanharan, Mid Glamorgan (tel Llantrisant [0443] 226253). 7m E of Bridgend on A473. ST 0083 (OS 170). Mainly Georgian country house with notable plasterwork, furniture and and portraits, and a distinctive spiral staircase. There is a fine garden, with hill walks from the house. Open July to mid-Sept W and Su pm; also Bank Hol Su and M in May and Aug. ⊖ 🅿 WC 🚻 (by appt) ♦

Lower Brockhampton House, Bromyard, Hereford and Worcester (tel Bromyard [088 52] 2258). 2 m E of Bromyard on A44, turn N. SO 6854 (OS

149). Small manor house surrounded by a moat, and with a small timber-framed gatehouse, of the 15th century. There is a ruined 12th-century chapel. Open Apr to Oct W-S and Bank Hols am and pm, Su pm; other times by appt. ⊖ 🅿 WC ♿ 🚻 (by appt)

Moccas Court, Moccas, Hereford and Worcester (tel Moccas [098 17] 381). 18 m W of Hereford on B4352, turn N. SO 3543 (OS 161). Small red-brick country house built in the late 1770s for the Cornewall family, with details by Robert and James Adam. The interior is elegant, and the house overlooks the River Wye, across a park designed by Capability Brown. Open Apr to Sept Th pm; other times by appt. 🅿 WC ♿ 🚻 (by appt) ♦

Montgomery Castle, Montgomery, Powys. 10 m E of Newtown on B4386. SO 2296 (OS 137). Castle begun in the 1220s, with two distinct enclosures, linked by a causeway over a ditch, within the curtain walls. The castle was slighted in the Civil Wars, and has been excavated since the 1960s. Open daily am and pm (Su pm only). ⊖ 🅿

Old Beaupré Castle, St Hilary, near Cowbridge, South Glamorgan. 2 m SE of Cowbridge. ST 0072 (OS 170). Fortifications of around 1300, built into a mid 16th-century manor house. There is a distinctive Italianate gatehouse, now part of the south wing of the house; and a three-storeyed porch of about 1600. Open daily am and pm (exc Su). 🅿 ★

Old House, High Town, Hereford, Hereford and Worcester (tel Hereford [0432] 68121 ext 207). In town centre. SO 5140 (OS 149). Jacobean house of 1621, once one of a row of timber-framed houses, now restored as a private house with 17th-century furnishings, including much oak furniture. Open M-F am and pm (M am only). ⊖ 🅿 ♿

Owlpen Manor, near Dursley, Gloucestershire. 6 m SW of Stroud on B4066, turn E. ST 7998 (OS 162). Medieval stone-built house, with a hall and chamber of the mid-16th century and a Jacobean wing. Open by appt only. 🅿

Painswick House, Painswick, Gloucestershire (tel Painswick [0452] 813646). 6 m S of Gloucester on B4073. SO 8610 (OS 162). Palladian-style country house, built in the 1730s, and enlarged a hundred years later. The drawing room contains 18th-century Chinese wallpaper. The old kitchen houses a modern art studio. Open Aug daily pm; groups by appt at any time. ⊖ 🅿 WC 🔊 🚽 🐾

Pembroke Castle, Pembroke, Dyfed (tel Pembroke [0646] 684585). To NW of town centre. SM 9801 (OS 158). Powerful castle ruins, with a massive early 13th-century keep, some 80ft high and with a battered base. The site was first fortified in the late 11th century, and stone walls were added soon after. The castle has both an outer and inner bailey, each with its own gatehouse. Open daily am and pm (exc Su, Oct to Easter). ⊖ 🅿 WC 🔊 🚽

Peover Hall, Over Peover, Knutsford, Cheshire (Lower Peover [056 581] 2135). 3 m S of Knutsford on A50, turn E. SJ 7773 (OS 118). Stone Elizabethan house of 1585, built for Sir Ralph Mainwaring, with a notable kitchen and 17th-century stables with original stalls. There is an Elizabethan garden with topiary, summer-house and lily pond, and an 18th-century landscaped park. The hall was used by General Patton as American 3rd Army HQ in 1944. Open May to Sept M pm (hall, stables and gardens); Th pm (stables and gardens only). ⊖ 🅿 WC 🐾 🐾

Plas Mawr, High St, Conwy, Gwynedd (tel Conwy [0492 63] 3413). In town centre. SH 7877 (OS 115). Sometimes described as the finest Elizabethan town house in Britain, built by Robert Wynne in the Dutch style between 1576 and 1595. It has been resotred to its original condition, with fine furniture and plasterwork ceilings. There is a cockpit in the courtyard. Open daily am and pm (exc Christmas and New Year). ⊖ 🅿 WC 🔊 🐾

Plas Newydd, Isle of Anglesey, Gwynedd (tel Llanfairpwll [0248] 714795). 1 m S of Llanfairpwll on A4080. SH 5269 (OS 115). 18th-century house built by James Wyatt overlooking the Menai Strait, and decorated in Gothick style. In the dining room is a large fantasy mural painted in the 1930s by Rex Whistler, and there is a room devoted to a Whistler Museum. There is also an Anglesey Museum, with objects related to the 1st Marquess of Anglesey, wounded at Waterloo. The gardens are well known for their sweeping lawns and spring flowers. Open Apr to Nov daily (exc S) pm. ⊖ 🅿 WC 🔊 🚽 (by appt) 🎱 🐾

Raglan Castle, Raglan, Gwent (tel Raglan [0291] 680228). 9 m SW of Monmouth on A40. SO 4108 (OS 161). Later in date than many Welsh castles, Raglan was rebuilt in the mid-15th century on the site of a Norman motte-and-bailey. It has a hexagonal great tower, and complex forebuildings grouped around two courtyards. The rebuilding continued in the Tudor period, from which the

great hall dates. In the 16th and 17th centuries the castle was the property of the Earls of Worcester, who held it against the Parliamentarians in the Civil War. The castle was slighted in 1646. Open daily am and pm (Oct to March, Su pm only). ⊖ 🅿 WC 🔊

Rode Hall, Scholar Green, Stoke-on-Trent, Cheshire (Alsager [093 63] 3237). 5½ m SW of Congleton on A34, turn W. SJ 8157 (OS 118). 18th-century country house, modified by Samuel Wyatt and Darcy Braddell, with a distinctive Georgian stable block. Open Apr to Sept T and Bank Hols pm. ⊖ 🅿

Shipton Hall, Much Wenlock, Shropshire (tel Brickton [074 636] 225). 8 m SW of Much Wenlock on B4378. SO 5693 (OS 137). Attractive Elizabethan manor house in a large park. The interior was modified with a new hall and staircase in the 1760s, when a stable block was also built. There is a stone walled garden, medieval dovecote, and the parish church is also in the grounds. Open July and Aug Th and Su pm; May, June and Sept Th and Su pm; Bank Hol Su only; other times by appt. ⊖ 🅿 WC 🚽 (by appt) 🐾 🐾 (by appt)

Shrewsbury Castle, Castle Gardens, Shrewsbury, Shropshire (tel Shrewsbury [0743] 52019). In town centre. SJ 4912 (OS 126). Early Norman castle later rebuilt in stone in the 12th century. The gatehouse was added in the 13th century. The castle fell into disrepair in the 14th century, and only a few traces of the earlier building remain. Thomas Telford made alterations after 1780. Open daily am and pm (Oct to Easter not Su). ⊖ 🅿

Skenfrith Castle, Skenfrith, Gwent. 7 m NW of Monmouth on B4521. SO 4520 (OS 161). Norman Marcher castle above the River Monnow, with a 13th-century great tower in an enclosure of curtain walls and strong corner towers. The tower was originally of three storeys. Open daily am and pm. ⊖ 🅿 ★

Tretower Court, near Crickhowell, Powys (tel Brecon [0874] 730279). 3½ m NW of Crickhowell off A40. SO 1821 (OS 161). Remarkable 14th- and 15th-century fortified manor house by the ruins of an earlier cylindrical castle keep. There is a 15th-century great hall, and a small gatehouse. Open daily am and pm; Su pm only). 🅿

Trewyn, Abergavenny, Gwent (tel Crucorney [087 382] 541). 6 m N of Abergavenny on A465. SO 3322 (OS 161). William-and-Mary mansion built on a medieval site, undergoing restoration. There is notable oak panelling, staircase and minstrels gallery. The grounds include varied ornamental gardens, walks and an aboretum. House open by appt only; gardens open March to Oct daily (exc M) am and pm. ⊖ 🅿 WC 🚽 (by appt) 🐾 🐾

Tudor House, Friar Street, Worcester, Herefordshire and Worcestershire (tel Worcester [0905] 25371). In city centre. SO 8555 (OS 150). 16th-

century timber-framed building, overhanging the street. It houses a museum of local life, with period settings (notably relating to the Victorian age, and to life in the Second World War) and a display of farming implements. Open all year M-W, F-S am and pm; closed Christmas and New Year. ⊖ 🅿 ★

Upper Slaughter Manor House, Cheltenham, Goucestershire (tel Bourton-on-the-Water [0451] 20927). 1½ m W of Stow-on-the-Wold on B4068, turn S. SP 1522 (OS 163). Medieval manor house rebuilt from 1539 by the Slaughter family, and restored in 1913. There are fine terraced gardens on the steeply-sloping site. Open May to Sept F pm. ⊖ 🅿 WC 🐾

Upton Cressett Hall, Bridgnorth, Shropshire (tel Morville [074 631] 307). 4 m W of Bridgnorth on A458, turn SW. SO 6592 (OS 138). Medieval timber-framed manor house modified in the Elizabethan era, displaying original timberwork in the upper rooms. There is also an Elizabethan gatehouse and a medieval garden with peacocks. A Norman church stands in the grounds. Open May to Sept Th pm. 🅿 WC 🚽 (by appt) 🐾 🐾 🄰

Vale Royal Abbey, Whitegate, Northwich, Cheshire (Sandiway [0606] 888684). 2 m NW of Winsford on A54, turn N. SJ 6369 (OS 118). Cistercian abbey founded 1281, but rebuilt as a private house in the 16th century. The interior is presently undergoing extensive restoration. Attractive grounds, with the nun's grave, an historic monument. Open S, Su and Bank Hols, am and pm, by appt. ⊖ 🅿 WC 🐾 🐾

Weobley Castle, Llanrhidian, West Glamorgan. 6 m W of Swansea on A4118, turn onto B4271 for 9 m then turn W. SS 4792 (OS 159). Fortified manor house of the 12th-14th centuries, overlooking the Loughor estuary. The main fortifications were begun in the late 13th century, with a great tower. A number of other buildings were put up around it in the ensuing centuries. Open daily am and pm (Su pm only). 🅿

Wilderhope Manor, Wenlock Edge, Shropshire (tel Longville [069 43] 363). 9 m SW of Much Wenlock on B4371, turn S for 1¼ m then NE. SO 5492 (OS 138). Limestone-built Tudor manor house, similar in appearance to Shipton Hall. There are 17th-century plaster ceilings, and the house is set in deep woods. It is now used as a Youth Hostel. 🅿 WC 🚽

Witley Court, Great Witley, Hereford and Worcester. 5 m SW of Stourport on A451. SO 7666 (OS 150). Ruins of a grand country house, destroyed by fire in 1937, but originally built for Lord Ward in the 1860s on an older house with a portico by John Nash. The terraced gardens include a huge equestrian statue of Perseus by James Forsyth. The chapel, built in the 1730s, is now Great Witley parish church. Open daily am and pm. 🅿 ★

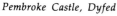
Pembroke Castle, Dyfed

Bamburgh Castle, Northumberland

The North

The North

0 10 20 30 40 50 Kms
0 10 20 30 Miles
Scale 1:1,330,000

1 Knaresborough Castle
2 Maister House Wilberforce House
3 Red House
4 Oakwell Hall
5 Heaton Hall
6 Platt Hall
7 Croxteth Hall

NORTH SEA

St Andrews
Kirkcaldy
Dunfermline
EDINBURGH
Dunbar
Peebles
Galashiels
Jedburgh
Hawick
Berwick-upon-Tweed
Holy Island
Lindisfarne Castle
Norham Castle
Coldstream
Wooler
Bamburgh Castle
Bamburgh
Preston Tower
Dunstanburgh Castle
Callaly Castle
Alnwick Castle
Howick Hall
Rothbury
Alnwick
Warkworth Castle
Cragside
Amble-by-the-Sea
Otterburn
NORTHUMBER-LAND
Wallington House
Ashington
Morpeth
Meldon Park
Belsay Hall
Blyth
Seaton Delaval
NEWCASTLE UPON TYNE
Haltwhistle
Hexham
Prudhoe Castle
Tynemouth Castle
Tynemouth
South Shields
Corbridge
TYNE & WEAR
SUNDERLAND
Naworth Castle
Brampton
Gateshead
Stanley
Washington Old Hall
Seaham
Carlisle Castle
Carlisle
Corby Castle
Consett
Houghton-le-Spring
Dumfries
Wigton
Hutton-in-the-Forest
Alston
Stanhope
Durham Castle
Durham
Maryport
Wordsworth House
Cockermouth
Penrith
Middleton in Teesdale
DURHAM
Crook
Bishop Auckland
Hartlepool
Workington
Keswick
Dalemain
Brougham Castle
Raby Castle
Stockton-on-Tees
Billingham
Redcar
CLEVELAND
Whitehaven
CUMBRIA
Appleby-in-Westmorland
Appleby Castle
Barnard Castle
Barnard Castle
Darlington
MIDDLESBROUGH
Ormesby Hall
Egremont
The Lake District
Shap
Brough Castle
Brough
Bowes Castle
Whitby
Dove Cottage
Rydal Mount
Kirkby Stephen
Richmond
Robin Hood's Bay
Ambleside
Townend
Kiplin Hall
Windermere
Abbot Hall
Bolton Castle
Richmond Castle
Northallerton
North York Moors
Muncaster Castle
Belle Isle
Brantwood
Hill Top
Kendal Castle
Leyburn
Bedale
Scarborough
Rusland Hall
Sizergh Castle
Middleham Castle
Osgodby Hall
Helmsley Castle
Pickering
Ebberston Hall
Scarborough Castle
Levens Hall
Sedbergh
Hawes
NORTH
Thirsk
Shandy Hall
Nunnington Hall
Filey
Ulverston
Holker Hall
Kirkby Lonsdale
YORKSHIRE
Norton Conyers
Gilling Castle
Leighton Hall
Ingleton
Ripon
Newburgh Priory
Malton
Sewerby Hall
Barrow-in-Furness
Swarthmoor Hall
Carnforth
Settle
Markenfield Hall
Newby Hall
Sutton Park
Castle Howard
Norton
Flamborough Head
Burton Agnes Hall
Bridlington
Morecambe
Grassington
Ripley Castle
Boroughbridge
Beningbrough Hall
Sledmere House
Norman Manor House
Lancaster Castle
Skipton Castle
Manor House
Harrogate
Knaresborough
York
Great Driffield
Thurnham Hall
Skipton
Ilkley
Otley
Treasurer's House
Hornsea
Fleetwood
Browsholme Hall
Broughton Hall
East Riddlesden Hall
Wetherby
Stockeld Park
Pocklington
LANCASHIRE
Clitheroe
Keighley
Harewood House
Tadcaster
Market Weighton
Lairgate Hall
Blackpool
Whalley Abbey
Gawthorpe Hall
Brontë Parsonage
Temple Newsam
Lotherton Hall
Selby
Beverley
Burton Constable
Chingle Hall
W.
Bramham Park
HUMBERSIDE
Lytham St. Anne's
Samlesbury Hall
Burnley
YORKSHIRE
LEEDS
KINGSTON UPON HULL
Preston
Blackburn
Bolling Hall
Carlton Towers
Blaydes House
Withernsea
Meols Hall
Astley Hall
Hoghton Tower
Shibden Hall
BRADFORD
Pontefract Castle
Goole
Southport
Chorley
Rawtenstall
Halifax
Wakefield
Pontefract
Nostell Priory
Normanby Hall
Barton-upon-Humber
Rufford Old Hall
Turton Tower
Hall i'th' Wood
Rochdale
Huddersfield
Sandal Castle
Thorne
Ormskirk
Formby
Smithills Hall
Wigan
Bolton
GR.
MANCHESTER
Oldham
Cannon Hall
Barnsley
Cusworth Hall
Scunthorpe
Grimsby
Spurn Head
LIVERPOOL
MERSEYSIDE
Leigh
MAN.
Ordsall Hall
Foxdenton House
Ashton-under-Lyne
SOUTH
Conisbrough Castle
Doncaster
Old Rectory
Wallasey
St Helens
Fletcher Moss
Newton Hall
YORKSHIRE
Rotherham
Bawtry
Gainsborough
Birkenhead
Altrincham
Dunham Massey
Stockport
Wythenshawe Hall
Stocksbridge
Bluecoats Chamber
Widnes
SHEFFIELD
Worksop
Speke Hall
Macclesfield
Lincoln
Chester
Northwich
Buxton
Chesterfield
Mold
Congleton
Ruthin
Leek
Matlock
Mansfield
Llangollen
Wrexham
Nantwich
STOKE-ON-TRENT
Ashbourne
Newark-on-Trent
Whitchurch
Sleaford
Boston
NOTTINGHAM
DERBY
Grantham

The Pennines

Alnwick Castle

Alnwick, Northumberland

Though twice restructured in relatively modern times, Alnwick reveals the plan of the original Norman castle: a large, centrally-placed motte surrounded by two baileys which enclose five acres. From the beginning it was larger than most castles. During the first half of the 12th century a stone shell-keep on the motte and stone curtain walls round the baileys replaced whatever timber structures had served up to that time. Stonework of that period can still be seen in several stretches of the curtain wall.

Left, the 15th-century gatehouse of Alnwick is permanently but precariously manned by stone figures, placed there in 1764.

Above, Alnwick Castle mainly dates from the 14th century, when the Percy family took over and rebuilt the Norman castle.

Left, like Arundel Castle, Alnwick displays the accumulation of the building works of many centuries; the main internal arrangements date from the 19th century.

Opposite above, the armoury room, and opposite below, the library, two of the Italianate interiors created by the 4th Duke of Northumberland in the mid-19th century.

In 1309 Henry de Percy, whose ancestors had come over from Normandy soon after the Conquest, acquired the castle and became the 1st Lord Percy of Alnwick. During the next fifty years of never-ending forays and battles against the Scots, Henry and his son turned the castle into the dominant stronghold of the Scottish border. Commanding the eastern route into England, it could halt an invasion and be used for assembling forces to strike northwards.

The defensive power of the keep was increased in the early 14th century by adding semi-circular towers and strengthening the gatehouse. Several towers were also built on the curtain wall and a new gateway to guard the entrance to the eastern bailey. A splendid gatehouse and barbican to the western bailey incorporated many of the features of Edward I's powerful fortifications in Wales. The castle then remained unchanged, except by neglect, for four hundred years.

The 4th Lord Percy was created Earl of Northumberland and appears in Shakespeare's *Richard II* and *Henry IV*, a well-nigh independent baron, a maker and unmaker of kings. Shakespeare vividly dramatised the death of his son Hotspur at Shrewsbury in 1403, and the Earl too died in battle a few years later. Hotspur's son became the 2nd Earl and he and the 3rd Earl both also fell in battle, victims of the medieval aristocracy's self-destruction in the Wars of the Roses. The 4th Earl survived the wars and imprisonment in the Tower of London only to be murdered by a mob protesting against an unpopular tax.

During the 16th century the Earldom became extinct for twenty years and was then restored by Queen Mary to Thomas Percy, a devout Catholic. After the Catholic Rising against Elizabeth I in 1569 he was beheaded at York, and was beatified as a martyr by the Catholic Church.

Towards the end of the century the family ceased to reside at Alnwick and it was beginning to fall into decay. The decline continued until the 18th century when the estates had passed to the 1st Duke. He employed Robert Adam and other craftsmen to turn the keep into a comfortable, pseudo-Gothic mansion, suitably furnished. Adam reorganised the rooms and designed the pointed windows for the keep and its towers. He ornamented some of the curtain towers with 'picturesque' turrets and placed figures of soliders on the battlements of the keep and curtain wall in imitation of the 14th-century figures on the keep gatehouse.

All Adam's interiors were swept away when the 4th Duke began another major reconstruction in the second half of the last century. Under the general direction of Anthony Salvin (1799-1881), a pupil of John Nash, the present palatial apartments were created. Salvin was assisted by several Italian artists and the design was inspired by modernised Italian interiors that the Duke had admired on his travels.

The entrance to the keep, however, remains genuinely medieval and formidable: two lofty octagonal towers dominate the approach and dwarf the gatehouse behind. The main door to the apartments is across the

courtyard and then, after passing through two un-remarkable halls, the great Victorian staircase is a surprise, the first hint of splendours to come. The steps, quarried at Rothbury a dozen miles away, rise gently beneath a groined vault with stucco ornamentation. Each step is 12 foot wide, the landing a single slab 12 foot square. Carrera marble and family portraits cover the walls. At the head of the stairs two pairs of round-headed windows match the lines of ceilings and walls. Through them a section of the keep's rugged exterior can be seen in sharp contrast to the opulence of the staircase.

All thought of the Middle Ages vanishes on entering the vestibule called the guard chamber. The mosaic floor, the stucco ceiling of octagonal panels, marble statues of Britannia and Justice and the gilded furniture begin a riot of Victorian extravagance. Fine pictures are displayed: two by Canaletto, a typical harbour scene by the 17th-century French landscape painter Claude Lorraine and, best of all, Van Dyck's swaggering portrait of the 10th Earl. He had been made Lord High Admiral of England in 1637, but sided with the Parliamentarians in the Civil War. He opposed the execution of Charles I and lived to assist in the restoration of Charles II.

The small ante-chamber to the main apartments is also distinguished by its paintings, an *Ecce Homo* of Tintoretto, portraits by Palma Vecchio and Titian and part of a fresco by Sebastian del Piombo. A small billiard table and two writing tables designed by Robert Adam are survivors from the 18th-century furnishings.

Above, the apse of the chapel.

The library is another magnificent 19th-century room, occupying a whole floor of the Prudhoe tower. This was a bold addition to the older towers of the keep, erected in 1854. Sixteen thousand volumes are housed in oak bookcases with marble inlays. Measuring 56 by 24 feet, the room has the luxury of three fireplaces. These are surmounted respectively by busts of Shakespeare, Bacon and Sir Isaac Newton, all executed by Italian artists.

The profusion of decoration and furnishing continues through the remainder of the apartments. In the drawing room an endearing self-portait by Andrea del Sarto and a proud Venetian nobleman by Tintoretto look down on two large ebony cabinets dated 1683. In the dining room, on the site of the medieval great hall,

the ceiling and frieze are of pinewood from New Brunswick. Two magnificent Meissen dinner services depict birds and animals and scenes from Aesop's Fables. Full-length portraits of the 1st Duke and his Duchess by Reynolds hang over the prestigious fireplace. But though so sumptuous and peaceful within, the older walls and towers, majestic on the plateau above the River Aln, ensure that the turbulence of earlier events is not forgotten.

☎ Alnwick (0665) 602207

In N outskirts of Alnwick

NU 1813 (OS 81)

Open May to end Sept daily exc S 1300-1700

⊖ P WC ⊟ ✦ ⊼ ◆ ※ ⚔

● (not in castle)

Castle Howard

From the high ground a few miles west of Malton, North Yorkshire, the mellowed, creamy mass of Castle Howard dominates the countryside.

The estate came into the possession of the Howard family when Lord William Howard, a younger son of the 4th Duke of Norfolk, married Elizabeth Dacre in 1577. It was an ancient seat of the Dacre family and known as Henderskelfe Castle, the buildings lying where the obelisk stands to the west of the present house. The great-grandson of William and Elizabeth was created Earl of Carlisle in 1661. After a fire at the castle in 1693 the 3rd Earl, a distinguished statesman, decided to build a new house and to call it Castle Howard.

The chimney-piece of the entrance hall, more cathedral than house.

Left, Castle Howard was very carefully sited by Vanbrugh and given an avenue approach.

Below, the cupola, reminiscent of that on St Peter's Rome, is visible from much of the park.

The Earl's choice of architect surprised everyone. John Vanbrugh was a soldier who had turned dramatist, achieving instant fame with the first of his witty and licentious comedies. Along with other well-known writers he frequented the famous Kit-cat Club where the leading Whig politicians met, among them the Earl of Carlisle. The friendship which developed between the rich, intellectual landowner and the adventurous Captain and playwright led to Vanbrugh's first commission as an architect.

Van's genius, without thought or lecture,
Is hugely turned to architecture
commented Dean Swift.

Wisely Vanbrugh chose for his assistant Nicholas Hawksmoor, who had been employed by Sir Christopher Wren for twenty years. Vanbrugh supplied the grand design, the inspiration and drive to push the work forward, but there is little doubt that Hawksmoor, a trained and able architect, translated Vanbrugh's ideas into working plans and added many personal touches. It proved an ideal and harmonious partnership, continued soon afterwards at Blenheim Palace.

Vanbrugh's design centred on a domed hall inside a monumental entrance. Three flights of steps lead up to the main door. Towering pairs of Doric pilasters, with statues in niches between each pair, separate the row of tall windows in the channelled walls. Statues on a balustrade above the entablature and the great lanterned dome rising behind on an octagonal drum are reminiscent of St Peter's in Rome.

Beyond the domed hall a long wing, single-storeyed over a basement, contained the principal apartments. They all faced south over the gardens and were comparatively small, to be easier to heat in the sharp climate of North Yorkshire. On either side of the entrance two wings were to extend forwards to form a large forecourt.

Work began in 1700 and continued until Vanbrugh's death in 1726. The central block and the east wing were completed but only the foundations laid for the west wing. The Earl in his later years became more interested in the gardens and park and completion of the house was left to his son, the 4th Earl. The west wing was built in the 1750s by the Earl's brother-in-law, Sir Thomas Robinson, in the Palladian style then prevailing, noticeably less exuberant than Vanbrugh's Baroque. It was a serious misfortune that Vanbrugh's design was not adhered to. The intrusion of another style, though satisfactory in itself, detracts from the splendour of the entrance front.

Another disaster was to overtake Vanbrugh's work during the Second World War. By this time the estate had passed through a younger son of the 9th Earl of Carlisle to Mr Geoffrey Howard, later created a life peer with the title of Lord Howard of Henderskelfe for his services as a Governor and then Chairman of the BBC. While he was away serving in the local regiment, the Green Howards, a girls' school was evacuated to the castle. During their occupancy a fire destroyed most of the apartments in the south wing and Vanbrugh's dome crashed into the hall, causing serious damage. After the war, under the skilled direction of Lord Howard, the dome and lantern were replaced with scrupulous regard to the originals and the damage to the hall repaired. It continues to impress as one of the most daring interiors in England.

The house contains collections of furniture, ceramics and Dutch and Italian paintings of importance. The English obsession with portraiture is well represented, from Holbein to Reynolds and Gainsborough. An abundance of Classical statuary came from Rome, where the 4th Earl resided for some years. The 19th-century chapel, full of Victorian colour, has some stained glass made by William Morris to designs of Burne-Jones. Castle Howard also has the largest collection of costume in private hands.

The 3rd Earl laid out the gardens and park to give good views from the house and to enhance its setting. The formal gardens were redesigned later but the landscaping of the park bears the stamp of the 18th century. A broad lake to the north of the house, the ponded river to the south crossed by a Palladian bridge leading nowhere, an obelisk commemorating the building by the 3rd Earl, crenellated walls and towers defending nothing – these can be matched elswhere. Two of the park's features, however, are of exceptional interest.

The Belvedere, known as 'The Temple of the Four Winds', stands on a knoll south-east of the house and reveals an unexpectedly light touch for Vanbrugh. It was built after his death but no doubt he approved the site with its all-round views over the park. A square building with four Ionic porticos and surmounted by a dome and small lantern, its proportions have been

criticised yet it remains one of the best 'garden' buildings in England.

The second building, visible from the Belvedere as part of the grand layout, was also completed after the death of its architect, Hawskmoor, the other member of the partnership. The mausoleum is a good example on a small scale of his skills. A circular chapel is surrounded by a Classical colonnade and roofed by a flat dome. In the crypt below lies the 3rd Earl to whose ideas and informed instruction the partnership owed much.

☎ Coneysthorpe (065 384) 333

11½ m NE of York on A64 turn N at Barton Hill for Welburn

SE 7170 (OS 100)

Open late Mar to end Oct daily 1100-1630; reduced rates for parties

P WC 🚹 🛋 D ♣
🍴 (by appt) ◆ 🐕 ✳

Above, the Temple of the Four Winds; and opposite above, the view from the temple. This was intended as a summer house for refreshments, and is a Baroque interpretation of Palladio's Villa Capra at Vicenza.

Below, Lady Georgiana's bedroom, furnished in the style of the late 19th century.

Opposite below, the tapestry room, with a fine pinewood frieze and portraits by Reynolds, Gainsborough and Ramsay.

Temple Newsam House
Leeds, West Yorkshire

The house is now unashamedly a museum. Situated only four miles from the centre of Leeds, in 1922 it was purchased by the City, together with nine hundred acres of parkland. It forms part of the City Art Galleries and is an educational and research centre as well as a permanent exhibition of paintings, furniture and the decorative arts.

The estate has been identified with the fortified preceptory of the Knights Templars called Templestowe in Sir Walter Scott's *Ivanhoe*. The Knights were the owners from the 11th century until 1307, hence the addition of Temple to the name Newsam which originated before the Norman Conquest. Edward II confiscated the estate when the Templars were suppressed in 1312, and Edward III later gave it to the Darcy family. The oldest part of the present building was built by Thomas, Lord Darcy, early in the 16th century.

The Tudor house was four blocks round a courtyard, built of brick with stone quoins and mullioned windows. After Lord Darcy's execution for treason in 1537 the estate was forfeit and Henry VIII gave it to the Earl of Lennox, the husband of his niece Lady Mary Douglas. Their son, Henry Stewart, Lord Darnley and husband of Mary, Queen of Scots, was born at Temple Newsam in 1545. After his marriage Elizabeth imprisoned his mother and appropriated the estate. It remained in royal hands until James I, Darnley's son, bestowed it on a cousin who, to pay his debts, sold it.

The purchaser was Sir Arthur Ingram, a wealthy merchant and financier of Yorkshire descent and Comptroller of the Port of London. In the house his portrait by George Geldorp shows the portly figure and shrewd, self-possessed face of a City worthy. He rebuilt Temple Newsam between 1622 and 1637 in Jacobean

Left, Temple Newsam was easily the greatest Tudor house in Yorkshire, and was rebuilt in a conservative style in the 1630s.

Above, the Prince's room, with an early-19th-century bed made by Gillows of Lancaster.

style. The east wing was demolished and replaced by a wall and gateway. The north and south wings were rebuilt and the Tudor west wing extended at each end to tie in with them. Brick walls and mullioned and transomed windows were designed to blend with the earlier work so that, superficially, the whole house resembled a Tudor mansion. Stone balustrades running round the roofs of the three wings held the building together. But details reveal the later work. The ornate porch, the entrance to the south wing, has coupled Ionic columns and cannot be mistaken for early 16th-century work. The older part of the west wing has rectangular bays and widely-jointed bricks decorated by diaper work, darker bricks laid as headers to form patterns. In contrast the later north and south wings have canted bays and plain, close-set brickwork.

Many alterations have been made at different times to the interior so that it no longer resembles a 17th-century mansion. The exterior too has been reorganised, the east wall demolished, a cupola added to the west wing, and both south and north fronts altered. But on the whole the external aspect, particularly to the courtyard, remains much as in Sir Arthur Ingram's time.

The Ingrams continued to own the estate for nearly three hundred years. Sir Arthur's grandson was created Viscount Irwin, and the 3rd Viscount had nine sons of whom five succeeded in turn to the title over a period of sixty years. The last of them, an ageing Canon of Windsor, died in 1763 and the estate went to a nephew Charles, the 9th Viscount. He called in Capability Brown to deal with the park and thoroughly changed the layout of the south wing. On the death of his widow their eldest daughter Isabella, wife of the second Marquis of Hertford, inherited the estate. She is best known as one of the Prince Regent's confidants; they had met when he visited Temple Newsam in 1806. A superb full-length portrait of her, one of Reynolds' best works, is displayed in the south bedroom.

The last private owner was Edward Lindley Wood, son of the 2nd Viscount Halifax. As a young man of 23 he inherited from an aunt in 1904. Later he would become Viceroy of India, taking the title of Viscount Irwin of the second creation, and later still as Lord Halifax held the important post of Ambassador to the United States during the Second World War. Meanwhile he had sold the estate to the City in 1922. Although most of the contents were dispersed at that time, a nucleus of family portraits and furniture remained. They have been supplemented over the years by discriminating purchases from other houses and by gifts, including many from Lord Halifax.

Most of the original furniture has been recovered for the 18th-century saloon, a delightful room formed from part of the Jacobean long gallery which had stretched the whole length of the north wing. The unique set of Rococo chairs and settees upholstered in floral needlework was made in 1745-46 by James Pascall, of whom little is known. He also made the candle stands and the gilded pinewood wall-lights depicting a hound attacking a stag. The two plaster chimneypieces, rising to the frieze and ingeniously incorporating paintings by Antonio Ioli, are from designs by William Kent.

The attractive Chinese drawing room in the south wing has the hand-painted wall-paper presented by the Prince Regent on his visit and subsequently hung by Lady Hertford. The whole room evokes, in a restrained way, the tastes of the Prince Regent.

The Tudor room in the earliest part of the house has contemporary linenfold panelling, a cupboard and a bed brought from an early Tudor house elsewhere. Other rooms have been similarly restored and furnished, not only with articles of furniture but with copies of original wallpapers and hangings, contemporary paintings, ceramics and silverware, to show the development of styles during the long occupation of the house.

The changing use of many rooms is illustrated by the history of the library in the north wing, also originally part of the Jacobean long gallery. The 7th Viscount divided it off and turned it into a library in the mid-18th

century. In 1877 the Hon. Mrs Meynell Ingram, aunt of the future Lord Halifax and a High Church Victorian lady, decided to change it into a chapel. She employed the well-known ecclesiastical architect George Frederick Bodley and the result was a typically lavish Victorian interior. In 1974 the present owners recreated the 7th Viscount's beautiful Palladian library. It is one of the most impressive of the thirty rooms open to the public and representative of the painstaking care of continuing restoration of the house fabric.

☎ Leeds (0532) 641358

4½ m E of Leeds on A63, turn S at Malton

SE 3532 (OS 104)

Open throughout year Tu-Su and Bank Hol M 1030-1815 (dusk if earlier); May to Sept W 1030-2030

♿ 🅿 WC ♿ (limited access) 🚌 D ♣ 🍴 ☂ ◆ ❀ ✻ ● (by permission only)

Above, the long gallery, or, more exactly, the saloon made from part of the Jacobean long gallery in the 1740s. The exceptional furniture in this room is original to the house.

Above right, the Chinese drawing room, as it was decorated in the 1820s using hand-painted wallpaper presented to the family by the Prince Regent some 20 years before.

Right, the stable block was built in Palladian style in 1742 to the designs of Daniel Garrett.

Bamburgh Castle

Bamburgh, Northumberland

Bamburgh Castle, crouched on its rocky outcrop on the Northumberland coast, blends into its bleak but beautiful landscape as if it grew there. However, although it was an important stronghold from at least Saxon times, what we see today is almost entirely Victorian. The Saxon castle was besieged by William II at the end of the 11th century, and deserted by its lord, Robert de Mowbray, 3rd Earl of Northumberland, whose wife Matilda surrendered only when he was recaptured and threatened with death. The new Norman castle, built over the next hundred years, was more or less complete by the reign of Henry III (1207-72), who made important additions to it, including the double-towered east gate. The age of the great fortified castles was over by the 15th century, and by Tudor times Bamburgh was decayed and ruinous. Early in the 18th century Lord Crewe, Bishop of Durham, bought it for the Crown, and it came under the trusteeship of the remarkable Dr John Sharp, Archdeacon of Northumberland, who spent a great deal of his own money on restorations. In 1894 it was bought by Lord Armstrong, the arms manufacturer, and the present building is largely the result of his extensive restorations, completed in 1903. The interior is a splendid display of Victorian medievalism, the centrepiece being the great king's hall with its fine hammerbeam roof. The guardroom at the bottom of the keep contains an important collection of weapons and armour as well as some good tapestries and porcelain.

☎ Bamburgh (066 84) 20208
16 m N of Alnwick on A1 turn E onto B1341
NU 1835 (OS 75)

Open Easter to end Oct daily 1300-variable closing; phone for details

⊞ WC 🚻 ♿ ✕ ✗

Belle Isle

Windermere, Cumbria

This appropriately named house, standing on the largest island in Lake Windermere, is very unusual, being the first and almost the only house to be built on a circular plan. It was built in 1774, and copied at Ickworth some twenty years later. Belle Isle was designed by a then unknown architect, John Plaw, for a Mr English, who had just bought the island. Built of a very hard stone from the nearby Ecclerigg quarry, it is three storeys high and a true circle, 54 feet in diameter, with only the portico projecting. Plaw wanted the house to look perfect from every angle, and coped with the problem of deliveries and waste disposal by planting the house in a small sunken area, which also concealed the kitchens and servants' accommodation. In 1800 a new kitchen was built at the back, slightly marring the perfection of the plan, but this extension blends in quite well. Visitors are shown round the ground floor rooms only, which are small, with fine Adam plasterwork. An elegant staircase rises in the middle of the house. When it was first built, the house did not seem to accord with contemporary taste and aroused a storm of protest – the poet Wordsworth condemned the destruction of the natural beauty of the island – and Mr English sold the entire property for £1,720 to Miss Isabella Curwen in 1781 (he had spent £6,000). Much of the furniture, made in the 18th century by the well-known firm of Gillow, comes from the Curwens' other house, Workington. Bills for the furniture making are on show in the house.

☎ Windermere (09662) 3353
On Lake Windermere 2 m S of Windermere, boat from Bowness Promenade nr Cockshott Point
SD 3997 (OS 97)

Open May to Sept Su, M, T and Th 1030-1700; parties at other times by appt

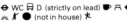
♿ WC 🚻 D (strictly on lead) ♿ 🛋 ◆
✕ ✗ ● (not in house) ⚓

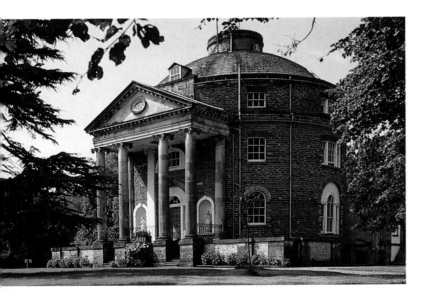

Brontë Parsonage

Haworth, Keighley, West Yorkshire

This rather bleak Georgian house, built in 1778, was the home of the Brontë family, and although the north wing was added in the 1870s, the rest of the house is just as it was in their time. The building was presented to the Brontë Society in 1928, and the north wing now houses the library and exhibition room, while the older part of the house contains the Brontës' furniture and personal possessions. Charlotte made various alterations to the house, enlarging the dining room and bedroom above it; the dining room was where the sisters did most of their work. The room contains the rocking chair where Anne used to sit, the sofa on which Emily died, and a portrait of Charlotte's hero, the Duke of Wellington. Another of Charlotte's alterations was the creation of a study for her fiancé Mr Nicholls, and she wrote to a friend about 'the new little room' with its green and white curtains. Sadly, she survived only a year of married life. The bedroom in which the girls' mother died was also the room in which 'Aunt Branwell' taught the sisters fine needlework, and there are examples on show, together with family china, Charlotte's baby shoes and other items. Some of their toys, which were found under floorboards during repair work, are displayed in the nursery, and 'Branwell's room' contains some of his drawings and paintings. The Bonnell room houses the extensive collection of books, manuscripts and drawings by the Brontës left to the Brontë Society by Henry Houston Bonnell of Philadelphia.

☎ Haworth (0535) 42323
3½ m S of Keighley on A6033, turn W to Haworth
SE 0237 (OS 104)

Open Apr to end Sept daily 1100-1730, Oct to end March daily 1100-1630; closed 24, 25, 26 Dec

♿ ♿ (by appt) 🚻 (by appt) ♿ ◆ ✕
● (by permission)

Burton Agnes Hall

Driffield, Humberside

The lovely proportions of this fine red-brick Jacobean house suggest the hand of a professional designer, and the architect was indeed Robert Smythson, builder of Longleat, Wollaton and Hardwick Hall. Burton Agnes was designed for Sir Henry Griffiths and built between 1601 and 1610. The house is remarkable in that it has been so little altered, though sash windows have replaced the mullioned ones in places, and those at each end of the gallery are 18th century. The brick gatehouse, built in 1610 and bearing the arms of James I flanked by allegorical figures, is a particularly fine example of Tudor architecture. The entrance door, set in the side of a bay, leads into a screens passage and then into the great hall, which contains some truly breathtaking Elizabethan allegorical carving, plasterwork and panelling as well as a fine Nonsuch chest. There is more woodcarving in the drawing room, the centrepiece being a somewhat gruesome Dance of Death over the fireplace. The other rooms were renovated in the 1730s, and reflect mainly 18th-century taste, but the recently redecorated dining room has a splendid carved Elizabethan chimneypiece which was originally in the long gallery, and the staircase, one of the most remarkable features of the house, has been untouched since Tudor times. Like most country houses, Burton Agnes contains some fine paintings, and there is an impressive collection of Impressionist and later paintings. These are on display in the house, many in the long gallery, recently restored and with a lovely barrel ceiling.

☎ Burton Agnes (026289) 324
6½ m SW of Bridlington on A166 at Burton Agnes
TA 1063 (OS 101)

Open Easter weekend and late Apr to end Oct daily 1100-1700; subject to closure at short notice

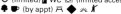
♿ (limited) 🅿 WC 🚻 (limited access) 🚌 D
🌸 🍴 (by appt) 🎪 ♦ ✲ 🏌

Burton Constable

Sproatley, near Hull, Humberside

A large brick Tudor house with two battlemented towers rising above the roofline, it was mainly built around 1600 for the Constable family, on an earlier house. During the 18th century the main door was moved to the centre and a new top storey added, as well as two bay windows. The interior of the house is the real surprise, as nearly all the interiors are 18th century and very opulent. A large number of architects and craftsmen worked here replacing the original decorations with their own work, and the numbers were added to during the 19th century, when Lady Constable carried out redecorations. The long gallery was made from a series of bedrooms after 1740 with plaster ceilings copied from the Bodleian Library in Oxford; the staircase was built by Timothy Lightholer, who also designed the plasterwork in the hall, the stable block and the new top storey; the lovely ballroom was designed by the young James Wyatt, and the blue drawing room, with its rich Victorian upholstery, was made by Thomas Atkinson in the 19th century. Designs were commissioned but not used from both Robert Adam and Carr of York, and Capability Brown's ceiling design for the great hall was later used at Corsham Court. The furniture is as rich and diverse as the rooms, and there are some good paintings collected by William Constable. The park with its two lakes was laid out by Capability Brown's pupil Thomas White, though Brown advised on it.

☎ Skirlaugh (0401) 62400
9 m NE of Kingston upon Hull on B1238 turn N after Sproatley to Burton Constable
TA 1836 (OS 107)

Open Good Fri to end Sept S, Su and Bank Hol M 1330-1700

♿ 🅿 WC 🚻 (preferably by appt) 🚌 (by appt)
🌸 🍴 🎪 ♦ ✲

Carlton Towers

Carlton, North Yorkshire

At first sight this is an uncompromisingly Victorian house, with its amazing array of towers, turrets, pinnacles and gargoyles; but beneath its 19th-century veneer Carlton Towers is very much older. The home of the Dukes of Norfolk, it has passed down by inheritance since the Norman Conquest, and may even still retain some of the medieval masonry, while the Jacobean house, Carlton Hall, can be seen to the left of the entrance. The two men responsible for the house's present appearance were Lord Beaumont and his architect E. W. Pugin, son of the more famous A. W. N. Pugin. Pugin remodelled and refaced it in the 1870s, but he and Lord Beaumont, both eccentrics, then quarrelled, and Pugin was replaced by John Francis Bentley, designer of Westminster Cathedral, who was responsible for most of the interiors, which remain more or less unchanged. His rooms, with their dark, rich colour schemes, took fifteen years to complete, and he designed every detail, right down to such things as curtains, towel rails and firedogs. The most sumptuous room is the pink, green and gold Venetian drawing room, one of the most complete Victorian interiors in existence. The dado panels are painted with scenes from the *Merchant of Venice* by Westlake, the upper parts are covered with moulded and gilded plaster, and the vast chimneypiece is decorated with heraldry and painted panels, again by Westlake. In contrast, several smaller rooms, which retain their 18th-century and Edwardian decoration, give the house a lighter and more 'lived-in' feeling.

☎ Goole (0405) 861662
1 m N of Snaith on A1041
SE 6623 (OS 105)

Open May to end Sept Su and Bank Hol weekends 1030-1730; other times by appt

♿ 🅿 WC 🚌 (by appt) D 🌸
🍴 ♦ ✲ 🏌

In centre of Conisbrough

SK 5198 (OS 111)

Open daily throughout year; Mar to Oct 0930-1830,
Oct to Mar 0930-1600 (Su 1400-1600)

♿ 🅿 (limited access) 🚻 D ♠ ☂

Conisbrough Castle

Conisbrough, South Yorkshire

The castle is ruined, but it is still an impressive sight, and the keep itself is an extremely unusual construction. It was built about 1180 by Hamelin Plantagenet, the half-brother of Henry II, at about the same time as the great square keep of Dover Castle was being built, and is one of the first circular keeps in Britain. A further unusual feature is the six massive wedge-shaped buttresses which support it and rise above roof level as turrets. These appear to serve no practical purpose, as all except one, which has a small chapel set into it, are solid, but they must have provided an effective defence as not only does the keep still stand, but the stonework is extremely well preserved. The base of the keep is splayed for extra strength, and the semi-circular bailey surrounding it on three sides is enclosed by a high curtain wall, also splayed at the base and reinforced by solid towers. Inside the walls, the foundations of living quarters can be seen in the grass, but nothing is standing except the keep. Access is at first-floor level via a modern flight of steps, and below is a vaulted basement reached only from above. There were originally four storeys above this, though all the floors have now gone, and they are reached by a stone stairway in the thickness of the walls. The third and fourth storeys were evidently the main living rooms, and the fireplaces can still be seen. The upper room gives into the little chapel, which is partly in the thickness of the wall and partly in the buttress behind it.

☎ Liverpool (051) 228 5311

7 m NE of Liverpool on A580 turn S

SJ 4094 (OS 108)

Open Good Fri to end Sept daily 1100-1700

♿ 🅿 WC 🅿 (limited access) 🚻 (by appt)
D ♠ ♨ (limited opening) ◆ 🏕
☂ 🎣 ● (no tripods or flash) ⚲

Croxteth Hall

Country Park, Liverpool, Merseyside

Until recently the home of the Molyneux family, Earls of Sefton, Croxteth is now under the administration of Merseyside County Museums, and the 500-acre estate inside the city boundaries is organised as a country park. The house was begun in about 1575 for Richard Molyneux, but only a small part of the original Elizabethan house remains, as there were several later and larger additions. The first of these, built between 1702 and 1714, and known as the Queen Anne wing, is today the house's most attractive façade. Raised on a wide terrace and embellished with decorative stonework incorporating the Molyneux arms, it transformed the house into an imposing mansion. Further extensions were made in about 1800, and there were Victorian and Edwardian additions, the north range dating from the 1870s and the west front from 1902. In 1952 the finest rooms in the Queen Anne wing were destroyed by fire, and most have not been restored. There are relatively few outstanding rooms inside, partly because of the fire and partly because most of the contents were sold at auction, but the ground floor has been arranged as the 'Croxteth Heritage' exhibition, which explains the history of the park and the lifestyle of an Edwardian estate. Furniture and other items are being collected for the house, and the rooms are partly furnished, with some of the paintings which originally hung there back on the walls and others on loan from the Walker Art Gallery. Special exhibitions of costume are held from time to time in the main rooms.

☎ (061) 941 1025

1½ m W of Altrincham in Dunham Town

SJ 7387 (OS 109)

Open Apr to end Oct daily exc F (but inc Good Fri)
1300-1700; reduced rates for parties of 15 or over

♿ 🅿 WC 🅿 (limited access) 🚻 (by appt)
D ♠ ♨ 🚃 ◆ ☂

Dunham Massey

Altrincham, Greater Manchester

Dunham Massey, a low, plain, red-brick house, was mainly an 18th-century rebuilding of an Elizabethan moated manor house built by George Booth, close to the site of a Norman castle. The rebuilding was done by another George Booth, the 2nd Earl of Warrington, using a little-known architect, John Norris. By 1721 he had made extensive alterations to the interiors and laid out much of the park, and in the following years the old Tudor house was completely rebuilt. The arrangement of the new house, however, was dictated by the original Tudor building – today's house still has its open central courtyard, and the great hall is still basically the Tudor hall, though it retains none of its original decorations. Some further alterations were carried out between 1905 and 1909 by the architect J. C. Hall, who added the elaborate stone centrepiece on the south front, and the state rooms were superbly redecorated early in this century under the supervision of the furniture historian Percy Macquoid. Dunham Massey is particularly noted for its fine collections of furniture, silver and paintings, some of which were amassed by the 1st Earl, and others, particularly the pictures, by the 5th Earl of Stamford about 1760. Succeeding generations have added to and cherished the collections. The silver is displayed in Queen Anne's room, the Stamford gallery contains lovely walnut furniture, and there is a collection of paintings of the house in the gallery. The deer park contains an Elizabethan mill in working order, built by the first George Booth.

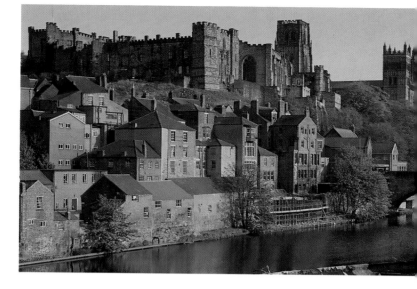

Durham Castle

Durham, Co. Durham

Durham Castle stands beside the cathedral on high ground above the river; both were begun about the same time, in the 11th century. The stronghold was given to the Bishop of Durham and became a palace of the prince bishops who, in return for the absolute power they held over their territory, were expected to produce an army, when necessary, to counter any threat from the Scots moving south. Little remains of the Norman building except for the chapel, but the castle still follows the original Norman pattern. In the 19th century the last of the prince bishops, William van Mildert, gave it to the newly founded University of Durham, and it is now a postgraduate college. The keep, which was extensively restored in 1831, is not open to the public, but the buildings of the various bishops can be visited. These were constantly altered and modernised by their successive owners, and display a variety of architectural styles, the common factor being a superlative standard of workmanship. Each bishop left his mark on his particular building or improvement by carving his personal coat-of-arms into the stone – on walls, over doorways or wherever else they would fit. A 17th-century porch in the courtyard leads to a screens passage with the kitchen on one side and the great hall on the other. The hall has 19th-century panelling and stained glass but its walls are 14th century, and parts of the undercroft are Norman. Two of the castle's best features are the black staircase, with its lovely carved wooden tracery, and the Norman chapel.

☎ Durham (0385) 65481
In centre of Durham
NZ 2742 (OS 88)

Open Apr, July, Aug, Sept M-S 1000-1200 and 1400-1630; other months M, W, S 1400-1800

Harewood House

Harewood, Leeds, West Yorkshire

Harewood, a showpiece of all that is best in 18th-century architecture and decoration, was built between 1759 and 1771 to the designs of John Carr of York, who also built the stable block and the village. In the 1760s Robert Adam returned from Italy full of ideas and suggestions for improvements, and was given the responsibility for all the interiors, and in 1772 Capability Brown began to landscape the park. The Palladian perfection of the house was slightly marred in the 19th century when Charles Barry built additional floors, modified the south front and removed some of Adam's interior work, but the house is still very impressive, and the interiors are among Adam's finest. The hall shows his mature style, with great Doric half-columns and Neo-Classical plasterwork, while the other rooms are lighter in style, with delicate plasterwork by Joseph Rose and paintings by Angelica Kauffmann. The long gallery, with a lofty ceiling decorated with mythological paintings, was designed for pictures, and contains striking portraits by Reynolds, Gainsborough, Romney and others as well as a collection of Chinese porcelain. Harewood is particularly famous for its superb furniture, most of which was made for the house by Thomas Chippendale, who also designed and made the pelments in the library, carved and painted to resemble drapery. The house also contains a good collection of Italian – mainly Venetian – paintings, and there are several delightful watercolours of the house and park by Turner, Girtin and John Varley.

☎ Harewood (0532) 886225
10½ m S of Harrogate on A61, turn W ay junction with A659
SE 3144 (OS 104)

Open Apr to end Oct daily, Feb, March, Nov Su 1100-dusk

(1 mile walk)

Heaton Hall

Heaton Park, Prestwick, Manchester

Heaton Hall (or House as it was formerly known) is the masterpiece of James Wyatt, one of the greatest architects of the 18th century. His client was Sir Thomas Egerton, later 1st Earl of Wilton, who had inherited the house in 1756 while still a minor. In 1771 Wyatt burst upon the fashionable world with his simplified version of Adam's Neo-Classicism, and Sir Thomas, a man of taste and fashion, commissioned him to prepare designs for the rebuilding of Heaton Hall. The garden front is one of the best examples in the country of the style, and the interior decoration is also very charming, a 'prettier' version of Adam's manner, which was becoming less popular. In 1902, after 200 years of ownership, the Egerton family sold the house to Manchester City Corporation. This was long before the concept of country-house visiting had been born and the entire contents were auctioned off and the house itself used for a variety of unsuitable purposes. However, since 1972 much restoration work has been carried out, and the house is now used as a museum, with good 18th-century paintings and furniture in many of the rooms. A fine central staircase leads to the first floor, where there is a bow-ended room exquisitely decorated in the Etruscan style by Biagio Rebecca. This originally contained gilt and painted chairs and sofas, window seats and a circular carpet.

☎ (061) 236 9422
5½ m N of Manchester city centre on A576 turn W to Heaton Park
SD 8304 (OS 109)

Open spring and summer, phone for information

WC (limited access)

● (by permission only, no use of flash)

☎ Hoghton (025485) 2986

4 m W of Blackburn on A675

SD 6226 (OS 103)

Open Easter weekend, then to end Oct Su and Bank Hol M also S in Jul and Aug

⊖ 🅿 WC 🚻 (by appt) D ♣ 🍴 (by appt) 🛏 ◆ ✈ 🗡 (compulsory) 🕊

Hoghton Tower

Hoghton, Preston, Lancashire

The name means 'the house on the hill', and Hoghton, visible for miles in every direction, presents a dramatic sight with its castellated front and crowded chimneys silhouetted on the skyline. The Hoghton family had lived in a house on the site since at least the 12th century, and when Thomas Hoghton began to build his new house in 1565 he built it in a rather old-fashioned medieval style; it was completed by his son in the following century. The house was not lived in during the 18th century as the family moved out in 1710, so it was spared the usual 18th-century rebuilding. However, it did become fairly dilapidated, and the Hoghtons, who moved back again at the end of the 19th century, had to carry out extensive restorations to render it habitable again. The house has two courtyards: the battlemented gatehouse leads into an outer courtyard formed by the stables and service blocks, while the main living rooms are arranged around an inner courtyard. The two were once separated by the great tower that gives the house its name, but this was destroyed during the Civil War. The great hall, with stone walls and an oak roof, contains furniture of its period and relics of James I's visit in 1612 (it was here that he reputedly knighted a piece of beef, thus inventing the word 'Sirloin'). The other rooms are panelled in the 17th-century style. A fire in the 19th century destroyed the best of the furniture and paintings, but there are family portraits, pictures of local interest, and an excellent collection of dolls and dolls' houses.

☎ Flookburgh (044853) 328

6½ m S of Haverthwaite on B5278

SD 3577 (OS 97)

Open Easter to end Oct daily exc S 1030-1800; reduced rates for parties

⊖ (1 m walk) 🅿 WC 🚾 (limited access) 🚻 D ♣ 🍴 🛏 ◆ 🐾 ✈ 🗡 🕊

Holker Hall

Cark-in-Cartmel, Grange-over-Sands, Cumbria

Formerly the home of the Dukes of Devonshire, Holker Hall dates originally from the 17th century, but it was altered and refaced in 1840 by Lord Burlington to give it a Gothic look, with tall ornamental chimneys, gables and mullioned windows. This part, known as the old wing, is closed to the public. In 1871 a fire broke out, destroying the entire west wing before it could be brought under control, and soon afterwards the 7th Duke began plans for rebuilding. A grand new wing was designed by Paley and Austin of Lancaster, who have been described by Pevsner as 'the best architects living in the country'. The new wing, built of red sandstone in the Elizabethan style, is their outstanding work; the craftsmanship is superb and there are many delightful details. The interior of the house, which contains a mixture of Georgian and later furniture, is spacious, and visitors can walk round quite freely. The chimneypieces of local marble are beautifully worked, and there is an elaborately carved staircase and some fine woodwork. The spacious pleasure grounds – 120 acres of park and 22 acres of garden – hold numerous attractions, including a herd of fallow deer established in the 18th century and a more recently introduced herd of red deer; the Lakeland Motor Museum; the Crafts and Countryside Museum; a baby animal house and an adventure playground. The garden contains rare trees and shrubs as well as the oldest monkey-puzzle tree in England, grown from the original seed first brought into the country by Joseph Paxton in the mid-19th century.

☎ Carnforth (0524) 734474

10½ m N of Lancaster on A6 turn W to Yealand Conyers

SD 4974 (OS 97)

Open May to Sept Su, Bank Hol M, T-F 1400-1700

🅿 WC 🚾 (limited access) 🚻 (by appt) D ♣ 🍴 (by appt for parties) 🛏 ◆ 🐾 🗡 (compulsory) Falconry in park

Leighton Hall

Carnforth, Lancashire

No finer setting for a house could be imagined: the Lake District mountains rise blue behind, the park in front slopes gently down to the house, and the building itself, in brilliant white limestone, shines in the sun. The house was given its fairy-tale castellated look in the early 1800s; previously it had been a Classical-style house with a sober façade. The additions were made by Harrison of Chester, who built turrets and pinnacles and gave the stables a tall, pointed window so that they look like a chapel from the outside. A projecting wing with a high tower was added in 1870 by Paley and Austin, the best architects in the north-west at the time. The house was bought in 1822 by Richard Gillow, whose father had founded the firm of Gillow of Lancaster; one of its main features is the large amount of very fine furniture made by this firm. Although Gillows are perhaps best known today for their 19th-century work, they were in business by 1730, and there are some excellent Georgian pieces in the house, including an altar in the small private chapel. The interior generally is attractive without being out of the ordinary. The entrance hall has a delicate screen of clustered columns dividing it from the elegant curved stone staircase; the dining room, once a billiards room, still has its central skylight, and the drawing room gives a breathtaking view of the mountains. The gardens and grounds are both open to visitors, and birds of prey are flown in the park whenever weather permits.

Levens Hall

Kendal, Cumbria

Grey, gabled, irregular and mainly Elizabethan, Levens, like many houses in this region, began life as a pele tower (a square fortified tower house). The base of the tower can still be seen in the undercroft, now the shop. But the façade and most of the rest of the house date from about 1580 when it came into the hands of the Bellingham family, who were also responsible for the house's most outstanding feature, the lavishly decorated series of rooms on the ground floor. The house has been little altered since that time, although a south front was added about a century later by a new owner, Colonel James Grahme, who also made the garden and acquired some fine furniture. The entrance hall leads straight into the great hall, which has a deep plaster frieze decorated with the coat-of-arms of Elizabeth I, animals and heraldic shields. The other ground-floor rooms are beautiful, and most have panelling, carved chimneypieces and moulded plaster ceilings, though in the dining room the walls are covered with Spanish leather, introduced by Colonel Grahme, who probably also bought the fine Stuart chairs. The drawing room, dated 1595, is a particularly rich example of late Elizabethan taste, with heraldic glass, geometric plaster ceilings and an amazing chimneypiece incorporating panels of heraldry and the Orders of Classical architecture. The topiary gardens were laid out in 1690 by Monsieur Beaumont, gardener to James II at Hampton Court. They fortunately escaped the 18th-century craze for landscaping, and remain much as they were planned.

☎ Sedgwick (0448) 60321

6 m S of Kendal on A6 just after junction with A590

SO 4985 (OS 97)

Open Easter to end Sept Su-Th 1100-1700; evening parties by appt

 (by appt for parties) ● (not in house) 大

Lindisfarne Castle

Holy Island, Berwick-upon-Tweed, Northumberland

The great crag on Holy Island, suitable though it was as a castle site, was surprisingly not fortified until 1542, when gunposts were set up to defend the harbour against the marauding Scots. The castle was completed by 1550, built from the stone of the ruined priory situated conveniently nearby, but the expected attack never came. There was just one dramatic incident in 1725, when the garrison had shrunk to seven men, and the castle was seized by Jacobite supporters, but they were speedily ejected and the castle went back to sleep. In 1819 its guns were removed and it fell into disuse, but in 1901 Edward Hudson, the founder of *Country Life* magazine, bought it and engaged Edwin Lutyens, then the leading country-house architect, who had begun to show a particular skill in romantic reconstructions using traditional materials. Lutyens's task was to make a comfortable house within the ramparts, and the result was a series of small vaulted chambers and rock passages, a slightly odd mixture of the medieval and the cosy. The views from most of the curiously shaped rooms are superb, and the rooms themselves contain some fine furniture chosen by Lutyens and Hudson, mainly 17th-century English and Flemish oak. One piece, the oval dining table, was designed by Lutyens. The castle is certainly romantic, but it seems that not everyone found it comfortable, and some of Mr Hudson's house guests complained of the intolerable cold.

☎ Berwick (0289) 89244

13 m SE of Berwick-upon-Tweed on A1 turn E at West Mains Inn to Holy Island

NU 1341 (OS 75)

Open Apr to end Sept daily exc F (but inc Good Fri) 1100-1700; Oct S and Su 1400-1700

⊖ (limited) D

Meols Hall

Southport, Lancashire

This is a brick manor house that is essentially late 17th century in character, though its history goes back much further. There was certainly a house on the site during the reign of King John, when most of the manor of North Meols was granted to Robert de Coudray. It passed by marriage from the de Coudrays to the Aughtons in the 14th century, and in the 16th century to the Heskeths. Like many of the Lancashire gentry, the Heskeths remained Catholics after the Reformation, and there are still traces of a 'priest's hole' at Meols; the famous Jesuit missionary St Edmund Campion is said to have used it. Roger Hesketh and his wife were imprisoned for a time after the Jacobite rising of 1692 in Lancashire, but there nevertheless seems to have been much new building at about this time: an inventory made in 1675 suggests a markedly different arrangement of rooms from the present one, and a back gable on the house, carrying the date 1695, also indicates that changes substantial enough to warrant recording must have been made. In the 18th century the Heskeths married into the Fleetwood family, and Meols was rather neglected in favour of the Fleetwoods' great Rossall estate. But in the 1840s, after the head of the family, Sir Peter Fleetwood-Hesketh, lost most of his fortune, his younger brother Charles managed to save Meols from the wreck. The large Rossall collection (paintings, furniture and *objets d'art*) eventually came to Meols and is the principal attraction of the interior.

☎ Southport (0704) 28171

1 m N of Southport off A565

SD 3720 (OS 108)

Open Apr to end Sept Th and Bank Hol M 1400-1700

⊖ WC D

☎ Ravenglass (065 77) 614/203

18 m S of Whitehaven on A595

SD 0996 (OS 96)

Open Good Fri to end Sept daily exc M (but inc Bank Hols) 1330-1630; other times by appt

⊖ 🅵 WC ♿ 🚻 D ♣ 🍴 ◆ ⚘ 🗡
● (not in house) ⚘

Muncaster Castle

Ravenglass, Cumbria

Muncaster Castle, which guards the entrance to Eskdale, is ancient in origin; the lands were granted to Alan de Penitone in 1208. The original castle was built about 50 years later and enlarged by the addition of a pele tower in 1325. However, although the present house incorporates the medieval tower, it is almost entirely the creation of Anthony Salvin, who rebuilt it in the 1860s for the 4th Lord Muncaster. Salvin specialised in restoring castles, and the pink granite building harmonises well with the heather-clad hills and the rhododendrons for which the gardens are famous. The interiors are mainly Victorian, but there is some excellent 17th-century furniture and many good paintings. The house is full of treasures collected over the generations, including Flemish woodcarvings, tapestries and silver. One of the most interesting rooms is the large octagonal library with its coved ceiling. Standing over the site of the medieval kitchens, it dates from about 1780, but was altered by Salvin, who also changed the exterior so that it cannot be seen as an octagon from the outside. The drawing room, with a lovely barrel ceiling decorated with plasterwork by Italian craftsmen, contains one of the finest collections of family portraits in the country. Upstairs is a magnificent Elizabethan bed in the west bedroom, with carved and inlaid scenic panels, and the curtains are hand-painted silk. The carved fireplace is Tudor, as is the one in the tapestry room, and the King's bedroom has 16th-century carved panelling.

☎ Brampton (069 77) 2621

12 m E of Carlisle on A69 turn N

NY 5662 (OS 86)

Open Easter Su and M, May to end Sept W, Su and Bank Hols; parties at other times by appt

⊖ 🅵 WC 🚻 (by appt) ♣

Naworth Castle

Brampton, Cumbria

Naworth stands on a good defensive site beside the River Irthing, with the ground falling away steeply on three sides. The first stone fortress there was built after 1335, when Edward III granted Ranulph de Dacre a licence to crenellate his house; Dacre added a tower and a walled enclosure. Although the Dacres were a powerful family, Naworth was neglected until the time of Thomas, Lord Dacre, a warrior who distinguished himself at the battle of Flodden (1513) and remained much concerned with the defence of the North. Lord Thomas rebuilt and heightened Ranulph's tower (now called the Dacre Tower) and gave Naworth essentially its present form. This consists of an irregular quadrangle with towers at each end of the main façade, on the most vulnerable side; the rectangular Dacre Tower projects right out from the walls, extending the façade. In front of it stand once-formidable outer defences that include a moat and a gatehouse. The most notable of the courtyard buildings is the very large great hall, measuring 78 by 24 foot. By 1588 Naworth was again 'in very great decay in all parts', and a second restoration was undertaken by Lord William Howard, who had married a Dacre heiress in 1604. He converted the tower into luxurious private apartments, fitted with a superb 14th-century ceiling taken from Kirkoswald Castle. Fortunately this survived the disastrous fire of 1844, though much else was lost. However, Naworth's owner, the Earl of Carlisle, called in the architect Anthony Salvin, who restored the original with great fidelity.

☎ Coxwold (034 76) 435

3½ m SE of Thirsk on A19 turn E to Coxwold

SE 5476 (OS 100)

Open mid May to end Aug W and Su in Aug 1430-1700; parties of 20 or over on other days by appt

🅵 WC 🚻 D ♣ 🍴 ⚘

Newburgh Priory

Coxwold, North Yorkshire

This large stone house is a mixture of styles, Tudor, Jacobean and 18th century, with little remaining of the original Augustinian priory founded in 1145. After the Dissolution Henry VIII sold the buildings to his loyal chaplain Anthony Bellasis, and he began to turn the priory into a mansion, a process that continued until the 18th century. Only some parts of the building can be accurately dated: the porch and mullioned windows are Elizabethan; parts of the courtyard were remodelled in 1720, and the drainpipes on the east front are dated 1732. The ground floor rooms are shown to visitors, and one room upstairs containing Oliver Cromwell's tomb. Thomas Bellasis, the 2nd Viscount Fauconberg, married Cromwell's daughter Mary, but no one really knows why – or even if – the Protector's body was brought here for burial. One of the most notable features of the rooms is the elaborate carved overmantel in the dining room, dated 1615 and made by Nicholas Stone in a style advanced for its time. The black gallery contains good family portraits, including one of Cromwell, and there is a charming 18th-century painting of Earl Fauconberg and his family in the justice room (where the Court Leet was held). More family portraits are hung throughout the rooms and on the stairs, among them two of Mary Cromwell, one showing her in her court robes after her marriage, holding a plan of the drawing room. The two panelled rooms on the garden front were rebuilt after a fire in 1757, and have pretty plaster ceilings and a set of Georgian chairs with needlework covers.

Newby Hall

Ripon, North Yorkshire

This large, red-brick house built in the 1690s for Sir Edward Blackett, was bought in 1748 by the Weddell family. William Weddell, a man of great taste and knowledge, returned from the Grand Tour in the 1760s, determined to alter and enlarge the house for his collection of sculpture and tapestries, and he commissioned the most fashionable architect of the time, Robert Adam. Adam added the two wings to the east of the house, one containing the sculpture gallery and the other the kitchens, and completely redesigned the interiors of the main rooms. Around 1800, Lord Grantham, an amateur architect, turned Adam's dining room into a library and added the 'Georgian dining room' on the north-west corner, and his grandson built the Victorian wing and the billiards room above the dining room. The interiors at Newby Hall provide one of the finest complete examples of the Adam style to be found anywhere, the climax being the great domed sculpture gallery with delicate stucco work in the 'antique' style. This still contains the Roman marbles it was built to display, and Weddell's other collections are also intact – the Gobelin tapestries in the tapestry room were ordered by him in Paris in 1765. The superb furniture was made for the house by Thomas Chippendale, much of it to Adam's own design. The charming bedrooms, several of which have been skilfully refurbished in recent years, also contain fine furniture and decorations. On the back stairs there is a collection of chamber-pots, some very rare, from all over Europe and the Far East.

☎ Boroughbridge (090 12) 258
2½ m SE of Ripon on B6265 turn S before Bridge Hewick to Great Givendale
SE 3467 (OS 99)

Open Apr to end Sept daily exc M but inc Bank Hol M 1300-1700
⊖ (1 m walk) 🅿 WC 🚻 🖾 🍴 🍽 🎋 ◆ 🐾 ● (not in house) ☂

Normanby Hall

Scunthorpe, Humberside

This fine Regency building, set in a 350-acre park, was built for the Sheffield family, formerly Dukes of Buckingham (and owners of Buckingham Palace). It was designed by Robert Smirke to replace an older house, and was completed about 1830. The rear wing, in the Baroque style, was added by Walter Brierley in 1906, as part of a major programme of enlargement including an east wing with a ballroom and complete range of bedrooms. Much of Brierley's work, however, was demolished after the last war, and the Sheffields themselves left the house in 1963. Since then it has been leased to Scunthorpe Borough Council, and has been completely refurnished in the style of the 1820s. Although it is run as a museum – it contains fine collections of furniture, textiles, uniforms, costumes, paintings, ceramics and silver – the richly decorated rooms have a pleasant 'lived-in' feeling, and there are no rope barriers. The park, which includes a deer park with free-roaming herds of red and fallow deer, has numerous attractions including a golf course, a swimming pool and facilities for horse riding. There are four nature trails, a large wooded picnic area and a centre for traditional crafts, where visitors can watch the potter or the blacksmith at work.

☎ Scunthorpe (0724) 720215
5 m N of Scunthorpe off B1430
SE 8816 (OS 112)

Open Nov to Mar M-F 1000-1230, Su 1400-1700; Apr to Oct M, W, Th, F 1000-1230 and 1400-1730
⊖ 🅿 WC 🖾 (limited access)
🍴 D 🍽 🎋 ◆ 🐾 ☀ (evenings only) ☂ ☖

Raby Castle

Staindrop, Darlington, Co. Durham

Raby Castle, with its great, long, battlemented front and its encircling protective walls, readily evokes the spirit of medieval England. It is first recorded as belonging to King Canute, and was evidently fortified some time before Lord Neville was granted a licence to crenellate in 1378, as the oldest parts of today's building date from the 12th century. The power of the Neville family was destroyed after the 'Rising of the North' in 1569 against Elizabeth I, and Raby was acquired by Sir Henry Vane, whose family still own it. Although it still gives the appearance of a 14th-century castle most of the buildings have been turned into something more like a country house. The most complete medieval parts are on the west side, where a drawbridge once led across the moat to the Neville gateway and the inner court. Some of the walls here are 20 feet thick. A good deal of alteration was done in the 1780s by Carr of York, and much of his work was in turn altered by William Burn in the 1840s, so the interiors are a mixture of late 18th-century and mid-19th-century revival styles. The great, Gothic-style entrance hall with its pointed vault and dark red pillars is Carr's work, while the octagonal drawing room with its gilded 'Jacobean' strapwork, silk-hung walls and vast mirrors is the most impressive of Burn's rooms. The house contains a good collection of paintings and furniture as well as some fine Meissen porcelain and the statue of a naked and manacled slave girl by Hiram Powers, which caused a sensation when it was first exhibited in 1851.

☎ Staindrop (0833) 60202
6 m SW of West Auckland on A688 turn N at Maltkiln Cotts
NZ 1221 (OS 92)

Open Apr, May, Jun W, Su; Jul, Aug, Sept daily exc S also Bank Hol weekends S-T
⊖ 🅿 WC 🖾 🍴 D 🍽 🎋 ◆ ☀
☂ (by appt for parties only)

In centre of Richmond on N bank of River Swale

NZ 1700 (OS 92)

Open daily throughout year; Mar to Oct 0930-1830
Oct to Mar 0930-1600 (Su 1400-1600)

⊖ WC ♿ ⚹

Richmond Castle

Richmond, North Yorkshire

In spite of its formidable appearance and dramatic cliff-top site above the River Swale, the history of Richmond Castle has been a quiet one, and it never saw military action. Its ruin was due to gradual neglect from the 16th century when, no longer serving any military purpose, it was simply left to decay. However, it is an interesting castle, and has some very early remains. Before the Conquest, the site belonged to Edwin, Earl of Mercia, but it was granted to Alan the Red of Brittany in about 1080, and he was responsible for the early building works, the first of which were the enormously thick curtain walls, triangular in plan to follow the oddly-shaped site. Scolland's hall, the hall block of the castle situated in a corner of the courtyard, was built soon after, and is believed to be the oldest castle hall in Britain. Before the keep itself was built, this would have served a similar purpose, with the ground floor used for storage and possibly as a servants' hall. The hall itself was at first-floor level, approached by a flight of steps, with the solar, or withdrawing room, at the eastern end. Adjoining the building, in an extension of the curtain wall, is the gold tower, which contained garderobes (lavatories). The great keep, Richmond's dominant feature, was added about a century later, possibly by Henry II, and was built as an upwards extension of the existing gatehouse, retaining the fine 11th-century archway. It is extremely well preserved, with all its walls intact, and the top provides a fine view of the town and countryside.

☎ Skipton (0756) 2442

In centre of Skipton

SD 9951 (OS 103)

Open throughout the year M-S 1000-1800, Su 1400-1800 (or dusk if earlier). Closed Good Fri and 25 Dec

⊖ Ⓟ WC ⊟ D ★ ⚹ (available in foreign languages) ⚔ (by appt for parties)

Skipton Castle

Skipton, North Yorkshire

The great round towers of the castle's main gate rise at the end of the sloping high street to dominate the small market town, and the castle itself lies slightly behind. The castle was granted to Robert de Clifford in 1284, and he began a family tenure which was to be unbroken for fourteen generations, rebuilding the castle before his death at Bannockburn in 1314. The Cliffords, at one time castellans of the Castle of York, and builders of Clifford's Tower, were intensely loyal to the Crown and it is fitting that Skipton Castle should have been the last northern stronghold to capitulate to the Parliamentary forces. It held out for three years until December 1645, and was then slighted (had its defences destroyed). Its excellent condition today is largely due to Lady Anne Clifford, the last of the line, who restored it, together with several other castles. A tablet over the entrance records her work, which was completed in 1658. The castle is D-shaped, with six round towers on the curve, and the straight edge along the cliff above the river. The delightful inner courtyard with a yew tree in the centre, known as the conduit court, owes much of its character to a rebuilding carried out about 1500, but on its north side are the original domestic buildings of about 1300, all of which are open to the public. The range of buildings to the right of the castle, now a self-contained residence and not open to the public, was built as an extension to the castle in 1535 on the marriage of Henry Clifford to Eleanor Brandon.

☎ Driffield (0377) 86208

12 m SE of Malton on B1248 turn NE on B1251

SE 9364 (OS 101)

Open Apr Easter weekend and Su; May to end Sept daily exc M and F (but inc Bank Hol M) 1330-1730

Ⓟ WC ♿ (preferably by appt) ⊟ D ♣
Ⓟ (by appt for parties) ◆ ⚹

Sledmere House

Driffield, Humberside

A large 18th-century house standing in a park with great trees, laid out by Capability Brown in 1777. The Sykes family inherited the property in 1748, and the whole ensemble, house, park and village, has been created by them. The village originally lay at the bottom of the valley, but was removed to dry ground out of sight of the house. The square core of the house was built by Richard Sykes, and a generation later Sir Christopher improved it by adding two wings and a pediment. The exterior was finished by 1786, and a year later the interior was decorated with plaster ornament in the Adam style. The plasterer was the famous Joseph Rose, who had worked with Adam on several major houses. Tragically, the house was gutted by fire in 1911, but all the furniture and sculpture and many of the fittings were rescued by the villagers, and the plasterwork was brilliantly restored by the architect Walter Brierley. The staircase hall, drawing room and dining room are all on a grand scale and very fine, and the contents are altogether of a very high quality. Much of the furniture was made for the house, and there are some good paintings, including Elizabethan portraits and 17th-century Italian works. The finest room of all is the library on the first floor, which takes up the whole of the park front. Sir Tatton, son of Sir Christopher, whose collection of books the room was built to house, used to take his exercise here on rainy days, covering miles by walking up and down. The room has a great arched vault based on the baths of ancient Rome, and a lovely parquet floor of 1911.

Speke Hall

The Walk, Liverpool, Merseyside

Sandwiched between Liverpool's industrial buildings and a runway of the airport, Speke Hall is an amazing survival – an unspoilt, picturesque Tudor mansion set in its own gardens and woodlands. Built for the Norris family between about 1490 and 1613, it has been remarkably little altered, and the buildings, although of different dates, are all of the same style, the black-and-white half-timbering typical of Cheshire and Lancashire. The house has four wings surrounding a cobbled courtyard in which there are two yew trees older than the house. The great hall is the oldest part of the house, though no one is quite sure of its date. It has a huge battlemented Tudor fireplace at one end, while at the other is sumptuous Flemish panelling containing carved busts of Roman emperors. The parlour has an odd overmantel with a relief representing three generations of the Norris family, and a rich Elizabethan plaster ceiling. The house contains a number of secret hiding places and priest holes, and in most of the rooms there is good oak furniture amassed by the Watt family. Richard Watt bought the house in 1796, and he and his family restored it lovingly, most of the furniture and fittings introduced in the 19th century being in the various Victorian revival styles. Miss Adelaide Watt bequeathed it to descendants of the Norrises, the original owners, and the National Trust received it in 1944. It is now leased to Liverpool Corporation as an historic museum.

☎ Liverpool (051) 427 7231
10 m SE of Liverpool on A561 turn S to Speke Airport
SJ 4182 (OS 108)

Open M-S 1000-1700, Su 1400-1700 (Apr to end Sept 1400-1900) Bank Hols 1000-1900
⊖ (1 m walk) 🄿 WC 🅐 � (by appt) ♦
📹 (limited opening) ♦ 🕸 ✗ ◆

Thurnham Hall

Lancaster, Lancashire

Thurnham Hall has an elegant Gothic-style façade, sash windows, turrets and a castellated parapet, all of about 1823, with the chapel at one side added in 1854; but all this is merely a skin on a much older building. The main part of the house is 16th century, and this house was itself built around a much earlier dwelling, a 13th-century pele tower. The house was the seat of the Catholic Dalton family for over four hundred years, but unfortunately it was allowed to decay from the late 19th century, and a fire in 1959 damaged it still further. When its present owner bought it in 1973 it was virtually a ruin, but he and his family set about restoring it, and although the work is not yet finished, it is once again a fine country house and much of the early fabric is being revealed under its Victorian accumulations. The best of the interiors is the great hall, with a particularly fine Tudor fireplace (one of several in the house), oak panelling, an Elizabethan plaster ceiling and roundels in the windows bearing the Dalton arms. Most of the rooms contain old oak furniture, and there are several Dalton portraits on the walls. The once-Victorian bedroom, now restored to its Tudor character, has a priesthole behind the fireplace and is said to be haunted by a lady in green, who will appear to give warning of any impending tragedy at Thurnham. The house is of particular appeal to anyone interested in the processes of restoration, and the owners give a slide show of the repair work before the guided tour commences.

☎ Lancaster (0524) 751766
8 m S of Lancaster on A588 at Upper Thurnham
SD 4654 (OS 102)

Open Good Fri to end Sept daily exc S 1400-1700
⊖ 🄿 WC 🅐 (limited access)
� D ♠ 📹 🎄 ◆ 🕸 ✗ (compulsory)

Warkworth Castle

Warkworth, Northumberland

Warkworth presents a fine and dramatic sight, perched on its mound above the town and overlooking the winding River Coquet on the other side. Though small, it has played a major part in England's history. There was almost certainly a Saxon stronghold on the site, and the basic layout of today's castle was established as early as the 12th century. King John stayed here in 1214, by which time it had become an important military base, complete with walls, gatehouse, hall and chapel, and in 1332 his great-great-grandson Edward III sold it to Henry, 2nd Lord Percy of Alnwick. The Percy lords improved, enlarged and strengthened it, turning the keep into a small palace and building the tower known as the 'Grey Mare's Tail'. The 'lion tower', which covers the entrance to the hall, is named after the Percy lion carved on the central boss of its vault. The 3rd Lord Percy, a renowned soldier, was created Earl of Northumberland by Richard II, and he and his son Harry 'Hotspur' first supported and then conspired against Henry IV. The conspiracy was hatched within the castle walls, and in 1405 Henry besieged and took Warkworth, giving it, to his brother John, later Duke of Bedford. In 1416 Henry Percy, son of Hotspur, was pardoned and restored to his lands, and thereafter Percys came and went, making alterations and additions to the castle throughout the 14th and 15th centuries. In 1572 Sir Thomas Percy was beheaded for his part in the 'Rising of the North' against Elizabeth I, and the castle finally declined and fell into decay.

10 m SE of Alnwick on A1068
NU 2405 (OS 81)

Open daily throughout year; Mar to Oct 0930-1830, Oct to Mar 0930-1600 (Su 1400-1600)
⊖ (limited) 🄿 WC 🅐 (limited access) � D ♠ 🕸

Abbot Hall Art Gallery, Kendal, Cumbria (tel Kendal [0539] 22464). In town centre, by the River Kent. SD 5192 (OS 97). House built in 1759 for Col. George Wilson. The ground floor has been restored in 18th-century style, and the upper floor is a gallery for modern art. The stable block contains a museum of Lakeland life and industry. Open daily am and pm (S and Su pm only); closed for two weeks over Christmas. ⊖ WC ♿ ♣ ☞

Appleby' Castle, Appleby, Cumbria (tel Appleby [0930] 51402). In town centre. NY 6819 (OS 91). Norman castle with an 80ft high square keep of 1100 and later, 14th-century outhouses, and a 15th-century gatehouse. The grounds contain a collection of exotic birds, and rare and historic breeds of domestic animals. Open May to Sept daily am and pm. ⊖ 🅿 WC ♿ ♣ ☞

Astley Hall, Chorley, Lancashire (tel Chorley [025 72] 62166). 2 m NW of Chorley town centre on A581, turn N onto B5252 for ½ m, then turn E. SD 5718 (OS 108). Elizabethan house with many-windowed façade set in a large park. The interior contains highly elaborate Restoration plasterwork, Cromwellian furniture, Flemish tapestries and a magnificent long gallery. Open all year M-F pm, S and Su am and pm. ⊖ 🅿 WC ♿ ♣ ☞

Barnard Castle, County Durham. In centre of Barnard Castle town. NZ 0516 (OS 92). Ruined castle, mostly of 1250-1350, on a cliff above the River Tees. Originally built by the Baliol family, it eventually passed to royal control in the 15th century. The most striking feature is the cylindrical, early 13th-century, round tower. Open daily am and pm. ⊖ 🅿

Bedale House, Bedale, North Yorkshire (tel Bedale [0677] 23131). 10 m SW of Northallerton on A684. SE 2688 (OS 99). Mid-Georgian mansion, with fine plasterwork; the outstanding room is the ballroom, which has a fine decorated ceiling. There is also a collection of items of local interest. Open May to Sept T pm; other times by appt. ⊖ 🅿 WC ♿ ★

Belsay Hall, Belsay, Northumberland. 14 m NW of Newcastle on A696. NZ 3078 (OS 81). Early 19th-century Neo-Classical house built in the grounds of a 14th-century tower-house castle. Sir Charles Monck designed the Hall in immense detail and planned its gardens. The stable block, servants wing, gardens and castle are all open to the public. Open Apr to Sept daily am and pm (Su pm only). ⊖ 🅿

Beningbrough Hall, Shipton-by-Beningborough, North Yorkshire (tel York [0904] 470715). 8 m NW of York on A19, turn W. SE 5158 (OS 105). Attractive red-brick Queen Anne house built in 1716, with carved woodwork by William Thornton. The house is used to display a collection of 100 portraits of the period 1688-1760 belonging to the National Portrait Gallery. The Victorian laundry carries a display of 19th-century domestic life. Open Apr to end Oct T-Th, S, Su and Bank Hol M pm. ⊖ 🅿 WC ♿ 🚻 (by appt) ♣ ☞

Blaydes House, High St, Hull, Humberside (tel Hull [0482] 26406). In town centre. TA 0927 (OS 107). Merchant's house of the mid-Georgain period, with a fine staircase and panelled rooms, restored by the East Yorkshire Georgian society. Open all year M-F am and pm by appt. ⊖

Bluecoats Chamber, School Lane, Liverpool, Merseyside (tel 051-709 5297). In city centre. SJ 3591. (OS 108). A fine building of the early 18th century with a cobbled quadrangle and a garden courtyard. It was originally a charity school but now serves as a gallery and concert hall. Open M-S am and pm. ⊖ ♣ ☞ ★

Bolling Hall, Bowling Hall Rd, Bradford, West Yorkshire (tel Bradford [0274] 723057). 1½ m SE of town centre. SE 1831 (OS 104). 15th-century manor house and tower, extended in the 17th and 18th centuries. The house is now a museum containing period furniture (including several pieces by Chippendale) and displays of local life. Open T-Su and Bank Hol M am and pm (not Christmas or New Year). ⊖ 🅿 WC ♿ 🚻 ♣ ★

Bolton Castle, Castle Bolton, near Leyburn, North Yorkshire (tel Wensleydale [0969] 23408). 10 m S of Richmond on A6108, turn SW. SE 0391 (OS 98). Castle built in the late 14th century for Lord Scrope, the Chancellor of Richard II, on a compact quadrangular plan. The castle was beseiged by Parliamentary forces in the Civil War. It is now partly used as a restaurant. Open T-Su and Bank Hol M am and pm. ⊖ 🅿 WC ☞

Bowes Castle, Bowes, County Durham. In village centre, 5 m SW of Barnard Castle on A67. NY 9913 (OS 92). 12th-century castle built by Henry II on the site of a Roman fort guarding the Stainforth Pass. It comprised a single, massive tower, without outer walls, and is now ruined. Open daily am and pm. 🅿 ★

Bramham Park, Wetherby, West Yorkshire (tel Boston Spa [0937] 844265). 7 m S of Wetherby on A1, turn W. SE 4041 (OS 105). Queen Anne mansion built by Robert Benson in the Italian manner. The interior was restored in an authentic style in the early 20th century after a fire in 1828. The park retains its original Classical layout, incorporated excellent vistas inspired by Versailles. Open mid-June to end Aug Su, T-Th and Bank Hol M pm. ⊖ 🅿 WC 🚻 D 🌲

Brantwood, Coniston, Cumbria (Coniston [096 64] 396). 6 m SW of Ambleside on B5285, turn W. SD 3195 (OS 96). Mainly 19th-century house that was the home of John Ruskin from 1872 to 1900, with an exceptional view over Coniston Water. The house has a collection of Ruskin's water-colours and memorabilia. The grounds contain a fine nature trail. Open March to Nov daily am and pm; Nov to March W to Su, am and pm. ⊖ 🅿 WC ♿ ♣ ☞

Brough Castle, Brough, Cumbria. In village centre, near junction of A66 and A685. NY 7914 (OS 91). Ruined castle on a steep escarpment. The first fort on the site was Roman; the present keep was built in the late 12th century, and the walls repaired and extended many times from the 11th to the 17th century. Open daily am and pm (Su pm only). 🅿

Brougham Castle, Brougham, Cumbria. 1 m S of Penrith on A66, turn E onto B6262. NY 5328 (OS 90). Stone castle begun in the reign of Henry II, controlling the crossing over the River Lowther. It was expanded over the centuries and converted in the late 17th century by Lady Anne Clifford. Open daily am and pm (March to Oct Su pm only). ⊖ 🅿

Broughton Hall, near Skipton, North Yorkshire (tel Skipton [0756] 2267). 3½ m W of Skipton on A59. SD 9450 (OS 103). Georgian house built in the Classical style 1750-1810 for the Tempest family. There are many interesting family portraits, and a private chapel. The conservatory dates from 1855, as does the Italian garden. Open June M-F pm, and Spring and Summer Bank Hols am and pm; other times by appt. ⊖ 🅿 WC ♣

Browsholme Hall, near Clitheroe, Lancashire (tel Stonyhurst [025 486] 330). 5 m NW of Clitheroe off B6243. SD 6844 (OS 103). 16th-century house, with early and late 18th-century additions. It has been the home of the Parker family ever since it was built, and contains a wide-ranging collection of antiquities, furniture and portraits. The grounds were landscaped in the early 19th century. Open Easter Week, Spring Bank Hol S-M; June and July S pm; Aug daily pm; parties at other times by appt. 🅿 WC ♿ 🚻 (by appt) ♣ 🌲

Callaly Castle, Whittingham, Northumberland (tel Whittingham [066 574] 663). 12 m SW of Alnwick on B6341, turn NW. NU 0509 (OS 81). Mansion incorporating an earlier pele tower. The south front dates from the 1670s, the rest of the house from the first half of the 18th century. The castle was the home of the Catholic Clavering family from 1271 to 1877. The drawing room, dated 1757, was probably the work of James Paine. Open May to mid-June and July to mid Sept S, Su and Bank Hols pm. 🅿

Cannon Hall, Cawthorne, South Yorkshire (tel Barnsley [0226] 790270). 6 m W of Barnsley on A635, turn NW. SE 2708 (OS 111). Modest house, mainly built in the 1760s by John Carr of York, with a Jacobean-style ballroom of the 1890s. It is now a museum, housing 18th-century furniture, glassware, paintings of the Dutch Old Masters, and the regimental museum of the history of the 13th/18th Royal Hussars. There is a large park. Open daily am and pm (Su pm only). ⊖ 🅿 WC ♿ 🚻 ♣ ★

Brantwood, Cumbria

Carlisle Castle, Carlisle, Cumbria. In N outskirts of Carlisle. NY 3956 (OS 85). Castle first built by William Rufus in the late 11th century, and rebuilt in the mid-12th century, with a 14th-century gatehouse. It was converted into a barracks in the 19th century now houses a museum of the Border Regiment. Open daily am and pm (Su pm only). ⊖ ▯ WC ⅍

Castletown House, Rockcliffe, Carlisle, Cumbria (tel Rockcliffe [0228 74] 205). 5 m NW of Carlisle on W side of A74. NY 3562 (OS 85). Georgian country house in attractive grounds. There is a display of naval paintings. Open Apr to Sept W and Bank Hol M 2-5; other times by appt. ⊖ ⅍

Chingle Hall, Goosnargh, near Preston, Lancashire (tel Goosnargh [077 476] 216). 5 m N of Preston on A6, turn E onto B5269. SD 5535 (OS 102). Medieval manor house with 13th-century door. It is claimed to be the most haunted house in Britain. Open T-Th, S-Su and Bank Hols pm. ⊖ WC ⅍

Corby Castle, Great Corby, Cumbria (Wetheral [0228] 60246). 4 m E of Carlisle off B6263. NY 4785 (OS 86). Ancient pele tower incorporated into a 17th-century house, again modified in the 1810s by Peter Nicholson. Grounds open Apr to Sept daily pm. ▯

Cragside House and Country Park, Rothbury, Northumberland (Rothbury [0669] 20333). 1 m E of Rothbury on B6341, turn N. NU 0702 (OS 81). House built by Richard Norman Shaw for Lord Armstrong in the late 19th century; the first house to be lit by water-generated electricity. It contains Arts and Crafts furniture, and is set in a 900-acre country park. Open Apr to Sept daily am and pm; Oct W, S and Su pm only (house closed am and all day M). ▯ WC ⅍ D ♣ ♥

Cusworth Hall, Doncaster, South Yorkshire (tel Doncaster [0302] 782342). 2 m NW of town centre on A638, turn SW. SE 5403 (OS 111). Mid 18th-century house built for the Wrightson family, with wings added by James Paine. There are fine plaster ceilings and chimneypieces, and the house is used as a museum of South Yorkshire life. There is a large park with many facilities. Open M-Th, S am and pm; Su pm only. ⊖ ▯ WC ⅍ ☐ ✿

Dalemain, near Penrith, Cumbria (tel Pooley Bridge [085 36] 450). 1 m W of Penrith on A66, turn SW onto A592. NY 4726 (OS 90). Georgian manor house built on the site of an older manor house. The drawing room has hand-painted Chinese wallpaper, and Chinese Chippendale furniture. The fireplace in the drawing room is by Grinling Gibbons. The Norman tower of the old house contans a museum of the local regiment. Open Easter Su to mid-Oct daily exc F and S pm. ⊖ ▯ WC ⅍ ☐ D (on leads) ♣ ♥ ★

Dove Cottage, Grasmere, Cumbria (tel Grasmere [096 65] 464). ½ m SE of Grasmere village on A591, turn SE. NY 3407 (OS 90). The home of William Wordsworth from 1799 to 1808, after which it was the home of Thomas de Quincy until 1835. It has been preserved as a Wordsworth memorial since 1890. The house reconstructs the life of the late 18th century and contains a collection of manuscripts. Open March to Oct daily (exc Su) am and pm. ⊖ WC ♣

Dunstanburgh Castle, Embleton, near Craster, Northumberland. On coast, 12 m N of Alnwick. NU 2522 (OS 75). Ruined castle on the coast (originally protected by an inlet of the sea) with a huge gatehouse of the early 14th century. The plan, which covers 11 acres, was modified by John of Gaunt in the 1370s and 1380s. During the Wars of the Roses the castle was besieged and suffered heavy damage. Open daily am and pm (Oct to Apr Su pm only). WC D

East Riddlesden Hall, near Keighley, West Yorkshire (tel Keighley [0535] 607075). 2 m NE of Keighley on A650. SE 0742 (OS 104). 17th-century manor house, with a fine banqueting hall, plasterwork, panelling and a Restoration-period staircase. The grounds contain a timber-framed tithe barn, considered one of the best in the country, with a collection of farm implements. Open July and Aug W-Su and Bank Hols am and pm; Sept and Oct pm only. ⊖ ▯ WC ⅍ ☐ ♣

Ebberston Hall, Scarborough, North Yorkshire (tel Scarborough [0723] 85516). 14 m SW of Scarborough on A170. SE 8983 (OS 101). Palladian villa designed by Colen Campbell in 1718 as a pavilion for a large garden that mostly no longer survives. The interior contains some bold wood-carving. Open Easter to Sept daily am and pm. ⊖ ▯ WC ♣

Fletcher Moss, Wilmslow Rd, Didsbury, Greater Manchester (tel 061-236 9422). 5 m S of city centre on A5145. SJ 8491 (OS 109). Small parsonage built in the early 19th century, now preserved as a local heritage centre, with works of art by artists of the north west. The house is set in an attractive small garden. Open Apr and May W-Su am and pm. ⊖ WC ♣ ★

Foxdenton House, Foxdenton Park, Chadderton, Greater Manchester (tel Royton [061-620] 3505). 5 m NE of city centre on B6189. SD 9005. (OS 109) Small mansion of red brick built between 1710 and 1730. The house was restored in the 1960s. Open T, Su and Bank Hols pm. ⊖ ▯ ★

Gawthorpe Hall, Padiham, near Burnley, Lancashire (tel Padiham [0282] 78511. 2 m W of Burnley on A6061, turn N to E outskirts of Padiham. SD 8034 (OS 103). Fine early 17th-century manor house restored in the 1850s by Sir Charles Barry. It was built around a pele tower, is unusual in having the great hall at the back of the building, and has a minstrel gallery. The house contains the Kay-Shuttleworth collection of textiles and embroidery, mainly of the 19th and early 20th centuries. There is also a collection of early European furniture. Open March to Oct W, S, Su and Bank Hols pm; also T in July and Aug. ⊖ ▯ WC ☐ (by appt) ♣ ♥

George Stephenson's Birthplace, Wylam-on-Tyne, Northumberland (tel Wylam [06614] 3457). 8 m W of Newcastle on A69 turn S at Wylam. NZ 6350 (OS 88). A small stone-built cottage, built in the mid-18th century and furnished in late 19th-century style. The inventor was born there in 1781. Open Apr to end Oct W, Th, S and Su pm; other times by appt. ⊖ ▯ (500 yds)

Gilling Castle, Gilling East, near Helmsley, North Yorkshire (tel Ampleforth [043 93] 238). 18 m N of York. SE 6176 (OS 100). Norman keep incorporated into 16th-century tower house built for Sir William Fairfax, and again modified in the early 18th century. There is a Tudor great chamber, with notable stained glass. Open M-F am and pm. ▯ ♣ ★

Hall i' th' Wood, Crompton Way, Bolton, Greater Manchester (tel Bolton [0204] 51159. 2 m NE of town centre on A58. SD 7211 (OS 109). Black-and-white timber-framed house from the 1480s, with additions in 1591 and 1648. It was the home of Samuel Crompton, inventor of the cotton spinning machine in 1779. The house was restored in the early 20th century by Lord Leverhulme as a

17th-century home. Open M-W, F-S am and pm, also Apr to Sept Su pm. ⊖ ▯ WC ☐

Helmsley Castle, Helmsley, North Yorkshire. In town centre, 20 m N of York. SE 6183 (OS 100). 12th-century castle with ruined great tower and large earthworks, perhaps the relics of an earlier fortification. A square west tower survives and was remodelled in the Tudor period. The castle suffered badly in the Civil War. Open daily am and pm (Su pm only, Oct to March). ⊖ ▯

Hill Top, Near Sawrey, Hawkshead, Cumbria (tel Hawkshead [096 66] 269). 3 m S of Hawkshead on B5285, in village of Near Sawrey. SD 3795 (OS 97). 17th-century farmhouse, the home of children's author and illustrator Beatrix Potter until 1913, and retained unaltered since that date. A collection of her illustrations is on display. Open Apr to Oct daily (exc F), am and pm (Su pm only). ▯ ☐

Howick Hall, Howick, Northumberland (tel Longhoughton [066 577] 285). 4 m NE of Alnwick, on B1340; turn onto B1399 for 1 m then turn E. NU 2517 (OS 81). Late 18th-century house with fine grounds laid out by Earl Grey, including many shrubs and rhododendron gardens. Open Apr to Sept daily am and pm. ⊖ ▯

Hutton-in-the-Forest, Penrith, Cumbria (tel Skelton [085 34] 207). 3 m N of Penrith on A6 turn W onto B5305 for 5 m. NY 4635 (OS 90). 14th-century pele tower with many later additions; the house was greatly rebuilt in the early 17th century. The interior was remodelled by Anthony Salvin in the 19th century. The gardens date from the 17th century. House open late May to mid-Sept Th, F, Su and Bank Hol M pm; parties at other times by appt; grounds open daily am and pm. ▯ WC ☐ ♣ ♥

Kendal Castle, Kendal, Cumbria. In town centre on River Kent. SD 5292. Ruins of 12th-century castle, comprising a great tower, curtain walls with round corner towers, and a gatehouse with a bridge over the moat. It was the birthplace of Henry VIII's wife Katherine Parr. Open daily am and pm. ⊖ ▯ D ♣ ★

Kiplin Hall, near Richmond, North Yorkshire (tel Richmond [0748] 818178). 7 m E of Richmond on B6271. SE 2797 (OS 99). Small house with lively skyline, built for the 1st Lord Baltimore in 1625. The interior was redesigned in the early 18th century, when a new staircase was installed. Open May to Sept W and Su pm. ▯ WC ⅍ ♥

Knaresborough Castle, Knaresborough, North Yorkshire (tel Harrogate [0423] 504684). On W outskirts of Knaresborough. SE 3456 (OS 104). 14th-century royal castle built by Edward II and III on a high rock overlooking the River Nidd, to replace an earlier Norman enclosure. Parts of the keep and the gatehouse remain. The old court-house museum is in the castle grounds. Open Easter, Spring Bank Hol to Sept daily am and pm. ⊖ ▯ ☐ (by appt)

Dalemain, Cumbria

Lairgate Hall, Lairgate, Beverley, Humberside (tel Hull [0482] 882255). In town centre. TA 0339 (OS 107). Large house built for the Perryman family in about 1700, now used as council offices. The upstairs room that is now used as the council chamber contains fine 18th-century plasterwork and wallpaper. Open M-F am and pm. ⊖ 🅿 ♿ ★

Lancaster Castle, Lancaster, Lancashire (tel Lancaster [0524] 64998). In town centre. SD 4762 (OS 97). 12th-century castle on a hill above the River Lune, the site of an earlier Roman fort. There is a fine gatehouse, with twin-octagonal towers, machicolations and turrets, which was built by Henry IV after 1399. The castle was converted into the County Court and prison in about 1800 and the neo-Gothic shire hall houses a display of the coats-of-arms of the monarchs, constables and high sheriffs since 1129. The hall and court contain a collection of ancient instruments of extracting justice and of prison life. Open Easter, late May to late Sept daily am and pm (only some parts open when court is in session). ⊖ WC

Lotherton Hall, Aberford, West Yorkshire (tel Aberford [0532] 813259). 10 m E of Leeds, on B1217. SE 4436 (OS 105). Edwardian house created in Neo-Classical style around an 18th-century building. It is now a museum, containing a collection of 18th-century paintings, Chinese ceramics and 19th- and 20th-century furniture, including modern works. There is also a costume gallery, and a collection of silver race cups. The gardens are attractive. Open T-Su and Bank Hol M, am and pm. ⊖ 🅿 WC ♿ ♠ ☞

Maister House, High St, Hull, Humberside (tel Hull [0482] 24114). In city centre. TL 1028 (OS 107). Merchant's house built in 1744 in the Palladian manner; its staircase hall is distinctive, decorated by Joseph Page with ironwork by Robert Bakewell. Open M-F am and pm (closed Bank Hols). ⊖

Manor House, Castle Yard, Ilkley, West Yorkshire (tel Ilkley [0943] 600066). In town centre. SE 1147 (OS 104). Elizabethan manor house built on the site of a Roman fort, with some of the Roman foundations visible. There is a display of Roman materials, and a programme of exhibitions by local artists and craftsmen. Open T-Su and Bank Hol M am and pm. Closed Christmas and New Year. ⊖ 🅿 ♿ ★

Markenfield Hall, Ripon, North Yorkshire. 4 m S of Ripon off A61, turn W. SE 2967 (OS 99). Medieval moated manor house, with a great hall of the early 14th century; the house was abandoned in the 1560s, but restored in the 19th century and now empty again. Open Apr to Oct M am and pm. ⊖ 🅿

Meldon Park, Morpeth, Northumberland (tel Hartburn [067 072] 661). 7 m W of Morpeth on B6343. NZ 1085 (OS 81). Neo-Classical house built in 1832 by John Dobson for the Cookson family. The rooms have spacious views over the countryside, and the 10-acre wooded grounds are famous for their rhododendrons. Open June daily and Aug Bank Hol pm. 🅿 ♿ ♠ ☞ 🍴

Middleham Castle, Middleham, near Leyburn, North Yorkshire. In town centre, 24 m NW of Ripon on A6108. SE 1287 (OS 99). Ruins of one of the largest keeps built in Britain, dating from about 1170 and containing the main castle living quarters. Curtain walls and the gatehouse were added in the 13th century, as was the moat. The castle passed to the Neville family in the 15th century, and was slighted in the Civil War; it is now a ruin. Open daily am and pm. ⊖ 🅿

Newton Hall, Dukinfield Rd, Hyde, Greater Manchester (tel 061-308 2721). 7 m W of city centre, 1½ m N of Hyde on B6170. SJ 9596 (OS 109). 14th-century timber-framed manor house, comprising a single large hall. It has been thoroughly restored, and is set in large open grounds. Open M-F am and pm. ⊖ 🅿 ♿ ♠ ★

Norman Manor House, Burton Agnes, Humberside (tel Burton Agnes [026 289] 324). 6 m SW of Bridlington, on A166. TA 1064 (OS 101). Manor house dating from the Norman period, with original architectural features within its 18th-century façade. Open daily am and pm. ⊖ 🅿 ★

Nunnington Hall, North Yorkshire

Norton Conyers, Ripon, North Yorkshire (tel Melmerby [076 584] 333). 1½ m N of Ripon on A61, turn N. SE 3176 (OS 99). Attractive house of the early 16th century with an 18th-century façade. It has been the home of the Graham family since 1624. The James II bedroom contains notable 17th-century furniture. There is a walled garden, specialising in 18th-century and unusual hardy plants. Open June to Sept Su; also Bank Hol Su and M; and last week in July daily. ⊖ 🅿 WC ♿ ⏚ (by appt) 🎨 ☞

Nostell Priory, Wakefield, West Yorkshire (tel Wakefield [0924] 863892). 8 m SE of Wakefield on A638, turn N. SE 4017 (OS 111). Palladian house built on the site of an old abbey by the young James Paine in the 1730s, and extended by Robert Adam in 1766. The state rooms are all by Adam and include fine plasterwork, and furniture made especially for the house by Thomas Chippendale. There is a large park, with fine trees, a museum of vintage and veteran motor cycles, and an aviation museum. Open July and Aug daily exc F pm; Apr to June, Sept and Oct Th, S and Su pm. ⊖ 🅿 WC ♿ ⏚ ♠ ☞

Nunnington Hall, near Helmsley, North Yorkshire (tel Nunnington [043 95] 283). 14 m SE of Helmsley on B1257, turn E. SE 6779 (OS 100). Large manor house of the 17th century and earlier, rebuilt by Lord Preston after 1688. There is much woodwork of this date, and a fine chimneypiece in the panelled hall. A collection of miniature rooms, fully furnished in the style of various periods, can be found in the attic. Open Apr to end Oct T-Th, S and Su pm; also Bank Hol M am and pm. ⊖ 🅿 WC ⏚ (by appt) ☞ 🍴

Oakwell Hall, Birstall, West Yorkshire (tel Batley [0924] 474926). 6 m SW of Leeds, off A652. SE 2226 (OS 104). Moated manor house dated 1583. The house retains its 17th-century decoration and oak furniture. The house features in Charlotte Brontë's novel *Shirley*. Open daily am and pm (Su pm only). ⊖ 🅿 ♿

Old Rectory, Epworth, Humberside (tel Epworth [0427] 872268). 13 m SW of Scunthorpe. SE 7804 (OS 112). Birthplace and early home of John and Charles Wesley; restored in 1957, with objects associated with Wesley and the Methodist movement. Open March to Oct daily am and pm (Su pm only). 🅿 ★

Ordsall Hall, Taylorson St, Salford, Greater Manchester (Tel 061-872 0251). 2 m SW of Manchester city centre on A57. SJ 8197 (OS 109). Fine timber-framed house of 16th and 17th centuries, with intact great hall, and fully-equipped Victorian kitchen. On the upper floor is a display of local social history and artefacts. Open M-F, am and pm, Su pm only (closed Christmas, New Year's Day, Good Fri). ⊖ 🅿 WC ♿ ★

Ormesby Hall, near Middlesbrough, Cleveland (tel Middlesbrough [0642] 324188). 3 m SE of Middlesbrough on A171, turn NE onto B1380. NZ 5216 (OS 93). Mid-18th century house showing the typical lifestyle of the country gentry. The house includes a 17th-century wing; the main house includes fine plasterwork, and a display of 18th-century costume. The 18th-century stable-block is notable. Open W, S, Su and Bank Hols pm, Apr to Oct. ⊖ WC ♿ ⏚ (by appt) ♠

Osgodby Hall, near Thirsk, North Yorkshire (tel Thirsk [0845] 597534). 4 m E of Thirsk on A170, turn S. SE 4981 (OS 92). Small and elegant Jacobean house, with a broad 17th-century staircase. The fine forecourt remains as it was built in 1640. Open Easter to Sept S, Su and Bank Hols pm. 🅿 ⏚ (by appt) ♠ ☞ (by appt)

Platt Hall, Platt Fields, Rusholme, Greater Manchester (tel 061-224 5217). 3 m SE of city centre off A6010. SJ 8594 (OS 109). Mid 18th-century house built by Timothy Lightoler of red brick. The interior contains a large and important gallery of English costume, with clothing items, accessories and related books from the 17th century to the present day. Open Apr to Sept daily am and pm (Su pm only). ⊖ 🅿 WC ♿ ★

Pontefract Castle, Pontefract, West Yorkshire. In town centre. SE 4622 (OS 105). Ruins of a Norman motte-and-bailey castle mostly rebuilt in the 14th century. It was the major royal castle in the north, and the place of the death of Richard II. The castle was demolished in 1649. Open daily am and pm; Su pm only. ⊖ 🅿

Preston Tower, Chathill, Northumberland. 7 m N of Alnwick on A1, turn E. NU 1825 (OS 75). Fortified pele tower, one of the few that remains intact from the 15th century. It is furnished in original style, and contains a display of local history. Open Apr to Sept daily am and pm. ⊖ 🅿

Prudhoe Castle, Prudhoe, Northumberland. 10 m W of Newcastle upon Tyne, on A695, turn N. NZ 0963 (OS 88). Castle above River Tyne begun in the Norman period as a motte-and-bailey, and receiving a stone tower in 1175. The castle was extended in the 13th and 14th centuries, with a fine gateway and barbican, and possibly the earliest oriel window in England. A Classical house was built into the castle, and only the pele yard can be visited. Open daily am and pm (Su pm only). ⊖

Red House, Gomersal, West Yorkshire (tel Cleckheaton [0274] 872165). 7 m SE of Bradford on A651. SE 2026 (OS 104). Red-brick house of the Restoration period, often visited by Charlotte Bronte who described it in *Shirley*. It is furnished in the style of that period. Open daily am and pm (Su pm only). ⊖ 🅿 WC ♿ ★

Ripley Castle, Ripley, North Yorkshire (tel Harrogate [0423] 770152). 3½ m N of Harrogate, on A61. SE 2860 (OS 99). The home of the Ingilby family for 600 years, the castle is now an 18th-century mansion built around a 15th-century tower. The original gatehouse of the 1410s survives. The gardens are 18th-century and the model cottages of the village were created in the 1820s. The house contains an exhibition of Civil War armour and weapons, and other curiosities. Open June to Sept T-Th, S and Su pm; Easter to end May S and Su pm; Bank Hols am and pm. ⊖ 🅿 WC 🅿 🖪 (by appt) ♣ 🖝

Rufford Old Hall, Rumford, near Ormskirk, Lancashire (tel Rufford [0704] 821254). 9 m NE of Ormskirk on A59. SD 4616 (OS 108). Elizabethan half-timbered house with later wings. There is an exceptional 15th-century great hall with carved timber roof and a unique movable screen. The house also contains collections of Tudor arms and armour, 17th-century furniture and the Rufford village museum of social history. Open Apr to end Oct daily (exc F) pm. ⊖ 🅿 WC 🅿 (by appt) 🈁 🖝

Rusland Hall, near Newby Bridge, Cumbria (tel Satterthwaite [022 984] 276). 5 miles NW of Newby Bridge. SD 3488 (OS 97). 18th- and 19th-century house, containing a collection of early photographic equipment and mechanical musical instruments, many in working order. Open Apr to Sept daily (exc S) am and pm. 🅿 ♣

Rydal Mount, Ambleside, Cumbria (tel Ambleside [096 63] 3002). 3 m N of Ambleside on A591, turn N. NY 3606 (OS 90). The home of William Wordsworth from 1813 to 1850, containing a collection of books and personal effects. The garden was laid out by Wordsworth himself and is particularly attractive. Open daily am and pm. ⊖ WC 🖪 ♣

Samlesbury Hall, Samlesbury, near Preston, Lancashire (tel Mellor [025 481] 2010). 6 m E of Preston on A677. SD 6230 (OS 102). 14th-century black-and-white timber-framed manor house, partly rebuilt in the 19th century. The hall has an elaborate timber screen of 1532. The house contains exhibitions run by the Council of the Preservation of Rural England, often with antiques for sale. Open T-Su all year, am and pm. ⊖ 🅿 WC 🖪 🅿 (by appt) ♣ 🖝 🎋

Sandal Castle, near Wakefield, West Yorkshire. 2 m S of Wakefield on A61, turn N. SE 3318 (OS 111). Recently excavated castle, dating originally from the 12th century with stonework added in the 13th century. It comprised a great tower with barbican within an enclosure in which were also a great hall and pantries, etc. These buildings date from the late 14th century. The castle was decayed by Elizabeth's reign, and slighted in the Civil War. Open daily am and pm (Su pm only). ⊖ 🅿

Scarborough Castle, Scarborough, North Yorkshire. To the E of town centre. TA 0589 (OS 101). Castle begun in the 1130s and rebuilt by Henry II in the 1150s, from which date are the ruins of the great tower. There is a mid 13th-century barbican. The castle saw action in the reign of Henry VIII, and the Civil War, and was damaged again in the First World War. Open daily am and pm (Su pm only). ⊖ 🅿

Seaton Delaval, Northumberland (tel Seaton Delaval [0632] 481759). 12 m NE of Newcastle on A190. NZ 3276 (OS 88). Villa built in the 1720s by Vanbrugh for Admiral Delaval near the coast, in a dramatic style combining Classical and Elizabethan features. Much of the house was ruined by fire in the 19th century, but part has been restored and houses a collection of paintings. There are fine stables in one wing. Open May to end Sept W and Su pm. ⊖ 🅿 WC ♣

Sewerby Hall, Bridlington, Humberside (tel Bridlington [0262] 7855). 2 m NE of Bridlington on B1255, turn S for ½ m. TA 2068 (OS 101). Manor house rebuilt in about 1715 and adapted in the early 19th century. The interior contains old furniture, an art gallery and a collection of Amy Johnson relics. The gardens are of great botanical interest, with an Old English walled garden. There is also a miniature zoo and aviary. House open Easter to Sept daily am and pm (S pm only);

park daily am and pm. ⊖ 🅿 WC 🖪 🅿 (by appt) ♣ 🖝

Shandy Hall, Coxwold, North Yorkshire (tel Coxwold [034 76] 465). 4 m SE of Thirsk. SE 5377 (OS 100). Small medieval hall that was the home of Laurence Sterne from 1760 to 1767, the place where he wrote *Tristram Shandy* and *A Sentimental Journey*. It is not kept as a museum to Sterne, but as a 'lived-in house full of relevant books, pictures, memorabilia – and surprises!'. There is an attractive walled garden. Open June to Sept W and Su pm. ⊖ 🅿 WC 🖪 ♣

Shibden Hall, Halifax, West Yorkshire (tel Halifax [0422] 52246). 1 m E of town centre, on A58. SE 1025 (OS 104). An early 15th-century timber-framed house with later additions. The interior contains period rooms of the 16th-18th centuries. The 17th-century barn and outbuildings contain the West Yorkshire Folk Museum, with a collection of old agricultural implements and craft workshops. Open March to Nov daily am and pm (Su pm only). ⊖ 🅿 WC 🅿 ♣ 🖝

Sizergh Castle, near Kendal, Cumbria (tel Sizergh [0448] 60285). 3½ m S of Kendal on A6, turn W. SD 4987 (OS 97). Home of the Strickland family since 1239, and built around a good example of a 14th-century pele tower. The great hall dates from about 1450, and the two wings from the 16th century. The interior contains excellent examples of Elizabethan woodwork, panelling and chimney-pieces, and a notable collection of paintings. The grounds include a fine rock garden laid out in the 1920s. Open Apr to Sept W, Th, Su and Bank Hols pm; garden only Oct W and Th pm. ⊖ WC ♣

Smithills Hall, Smithills Dean Road, Bolton, Greater Manchester (tel Bolton [0204] 41265). 2½ m NW of Bolton centre on A58, turn N. SD 6911 (OS 109). One of Lancashire's oldest manor houses, dating in part from the 14th century, though added to over the years. The great hall is 15th-century, with a fine exposed timber roof. The extensive grounds include a nature trail and associated museum. Open daily am and pm (exc Th, Su am, and Christmas, New Year and Good Fri). ⊖ 🅿 WC 🖪 🅿 ♣

Stockeld Park, Wetherby, North Yorkshire (tel Wetherby [0937] 66101). 8 m SE of Harrogate on A661, turn SW. SE 3849 (OS 104). Small country mansion, a notable example of the work of James Paine and built between 1758 and 1763. The central hall and staircase are impressive. Open mid-July to mid-Aug daily (exc M) pm. ⊖ 🅿 ♣ 🖝

Sutton Park, Sutton-on-the-Forest, North Yorkshire (tel Easingwold [0347] 810249). 12 m N of York on B1363. SE 5864 (OS 100). Early Georgian house of about 1730, built in the Palladian style. There is interesting 18th-century plasterwork, furniture from both England and France, and a collection of porcelain. Open May to end Sept T-Th, Su and Bank Hols pm; also Su in Apr and Easter weekend. ⊖ 🅿 WC 🖪 ♣ 🖝

Swarthmoor Hall, near Ulverston, Cumbria (tel Ulverston [0229] 53204). 1 m SW of Ulverston on A590, turn E. SD 2877 (OS 96). Early 17th-century hall built by George Fell and with early associations with the Quakers. The interior contains 17th-century furniture and relics of the early history of the Society of Friends. George Fox, who married Fell's widow Margaret, built the Meeting House here in 1668. Open March to Oct M, T, W, S am and pm; other times by appt. 🅿 WC ♣ ★

Townend, Troutbeck, Cumbria (tel Ambleside [096 63] 2628). 3 m SE of Ambleside, in Troutbeck village. NY 4002 (OS 90). Small farmhouse built by George Browne in 1626, occupied by his family until 1944 and typical of Lakeland houses. The interior contains a rich and diverse collection of woodwork carved by the Browne family over the centuries. The dairy houses old farm equipment. Open Apr to Oct daily (exc M and S) pm. ⊖ WC 🅿 (by appt)

Treasurer's House, Chapter House St, York, North Yorkshire (tel York [0904] 24247). In city centre, to N of Minster. SE 6052 (OS 105). Large house of the 1630s, built for the treasurer of the Minster. It was restored in 1900, but the interior retains many 18th-century features. The house

contains period furniture, paintings and a display of its historical associations. There is a small formal garden. Open Apr to Oct daily am and pm. ⊖ WC 🅿 ♣

Turton Tower, Turton, Lancashire (tel Bolton [0204] 852203). 5 m N of Bolton on B639. SD 7315 (OS 102). 15th-century pele tower with an Elizabethan farmhouse attached. There is a display of armour and local history. The house stands in 8 acres of grounds. House open S-W pm; gardens open daily throughout year. ⊖ 🅿 WC ♣ 🅿

Tynemouth Castle, near Newcastle upon Tyne, Tyne & Wear. NZ 3769 (OS 88). 13th- and 14th-century castle forming a unified complex with Tynemouth Priory. It stands on a headland at the mouth of the river, and has a late 14th-century gatehouse and barbican, and a curtain wall enclosing the priory. Open daily am and pm (Oct to March Su pm only). ⊖ 🅿

Wakefield Castle, Wakefield, West Yorkshire. In town centre. SE 3219 (OS 105). Mid 12th-century motte-and-bailey castle, which never was given stone walls or tower. The castle now stands in a public park. Open daily am and pm. ⊖ 🅿

Wallington House, Cambo, Northumberland (tel Scots Gap [067 074] 283). 15 m W of Morpeth on B6343, turn S onto B6342. NZ 0384 (OS 81). House built in 1688, in Classical style, modified in the mid-18th century with fine wood- and plaster-work. A central hall, added in the 19th century, was decorated by William Bell Scott and John Ruskin. There is a display of Victorian dolls' houses, and of old coaches. The grounds were laid out by Capability Brown, and include a walled terraced garden, woodlands and lakes. House open Apr to Sept daily (exc T) pm; Oct W, S, Su pm. Grounds open daily am and pm. ⊖ 🅿 WC 🖪 🅿 (by appt) D (park only) ♣ 🖝

Washington Old Hall, Washington, Tyne & Wear (tel Washington [0632] 466879). 5 m W of Sunderland on A182. NZ 3156 (OS 88). Jacobean manor house, with parts dating back to the 12th century. It was the home of the Washington family, of which George Washington was a member. The house has been restored since the 1930s and furnished in 17th-century style. Open March to end Oct daily (exc W pm; Nov to end Feb S and Su pm. ⊖ 🅿 WC 🖪 🅿 (by appt) ♣ 🖝

Whalley Abbey, near Blackburn, Lancashire (tel Whalley [0254 82] 2268). 8 m N of Accrington on A680, turn W onto B6246, for ½ m then S. SD 7235 (OS 103).Ruined Cistercian abbey built in the early 14th century; little of the church remains, but some of the monastic buildings survive including the 14th-century gatehouse, and among them is a 16th-century manor house now used as a retreat and conference centre. The grounds stretch down to the River Ribble. Open daily am and pm. 🅿 🖪 🅿 (by appt) ♣ 🖝 (for parties only) 🅿

Wilberforce House, High St, Hull, Humberside (tel Hull [0482] 223111 ext 2737). In city centre. TL 0928 (OS 107). 17th-century town mansion, the birthplace of William Wilberforce in 1759. It contains a local history museum, and a display connected with the slave trade and Wilberforce's campaign for Emancipation. Open M-S am and pm, Su pm only. ⊖ 🅿 WC 🖪 ♣ 🅿 ★

Wordsworth House, High Street, Cockermouth, Cumbria (tel Cockermouth [0900] 824805). In town centre. NY 1230 (OS 89). Mid-Georgian house where William Wordsworth was born in 1770. The house contains 18th-century furniture, and objects connected with the poet. The garden leads down to the River Derwent. Open Apr to Oct daily (exc Th and Good Friday) am and pm. ⊖ WC ♣ 🖝

Wythenshawe Hall, Northenden, Greater Manchester (tel 061-236 9422). 7 m S of city centre on A560, turn N onto B5167. SJ 8189 (OS 109). Timber-framed manor house with Georgian additions, the home of the Tatton family for many centuries. It houses a wide-ranging collection of *objets d'art*, including paintings, arms and armour, ceramics, ivories and Japanese prints. The house stands in an attractive park. Open Aug and Sept W-Su am and pm. ⊖ 🅿 ♣ 🖝 ★

Caerlaverock Castle, Dumfries and Galloway

Scotland

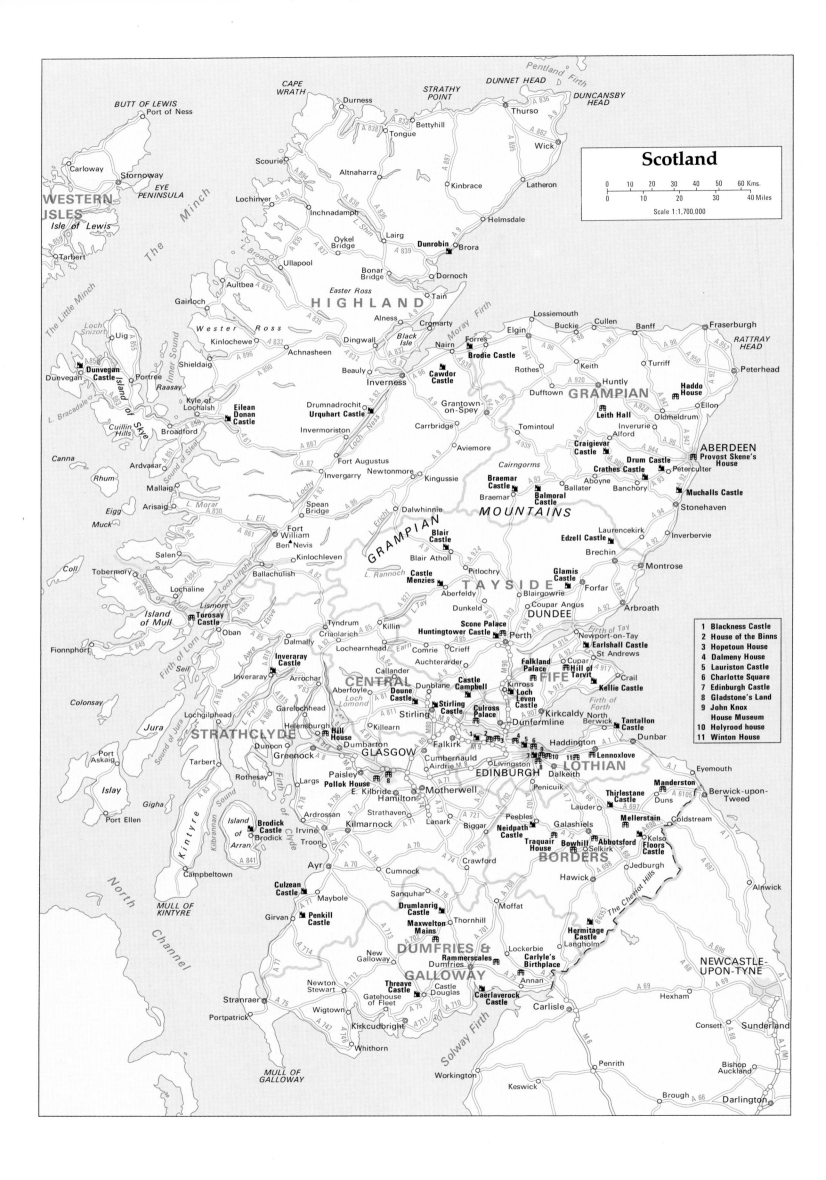

Scotland

	0	10	20	30	40	50	60 Kms.
0		10		20		30	40 Miles

Scale 1:1,700,000

Pentland Firth

CAPE WRATH
STRATHY POINT
DUNNET HEAD
DUNCANSBY HEAD

BUTT OF LEWIS
Port of Ness

Durness
Bettyhill
Tongue
Thurso
Wick

Carloway
Stornoway
EYE PENINSULA

WESTERN ISLES
Isle of Lewis

Scourie
Altnaharra
Kinbrace
Latheron

The Minch

Lochinver
Inchnadamph
Lairg
Helmsdale

Tarbert

L. Shin
Oykel Bridge

Dunrobin
Brora

Ullapool
Bonar Bridge
Dornoch

Aultbea
Easter Ross
Tain

The Little Minch

Gairloch
L. Broom
Alness
Cromarty
Moray Firth

Loch Snizort
Uig
Kinlochewe
Wester Ross
Dingwall
Black Isle
Nairn
Forres
Lossiemouth
Buckie
Cullen
Banff
Fraserburgh

HIGHLAND

Dunvegan
Dunvegan Castle
Portree
Achnasheen
Beauly
Inverness
Brodie Castle
Elgin
Keith
Turriff
RATTRAY HEAD
Peterhead

Island of Raasay

Shieldaig
Cawdor Castle
Rothes
Dufftown
Huntly
GRAMPIAN
Haddo House

Kyle of Lochalsh
Eilean Donan Castle
Drumnadrochit
Urquhart Castle
Grantown-on-Spey
Ellon

Cuillin Hills
Broadford
Loch Ness
Leith Hall
Inverurie
Alford
Oldmeldrum

Canna
Ardvasar
Island of Skye
Sound of Sleat
Invermoriston
Carrbridge
Tomintoul
Craigievar Castle
ABERDEEN
Provost Skene's House

Rhum
Mallaig
L. Morar
Fort Augustus
Aviemore
Drum Castle
Peterculter

Eigg
Arisaig
A 830
L. Eil
Invergarry
Newtonmore
Kingussie
Cairngorms
Crathes Castle
Aboyne
Banchory
Muchalls Castle

Muck
Fort William
Ben Nevis
Spean Bridge
Braemar Castle
Balmoral Castle
Ballater
Stonehaven

Coll
Tobermory
Salen
Kinlochleven
Dalwhinnie
GRAMPIAN
MOUNTAINS
Laurencekirk
Inverbervie

Lochaline
Ballachulish
L. Rannoch
Blair Castle
Blair Atholl
Edzell Castle
Brechin
Montrose

Island of Mull
Lismore
Torosay Castle
Castle Menzies
Pitlochry
Glamis Castle
Forfar

Fionnphort
Oban
Loch Linnhe
Aberfeldy
Blairgowrie
TAYSIDE
Arbroath

Colonsay
Dalmally
Tyndrum
Killin
Dunkeld
Coupar Angus
DUNDEE

Crianlarich
L. Tay
Scone Palace
Huntingtower Castle
Perth
Firth of Tay
Newport-on-Tay
Earlshall Castle
St Andrews

Lochearnhead
L. Earn
Comrie
Crieff
Auchterarder
FIFE
Cupar
Hill of Tarvit
Crail

INVERARAY
Inveraray Castle
CENTRAL
Callander
Aberfoyle
Loch Lomond
Doune Castle
Dunblane
Castle Campbell
Falkland Palace
Kinross
Loch Leven Castle
Kellie Castle

Jura
Lochgilphead
L. Fyne
Arrochar
Garelochhead
Stirling Castle
Culross Palace
Kirkcaldy
North Berwick
Tantallon Castle

Colonsay
Hill House
Helensburgh
Killearn
Stirling
Dunfermline
Dunbar

Port Askaig
Tarbert
Lochgoilhead
Dunoon
Greenock
Dumbarton
GLASGOW
Falkirk
Haddington
Lennoxlove
LOTHIAN

Islay
Rothesay
Largs
Paisley
Pollok House
Cumbernauld
Airdrie
Livingston
EDINBURGH
Dalkeith
Eyemouth

Port Ellen
Gigha
E. Kilbride
Motherwell
Hamilton
Penicuik
Manderston
Berwick-upon-Tweed

Kintyre
Kilmarnock
Strathaven
Lanark
Peebles
Thirlestane Castle
Lauder
Duns
Coldstream

Island of Arran
Brodick Castle
Brodick
Irvine
Troon
Biggar
Neidpath Castle
Galashiels
Mellerstain
Kelso
Floors Castle

MULL OF KINTYRE
Campbeltown
Ayr
Cumnock
Crawford
Traquair House
Bowhill
Abbotsford
Selkirk
Jedburgh
BORDERS

Culzean Castle
Maybole
Sanquhar
Moffat
Hawick
The Cheviot Hills
Alnwick

North Channel
Girvan
Penkill Castle
Drumlanrig Castle
Thornhill
Lockerbie
Langholm
Hermitage Castle
NEWCASTLE-UPON-TYNE

Maxwelton Mains
Moffat
Hexham

DUMFRIES & GALLOWAY
New Galloway
Rammerscales
Dumfries
Carlyle's Birthplace
Annan

GALLOWAY
Newton Stewart
Threave Castle
Castle Douglas
Caerlaverock Castle
Carlisle

Stranraer
Gatehouse of Fleet
Wigtown
Solway Firth
Penrith
Consett
Sunderland

Portpatrick
Kirkcudbright
Whithorn
Workington
Bishop Auckland

MULL OF GALLOWAY
Keswick
Brough
Darlington

1 Blackness Castle
2 House of the Binns
3 Hopetoun House
4 Dalmeny House
5 Lauriston Castle
6 Charlotte Square
7 Edinburgh Castle
8 Gladstone's Land
9 John Knox
   House Museum
10 Holyrood house
11 Winton House

Edinburgh Castle
Edinburgh,
Lothian Region

The castle perches on a rocky promontory nearly 300 feet above the streets of the modern city. The approach is along the ridge through the Old Town to the esplanade, an open space the width of a bow-shot, in front of the curtain wall, where no building was allowed. Across this the gatehouse and wall rise behind a deep moat. On the other sides the rock falls precipitously from the walls.

Today the castle recalls the turbulence of Scottish history from earliest times down to the last Jacobite rebellion, in 1745, when Bonnie Prince Charlie was refused admittance and, lacking the means to assault or blockade, retired to hold court a mile away at Holyrood. Since then the castle has played little part in affairs. Once a year it forms a magnificent backdrop for the Military Tattoo held on the esplanade.

Edwin (r. 616-33), King of Northumbria, built a wooden fortress on the rock early in the 7th century and gave the place its name – Edwin's burgh. The oldest building surviving, however, is the little Chapel of St Margaret erected on the summit at the end of the 11th century.

Above, Edinburgh Castle, on top of its volcanic crag, was for centuries the focal point of Scottish history.

St Margaret was an Anglo-Saxon princess who fled to Scotland at the Norman Conquest and became the second wife of King Malcolm III (r. 1058-93), son of the Duncan whose murder Shakespeare immortalised in *Macbeth*. A pious and strong-willed lady, her civilising influence reformed the Scottish Church and led to her canonisation in 1250. She was lying ill at the castle, besieged by an army of Highlanders who were trying to capture it in her husband's absence, when news came of his death at Alnwick. A few days later she herself died and her body was smuggled down the west cliff and carried across the Firth of Forth for burial at Dunfermline Abbey. At that time Dunfermline was the capital of the kingdom but during the reign of Margaret's son David (r. 1124-53) the capital was moved to Edinburgh.

After the Reformation in the 16th century, St Margaret's Chapel was desecrated and used as an ammunition store for more than three centuries. It was restored in this century. The vaulted apse and mouldings of the nave arch are typical Norman work. The fine windows of saints and of the Scottish hero William Wallace are modern, the work of the stained-glass artist Douglas Strachan.

Not far from the chapel, on the north side of the castle courtyard, the Scottish National War Memorial commemorates the hundred thousand men killed while serving in Scottish units during the First World War. Designed by Sir Robert Lorimer and dedicated in 1927, it consists of a Shrine and Gallery of Honour. The stained glass in the Shrine is again by Douglas Strachan, and round the apse are reliefs depicting all the participants in the war, men and women, animals, pigeons, even the canaries and mice used to detect the presence of poison gas. The Gallery of Honour has separate bays for each of the famous Scottish infantry regiments, for women in war, and for the supporting services, artillery, sappers and cavalry. Windows at either end record the sacrifices of the Navy and Air Force.

The east side of the courtyard is occupied by the palace, mainly a restoration of the early 17th century. The older parts that survive include the small room on the ground floor where Mary, Queen of Scots gave birth in 1566 to the future James VI and I. The Palace houses the 'Honours of Scotland', the crown, sceptre and state sword of the Scottish kings. These survived the Civil War, luckier than their English equivalents, lying hidden for most of the time in the church at Kinnef on the Kincardine coast. After the Restoration of Charles II they were returned to the castle. The Act of Union of 1707 provided that they should be kept at Edinburgh and they were locked away in an oak chest at the castle and forgotten. Not until 1818, after much prodding by Sir Walter Scott, was royal permission obtained to open the chest. Sir Walter was one of those present when, to the joy of all Scots, the 'Honours' were found after a century of oblivion. They were last used in 1953 on the occasion of Elizabeth II's State visit to Edinburgh after her Coronation.

The great bastion east of the Palace, known as 'Half Moon Battery', was erected in 1573 and enlarged in the 17th century. In comparatively recent times it has been discovered that it stands on the remains of a tower built by King David II, the son of Robert Bruce, in the 14th century.

On the south side of the courtyard stands the banqueting hall, its outer wall an upward continuation of the precipitous rock. This was built by James IV, who was slain at Flodden in 1513. A fine hammer-beam roof has carved corbels and the heads of men and animals at the ends of the beams. Beneath the hall are vaulted chambers where French prisoners were kept during the Napoleonic Wars. Robert Louis Stevenson described this in his unfinished novel *St Ives*.

Though seemingly on an impregnable site, the castle was taken and retaken many times by Scots and English. In 1313 Randolph, Earl of Moray, captured it for Robert Bruce by a daring assault up the south face of the rock, probably helped by one of those mists that sometimes envelop it. Bruce ordered the demolition

of all the buildings except St Margaret's Chapel. By 1341 the castle was refortified and again in English hands. The celebrated medieval chronicler Sir John Froissart relates the events of that year. Sir William Douglas took two hundred Highlanders to Edinburgh by night. He and a dozen others disguised themselves as merchants with horses to carry sacks of oats, meal and coal. At daybreak this small band approached the Castle across the esplanade with Douglas at their head. He told the porter that they had taken great risks to bring supplies to the garrison. The porter, knowing how great the need for succour and thinking it too early to wake up any superior for orders, opened the gate. As Douglas and his men passed in they flung sacks of coal against the gate so that it could not be closed. The porter was slain and a blast on the horn summoned the remainder of the Highlanders to the castle. The garrison was also roused but Douglas and his 'merchants' held the gate until the rest of his force arrived. The garrison, except for the Governor and his squires, were slaughtered.

By comparison the last siege was a quiet affair. The castle surrendered after twelve days on terms negotiated between Governor Dundas and the Lord General Cromwell. 'It hath pleased God' wrote Cromwell to Speaker Lenthall on Christmas Eve 1650, 'to cause this castle of Edinburgh to be surrendered into our hands this day about eleven o'clock . . .'

In centre of Edinburgh at W end of High Street

NT 2573 (OS 66)

Open M-S Apr to end Sept 0930-1900; Oct to end Mar 0930-1600; opens 1400 Su

WC (limited access)

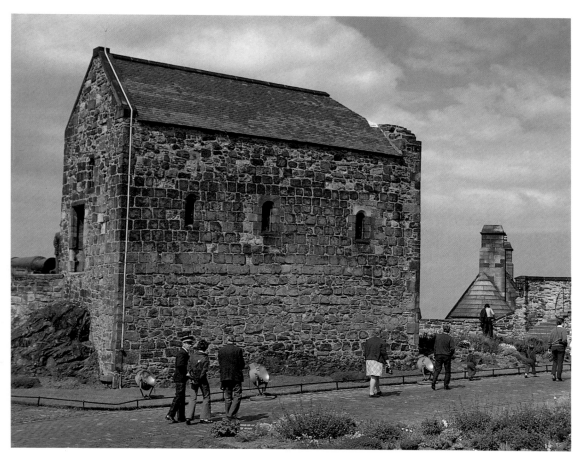

Above, the regalia of Scotland, including the 16th-century crown made for James V, are kept in the Palace where they were lost for more than 100 years.

Above right, Queen Margaret's chapel dates from the 11th century, the oldest building on the rock and a rare example of Scottish Romanesque architecture.

Right, the Edinburgh tattoo, an annual military spectacle which ends with massed bands of pipes and drums and a single piper on the castle battlements, is held on the castle esplanade.

Glamis Castle

Glamis, Tayside Region

Twelve miles north of Dundee, Glamis occupies unusually flat ground for a medieval fortress. At first sight, with its turrets and pinky-grey stones, it seems more like a fairy-tale castle or a *château* plucked from the banks of the Loire. But behind the French-influenced extensions and embellishments of the 17th century and subsequent alterations, a late-14th-century tower-house survives. This type of castle was still strongly fortified but at the same time more comfortable and spacious than the rugged keeps and fortified gatehouses that had served in previous centuries.

In 1372 King Robert II of Scotland granted the castle to his Keeper of the Privy Seal, Sir John Lyon, who within a few years married the king's daughter Joanna. The Lyon family have remained at Glamis by direct descent ever since.

The site had long been fortified by the Scottish kings and Malcolm II was reputed to have died there in 1034. What buildings existed at the time of the grant to Sir John Lyon is not known, because he effected a complete reconstruction. He built a strong, rectangular tower with a small wing on the south side, rising four storeys to battlements. The original entrance, now a window identifiable in the south wall, was at second-storey level, reached by an external stair. Inside the tower a straight flight of steps led down to the first storey and a narrow, spiral staircase up to the battlements. The great hall occupied the third storey, with a separate stair to the private chambers above it.

Sir John's grandson became Lord Glamis in 1445 and in 1606 Patrick Lyon, 9th Lord Glamis, was created Earl of Kinghorne. His grandson, another Patrick, added the

name of Strathmore to the title in 1677. During the 17th century, no doubt partly because of the family's advancement, large-scale developments began. Two wings were added to the original tower: a west wing which burnt down in 1800 and was rebuilt in its present form, and the east wing which survives today. The present main entrance was made at the foot of the tower's corner turret and an enlarged spiral stair carried up the turret from ground level to the roof. This staircase is easy of ascent and made of massive stone blocks on which five people can stand abreast, very different from the cramped, defensive stairs of medieval times. The height of the original tower was raised and roofed, and the attractive bartizans and cone-topped corner towers built. A chapel was made opening off the great hall.

On the first storey the crypt, the old kitchen and the so-called Duncan's hall are the least altered parts of the 14th-century castle. Weapons and armour are (appropriately) housed in the crypt and two small chambers in the thickness of the wall show how massive were the foundations of the original tower-house. The dungeon below has been adapted for use as a wine cellar.

The remodelled great hall became the drawing room. The dais was removed, the end fireplace blocked and the stone vault covered by a plasterwork ceiling dated 1621. A new fireplace, more than 13 feet in width, was built in the south wall. Its huge overmantel reaches to the springing line of the barrel ceiling. Many good portraits contribute to the handsome appearance of the room. A large painting of Patrick, the 3rd Earl, and his

sons rightly dominates the east wall. The important French artist François Clouet painted the smaller portrait of the 9th Lord Glamis, later the 1st Earl. Its reverse side has a picture of his loyal secretary George Boswell, ink-horn in hand and pen behind ear. John Grahame of Claverhouse, Viscount Dundee and the 'Bonny Dundee' of Sir Walter Scott's song, stares from his frame with a steely expression of arrogance. His bullet-proof vest is shown in another room. The castle at Claverhouse was only two miles away and the site became part of the Glamis estate in the last century.

Adjoining the drawing room, the simple, rectangular chapel has a series of paintings on the panels of both ceiling and walls. They were executed in the 17th century by the Dutch artist de Wet and include a striking rendering of Christ appearing to Mary Magdalene. Christ is shown resting His hand on the handle of a spade and wearing a large, black hat which is sharply silhouetted by His halo. He is the gardener for whom, according to St John's gospel, Mary at first mistook Him. Among many paintings of this subject few survive showing Christ wearing a hat.

King Malcolm's room is another remodelled part of the old castle, the later plaster ceiling and decorations concealing the earlier stone walls and vault. The blue linen hangings, once bed curtains, were embroidered

Opposite and below, Glamis began as a hunting lodge of the early kings of Scotland, and it was much expanded in the 14th century. Its turreted exterior, like the interior, owes most to the later 17th-century craze for 'Baronial' improvements.

in *petit point* by Helen, wife of the 3rd Earl. A large cabinet displays three sets of 18th-century Chien Lung armorial porcelain. One bears the coat of arms of the Lyon family with its blue lion, another the stringed bows of the Bowes family crest. The 9th Earl of Strathmore and Kinghorne married Mary Eleanor Bowes in 1767 and since then the family name has been Bowes Lyon. A third set of china commemorates this, showing three bows imposed on the Lyon coat of arms.

In the gardens an impressive sundial has stood in the centre of the lawn for three hundred years. It is over 20 feet high and topped by curving *fleurs-de-lis* supporting a coronet. Four lions and four twisted pillars decorate the large pedestal and the dial has a facet for each month of the year.

Glamis now has a special interest as one of the childhood homes of the much-loved Queen Elizabeth, the Queen Mother. She was the youngest daughter of the 14th Earl. A teenager during the First World War when the castle, like so many great houses, became a convalescent hospital for soldiers, she helped her mother to welcome and care for the wounded. After her marriage in 1923 to the Duke of York, who was to become King George VI thirteen years later, the royal apartments at Glamis were arranged for their use whenever they could get away from the pessure of royal engagements. Their sitting room and two bedrooms, not spacious by royal standards, display fine furniture, portraits and china. These comfortable quarters emphasise how the castle continues to evolve after more than six hundred years of occupation.

☎ Glamis (030 784) 242

6 m S of Kirriemuir on A928 turn E at Bridgend

NO 3848 (OS 54)

Open May to end Sept daily exc S 1300-1700; by appt only

♿ (limited) 🅿 WC ♿ (limited access) 🍴 D ♣ ☂ 🪑 ◆ ✿ ♣ (available in foreign languages) ● (not in house) ✗ (compulsory) ♿ ♿

Left, the chapel, built in the 17th century by the 3rd Earl of Strathmore and Kinghorne, was decorated by the Dutch artist de Wet with scenes from the life of Christ.

Opposite above, much of the fame of Glamis today derives from its association with Her Majesty the Queen Mother, whose living room this was.

Opposite below, the drawing room, fashioned out of the great hall by the 2nd Earl in the early 17th century.

Hopetoun House

On the south shore of the Firth of Forth, two miles west of the great Forth bridges, Hopetoun House is something of a surprise. At first sight it seems to be an English country mansion transported north of the Border. Yet it was designed and built by Scottish architects and craftsmen for a family of French origin who had been settled in Scotland for more than a hundred and fifty years.

The Hope family claim as their ancestor one John de Hope who came to Edinburgh about 1537 and established himself as a successful merchant. His grandson Thomas Hope was appointed Lord Advocate of Scotland by Charles I and a baronet two years later. Thomas's sixth son, James, another lawyer, acquired by

marriage some valuable lead mines south-west of Edinburgh at Leadhills, then known as Hopetoun. He adopted the title 'Sir James Hope of Hopetoun'. In 1678 his son John bought the lands at Abercorn where Hopetoun House now stands.

John Hope died in a shipwreck in 1682 when his son Charles was one year old. The house was planned during Charles' minority and the work entrusted to Sir William Bruce, the King's Surveyor in Scotland, who had already built Holyroodhouse. Charles was still a minor when building began. In 1703 he was created Earl of Hopetoun by Queen Anne at the early age of twenty-two, probably in recognition of some service rendered by his father to the Queen's father, James II, when

Left and above, Hopetoun is a vast house set in grounds designed in the style of Versailles, sweeping down to the Firth of Forth. William Adam, father of Robert, considered that his contribution to Hopetoun represented his finest work.

Duke of York. In the same year Bruce's house was completed. It was planned as a central block with two small wings, the latter joined to the front façade by convex rather than the usual concave colonnades. The central block remains, and the west or garden front is marvellously restrained and satisfying, with deep joints between the blocks of masonry and a semi-circular pediment over the entrance porch.

Some fifteen years later, however, the Earl commissioned William Adam, father of the famous Robert, to improve and enlarge the house. Work began in 1721 and continued until William Adam's death in 1748. He re-faced Bruce's east front and added the bays projecting from it. He built concave colonnades on either side and the large, pleasant wings, each enhanced by a tower with a cupola. After his death his sons Robert and John, who had been assisting him, put the final touches to the house and decorated the interior. Much of the original Adam decoration survives.

The family estates were expanded and developed by the 2nd and 3rd Earls. On the death of the latter in 1816 he was succeeded by his half-brother, General Sir John Hope, who had served with distinction in the West Indies, Holland and Egypt before commanding a division during the Retreat to Corunna. After the death of Sir John Moore he took command of the Army and directed its evacuation. Later he became one of Wellington's ablest generals in the Peninsular War. His portrait by Sir John Watson Gordon, the foremost Scottish portrait painter after Allan Ramsay (himself 'the Scottish

Reynolds') and Sir Henry Raeburn, hangs over the fireplace in the garden room. He is shown in the uniform of the Royal Company of Archers, the Sovereign's Bodyguard in Scotland.

John Adrian Louis, the 7th Earl, succeeded in 1873. A career in the public service led to his appointment as the first Governor-General when the Commonwealth of Australia came into being on 1st January 1901. He was created Marquis of Linlithgow in the following year. The 2nd Marquis had an even more notable career and was Viceroy of India during the difficult years from 1936 to 1943. The present Marquis is the elder of his twin sons. Both he and his brother saw active service in the Second World War.

The east entrance has a broad flight of steps up to a door which looks very modest in the vast façade of windows and towering Corinthian pilasters. The lack of a porch, the bare steps, the sheer functional simplicity is very impressive. The hall, built by William Adam and decorated by his sons with classical restraint, has full-length portraits of the 1st and the 2nd Marquis. It leads to the earlier ground floor rooms built by Sir William Bruce, the pine-panelled library with a fine collection of books, the garden room looking out on the west porch, and the 1st Earl's bedroom and closet. Next to the latter is the interesting charter room, entered through a low doorway and having a stone vault and iron window shutters for protection against fire. The shelves, deed boxes and the documents on display are all 18th century. The solid octagonal staircase is also Bruce's work, the banister and handrail of oak, the wall panelling of pine carved with fruit and flowers. The murals are a memorial to the present Marquis' first wife and were executed by the Scottish artist William McLaren in 1967. They blend admirably with the 18th-century panelling.

The yellow and red drawing rooms were decorated by Robert and John Adam and, together with the hall, are important examples of their early work. Only the furnishings are by an Englishman, James Cullen of London, a craftsman whose skills have been overshadowed by those of his contemporary, Thomas Chippendale. Chairs and settees, and particularly the mirrors and side-tables, all of which were made especially for Hopetoun, reveal the exquisite quality of Cullen's work. In the red drawing room the marble fireplace sculpted by Rysbrack and the gilded Adam ceiling are also noteworthy.

A typical view of Venice by Canaletto is one of a rich collection of paintings. Works by Van Dyck, Teniers and Cuyp, a Rubens, portraits by Ramsay, Raeburn and Gainsborough are exhibited. A very intriguing picture of four brothers of the Manaldini family, all musicians, is by the little known Passerotti. Some 17th-century tapestries from Antwerp decorate the west wainscot bedchamber, another of Bruce's rooms. More 17th-century tapestries, from the Aubusson factory in France, hang in the graceful Adam ballroom in the south wing.

In contrast to the 18th-century rooms, the state dining room is late Regency, created in about 1820 by the 4th Earl. Elaborate curtains and an over-decorated cornice, gold cloth on the walls and the chimney piece all make an interesting comparison with the furnishings of the

other rooms that are currently on show to the public.

The beautiful park bordering the shore of the Firth, laid out in the middle of the 18th century and little altered, is a proper setting for Scotland's largest country house with its important contents.

☎ Edinburgh (031) 331 2451

3 m W of Queensferry on A904 turn N to Abercorn at junction with B8020

NT 0879 (OS 65)

Open Easter weekend, then late Apr to late Sept daily 1100-1730

♿ (limited) P WC 🖼 (limited access by appt) ⊟ D ♣
🍽 ☂ ◆ ❀ ⚘ (available in foreign languages)
🏹 ● (by permission) ⚹

Top, the yellow drawing room, a rich, robust room designed by Robert Adam.

Above, the red drawing room, the climax to Robert Adam's suite at Hopetoun.

Opposite, the elegant sweep of the main staircase, a fine example of the work of Sir William Bruce, who was responsible for the original building work at Hopetoun in the late 17th century.

Traquair House

Innerliethen, Borders Region

A Charter signed by King Alexander I of Scotland (r. 1107-24) in the first year of his reign is the first record of Traquair's existence. Already a building must have occupied the beautiful site in the upper valley of the Tweed, only a day's ride from Edinburgh. The kings of Scotland continued to transact business there, to fish the river, to hunt boar, bear and wolf in the great forest of Ettrick for another three and a half centuries. Late in the 15th century James III (r. 1460-88) gave the estate to one of his favourites and not long afterwards it passed by purchase (the deed of sale is displayed in the museum room) to the Earl of Buchan. In 1491 the Earl presented Traquair to his son, James Stuart, who became the 1st Laird and whose descendants still live there.

James Stuart's castle was typical of the many small fortresses that sprang up in Scotland during the later Middle Ages: a strong, battlemented tower of three or four storeys with a walled courtyard but no other buildings or defences. The remains of the tower, thick walls, a narrow spiral staircase, a downstairs chamber where cattle and horses were herded at times of danger, form part of the present house.

Whatever plans the 1st Laird had for improvement of his austere home, nothing was done before his death beside his king, James IV, at Flodden Field in 1513. His son and grandson began the extensions which gradually transformed the medieval tower into the house that exists today. Other substantial additions followed in the 17th century. On the nail-studded front door the wrought-iron knocker is dated 1705 and little has been done since to alter the external appearance.

The main façade reveals a building wholly unlike any Tudor or Jacobean house in England. The low storeys, the small windows and steep roofs, the lack of embellishments save for dormer windows and small corner turrets, give an impression of dourness. The interior and its treasures maintain the contrast. This was not the home of a rich and powerful family but of people who unhesitatingly supported lost causes – Mary, Queen of Scots, Charles I, the Old and Young Pretenders – and who were prepared to suffer without compromise for their beliefs.

Mary, Queen of Scots (r. 1542-68) knighted the 4th Laird, John Stuart, and made him Captain of her Bodyguard. An oak carving of the Royal Arms of

Opposite, Traquair claims to be the oldest inhabited and most romantic house in Scotland, visited by no fewer than 27 reigning monarchs.

Below, the library at Traquair is a secluded 18th-century room containing a fine collection of books beneath the gaze of a frieze of ancient philosophers.

Scotland in the entrance hall commemorates her visit to Traquair in 1566, and the Laird supported her loyally until she fled to England two years later. Several of her personal possessions are shown, most movingly a rosary and crucifix, symbols of the religion for which later Lairds would accept poverty and danger. Traquair also has letters signed by the unhappy Queen and the carved cradle of her son, the future James VI of Scotland (r. 1567-1625) and James I of England (from 1603).

The Traquair Stuarts shared a brief prosperity with their royal kinsmen during the first part of the 17th century. The 7th Laird, another John Stuart, rose rapidly to high office. In 1623, at the age of 23, he was knighted by James I and ten years later created Earl by Charles I. In 1636 he became High Treasurer of Scotland, the most powerful man in Scotland under the King. But like other more famous servants of Charles I he did not weather the uneasy years leading up to the Civil War. In 1641 he was dismissed from office, fined and banished to his estate. He took no part in the Civil War. But in 1648 when the Scots invaded England, having regretted handing over Charles I to the English Parliament, the Earl and his son marched with them.

They were both captured during the running fight at Preston. Four years as a prisoner in Warwick Castle preceded the Earl's slow decline into penury. 'Put not your trust in princes' could well have been his epitaph when he died at Traquair in 1659.

His son, yet another John, was a devout Catholic at a time when the celebration of Mass was forbidden and local feeling against Catholics strong. His heir was five years old when he died but his second wife, Lady Anne Seton, stoutly brought up their children in the Catholic faith. Her portrait in the King's room does less than justice to this determined and courageous lady. In those days Mass was said in a small room at the top of the house while the approaches were watched for intruders. A secret staircase enabled the priest to leave if the house was searched. Not until Catholic emancipation in the 19th century could a chapel be consecrated in one of the wings.

Miniatures of the exiled Stuarts and a fine collection of Jacobite glass mark the active support of the Traquair Earls. Both the 4th and 5th Earls suffered imprisonment for their Jacobite loyalties, the latter spending two years in the Tower of London after the 1745 rising. Legend has it that Bonnie Prince Charlie visited Traquair, that when he marched away to England the famous Bear gates, 'The Steekit Yetts', were closed behind him with the promise that they would not be opened until the Stuarts were restored to the throne. These gates remain locked at the end of the avenue west of the house. The bears on the gate pillars represent the supporters of the family coat-of-arms. But an alternative, no less romantic, explanation for the closure of the gates suggests that they were shut in 1796 by the 7th Earl on the death of his wife. He ordered that the gates should not be opened again until another Countess lived at Traquair. But this was not to be. He did not remarry, his son died unmarried in 1861 and the Earldom became extinct. The Lairdship passed through the last Earl's sister to a cousin, Henry Constable Maxwell, a great-grandfather of the present Laird.

Traquair has many other treasures to show: historic documents, china, needlework, a unique harpsichord dated 1651, a late-15th-century Bible. Part of a Tudor mural of hunting scenes has been uncovered in the museum room. On the second floor the 18th-century library is a superb room; the books have not been rearranged for over two hundred years. In the brew house the Laird makes a potent ale. Yet the appeal of Traquair is surely more emotive than material. Long occupation by one family, the links with so many historical tragedies, have created an atmosphere at once evocative and serene.

☎ Innerleithen (0896) 830323

1 m S of Innerleithen on B709

NT 3235 (OS 73)
Open Apr to late Oct daily 1330-1730; July to mid Sept 1030-1730; parties at other times by appt

⊖ (1 m walk) WC ♿ (limited access) 🚻 D ♣ ☕ 🚪 ★ ⚕ (available in foreign languages) 𝄞 ● (not in house) ⚒ Craft workshops

Left, the famous Bear Gates, which are said never to have been opened since 1745.

Opposite below, the chapel was built in the 19th century for worship in the Catholic faith, for which the family had endured centuries of harrassment and obscurity.

Below, the unique early harpsichord, made in Antwerp in 1651.

☎ Galashiels (0896) 2043

2 m SE of Galashiels on A7 turn W onto B6360

NT 5034 (OS 73)

Open mid Mar to end Oct: M-S 1000-1700; Su 1400-1700; reduced rates for parties

⊖ 🅿WC 🅰 🚽 ♣ 🍴 🎏 ★ ✄

Abbotsford House

Melrose, Roxburghshire, Borders

Sir Walter Scott's home by the River Tweed could be called the original country house open to the public, for even before the novelist's death in 1832 it had become a target for tourists, and it was officially opened to visitors the following year. The king of the romantic historical movement in English literature created an 'antient' property where previously there had been a modest farmstead, and invented a new name for it invoking a far-off monastic tenure of the Abbey of Melrose. To love Scott is to love Abbotsford and its medieval-magpie interior. The place was rebuilt by him in 1822-24 with the enthusiasm of an amateur, and with the help of an undistinguished architect, and it reflects Scott and his interests in an entirely personal way. The exterior design is a Tudor/Scottish-traditional 'mixed salad', with big sash windows to let in plenty of light. Inside, the light is considerably dampened by the massive, dark-coloured panelling and furnishings, and the crowding together of relics, memorabilia and solid furniture. Scott had bought the farm in 1811, and it was here that he began to write the series of 'Waverley' novels in 1814. After the completion of Abbotsford in 1824, all of his work was written in his personally designed study on the ground floor. He enjoyed his fame, and the library (large bay windows giving on to the Tweed) and entrance hall (stained glass) are on a scale to accommodate that hospitality for large numbers of friends and admirers for which Scott was renowned.

4½ m NE of Linlithgow on A904, turn N onto B9109

NT 0580 (OS 66)

Open Apr to Sept W-S 0930-1900, Su 1400-1900, M 0930-1200; Oct to March closes 1600

🅿 WC 🅰 ♣

Blackness Castle

Linlithgow, West Lothian, Lothian

Blackness Castle dominates the village of Blackness, once a flourishing seaport on the south shore of the Firth of Forth. The first record of a castle on the site dates from the 15th century, as does the oldest surviving part. This is the keep or central tower; its turnpike (circular stairway) is a later feature, added when the castle began to be used as a prison. In the 16th century the keep was enclosed by a wall which was later modified and strengthened when massive artillery emplacements were installed. The entrance is notable for its old 'yett', an iron grille of a type once common in northern England and Scotland. In the 15th century Blackness was disputed between the Crichtons (who seem to have been the lawful occupants) and the Douglases. One fascinating but obscure episode occurred in 1452-53, when Sir George Crichton was created Earl of Caithness, only to resign his estates in the following year. Why he did so is a mystery – and his son was so outraged that he seized Blackness and held the Earl a prisoner there until the King forced him to surrender it. After this, Blackness became a royal castle. It was frequently used as a prison, mainly for eminent Scottish offenders, but remained of military significance; the Scots' French allies took it over in 1548, the English General Monk captured it in 1654, and it was still being garrisoned in the 18th century. In the 19th century it was used to store powder and other military supplies, until it became a public monument.

☎ Braemar (033 83) 219

1 m NE of Braemar on A93

NO 1592 (OS 43)

Open May to early Oct daily 1000-1800

⊖ (limited) 🅿 WC 🚽 D ♣ 🎏 ◆ ✄ (available in foreign languages) 🔨 ● (not in castle)

Braemar Castle

Braemar, Aberdeenshire, Grampian

There is no mistaking the military function of the place, with its hexagonal, loopholed salients on the 18th-century pattern, its soaring and partly blind walls, its overhanging roof turrets – all suggesting a frontier blockhouse garrisoned to repel marauders at the drop of a flint-lock. And that, very largely, is what it is. Although the site is in the traditionally feud-torn province of Mar, this castle was only begun in 1628 by John Erskine, Earl of Mar, as an operational base for fighting his rivals, the Gordons, the Forbes and, above all, the Farquharsons. It was burned and gutted in the failed Jacobite uprising of 1689 and remained a ruin until after the last Jacobite uprising of 1745. Its reconstruction started in 1748 as an army post to hold down the Highlands, and this is when it acquired the defences it still has today. The French Revolutionary Wars, together with the gradual pacification of the Highlanders, led to the withdrawal of the garrison in 1797 and soon the castle was restored to domestic use – this time by the Farquharsons themselves, whose descendants still live here. The interiors conform to the defensive plans of a fort, with low-ceilinged rooms stacked round the newel staircase which connects the floors. The decoration of the rooms is now entirely domestic, and a number of interesting paintings and relics of Braemar's history are on display. The annual Braemar Highland gathering and games takes place in the castle grounds.

Caerlaverock Castle

Caerlaverock, near Dumfries, Dumfries & Galloway

The extraordinary triangular castle, now a ruin, was the seat of the important Maxwell family for many centuries, and was built towards the end of the 13th century. Its formidable defences have seen much use, and it was besieged by Edward I very early in its history, surrendered and was held by the English for twelve years. After this it deteriorated for a time, but was rebuilt and much strengthened in the 15th century, and the great gatehouse was altered internally to make it residential. Towards the end of the 16th century gunports were put in, and these were put to the test in 1640 when the castle held out for three months against the Covenanters. Lord Nithsdale, the 'philosopher-earl', who held the castle for the King, had earlier been responsible for the last alterations to the building when he put up a three-storey residential block in the Classical Renaissance style inside the walls. Caerlaverock is the only triangular castle in Britain, but its plan is quite simple. It is shaped like a shield, its three huge curtain walls covered by the massive twin-towered gatehouse at one corner and angle towers in the other two. It was surrounded by an inner moat, with earth ramparts around this and then another moat with more ramparts, so that attackers had to cross two bridges before even approaching the heavily defended gatehouse.

12 m SE of Dumfries on B725 at Greenhead
NY 0265 (OS 84)

Open Apr to Sept M-S 0930-1900, Su 1400-1900;
Oct to Mar M-S 0930-1600, Su 1400-1600.
Closed F pm

🅿 D ♠ 🎋 ⚒

Cawdor Castle

Nairn, Highlands

This is a good example of an early Scottish tower-house with several interesting features, but its fame – as the home of Macbeth and the scene of King Duncan's murder – is historically unsubstantiated: though Macbeth reigned in Scotland in 1040-57 and was a contemporary of Edward the Confessor, the 1st Thane of the Calders or Cawdors came to the area late in the 13th century. The tower was built on a virgin site as a royal stronghold in about 1370. In the middle of the lower chamber stands an ancient hawthorn trunk, recalling the legend that the 1st Thane was told in a dream to let a donkey laden with gold wander until it lay down at nightfall, and there to build the new tower. It did so under a hawthorn tree, and scientific tests allow this to be that actual tree's trunk. The curtain wall surrounding the tower has been replaced by largely 17th-century buildings on the north and east, away from the burn that defends the western approach. The original entrance can be seen at first-floor level on the east side, but an even stronger entrance was constructed at ground-floor level, with a typical Scottish 'yett' or grille, seized by the 6th Thane from a rival's castle in 1456. A more civilised entrance was made through the 15th Thane's additions in 1663-76. Cawdor Castle is the family seat of the Campbells of Cawdor, and the rooms in the tower and the surrounding houses are comfortably furnished and display a large number of tapestries and interesting family portraits and relics.

☎ Cawdor (066 77) 615
4 m SW of Nairn on B9090 at Cawdor
NH 8449 (OS 27)

Open May to end Sept daily 1000-1730; reduced rates for parties

☻ (limited) 🅵 WC 🦽 (limited access) 🅿 ♠
♥ 🎋 ◆ ⚒ (available in German) ⚔

Crathes Castle

Banchory, Kincardineshire, Grampian

This is a well-preserved and hardly spoiled example of the traditional domestic 'castellated' tower of Scotland, of which the finest are at Glamis and Craigievar. Built usually on an L-plan, buildings such as these allowed a family and its retainers to retreat to safety in times of turmoil and brigandage. The lower parts, with a single entrance protected by an iron grille called a 'yett', were made bleakly defensive, but the further up you went, the more convenient the living rooms became (and the more ornament appeared on the exterior). At Crathes, the laird's gallery is on the very top floor, reaching the whole length of one wing. Panelled in oak (unique for Scotland, where pine is normal), it is the showpiece of the castle. Other rooms are impressive in different ways. The great hall is on the first floor – a vaulted chamber with walls that were once plastered and decorated with murals but are now stripped to the bare, rough masonry. The 'green lady's' room is supposed to be haunted, and has brightly coloured but unsophisticated paintings, with texts, all over the rafters and on the undersides of the boards between them, dated 1602. The tower was constructed in 1553-96 by the Burnetts of Leys, who had been granted lands by Robert the Bruce in 1323. The ivory Horn of Leys, granted to the family by the king as a token of tenure, still hangs in the great hall. With the coming of more settled times, a comfortable Queen Anne wing was added, but it does not detract from the sense of a more dangerous age that both the inside and the outside of the tower impart.

☎ Crathes (033 044) 525
2¾ m E of Banchory on A93
NO 7396 (OS 38)

Open Easter weekend, May to end Sept M-S 1100-1800, Su 1400-1800

☻ 🅵 WC 🦽 🅿 D ♠ ♥ (limited opening) 🎋
◆ (limited opening) ⚒ ⚔

☎ Kirkoswald (065 56) 269
11 m N of Girvan on A77 turn NW onto A719
NS 2310 (OS 70)

Open Apr to end Sept daily 100-1800; Oct daily 1200-1700; reduced rates for parties exc July and Aug

⊖ 🅿 WC 🚻 D 🌣 🍴 🚽 🏕 ◆ ☀ 🚶 🏃 🐕

Culzean Castle

Maybole, Ayrshire, Strathclyde

The castle, its great towers rising up sheer from the sea, looks from the north side like an archetypal medieval stronghold, but in fact it is an 18th-century 'Gothick' building by Robert Adam. It is the best-known example of Adam's castle style, but he was less at home with the Gothic Revival style than with his own brand of Classicism. The estate had been owned by the Kennedy family since the 14th century, and by the 1690s the old castle had already been turned into a mansion house, but the 10th Earl of Cassilis, who succeeded in 1775, called in Adam, and work began on the first stage, the south front, in 1777. This incorporated the older mansion house, and with the interior decoration of library and dining room was completed by 1782. The next stage was the lower range on the north side, followed by the great round tower on the north front, and finally this was linked to the south front by a huge oval staircase. Some alterations were made during the 19th century to Adam's brewhouse, and an entrance hall was added to the east front. The interiors show Adam at his best, and the great circular saloon and oval staircase are among his most inventive works. As usual, he supervised every detail and designed much of the furniture as well as the carpet in the saloon, and the craftsmanship throughout is superb. The country park, of 560 acres, includes the walled gardens laid out by the 10th Earl and decorated by Adam with picturesque mock-ruins, as well as woodland walks, lakes and picnic places.

☎ Thornhill (0848) 30248
25 m NW of Dumfries on A76 turn W to Drumlanrig Park
NX 8599 (OS 78)

Open Easter weekend; May and June daily exc F 1330-1700; Jul and Aug daily exc F 1100-1700, Su 1400-1800

🅿 WC 🚻 D 🌣 🍴 🚽 🏕 ◆ ☀ 🚶 🏃 🐕

Drumlanrig Castle

near Thornhill, Dumfriesshire, Dumfries & Galloway

The old castle of Drumlanrig in Nithsdale had belonged to the Douglases for over 300 years when, in the reign of Charles II, William Douglas, 3rd Earl of Queensberry, decided to build a new house. The ground plan retained the medieval notion of a moated castle. The new front – especially the flight of steps and the ornate doorway that together form the entrance – boasts Baroque decorative features, but the rest of the house consists of four solid corner towers around a four-sided courtyard, from which newel stairs lead to the upper floors through four narrow turrets. Even the barbizans on the roofs of the turrets have a belligerent air, though the large and pedimented windows below them are designed for essentially peaceful times. The visitor is likely to notice the Douglas badge carved in a variety of places: a winged heart surmounted by a crown. The explanation given for this is that Sir James, the 'Black Douglas', was entrusted with the heart of King Robert the Bruce in a silver casket at his death in 1329 and enjoined to take it on crusade in order to fulfil a royal vow; when he was fatally wounded fighting the Moors in Spain, he hurled it into the enemy with the words, 'Forward, brave heart!' The interior of Drumlanrig Castle is very rich in fine furniture and paintings. In 1810 the title passed to the 3rd Duke of Buccleuch, who possessed many treasures of the late 17th century, including a pair of Louis XIV cabinets, which are displayed here. The paintings – one a Rembrandt of 1655, *An Old Woman Reading* – are well worth the visit.

☎ Golspie (04083) 3177
1 m NE of Golspie on A9
NC 8501 (OS 17)

Open mid June to mid Sept M-S 1000-1730, Su 1300-1730; parties at other times by appt

⊖ (½ m walk; limited) 🅿 WC 🚻 (by appt)
D 🌣 🍴 🚽 🏕 ☀ ● (not in castle)

Dunrobin Castle

Golspie, Sutherland, Highlands

Looking out over the Dornoch Firth eastward into the expanses of the North Sea, the extravagant sham-château of the Dukes of Sutherland presents a challenge to our feelings: it is the expression of the immense wealth and political clout of an English landowner who conducted the 'clearance' of 5,000 Highland tenants from the Sutherland estates. The ancestry of the Earls of Sutherland when created in the first half of the 13th century already reached back into the Celtic past. They held a fort at Dunrobin before 1400, which evolved over the centuries as a typical Scottish castle. So it remained until about 1840. By then the inheritance had, after a complicated family history, passed to the new Dukes of Sutherland. The son of the 1st Duke, who 'cleared' the glens, was the author of the changes at Dunrobin: Barry, who designed the new Houses of Parliament, was brought in to design the palatial structure we see today – in a style imported from the Loire valley with some rugged touches to remind us of the Scottish tradition. The interior was modified in parts by Sir Robert Lorimer after a fire in 1915. The spaciousness and craftsmanship are impressive, and Lorimer's rooms somewhat humanise the scale of the interior. Apart from the usual family portraits, there is an interesting Elizabethan painting of an Irish chief by Michael Wright, a collection of obsolete utensils and a curious museum of game trophies with some carved Pictish stones. Dunrobin Castle is now the home of the Countess of Sutherland in her own right.

Dunvegan Castle

Dunvegan, Isle of Skye, Highlands

On its commanding rock where Loch Dunvegan opens north-westward to the Little Minch and beyond to the Hebrides, this clan-castle of the MacLeods enshrines their relic-hoard. It cannot matter how gaunt the castle looks from the outside when it contains such treasures as the Fairy Flag, Rory More's mazer, the MacLeod drinking horn, the MacCrimmon pipes and the stays of Flora MacDonald, the Jacobite heroine. Dunvegan has been the headquarters of the chief – the MacLeod of MacLeod – since around 1270, soon after the Scots recovered the Western Isles from the Norwegians. A fort was built here by the clan's first chief, Leod, son of a Viking king of Man. The silken flag with the battle-winning magic seems to have a 7th-century origin in the Near East, and may have been brought back in the 11th century by Harald Haardraade of Norway, who had been in the service of the Byzantine empress. From Leod's time until 1748 the only way in to Dunvegan castle was by steps up from the loch to the sea-gate with its portcullis. The landward side, being more vulnerable to attack, was a sheer wall with scarcely any openings even for windows. When Boswell and Dr Johnson were here in 1773, their hostess, Lady MacLeod, complained to them bitterly about her primitive living conditions, but soon after, General MacLeod began planting trees, and now the surroundings are softened by woods and gardens, while the Victorian extensions within the walls have ensured that the present chief and his family live here in civilised comfort.

☎ Dunvegan (047 022) 206
On Isle of Skye, 1½ m NW of Dunvegan on A580
NG 2449 (OS 23)

Open early Apr to mid May and Oct daily exc Su 1400-1700; mid May to end Sept daily exc Su 1030-1700
🅿 WC 🚽 (by appt) D ♣ 🎋 ⚘ 🗡

Earlshall Castle

Leuchars, St Andrews, Fife

The castle, which is believed to take its name from the ancient stronghold of the Earls of Fife nearby, was built in the 16th century as a fortified house rather than a castle. It is roughly on a Z-plan, with a circular tower at one end, and opposite this a platform tower commanding a sea view. This is connected to another tower by a high wall in which there is a fortified gateway bearing the arms of Sir William Bruce of Earlshall, and the third side of the courtyard (the fourth is open) is enclosed by a range of buildings added in the 17th century. The fame of Earlshall today rests on its fine restoration by Robert Lorimer in the 1890s. It was his first job; he was only 26 when he was asked to renovate the castle and create a garden, but it is one of his most successful restorations. Its finest feature is the long gallery with its magnificent coved ceiling painted with armorial devices and fabulous beasts, which Lorimer was able to save only by taking down every single piece of painted woodwork, replacing the missing bits and re-assembling the whole again. The garden, a romantic recreation of the 17th-century formal style, is totally enclosed, its walls shutting out the country beyond, so that house and garden seem to exist in their own world. The topiary work is dramatic and inventive, its highlight being a huge grass chessboard with all its pieces 'carved' in yew. The yew trees were transplanted, already shaped, from an Edinburgh garden, and are still kept in shape and cared for by the present owners of the castle.

☎ Leuchars (033 483) 205
16 m SE of Dundee on A92, E of Leuchars
NO 4621 (OS 54)

Open Easter weekend to end Sept Th-Su 1400-1800; reduced rates for parties by appt
🚌 (1½ m walk) 🅿 WC 🚽 ♣ 🍴 🎋 ◆
🎨 ⚘ ● (not in castle) 🗡

Eilean Donan Castle

Dornie, Wester Ross, Ross and Cromarty, Highlands

Eilean Donan, standing guard on a small rocky island at the junction of three lochs, and facing the Isle of Skye, looks just like everyone's dream of a romantic Scottish medieval castle. And so, in many ways, it is, but the building itself dates entirely from the 20th century, as it was rebuilt at enormous expense between 1912 and 1932 by Colonel John Macrae, a direct descendant of the last constable of the castle. The site may have originally been an old Pictish fort, but the castle proper was one of many built in 1220 by Alexander II to protect Scotland from the Norse raiders. It was held for centuries by the Earls of Seaforth (the Macraes were their hereditary constables) and met its doom in 1719 through loyalty to the Jacobite cause. It was garrisoned by Spanish troops supporting the Old Pretender, and they were bombarded by an English man-of-war, HMS *Worcester*, which reduced the castle to rubble. The story goes that the method of reconstructing the castle came to Colonel Macrae in a dream, which seems unlikely, but it is certainly very authentic-looking, with massive rough stonework, bare walls, and the usual collection of Highland Scottish objects – pistols, powderhorns, antlers and tartans.

☎ Dornie (059 985) 202
12 m E of Kyle of Lochalsh on A87 just S of Dornie
NG 8825 (OS 33)

Open Apr to Sept daily 1000-1230 and 1400-1800
🅿 🚽 D ♣ 🎋 ⚘

☎ Falkland (03375) 397

16 m SE of Perth on A912 at Falkland

NO 2507 (OS 59)

Open Apr to end Sept M-S 1000-1800, Su 1400-
1800; Oct S 1000-1800, Su 1400-1800; reduced
rates for parties

WC 日 ♣ ⚡

Falkland Palace

Falkland, Fife

Falkland passed to the Stuarts in 1370, and had become a favourite place for hunting and relaxation by 1500 when James IV began to build a new palace to the south of the old – probably 13th-century – castle. This building consisted of three oblong blocks ranged round a central courtyard, and the style is Scottish Gothic, but the additions and alterations made by James V between 1537 and 1542 are entirely different. His courtyard façade, far more advanced architecturally than anything else in Scotland or England at the time, is pure French Renaissance, reminiscent of the châteaux of Blois or Chambord. The reason for this surprising piece of building was James' visit to the French court in 1537 and his subsequent return with a French bride, Madeleine, daughter of François I. The architect was Sir James Hamilton of Finnart, who had himself spent several years at the French court, and all the craftsmen were either French or trained in France. The angels decorating the buttresses on the south range were carved in 1539 by 'Peter the Flemishman', and the medallions with busts on the east range, which local tradition claims as portraits of personages connected with the palace, were done in 1538 by a French craftsman, Nicholas Roy. Sadly, the only interior to survive of these magnificent state rooms is the Chapel Royal, and even here only the elegant screen is of this period; the rest of the decorations date from 1635, when the palace was redecorated for Charles I's visit.

☎ Kelso (0573) 2333

1 m NW of Kelso on A6089

NT 7134 (OS 74)

Open Easter weekend and late Apr to late Sept
Su-Th, also F in July and Aug

WC 日 D ♣ ⚡ ⛱ ◆ ⚙ ☀ ● (not in
house) ⚡

Floors Castle

Kelso, Roxburghshire, Borders

Floors – a romantic-baronial transformation act of the Victorian age – is a masterpiece of architectural imagination and space-handling. Everything that the Edinburgh architect W. H. Playfair added to the regular Georgian central block begun in 1721 for the 1st Duke of Roxburghe works admirably – if theatrically. The array of turrets on the wings, with their Tudor caps, even outdo Hampton Court, while their layout to the north gives amplitude to the Vanbrugh-like grandeur of the conception. The underlying 18th-century building (which can be seen as it was in 1809 in a painting in the sitting room) can be sensed in the arrangement of the rooms. Much of the furnishing is of that time, and a fine collection of French pieces and tapestries was brought over from New York by the American bride of the 8th Duke. One object inside which is in keeping with the supposed period of Playfair's exterior is a fine early-16th-century Brussels tapestry of Pentecost. The celebrated Roxburghe library, which the 3rd Duke had assembled, had to be sold in 1813 by the 5th Duke to meet the costs of a lawsuit settled by the House of Lords (there had been rival claimants to the title). The purchasers, all wealthy peers, formed the Roxburghe Club to issue their newly acquired treasures to each other in facsimile form, and in doing so created another kind of collector's item for the future. The gardens, to the west of the castle, are notable for carnations.

☎ Edinburgh (031) 556 73771

In centre of Edinburgh at E end of Canongate

NT 2673 (OS 66)

Open daily throughout year 1000-1700
exc part of May and mid Jun to early Jul

♿ WC 日 ⚡ ◆
☀ ● (not in house)

Holyroodhouse

Edinburgh, Lothian

Holyroodhouse has a long history, the name itself being the legacy of the 11th-century queen who was to become St Margaret of Scotland, who died here, bequeathing her precious relic of Christ's cross, the 'holy rood', to her son David. The splendid 17th-century palace we see today grew from the guesthouse attached to a medieval monastery, and was begun under James IV in 1501. After the Restoration of 1660 Charles II decided to rebuild the palace, though he never came to see the result, and the great period of building took place from 1671 to 1680 at his behest, under the supervision of Sir William Bruce. The oldest rooms are those in the James IV tower, home of Mary Queen of Scots, where Lord Darnley plotted and David Rizzio met his death. The Queen's inner chamber has a lovely oak coffered ceiling with 17th-century painted panels, while the outer chamber has a 17th-century chimneypiece and a timber ceiling commemorating Mary's marriage to the Dauphin François. The gallery, which extends along the whole northern range and joins the old apartments to the 17th-century wing, has portraits of eighty-nine Scottish monarchs set into the panelling. These were commissioned by Charles II, and painted by the Dutch artist Jacob de Witt, who worked on them at the palace for two years. The finest room of all is the privy chamber (now called the morning drawing room as Queen Victoria used it for this purpose) where the splendid plaster ceiling, intricately carved woodwork, and wallpaintings are all original.

Inveraray Castle

Inveraray, Argyll, Strathclyde

Inveraray is the seat of the Dukes of Argyll, and the fairytale 'Gothick' castle, much admired by Dr Johnson, was built by the 3rd Duke in the 18th century close to the old Campbell stronghold. Not content with this, he also rebuilt the town itself, so that the whole ensemble became a Georgian capital in miniature. The castle was begun in 1744, and the architect was Roger Morris, who had already built Clearwell Castle in Gloucestershire in the Gothick style; the work was supervised by William Adam and his sons John and Robert. In 1877 a fire gutted the upper floors, and the attic storey with dormer windows was added by Anthony Salvin after this. The interior of the castle is quite unlike the exterior. Graceful, light and classical, it was the work of Robert Mylne, who was called in by the 5th Duke in 1772 and redecorated all the main apartments in the most advanced 18th-century style, with delicate plasterwork, tapestries and painted panels. The finest room is the dining room, with a huge central ceiling rose and wall panels of *grisaille* surrounded by painted decoration by Biagio Rebecca. The drawing room, with its coloured and gilded ceiling, was designed for the seven Beauvais tapestries which still hang on the walls, and the saloon, hung with family portraits, has a frieze, doorcase and chimneypiece made by James Adam. All the main rooms contain superb furniture, and there are no less than ten sets of gilded chairs, several of them covered with Beauvais tapestry. The family portraits include works by Gainsborough, Hoppner, Opie and Batoni.

☎ Inveraray (0499) 2203

½ m NW of Inveraray on A819 turn NE

NN 0909 (OS 56)

Open Apr to mid Oct M-Th and S 1000-1300 and 1400-1800 Su 1300-1800

⊖ (limited) 🅿 WC ♿ (limited access)
🚻 ♨ ♠ 🎪 ⚒ 🏹

Manderston

Duns, Berwickshire, Borders

Manderston, a lavish Edwardian country house, is lived in by the descendants of James Miller, who largely created it in the 1900s. The first house, of the 1790s, was built by Dalhousie Weatherstone, and the estate was bought in 1864 by William Miller, who had made a fortune from trading in hemp and herrings. In 1893 his son Sir James married Lady Miller, daughter of Lord Scarsdale. The latter was the owner of Kedleston Hall in Derbyshire, one of Robert Adam's great achievements, and it was probably to impress his new father-in-law that Miller at once began to plan a new house entirely in the Adam style. His architect was John Kinross, who was given *carte blanche* in the matter of finance, an architect's dream come true. The stables were built first, in 1895, with the grooms' rooms panelled in mahogany and the horses' stalls in teak with marble plaques for their names. The house itself was given a new wing, a new entrance front and a service court. The interior, with its string of reception rooms designed for formal entertaining, is pure Adam, with one of the chimneypieces and the ballroom ceiling actually copied from Kedleston. The showpiece is the drawing room leading to the ballroom, with furniture in the Louis XVI style, white silk curtains and walls hung with silk brocade. Almost as much care was lavished on the servants' quarters: the basement, which runs the entire length of the house, is unchanged, and provides an interesting example of the sophisticated domestic arrangements of such a household.

☎ Duns (0361) 83450

1½ m E of Duns on A6105 continue on minor road to Buxley

MT 8154 (OS 67)

Open mid May to late Sept Th, Su and Bank Hol M also T in Aug 1400-1730

⊖ 🅿 WC D ♨ 🎪 ★ 🐕 ⚒
🏹 ● (not in house) ♿

Mellerstain

Gordon, Berwickshire, Borders

The foundations for a new mansion at Mellerstain were laid in 1725 for the owner, Lady Grisell Baillie, who had intended to build a modest Palladian house on the site of the old building. However, only the simple square wings, designed by William Adam, were built, and when Lady Grisell's nephew George Baillie inherited in 1759, he abandoned her project and called in Robert Adam, William's much more famous son, to complete the house. The exterior of the house is in the castle style which was then becoming popular, and which Adam had used at Culzean and elsewhere. The interiors, in Adam's most assured light Classical style, are a delight, and are still complete with their original ceilings, friezes and fireplaces. The library (completed in 1773), with its white carved-wood bookcases, mahogany doors and green-and-white marble fireplace, is one of the finest rooms Adam designed, and the dining room, music room and drawing room, all decorated in their original colours, show the highest degree of skill and craftsmanship. The long gallery, which is used to display a collection of 18th- and 19th-century costume, would certainly have been as fine as the library, but the long barrel-vaulted ceiling was never completed. The house contains some good 18th-century furniture, though Adam did not design it himself as he did in many cases, and there is also an exceptional collection of paintings, Italian religious subjects as well as works by Van Dyck, Gainsborough, Ramsay, Jacob Ruysdael and Constable.

☎ Gordon (057 381) 225

8 m NW of Kelso on A6089 turn W to Mellerstain

NT 6439 (OS 73)

Open Easter weekend and May to end Sept daily exc S 1230-1700; reduced rates for parties by appt

🅿 WC 🚻 D ♨ 🎪 ★ ⚒
🏹 ● (not in house)

Scone Palace

Perth, Perthshire, Tayside

Scone is the centre of Scotland both geographically and historically: the first recorded Scottish Parliaments were here, and here was kept the famous Stone of Scone upon which the kings of Scotland were crowned. There was an ancient religious foundation at Scone; its ruins formed the base of the house built in 1580 by the Ruthven family, Earls of Gowrie. After 1600 James VI gave the property to Sir David Murray, and it has remained in the family ever since. The present house, built between 1802 and 1813 for the 3rd Earl of Mansfield, was designed by William Atkinson, the pupil of James Wyatt. Built of red sandstone in a sober Gothic style, it is similar to Wyatt's earlier buildings. The interior is entirely consistent with the exterior, the hall being vaulted or beamed, with every detail in the Gothic manner. The palace contains an amazingly rich variety of objects and works of art, among the earliest being a 16th-century needlework panel and pieces of a set of embroidered bed-hangings worked by Mary Queen of Scots and her ladies. The dining room has a unique collection of European ivories and two carved ivory mirrors; the charming little ante-room, painted in white, silver and gold, contains Chinese vases and Chinese Chippendale chairs, but the most spectacular furniture is in the drawing room, where there are 18th-century *boulle* commodes, tables and clocks, a set of tapestry-covered Louis XV chairs and an exquisite marquetry writing-table made for Marie-Antoinette by Reisener and stamped with her own cipher.

☎ Scone (0738) 52300

3 m N of Perth on A93, turn SW at Scone

NO 1026 (OS 53)

Open Good Fri to mid Oct M-S 1000-1730 Su 1400-1730; parties by appt at other times

♿ (limited, not Su) WC ♿ 🚻 D ♣ ♥ 🚻 ◆ ⚹ ⚹ ⚹

Stirling Castle

Upper Castle Hill, Stirling, Stirlingshire, Central

Stirling, built on a high and narrow ridge of basalt at the gateway of the Scottish Highlands, was a more important stronghold even than Edinburgh. During the Wars of Independence it was constantly changing hands. The Scots managed to hold it from 1299 to 1304, the year of a great siege by Edward I; the English then held it for ten years, yielding it back to the Scots after their victory at Bannockburn in 1314. The castle that withstood so much was a timber and earthwork construction, which has now entirely disappeared: it was rebuilt in stone, the earliest parts now standing dating from the 15th century. It changed its character too, under the Stuart dynasty, becoming no longer a grim fortress but a splendid royal palace with ornamental gardens. Today's buildings reflect those days of glory. The great hall, built for James III (r. 1460-88) and designed by Robert Cochrane, was one of the first and finest 15th-century Renaissance buildings anywhere in Britain. The curtain wall and towers probably date from the same period; the great palace block with its lovely carved detail was built by James IV (r. 1488-1513) and continued by his son, and James VI rebuilt the royal chapel about 1594. James VI was baptised at Stirling, as was his son, Prince Frederick Henry, but after 1603 the court moved to England and the castle was more or less abandoned, though kept in readiness. It was besieged by General Monk in 1651 and again – ineffectively – by Bonnie Prince Charlie in 1745.

In the centre of Stirling

NS 7994 (OS 57)

Open Apr to end Sept M-S 0930-1800, Su 1030-1730; Oct to end Mar M-S 0930-1700, Su 1230-1620

♿ 🚻 D ⚹

Tantallon Castle

North Berwick, East Lothian, Lothian

Tantallon is one of the most famous and romantic of Scottish castles, ruined yet so substantial and well formed that it gives an impression of indestructibility. The grandeur of the rose-coloured ruins matches that of the site, a rugged cliff top looking out at the North Sea and mighty Bass Rock. It is protected by the sea on two sides, with earthworks and ditches barring other approaches. Once past these and other outworks, the attacker was confronted (as the visitor is today) with a daunting curtain wall flanked by round towers and entered only through a strong gatehouse. Tantallon was the stronghold of the Red Douglases, and probably dates from the late 14th century; its builder may well have been William, the first Earl of Douglas. The Douglases certainly needed a stronghold; their lives were crammed with intrigues, betrayals, rebellions and sieges, broken only by intervals of exile or uncharacteristically law-abiding behaviour. A typical example was the fifth Earl, Archibald 'Bell the Cat' Douglas, who withstood a royal siege at Tantallon one year, and was made Chancellor of Scotland the next. The career of his grandson, the Earl of Angus, was a forty-year epic of office, exile and rebellion (including another siege at Tantallon in 1528) that ended only with his death at Tantallon in 1557. The catle was garrisoned by the Covenanters from 1639, and badly damaged by the English General Monk's artillery in 1651. By the end of the century it had been abandoned altogether.

2½ m E of North Berwick on A198

NT 5985 (OS 67)

Open M-S Apr to end Oct 0930-1900; Nov to end Mar 0930-1600; opens 1400 Su

 🚻 D ⚹

Thirlestane Castle

Lauder, Berwickshire, Borders

Thirlestane Castle, home since 1228 of the Maitlands, Earls and Dukes of Lauderdale, is the product of three periods of building, the 1590s, the 1670s and the 1840s. The castle, which was built on the site of an old fort in 1590 by Chancellor Maitland, is an oblong block between four huge corner towers, with smaller stair turrets on the north and south sides. The Renaissance west front, the first work of Sir William Bruce, was built for the Duke of Lauderdale following his marriage to the Countess of Dysart in 1672, and the castle was extensively remodelled inside at the same time. The 19th-century building work, in the Scottish baronial style, extended the west front in both directions, added conical roofs to the towers and raised the central tower, giving the castle its fine turretted silhouette. The building was in a state of serious disrepair when the present owner succeeded in 1972, but a major rescue operation was put under way from 1978 to 1982. The most remarkable feature of the interior is the rich Baroque plasterwork, particularly the ceilings in the 17th-century state rooms. These amazing *tours de force*, with their deeply modelled wreaths and garlands of leaves and flowers hanging suspended just below, were the work of an English plasterer, George Dunsterfield, who worked at Thirlestane continuously for two years from 1674. Most of the furniture made for the house during the 17th-century remodelling was removed to Ham House, which the Duchess had recently inherited, but some good pieces remain.

☎ Lauder (05782) 254

3 m E of Lauder on A697

NT 5647 (OS 73)

Open May, June and Sept W and Su; Jul and Aug daily exc S 1400-1700

P WC (limited access) D (not in house)

Torosay Castle

Craignure, Isle of Mull, Argyll, Strathclyde

The parish of Torosay was acquired in the early 19th century by Colonel Campbell of Possil, who demolished the existing Queen Anne house and commissioned David Bryce, the Edinburgh architect who pioneered the Scottish baronial style, to build a much larger house on the same site. The 'castle' was completed in 1858, and was then called Duart House. The diary of a guest tells us the family were well pleased with it, and throughout the Victorian and Edwardian periods they entertained lavishly, well-known visitors to the house including Dame Nellie Melba and Lillie Langtry. In 1897 it was left to Walter Murray Guthrie, grandfather of the present owner, who put it on the market briefly before he visited it, then fell in love with it and withdrew it from sale. It was he who commissioned Sir Robert Lorimer to design and lay out the three Italian terraces and statue walk that now connect the house to the old walled garden. Torosay Castle has recently been restored and the interior reflects its heyday of prosperity. The front hall is hung with rows of red deer antlers, and there is a painting by Landseer at the top of the stairs; the main hall is dominated by a fine portrait by Poynter of Olive Guthrie, who lived here until 1945, and there are more family portraits in the other rooms, including the dining room, where there is also a painting by Sir John Leslie, Olive Guthrie's father, painted in 1855 and hung in the Royal Academy that year. The boudoir contains exhibits on the theme of the Loch Ness Monster.

☎ Craignure (068 02) 421

On Island of Mull, W of Duart Point on A849

NM 7235 (OS 49)

Open May to end Sept daily 1030-1730, Apr and Oct by appt

WC (by appt) D

Winton House

Pencaitland, East Lothian, Lothian

Winton House, secondary residence of the important Seton family, saw three main periods of building, the late 15th, the 17th and the early 19th centuries. The first house was built about 1480, and though it was later 'burnt by the English', the barrel-vaulted ground floor and lower part of the walls survived and are incorporated into the present house. The house may have been restored about 1600, but the lovely tall, gabled, Jacobean central part was built in 1620 by William Wallace, the King's Master Mason. A particular feature of this phase of building is the extraordinary carved and sculptured chimneys, very unusual as they are of stone rather than brick. The third building programme began in 1800, when Colonel Hamilton enlarged the house, building a new north (entrance) front in the 'Gothick' style, together with battlemented wings on the north and west. The entrance hall leads into the octagon hall, built above the original open courtyard and giving a good view of the carved window frames. An ante-room then leads into the east wing, which is part of the old house though the ceilings are mainly of the Jacobean period. The finest of these is in the library. The drawing room, originally the great hall, has a fine Renaissance chimneypiece and an ornate plaster ceiling with the arms of the Setons. A turret stair leads from the first-floor bedrooms in the tower to the top, which provides a fine close-up view of the chimneys, while six storeys below is the oldest room of all, the barrel-vaulted kitchen, now used as the dining room.

☎ Pencaitland (0875) 340 222

7½ m SW of Haddington on A6093 turn N on B6355 for 1 m then S

NT 4369 (OS 66)

Open throughout year by written appt

(1 m walk) WC (by appt)

(compulsory)

Balmoral Castle, near Ballater, Grampian Region (tel Crathie [033 84] 334). 8 m SW of Ballater on A93, turn S. NO 2595 (OS 44). Mid 19th-century castle in Baronial style, built for Queen Victoria and Prince Albert. The castle is the Highland residence of Her Majesty the Queen, and is set in fine forested grounds. The ballroom contains an exhibition of paintings and works of art. Open May to July daily (exc Su) am and pm. ⊖ 🅿 WC 🅰 ♣ 👝

Blair Castle, Pitlochry, Perthshire, Tayside Region (tel Pitlochry [0796] 81 356). 1 m NW of Blair Atholl off A9. NN 8666 (OS 43). The stronghold of the Earls and Dukes of Atholl since the 13th century, with one tower surviving from that date. The house was rebuilt as a mansion in the mid-18th century. The staircase, imported from London, is a famous feature. In the 19th century the castle was given a Gothic feel once more. Open Easter weekend; end Apr to mid Oct M-S am and pm, Su pm only. ⊖ 🅿 ♣

Bowhill, Selkirk, Borders Region (tel Selkirk [0750] 20732). 3 m W of Selkirk on A708, turn S. NT 4227 (OS 73). 18th- and 19th-century mansion, the home of the Scotts of Buccleuch. The house contains a famous art collection, including works by Leonardo, Guardi, Canaletto, Claude and Gainsborough, and many *objets d'art*. There are also relics of the Duke of Monmouth, Queen Victoria and Sir Walter Scott, and a collection of 16th- and 17th-century English miniature portraits. Open July and Aug daily (exc F) pm; Easter, May to June, Sept daily (exc T and F) pm. ⊖ 🅿 WC 🅰 ♣ 👝 🖼

Brodick Castle, Isle of Arran, Strathclyde Region (tel Brodick [0770] 2202). 2½ m N of Brodick pierhead. NS 0037 (OS 69). Castle dating originally from a Viking fort of the 12th century, though mainly rebuilt in the 19th century for the Duke of Hamilton. It contains a collection of paintings (including works by Turner and Watteau) and gardens known for their rhododendrons. Castle open mid-Apr to end Sept daily pm; grounds open all year daily am and pm. ⊖ 🅿 WC ♣ 👝

Brodie Castle, near Nairn, Grampian Region (tel Brodie [030 94] 371). 6 m E of Nairn off A96. NH 9858 (OS 27). 16th- and 17th-century castle rebuilt after being burned in 1645, and containing a fine collection of paintings, including Dutch Old Masters, Impressionists and others. House open Easter, May to end Sept daily (exc Su) am and pm; grounds open all year daily am and pm. ⊖ 🅿 🅰 🖼 ♣

Carlyle's Birthplace, Ecclefechan, Dumfries & Galloway Region (tel Ecclefechan [057 63] 666). 7 m SE of Lockerbie on A74. NY 1974 (OS 85). 18th-century artisan's house, built by Thomas Carlyle's father and uncle, in which the writer was born in 1795. There is a collection of mementos and personal relics. Open Apr to end Oct daily (exc Su) am and pm. ⊖ 🅿

Castle Menzies, Weem, Tayside Region (tel Aberfeldy [0887] 20982). 2 m W of Aberfeldy on B846. NN 8349 (OS 52). Late 16th-century fortified house built on the typical Scottish Z-plan. It is the ancient seat of the chiefs of the Menzies clan, and has associations with Bonnie Prince Charlie. It houses the clan museum. Open Apr to Sept daily am and pm (Su pm only). 🅿 🅰

Craigievar Castle, Lumphanan, Grampian Region (tel Lumphanan [033 983] 635). 7 m S of Alford on A980. NJ 5609 (OS 37). Tower-house built in the 1620s for William Forbes, built on an L-plan and seven storeys high. An excellent example of the Scots Baronial style, with turrets and gables. The house was intended more for domestic than military use, and the hall contains a magnificent plasterwork ceiling. House open May to end Sept daily (exc F) pm; grounds open daily am and pm. ⊖ 🅿 WC 🖼 (by appt) ♣

Culross Palace, Culross, Fife Region. 7 m W of Dunfermline, off A985. NS 9885 (OS 65). Royal palace built in the early 17th century on the site of an earlier palace and monastery. It had been the home of many medieval monarchs, and it was the birthplace of Charles I. There are fine painted wooden panels, and terraced gardens. Open daily am and pm (Su pm only). ⊖ 🅿

Balmoral Castle, Grampian Region

Dalmeny House, South Queensferry, Lothian Region (tel 031-331 1888). 7 m W of Edinburgh off A90. NT 1678 (OS 65). The first Gothic Revival house in Scotland, designed in 1814 by William Wilkins. The house contains collections of French furniture and porcelain, the Earl of Rosebery's collection of paintings, tapestries and a Napoleon room. Open Apr to end Oct daily am and pm; Nov, S and Su only. ⊖ 🅿 WC 🖼 (by appt) 👝

Drum Castle, near Aberdeen, Grampian Region (tel Drumoak [033 08] 204). 11 m W of Aberdeen on A93, turn N. NJ 7900 (OS 38). A 13th-century great tower (one of the oldest in Scotland), with a mansion built in 1619 by the Irvine family. There are woodland walks in the grounds. Castle open May to end Sept daily pm, grounds open all year daily am and pm. ⊖ 🅿 ♣

Edzell Castle, near Brechin, Tayside Region. 8 m N of Brechin. NO 5869 (OS 44). Ruined 16th-century castle built on a much earlier defensive site, with an exceptional 'pleasance', or early 17th-century formal walled garden including a bath-house and summerhouse. Open M, W, F, S am and pm, Th and Su pm. ⊖ 🅿 🅰 ♣

Georgian House, 7 Charlotte Square, Edinburgh, Lothian Region (tel 031-225 2160). In city centre. NT 2574 (OS 66). One of the houses of Robert Adam's designs for Charlotte Square, praised as his masterpiece of urban architecture. The house has been restored as a typical 18th-century mansion. Open Apr to end Oct M-S am and pm, Su pm only; Nov S am and pm, Su pm only. ⊖

Gladstone's Land, Lawnmarket, Edinburgh, Lothian Region (tel 031-226 5856). In city centre. NT 2573 (OS 66). House built in 1620 and furnished as a typical 'Old Town' house with remarkable painted wooden ceilings. It is named after Thomas Gledstanes, who acquired the house shortly after it was built. The ground floor contains a shop front and goods of the period. Open Apr to end Oct M-S am and pm, Su pm only; Nov, S am and pm, Su pm only. ⊖

Gosford House, near Longniddry, Lothian (tel Aberlady [08757] 201). 14 m E of Edinburgh, off A198. NT 4578 (OS 66). A Neo-Classical house built by Robert Adam and William Young. Open May to Sept W, S and Su. 🅿

Haddo House, near Methlick, Grampian Region (tel Tarves [065 15] 440). 24 m N of Aberdeen on B9005. NJ 8634 (OS 30). Classical house built in the 1730s by William Adam for the Gordons of Haddo. The house has an elegant front, with a divided, sweeping stair. The interior was restyled in the later 19th century. There is a fine collection of portraits, including those of many mid 19th-century statesmen; the chapel has stained glass by Burne-Jones. House open May to end Sept daily pm; grounds open all year daily am and pm. ⊖ 🅿 WC 🅰 ♣

Hermitage Castle, Liddlesdale, Borders Region. 21 m S of Hawick on B6399, turn W. NY 4996 (OS 79). 14th-century castle built around an earlier tower-house, held by the Douglas family until the late 15th century, and by the Earl of Bothwell in Mary's reign. The castle has been well restored, and has close-set towers linked by a solid wall of the same height, with massive arched entries. Open daily am and pm (Su pm only). 🅿

Hill House, Upper Colquhoun St, Helensburgh, Strathclyde Region (tel Helensburgh [0436] 3900). In town centre. NS 2982 (OS 56). Built in 1902 for Walter Blackie, one of the finest domestic houses built by the Glasgow Art Nouveau architect Charles Rennie Mackintosh. Its furnishings were all designed by Mackintosh; the house overlooks the River Clyde. Open daily pm. ⊖ 🅿

Hill of Tarvit, near Cupar, Fife Region (tel Cupar [0334] 53127). 2½ m SW of Cupar on A916, turn E. NO 3711 (OS 59). Old mansion house, heavily rebuilt in the early 20th century. It has a fine collection of furniture, tapestries, porcelain and paintings. House open Apr to end Sept daily (exc F) pm; Oct S and Su only, pm. Gardens open daily am and pm. 🅿 🅰 (byappt) ♣

House of the Binns, Linlithgow, Lothian Region (tel Philipstoun [050 683] 4255). 3½ m E of Linlithgow on A904. NT 0578 (OS 66). House begun in the 15th century, remodelled in the 17th in transitional style, and modified again in the 19th century. It is the home of the Dalyells. There are fine moulded ceilings dating from 1630, and a 19th-century folly in the grounds. Open Easter, May to Sept daily (exc F) pm. ⊖ 🅿 🛆 ♣

Huntingtower Castle, near Perth, Perthshire, Tayside Region. 3 m W of Perth, off A85. NO 0825 (OS 53). Castellated tower house of the 15th century beside the River Almond, originally known as Ruthven Castle. It is made up of two towers joined by a great hall built in the 17th century. There are 16th-century paintings on walls and ceiling of the hall. The castle was the scene of the Ruthven raid, when King James VI was kidnapped in 1582. Open daily am and pm (Su pm only). ⊖ 🅿

Kellie Castle, Pittenweem, Fife Region (tel Arncroach [033 38] 271). 3 m NW of Pittenweem, on B9171. NO 5205 (OS 59). Large castle of the 15th to 17th centuries, comprising three towers around a main block. It is a good example of Lowlands domestic architecture of this period, and contains fine 17th-century plasterwork and painted panelling. Castle open Apr to end Sept daily (exc F) pm; Oct, S and Su only, pm. Gardens open daily am and pm. ⊖ 🅿 🛆 (by appt) ♣

John Knox House Museum, 45 High St, Edinburgh, Lothian Region (tel 031-556 6961). In city centre. NT 2573 (OS 66). 15th- and 16th-century town house, probably the home of religious reformer John Knox from 1561 to 1572. The house has fine wooden galleries of the late 16th century, and a painted ceiling of the early 17th century. There is a collection of items relating to Knox, and pictures of the old Edinburgh. Open M-S am and pm. ⊖ 🛆 (by appt)

Lauriston Castle, Cramond Rd South, Davidson's Mains, Edinburgh, Lothian Region (tel 031-336 2060). 4 m W of Edinburgh on A490, turn N. NT 2076 (OS 66). Late 16th-century turreted tower-house with 19th-century mansion attached. It was the birthplace of the 18th-century financier John Law. The castle is now decorated in Edwardian style and contains a collection of antiques and *objets d'art*. Castle open Apr to Oct daily (exc F) am and pm; Nov to March S and Su only, pm. Grounds open daily (exc F) am and pm. ⊖ 🅿 WC ♣ 🖝 🛆

Leith Hall, Kennethmont, Grampian Region (tel Kennethmont [046 43] 216). 34 m NW of Aberdeen, on B9002. NJ 5429 (OS 37). Mansion begun in the 1650s, with wings added in the 18th and 19th centuries; the home of the Leith family. The house contains family relics. The garden is pleasant, with nature walks in the grounds. House open May to end Sept daily pm; grounds open daily all year am and pm. ⊖ 🅿 ♣ 🛆

Lennoxlove, Haddington, Lothian Region (tel Haddington [062 082] 3720). 1½ m SE of Haddington on A6137, turn E. NT 5172 (OS 66). Fortified tower house first erected in the mid-14th century and reworked by the Duke of Lauderdale in the reign of Charles II. The house is now the home of the Duke and Duchess of Hamilton. There is fine 17th- and 18th-century furniture, 18th-century porcelain, and many notable portraits. Open Apr to end Sept W, S, Su pm; other times by appt. 🅿 WC 🛆 (by appt) ♣ 🖝

Maxwelton House, near Moniaive, Dumfries & Galloway Region (tel Moniaive [084 82] 385). 13 m NW of Dumfries on B729. NX 8289 (OS 78). Early 17th-century house, incorporating an earlier tower; a stronghold of the Earls of Glencairn. It was the birthplace in 1682 of Annie Laurie, immortalised in song, and there is a museum of agricultural and early domestic life. Open W and Th pm. ⊖ 🅿 ♣

Muchalls Castle, Stonehaven, Grampian Region (tel Newtonhill [0569] 30217). 6 m N of Stonehaven on A92, turn W. NO 8991 (OS 45). Castle built in the 1620s, adding to the remains of a 14th-century tower. It was rebuilt after the Jacobite Rebellion of 1745. The plasterwork and chimney-pieces are notable. Open May to Sept T and Su pm. ⊖ 🅿

Neidpath Castle, near Peebles, Borders Region (tel Aberlady [087 57] 201). 1 m W of Peebles on A72. NT 2340 (OS 73). Large 14th-century tower-house built to the L-plan, with 16th- and 17th-century additions. The castle, which was originally built by the Frasers and later taken over by the Hays, overlooks the River Tweed. It was besieged and taken by Cromwell in the 1650s. Open mid-Apr to mid-Oct daily am and pm (Su pm only). ⊖ 🅿 🛆 (by appt)

Penkill Castle, Girvan, Strathclyde Region (tel Old Dailly [046 587] 261). 2½ m E of Girvan off A77. NX 2398 (OS 76). 16th-century tower house, rebuilt in the 19th century, and the home in the 1860s of painter William Bell Scott. There is a collection of Pre-Raphaelite paintings. The house has special connections with the Rossettis. Open Easter and Bank Hol M; May to Sept by appt. 🅿 🖝

Pollok House, Pollok Park, Glasgow, Strathclyde Region (tel 041-632 0274). 3½ m S of city centre. NS 5561 (OS 64). Mid-Georgian house extended in the early 19th century, and containing the Stirling Maxwell collection of Spanish and other European paintings, with works by El Greco, Murillo, Goya, Signorelli and Blake. Open daily am and pm (Su pm only). ⊖ 🅿 WC ♿ ♣ 🖝 ★

Rammerscales, Lockerbie, Dumfries & Galloway Region (tel Lochmaben [038 781] 361). 5 m W of Lockerbie, on B7020. NY 0877 (OS 85). Manor house built in 1760 for Dr James Mounsey. There is a fine circular staircase and elegant rooms, with a collection of relics of the Jacobite movement and of Flora Macdonald. Open June to Sept T-Th pm; also alternate Su in July and Aug. 🅿 🛆

Provost Skene's House, Aberdeen, Grampian Region (tel Aberdeen [0224] 641086). In Guestrow, off Broad St, in city centre. NJ 9305 (OS 38). 17th-century house, furnished with period rooms and displays of local history and domestic life. Open all year M-S am and pm. ⊖ 🅿 🖝 ★

Tenement House, Buccleuch St, Glasgow, Strathclyde Region (tel 041-333 0183). In city centre. NS 5865 (OS 64). A restored first floor flat in a Victorian tenement building, erected in 1892. Open Apr to end Oct daily pm, Nov to end March S and Su pm; all visits by appt only. ⊖

Urquhart Castle, Drumnadrochit, Loch Ness, Highland Region. 16 m SW of Inverness. NH 5328 (OS 26). 14th- to 16th-century castle, one of the largest in Scotland, by Loch Ness on a site probably fortified since the Iron Age. The castle had a massive gatehouse, a 15th-century great tower, separate domestic quarters and a motte within the enclosure. Open daily am and pm (Su pm only). 🅿 WC ♣ 🖝 🛆

Pollok House, Glasgow, Strathclyde Region

Index

Page numbers in italic refer to captions to illustrations.

Acknowledgements

Photographs
All photographs by John Bethell, St. Alban's, except for the following:
Aerofilms, Boreham Wood 198, 202-3; Ken Andrew, Prestwick 229 T, 238, 242 M, 244 T, 246 B, 249 T; Arundel Castle, The Trustees of 55; Athelhampton 25; Belle Isle 210 M; Boughton Monchelsea Place 76 B; The Bridgeman Art Library, London 13, 17 T, 19; British Tourist Authority, London 36 B, 73, 104 T&B, 105, 108 B, 109, 142 T, 219 T, 232, 234-5; Broadlands (Romsey) Limited 77 M; Peter Burton, Scarborough 155 T; Burton Constable – John R. Chichester-Constable 211 M; Eric Crichton – The Field Magazine 185 M; Castle Howard, York 204 B, 205 B; Cawdor Castle (Tourism) Limited 243 M; Chenies Manor House 145 M; Combe Sydenham Hall 37 M; Croxteth Country Park – E. E. Jackson 212 M; W.F. Davidson, Penrith 185 T, 188 M&B, 192, 200, 214 M, 216 M, 221, 246 T; Michael Dent, Twickenham 89 T; C.M. Dixon, Canterbury 26, 27 T; Detillens 79 T; East Midlands Tourist Board, Lincoln 151 M; Eastnor Castle 184 M; Edinburgh Military Tattoo 229 B; Eyhorne Manor 80 T; Focus Photography, Exeter, 39 M; Forde Abbey 39 T; Fotobank International Colour Library, London 199 T&B; Gainsborough's House Society, Sudbury 117 T; Gaulden Manor – J.H.N. Starkie 39 B; Greater London Council: Kenwood (The Iveagh Bequest), Marble Hill House 82 B, 85 M; John Green, London 36 T; Hamlyn Group Picture Library, Twickenham 17 B, 18 T right; Hanch Hall 147 B; Harewood House 213 M; Harrington Hall – Lady Maitland 117 B; Hatch Court 40 T; The Heart of England Tourist Board, Worcester 142 B, 146 T, 147 M, 154 M, 181 M, 183 T; Hoar Cross Hall 148 M; Eddy Ryle Hodges 217 B; Michael Holford, Loughton 9 right, 27 B, 101 T, 102-3, 138-9; Holkham Estate – Viscount Coke and the Trustees of the, 112; Holme Pierrepont Hall 148 B; Hopetoun House Preservation Trust, The Trustees of the 235, 236 T&B, 237; Jarrold, Norwich – by kind permission of Holkham Hall 111 B; Geoff Johnson, Walton-on-Thames 47, 65, 90 T, 91 M, 114 T, 141 T, 149 B; Ipswich Museums & Galleries, Ipswich 116 T; Judge's Limited, Hastings 85 B; A.F. Kersting, London 24, 35, 56, 56-7, 57, 67 B, 68-9, 69, 70 T&B, 71, 78 T, 83 B, 84 B, 113, 121 M, 140, 141 B, 143 M, 155 M, 201, 211 B, 213 B, 244 M; Andrew Lawson, Oxford 103, 197 B; Leicestershire Museums, Leicester 143 T; Leighton Hall 214 B; Longleat House 29, 30 T&B, 31; John Makepeace 42 T; Mapledurham 152 T; S. & O. Matthews, Tunbridge Wells 76 M, 85 T, 88 B; Melbourne Hall 152 M; Meols Hall 215 M; National Trust, London 8, 11 B, 12, 16, 18 B, 20-1, 40 M, 43 B, 87 M, 121 B, 157 M, 184 T; Newnes Books, Twickenham 62-3, 67 T, 74 B, 122 M, 183 M, 214 T, 231, 233 T&B, 250; Newburgh Priory 216 B; Newhouse 41 B; Normandy Hall 217 M; Oakleigh House 121 T; Christopher Orlebar, Oxshott 91 T; Parham Park 86 B; Pattyndenne Manor 87 T; Pencarrow 42 M; The Photo Source, London 33 T, 110, 177, 178-9 T, 197 T; Pat Pierce, Sunbury 81 T; Pilgrim Press Limited, Derby 230, 235, 236 T&B, 237; Poundisford Park 42 B; Powderham Castle – Lord Courtenay 43 T; Raby Castle – Lord Barnard 217 B; Rockingham Castle 153 B; Rex Features, London 169; Scone Palace – Earls of Mansfield 248 T; Scottish Tourist Board, Edinburgh 228-9, 241, 242 B, 244 B, 245 M, 246 M, 247, 248 M; Sheldon Manor 44 T; Edwin Smith, Saffron Walden 34 left & right, 118 B; South East England Tourist Board, Tunbridge Wells 80 M&B, 84 M; Southern Tourist Board, Eastleigh 76 T, 77 T, 89 B; Southwick Hall – Bill Richardson 154 B; Stonor Park 155 B; The Sulgrave Manor Board 156 T; Syndication International Limited, London 182 T; Temple Newsam House, Leeds 208-9, 209 T; Thames & Chilterns Tourist Board, Abingdon 150 T, 153 T; Bob & Sheila Thomlinson, Carlisle 54-5, 220, 240-1, 240 B, 245 B; Thurnham Hall 219 M; Judy Todd, London 28, 37 B, 43 M, 45 T&B, 63 T, 74-5, 81 M&B, 82 M, 89 M, 111 T, 139, 144 B, 151 B, 170, 183 B, 203, 204 T, 205 T, 210 B, 217 T, 222, 243 B, 251; Torosay Castle 249 M; Traquair, with kind permission of Peter Maxwell Stuart of 239; Unichrome (Bath) Limited, Bath 72-3; Wales Tourist Board, Cardiff 166-7, 168, 174-5, 178-9 B, 181 B, 182 B, 187 T, 188 T, 189 M, 193; West Country Tourist Board, Exeter 37 T; Weston Park 189 B; Whitehall 91 B; Jeffrey W. Whitelaw, Harpenden 94, 101 B, 115 M, 116 M, 122 T&B, 123 T, 143 B, 146 M, 151 M, 180 M, 206-7, 242 T; Whitmore Hall 157 T; Derek G. Widdicombe, Huddersfield 75, 144 M, 207, 218 M; Wilton House 35 T; Windsor Castle: The Grand Staircase – reproduced by gracious permission of Her Majesty The Queen 74; Wingfield Castle 123 M; Winton House – Sir David Ogilvy, Bt. 249 B; Woodmansterne – Clive Friend 43 T, 239, Jeremy Marks 248 T; The World Government of the Age of Enlightenment – Great Britain 152 B; Yorkshire and Humberside Tourist Board, York 209 B.

Illustrations
Cut-away drawings on pages 60-61, 134-5 and 172-3 by Jonathan Preston of the Maltings Partnerhip, Duffield.

Maps
Maps on pages 22-3, 52-3, 98, 128, 164-5, 196 and 226 by Thames Cartographic Services Limited, Maidenhead.